THE RULE OF REASON AND THE RUSES OF THE HEART

OTHER BOOKS BY RÉMY G. SAISSELIN:

Style, Truth and the Portrait (1963)
Taste in Eighteenth-Century France (1965)

The Rule of Reason
and the Ruses of the Heart

A Philosophical Dictionary
of Classical French Criticism, Critics,
and Aesthetic Issues

RÉMY G. SAISSELIN

1970
THE PRESS OF CASE WESTERN RESERVE UNIVERSITY
Cleveland/London

Preface

THIS BOOK is not so much a reading or interpretation of French literature of the Classical period as it is a repertory of the assumptions on which writers wrote, poets and painters depicted, critics judged, connoisseurs knew, and the public tasted. The term "Classical" is most commonly used by the French in referring to their literature of the seventeenth century, beginning about 1630 and ending, in most people's opinions, in the 1680s, when the so-called precursors of the Enlightenment begin to write and publish. These terminal dates may be questioned, however, and we shall here stretch the term "Classical" to include also the periods of Louis XV and Louis XVI. Of course this extension may also be questioned, though for other reasons. It has been argued, for example, that French literature of the seventeenth century has a Baroque as well as a Classical period, while the eighteenth century has lately been divided into a Rococo and an Enlightenment phase in addition to the pre-Romantic phase of its closing decades that in the fine arts is also called the Neoclassic period. While all these terms may be justified, and sometimes prove to be useful, it nevertheless remains the case that they pose questions concerning the limits in time to which they may be applied: with whom and when does the Classical phase begin? when does the pre-Enlightenment period start? the Rococo? the Neoclassic? Such questions and characterizations seem to me largely fruitless. One period is not replaced by another in a time sequence conceived as motion along a line. Each of these periods is justified theoretically by recourse to the same terms as the others, namely "beauty," "truth," "nature," "taste," "imitation," and others equally ambiguous, so that it might be better to conceive of the arts and writings commonly denoted as being Baroque, Rococo, Classical, or pre-Romantic merely as possible variations within a general style and aesthetic norm.

My approach is admittedly conservative. I am not rewriting history

along psychoanalytical or structuralist lines, but rather making an enquiry into the meanings of certain words. Classicism is associated with
the *ancien régime*, with monarchy, an aristocratic public, and academies
of the arts. The temporal limits of our subject correspond to the life of
such institutions of the *ancien régime*, as well as to the vocabulary with
which such institutions may be associated. It is true that the Académie
Française survived several revolutions and republics and that the Classical critical vocabulary was not completely abandoned after the French
Revolution: yet something did change after that event. I believe that
the language of criticism and the arts themselves were in greater correspondence before the Revolution than they have been since. Let us
put it this way: one does not really have to contend with *isms* in the
Classical period. However, while the critical vocabulary of the Classical
period does avoid the ambiguities of such terms as "Classicism," "Romanticism," "realism," "naturalism," and "Symbolism," it does not avoid
ambiguity. Nor, for that matter, did it prevent critical disputes, as witness the quarrels of the *Cid*, of the Ancients and Moderns, of the partisans of Italian versus those of French music. Yet all the disputes of
the critics of the Classical period, no matter how passionately debated
and no matter how ill-put the points at issue, were different from those
which opposed Romanticists to Classicists, or poets to society, in the
nineteenth century. Before the Revolution questions were posed and
debated within what may be described as a closed system of the arts,
within the same society and by people who generally agreed upon the
value of perfection and generally accepted that art was an imitation of
nature. Questions could arise as to who had produced the most perfect
imitations, as to what one meant by nature or by imitation, and whether
certain genres unknown to the ancients had right of entry into the
Temple of Fame. By the 1830s such questions were largely irrelevant,
and disputes were no longer purely aesthetic. What had been a family
quarrel in the *ancien régime* tended in the nineteenth century to develop into a class conflict, and the meaning and connotation of words
such as "art" and "beauty" changed from what they had been in the
ancien régime, along with the artist's and writer's public and the nature
of artistic and literary production.

I have used the dictionary form because I thought it best fitted to
render the material covered, but this in no way means that the book is
to be taken as either a dictionary of critical issues or for that matter as
a reference book. I have used this form, rather, because we live in a time
and society quite different from that which produced the Classical aesthetic, so that we may now see the latter as a whole or as a tableau; we

may thus think of such a work as this, in dictionary form, as a tableau of knowledge set forth in consecutive order. It seemed more practical to use this treatment than to attempt narrative histories of the terms and problems of Classical criticism. (Such histories do exist, of course, and some of the articles in this book are themselves short narratives of the fortunes of words.) I wished, then, to offer a view of the whole structure of aesthetics in the Classical period, allowing the reader to read where he wishes, not necessarily from the first to the last page. The words and terms which make up the Classical aesthetic cannot be isolated and treated separately: modifications in one imply changes in another; the putting of great value on genius implies new attitudes to taste; modifications in the concept of nature bring changes in those of art and imitation. The dictionary form takes care of this: various essays, under various headings, are thereby united in a common structure which corresponds to the French Classical aesthetic. Such dictionaries existed in the eighteenth century; mine differs from these in that after two centuries we have a certain perspective their authors did not possess.

The title of the book is borrowed from Rollin, Crébillon *fils*, and the Abbé Jacquin, all of whom used that telltale eighteenth-century phrase *le coeur et la raison*: the first of these authors in connection with the purpose of a literary education; the second, in relation to the passion of love and its effects on the heart and reason; and the last, as a warning against novels which purport to warn the reader of the *égarements du coeur et de l'esprit*, to use Crébillon's title of his most famous novel. The meaning of the book is the meaning of the title: throughout the Classical period one attempted to reconcile the aspirations of the heart with the requirements of reason. The attempt to do so on the level of theory led to the discovery of that delightful *terrain vague*, fruitful for speculation, joyful to the imagination, useful as a training ground for perception — the aesthetic realm where art, nature, and history join, where poets, painters, and philosophers converse, and where the public as hearers and readers wonder.

NOTE

THIS WORK is divided into two major parts. The first is made up of critical articles, the second of biographical and bibliographical sketches of some of the major and minor writers who produced essays, articles, or books that may be classified as aesthetics or criticism. Some of these writers are well known; what I have tried to do with men like Diderot, Fénelon, Fontenelle, Montesquieu, Rousseau, Voltaire, and so on is to place them within the general context of the aesthetics of their period and assess their importance in the development of aesthetic theory. I have not attempted to make résumés of all that they wrote on matters relating to aesthetics and criticism.

References to other articles in this book are appended, where useful, at the ends of the articles. Bibliographical information is handled as follows. Sources of importance for illustrating a single point are cited either in the text or in a footnote with full bibliographical information. Sources used more frequently are cited in the text in an abbreviated form, while full bibliographic information is given either at the end of a Part II article on the author of the work cited or in the supplementary bibliography of primary sources at the end of the book. The "Bibliography" notes at the ends of the Part I articles refer, by author's name, first to the bibliographical information in the Part II articles; then to the supplementary bibliographies, respectively; and finally, in detail, to other books of interest on the subject being handled.

Contents

PART I: CRITICAL ARTICLES   1

Academy
Amateur
Ancients and Moderns
Antique, Antiquity, *Retour à*
  l'Antique
Art, Arts, Fine Arts
Artist
Beauty
Beau Idéal
Bienséance or Decorum
Connoisseur
Convenance
Costume
Critical Theory and Criticism
Curieux, Curiosité
Decadence, Decline
Dramatic Poetry: Tragedy
  and Comedy
Eclogue or Idyll
Eloquence
Enthusiasm
Epic Poetry
Expression
Fable
Genius
Gothic
Grands Siècles

Harmony
Imagination
Imitation
Interest
Je Ne Sais Quoi
Machines, *Grandes Machines*
Method
Nature, *Belle Nature*
Novel
Ode
Opera
Ornament
Pantomime
Perfection, *Perfectionnement*
Perspective
Please and Instruct: *Plaire et*
  Instruire
Poetry and Poetic Theory
Public
Rules
Satire
Style
Sublime
Taste
Truth and Verisimilitude
Ut Pictura Poesis

                                                                  ix

PART II: BIOGRAPHICAL AND BIBLIOGRAPHICAL ARTICLES 225

Alembert
Aubignac
Cartaud de la Vilatte
Chabanon
Chapelain
Condillac
Corneille
Descartes
Diderot
Du Bos

Fénelon
Fontenelle
La Motte
Le Bossu
Montesquieu
Pascal
Perrault
Rousseau
Terrasson
Voltaire

SUPPLEMENTARY BIBLIOGRAPHY 302

PART I

Critical Articles

ACADEMY

THE TERMS "academy," "academic," "academicism" do not enjoy a high reputation today, and in the United States academic persons, despite higher salaries, more research grants, and lower teaching loads than previously, are still looked upon with amusement or annoyance, and hardly ever as persons to be taken seriously. There is some reason for this, for upon examination it turns out that our academics are not academicians at all: they are college and university professors, and these are quite different. The point is, we have forgotten what academies were supposed to be and do, and thus tend to overlook their significance in the history of the arts and sciences.

D'Alembert, member of the Académie Française, pointed out in the eighteenth century that an academy was not the same thing as a university:

Parmi les modernes, ce mot se prend ordinairement pour une société ou compagnie de gens de lettres, établie pour la culture et l'avancement des arts ou des sciences.

Quelques auteurs confondent les mots d'Académie et d'Université: mais quoique ce soit la même chose en latin, c'en sont deux bien différentes en français. Une Université est proprement un corps composé de gens gradués en plusieurs facultés; de professeurs qui enseignent dans les écoles publiques, de précepteurs ou maîtres particuliers, et d'étudiants qui prennent des leçons et aspirent à parvenir aux mêmes degrés; au lieu qu'une Académie n'est point destinée à enseigner ou professer aucun art, quel qu'il soit, mais à en procurer la perfection; elle n'est point composée d'écoliers que de plus habiles qu'eux instruisent, mais de personnes d'une capacité distinguée, qui se communiquent leurs lumières et se font part de leurs découvertes pour leur avantage mutuel ["Mélanges," in Oeuvres Complètes, IV, 478–79.]

We tend to think that the spirit of academies is antithetical to creativity and artistic genius. This is, of course, quite wrong, for it confuses an

1

academy with a school of fine arts or a humanities department in a university. The truth is that people who love art, taste, and self-mastery ought to love academies, while those who love nature, genius, and self-expression ought to dislike them.

Academies were the guardian institutions of true and universal standards of taste and canons of beauty. They preserved these standards by forming men capable of perpetuating them. (Similarly, the academies of science were consecrated to the pursuit of truth, or what sometimes were referred to as *les belles connaissances*.) In the realm of the arts true taste was thus defended and distinguished from the myriad and sometimes seemingly victorious forces of fancy and personal prejudice, and from the fluctuations of false taste. The academy was a suprahistorical institution; it stood above the chaos of time as well as of untamed nature, maintaining true beauty, true art, true taste against the work of time and change by way of the doctrine of imitation.

From our perspective academicians may be likened to curators in a premuseum society; they were essentially *conservateurs* of what had been and ought to continue to be, whereas curators in a museum society are merely the keepers of what can never be again. The existence of academies supposes an imitative theory of artistic creation, and along with this a certain vision of history based upon that theory (see article "*Grands Siècles*"). Academicians not only preserved, they also transmitted.

While today a great many artists make it a part of their professed creed to disdain academies, academicism and academicians, (even when they have no choice but to work in disguised academies of art called institutes), there was a time when artists strove to become members of academies. As St. Peter's in Rome was the center of the visible Church so, French academicians sometimes tended to think, the French Academy was the visible Temple of Fame. Being a member of the Academy meant prestige, honor, immortality, and for painters, sales. It was also a consecration: a man of letters, as an academician, could at last be accepted as a gentleman, while an artist, sculptor, or architect became a member of one of the liberal arts. The academician was a man who had excelled; his temporal role in the republic of arts or letters was recognized, and his immortality seemingly assured — indeed, the motto of the Académie Française was *A l'immortalité*. He was, among thousands of scribblers or mere artisans, one of the elect. Dignity was imparted to artistic work, since this was raised from the mechanical to the mental, and the poet's work also gained in dignity, since in the academy his inspiration was given form by the proper imitation of the masters.

It is possible to argue, too, that the establishment of official academies prompted reflection upon the various arts, which led to further reflection upon rules and genres, and upon such words as "art," "beauty," "taste," and "nature," thereby establishing at length the new discipline of aesthetics, or, if you wish, of criticism. It was at the request of ministers of state that such thinking was prompted in the seventeenth century; aesthetics owes as much to Richelieu and Colbert as it does to Baumgarten. It may also be argued that the prestige accorded academies, the use made of them by the state, made for a greater awareness among the *honnêtes gens* of court and town of the importance of art, while among savants and artists, reflection upon various arts made for a better understanding of their rather special nature. In short, the distinction between other arts and the fine arts, the latter being recognized as rather special forms of human activity, was in part due to the establishment of academies. For such an institution was, after all, neither a church, a palace, a chateau, nor a salon, and its concern was neither religion, statecraft, warfare, nor social pleasure. In effect, the academy was concerned with the purity of beauty, art, language, taste, or, if you wish, with what might also be called the distinterested activity of being civilized. In this matter the academy was considered the representative of the state: not so much an agent as an ornament of a state obviously conceived as a work of art itself. Artistic production and patronage were affairs of state. The Directeurs des Bâtiments du Roi were closely related to the various academies; the Directeur de la Librairie, obviously, was concerned with literary production. The academies thus transformed the sporadic and individual production of art in preacademy days into a state enterprise and gave artistic production a certain direction and purpose as well as continuity. This made for a unity of style and thought which eventually came to be referred to as official or academic art. But until the mid-eighteenth century what we have come to call academic art was quite simply considered as the right, universal, and true art. The official, because supposedly true and universal, doctrine of art was expounded in a specific form which is part of the body of aesthetic writings of the time, namely the academic discourse, of which those of Antoine Coypel in France and Reynolds in England are the best.

It is one of the ironies of history that while academies were created to insure the survival of a universal, atemporal style and canon of beauty, much academic art is now primarily of historical interest.

AMATEUR

BECAUSE OF the general disease of expertise and professionalism it is
now no longer praiseworthy to be considered an "amateur." This was
not always so. The *amateur* belonged to a society in which professionalism was not considered a virtue, in which pedants and savants were
kept in their place and the fine arts were thought to be for men, rather
than men for the expert study of the fine arts. Thus the *amateur* belongs
to that happy, if precarious, period of history in which the production
and judgment of works of art were still associated with academies and
taste, rather than with sales and graduate schools. The term had a
precise meaning in the eighteenth century: "On appelle ainsi," writes
Lacombe, "une personne qui se distingue par son goût et par ses lumières
dans quelqu'un des beaux-arts, quoiqu'il n'en fasse pas profession. Ce
nom semble particulièrement consacré à ceux qui ont du goût pour la
peinture et la sculpture" (*Dictionnaire portatif,* s.v. "Amateur"). They
were useful to the arts and the nation, Lacombe believed. Some *amateurs* became famous through collections that reflected their taste. Some
also wrote on the arts and thereby helped spread interest in the fine
arts. But *amateurs* were not merely collectors; they were active patrons
of the arts, in that they opened their collections to artists for study and
also to other *amateurs* and *curieux.* They thus played an important role
in the development of interest in the fine arts in the eighteenth century.
They complemented the artistic patronage of the crown and the Church,
and it is undeniable that eighteenth century French painting was largely
influenced by their taste.

In the early years of the century they were received into the French
Academy as special members, *conseillers-amateurs,* their number being limited to eight; later, another eight were added and called *associés
libres.* Praised in the early eighteenth century for supporting the arts,
they were blamed for what was considered a decline of taste at the end
of the century. Diderot, in one of his *Salons,* referred to them as a
maudite race. This change of attitude reflects a change of taste which
may be explained as follows on the theoretical level: the *amateur* loved
and supported the fine arts and artists for himself, for his own collection,
for his own pleasure and vanity, if you will — all of which does not
exclude a disinterested love of beautiful objects. But those who later
blamed the *amateurs* for the decline of taste loved abstractions, namely
Ideal Beauty and Art; the disparagement of *amateurs* corresponds to
the rise of the aesthetic of the *beau idéal.* Polemically, one may also say
that *amateurs* belonged to the *ancien régime,* while their critics were

men of the new regime in the making. It is well known that Diderot at his worst possessed a taste which may in retrospect be described as petit bourgeois.

✳ ✳ ✳

See also: *Connoisseur, Critical Theory, Curieux; Descartes.*
Bibliography: Caylus, Félibien, Lacombe, Watelet; and the following: Edmond Bonnafé, *Dictionnaire des amateurs français* (Paris, 1884); Ferdinand Boyer, "Les Artistes français et les amateurs italiens au XVIIIe Siècle" in *Bulletin de la Société de l'Histoire de l'Art Français*, 1936, pp. 210–30; R. G. Saisselin, "Amateurs Connoiseurs, and Painters," in *Art Quarterly*, XXVII, 429–45.

ANCIENTS AND MODERNS

> Le malheur des Modernes . . . est de n'être pas venu les premiers, et tout leur crime souvent, c'est de penser comme les Anciens, sans les avoir lus.   *1628-1702*
>
> *Bouhours*

> On aime à lire les livres des Anciens pour avoir d'autres préjugés.
>
> *Montesquieu*

WE SHALL NOT give a detailed account of the series of critical disputes which in the course of time came to be referred to as the *querelle des Anciens et des Modernes* or, in Swiftian terms, the Battle of the Books. Such accounts are readily available and the tale hardly needs retelling. Let us rather attempt to summarize the issues and then turn to a perhaps neglected psychological aspect of the quarrel.

From Perrault's *Parallèle des Anciens et des Modernes* it is clear that the disputes touched on or raised almost all aesthetic problems of the eighteenth century. Progress in the sciences and its relation to *perfectionnement* in the fine arts and poetry; the nature of the judgment of taste; the relation of history and society to the judgment of the arts and the merit of individual works; the value and nature of rules; the nature of beauty; the limits of criticism; the use of the marvellous in Christian poetry; the relative merit of ancient and modern works; the proper translation and appreciation of Homer: all were issues in that great phenomenon the Battle of the Books. The results for the participants were complex: there were some who learned how to read and others who learned to rely on their own judgments rather than those of the savants. Certain poets became suspicious of philosophy and philosophers, while philosophers wondered how poetry could survive in a mechanistic universe of causes and effects. And there were also those who learned nothing. Those who did learn, learned that the eighteenth century was modern, that it was quite different in mentality from antiquity. The age of Louis XIV was also accepted as a *Grand Siècle*. Certain poets and painters were admitted to Parnassus. The rules were largely discredited as an instrument with which to judge of the merit of works of the imagination, and taste replaced the rules. The veneration for the ancients survived the quarrel, but the works of the ancients were no longer accepted or read uncritically as perfect, or as superior to the works of the moderns, just because they were ancient. The nature of criticism was still unclear, and one may say that eighteenth-century aesthetics was largely an attempt to define it.

We may thus consider the quarrel as a passage, far from smooth, from an aesthetic constructed on the notion of rules (rationally deduced from the examination of the "perfect" works of the ancients and theoretically reversible so that the application of these same rules would be productive of equally perfect works) to an aesthetic founded upon the notion of taste. If we look at the quarrel within the context of social and historical change we may argue that we passed from an aesthetic that was largely the work of savants, in a world dominated by spiritual and secular authorities, to one associated with a new leisure class in a world no longer quite believing in the spiritual and secular authorities of the *Grand Siècle*. The shift implied alterations in the concept of beauty, nature, art, pleasure, and the role of the public in the elaboration of taste. But it also meant that one had to begin to think about the implications of this recently discovered modernity, so that in effect the critics of the early eighteenth century found themselves in the enviable position of sitting at a *table rase* loaded with blank paper upon which they might elaborate their new criticism. They found themselves in that situation because they had discovered that their veneration of the ancients had, after all, been a pleasant illusion.

Perrault's *Parallèle des anciens et des modernes*, written in the form of a dialogue between a *Président* from the provinces and a worldly Abbé and Chevalier, is not set in Versailles for nothing. The *Président* is brought there for a purpose. He must be exorcised, freed of a prejudice for antiquity which prevents true perception and judgment. He is incapable of believing that anything great, noble, or perfect can be achieved in the present. The Abbé, in effect, is telling the *Président* that he does not really see what he is looking at because he perceives as under a spell, because he is dominated by his imagination and is thus incapable of judging of the relative merits of the ancients and moderns. The *Président* has been to Italy. He visited Tivoli and Frascati, but the Abbé argues that he never truly looked at these places because he saw them through his poetic imagination. He was not really charmed by the statues, fountains, cascades, but rather by the thought of Maecenas and Augustus walking in those gardens where he himself was walking and resting. To the image of Augustus and Maecenas he added that of Horace reading one of his odes, so that ever since, his view of Tivoli has been inseparable from the images of Horace, Augustus, and Maecenas. It was not so much Tivoli he admired, but rather the remembrance of those three noble figures of antiquity.

La même chose est arrivée à Frascati; vous y avez vu Cicéron au milieu de ses amis, agitant ces questions savantes dont la lecture fait encore aujourd'hui nos délices, et je suis sûr qu'à votre égard l'éloquence de Cicéron entre pour une plus grande part dans la beauté de Frascati que tous ses jets d'eau et toutes ses cascades [*Parallèle*, I, 8–9].

The Abbé questions, not only the *Président*'s vision, which in this case is a form of his judgment, or at least affects his judgment, but also the value of the poetic imagination, and through it a mental universe still prevalent in his day. The value and worth accorded the ancients is not founded in reason; it is not the result of a critical examination of their work, but of opinion, hearsay, prejudice. It is an effect of the imagination, and indeed of a widespread and common human failing, that of preferring the past to the present. This prejudice not only affects vision, it even alters one's hearing: "Je ne puis m'empêcher d'admirer ceux qui se pâment de plaisir en prononçant les vers d'Homère, comme s'ils en entendaient l'harmonie, eux qui peut-être n'en prononcent pas un seul mot comme il faut, pas une syllabe, pas une lettre" (Ibid., III, 108). But the Abbé's criticism goes beyond the prejudice to those who perpetuate it, and in so doing he redefines the lines of demarcation between partisans of the ancients and partisans of the moderns. It is no longer a question of one set of poets supporting the ancients and another, less successful, the moderns. Perrault, in this respect, is more penetrating than Boileau, La Bruyère, or La Fontaine. He had a sense of history and realized that the quarrel was not purely aesthetic, critical, or psychological, but that it concerned education, the material interests of the participants, and patronage. The partisans of the ancients, the prejudice in favor of antiquity, are seen as closely involved with pedagogy. The Abbé makes this point with reference to two ancient authors, Quintilian and Cicero; the latter was a modern, but the former was not because he was a pedagogue: "Quintilien était un rhéteur et un pédagogue obligé par sa profession de faire valoir les anciens, et d'imprimer dans l'esprit de ses écoliers un profond respect pour les auteurs qu'il leur proposait pour modèles" (Ibid., I, 16–17). This same process has continued into the present and explains the general veneration for the ancients. Perrault may well be counted among those figures who are now considered as precursors of the Enlightenment, for it is obvious that his attitude towards the ancients made possible, and is part of, the *esprit critique* which is one of the distinguishing traits of the Enlightenment.

Perrault must have been convinced that the veneration for the ancients would not last, since the savants no longer held an undisputed sway over the public. There were two reasons for this: women had become part of the public, and there were more books. The women, who dared to consider the divine Plato a bore and to prefer Lucian, were not particularly respectful to savants and were not inclined to accept scholarly opinion without question. Yet, the Abbé thought, they had become the final arbiters of taste in those questions raised by the quarrel. As for the greater production of books, this too worked against the ancients and their savant supporters. Consider, for example, the reputation of Ronsard, so famous in his day, so disfavored in Perrault's: "Dès que le commun du peuple a commencé à savoir quelque chose, la poésie de Ronsard a paru si étrange, quoique ce poète eût de l'esprit et du génie infiniment, que du comble de l'honneur où elle était, elle est tombée dans le dernier mépris" (Ibid., I, 67). The point is that more books meant more readers, different reading habits, different values, different types of books. The greater production of books meant a decline in erudition, an increase in general discussion, and consequently more prominence given to individual, rather than established, opinions about poets and philosophers. The erudite ceased to appear as an extraordinary mortal standing above the crowd of vulgar, small, and ignorant minds. The increase of publication meant that those who bought books would be potential critics, so that the veneration for the savant, the man of erudition, the man who supposedly was initiated into the arcana of higher learning and knowledge, was no longer automatic. Public approval became more difficult to obtain, and, thanks to translations from the Greek and Latin, more and more people came to know the ancients directly. The rejoinder to the Abbé's argument was obvious, and was made with respect to the ancients, though not to

Ronsard: perhaps the *commun du monde* did not know how to read either Ronsard or the ancients. The greater production of books had posed the problem of reading, and the partisans of the ancients sought to rally on this issue.

The beauties of Homer could not be perceived in translation, and to judge of his quality properly it must be understood that he had lived in a society quite different from that of the moderns, so that he must be judged in terms of his own times rather than by the standards of the present. The partisans of the ancients thus sought to defend their position by a more careful approach to reading and by historicizing works of the imagination. Perrault, through his Abbé, answered by drawing certain distinctions which had a direct bearing upon definitions of poetry. He conceded that it was difficult, if not impossible, to judge of the merit of Greek and Latin poets in French verse translations, but that one could do better in prose. For it was possible to judge of the mores, actions, discourses, and sentiments of the heroes of a poem through a skillful translation, and the only elements which would escape or be lost in translation would be diction and style. This loss did not unduly bother the Abbé because he thought that each language had its particular graces and elegancies, and that in this respect French was not inferior to Latin or Greek. A translation thus became really an adaptation to the genius of another language, so that the Abbé could argue, further, that if one were really free of the prejudice in favor of the ancients one would find there was much to be gained through translations of their works. For he also believed that the dead languages were not so well understood as the savants usually pretended, and that when a reader read Latin in the original he had, in effect, to do two distinct mental operations: translate the original language into his own and understand the author he was translating or reading at the same time. If the reader were spared translating, he could concentrate better on the author's mind.

Perrault's argument was based on a scholastic distinction between essence and accident, the universal and the particular, which distinction in his case was used to further the cause of the moderns as follows: The thoughts or ideas of an author are the content or essence of the work. Diction and style are but accidental and particular to individual languages, and therefore also to historical, changing time. Since the universal is also the true and the rational, one may judge of the works of the ancients irrespective of historical time and change, purely on the basis of the ideas of the ancient authors. Perrault made fun of the partisans of the ancients at the expense of Homer. He pointed to inconsistencies of composition in the Iliad and Odyssey, and also to the immoral, irrational, indecorous, barbarous, and cruel behavior of the Greek heroes. Reading these pages of the *Parallèle*, one may readily see why he made many enemies and also why the question of the proper translation and evaluation of Homer turned out to be one of the more important phases of the long disputes over the ancients and the moderns. Perrault is also assuming that if historical time worked against the ancients it worked for the moderns in the form of progress. The works of the moderns were more perfect than those of the ancients. History was being used by the moderns to downgrade the ancients because it was associated with *perfectionnement*, though it must be stressed that history was being thought of, here, as *time* in which to learn and apply the true and proper rules of art whereby civilization is assured. History, we might say, was detached from accidents, particulars, colors, to be conceived as a sequence of purely mental acts which, once applied, made for material progress. If, for Benjamin Franklin, time was money, for Perrault and the partisans of the moderns, time was perfection.

The partisans of the ancients, and others who might be described as judicious and critical observers of the quarrel, devised an answer to this modern criticism which also involved time and history. It was put rather well by Montesquieu in one of his notebooks:

Je ne sais si les Anciens avaient de meilleurs esprits; mais, par le changement des temps, il est arrivé que nous avons quelquefois de meilleurs ouvrages. Mais pour juger des beautés d'Homère, il faut se mettre dans le camp des Grecs, non pas d'une armée française ["Mes Pensées," in *Oeuvres*, I, 1023].

In this case it is beauty which becomes relative, so that its evaluation, enjoyment, or perception requires a special act of the imagination, for the reader must in effect transport himself in imagination back into the past. Thus imagination, which for Perrault clouded true judgment, is being mobilized by the partisans of the ancients to save the beauties of Homer. Reading thus became something rather different from the true perception Perrault imagined, a reading which involved the critical faculty (as if the reader were ever to ask himself, as he read some work of the past, Is this or that reasonable or civilized?). Now, because the imagination was involved, reading became a voyage into the past so that Rollin, by the time he wrote his *Manière d'enseigner les belles lettres par rapport à l'esprit et au coeur* (Paris, 1741), could write:

La raison, le bon sens, l'équité demandent qu'en lisant les auteurs anciens on se transporte dans le temps et dans les pays dont ils parlent; et que par une bizarrerie d'esprit tout-à-fait injuste on ne se laisse point prévenir contre des coutûmes anciennes, parce qu'elles sont contraires aux nôtres [p. 400].

The difference between this type of historical imagination and that which the Abbé criticized in the *Président* is that it has now become a conscious tool of critical, and we may say poetical, appreciation of ancient works.

One of the positive results of the quarrel was thus a change in the use and value put on imagination: the mind grew in breadth of vision, and man became capable of dissociating himself from his present to imagine a past valued for itself. The past thus became of aesthetic interest in part because it *was* past. But this imaginative reading of the past and of its works also implies a certain historicizing of the aesthetic or critical judgment, while the pleasure taken in the contemplation or possession of that work of the past remained in the present. Perrault's criticism of the ancients rested on a judgment which was founded on reason and universality, but Du Bos, Rollin, Montesquieu, and Voltaire all supposed that such judgment must be attenuated by historical considerations. Present pleasure or displeasure in an object of the past, written or painted in other circumstances, must be helped or buttressed by knowledge of that past. Since Perrault had associated pleasure with the contemplation of perfection which was the result of progress or *perfectionnement*, he was enabled to dismiss the works of the ancients as inferior to those of the moderns, and the proof seemed to lie with the public, which obviously enjoyed the works of the moderns more than those of the ancients. For those inclined to scholarship and to consider the past and its works, we may say that the pleasures of the imagination could be extended beyond the present to encompass the past and transcend time. Perrault had criticized precisely this through his dialogues between the Abbé and the *Président*, but in doing so he also, unwittingly perhaps, showed the way to a new imaginative use of scholarship and an extension of criticism. This is true of Du Bos, Fénelon, Gibbon, Montesquieu. If the rules, supposedly deduced from the rational analysis of the works of the ancients, suffered in the course of the quarrel, the feeling for antiquity was born anew in compensation, and the past was poeticized. This is readily seen in the *Télémaque* of Fénelon, as well as in the writings of Montesquieu and Du Bos. Montesquieu is especially revealing as concerns this new poetic feeling for the past. He was enchanted by antiquity, his heart was charmed by it, but his mind examined the enchantment with nearly puritan scruples. Thus, there occurred in his soul a conflict between mind and heart which may perhaps be characteristic of criticism and aesthetic judgment in general, or, to be more precise, of its birth, for Montesquieu is at pains to stress that one must not be too analytical:

Il ne faut point entrer avec les Anciens dans un détail qu'ils ne peuvent plus soutenir, et cela est encore plus vraià l'égard des poètes, qui décrivent les moeurs et les coutumes, et dont les beautés, même les moins fines, dépendent, la plupart, de circonstances oubliées, ou qui ne touchent plus. Ils sont comme ces palais antiques dont les marbres sont sous l'herbe, mais qui laissent encore voir toute la grandeur et toute la magnificence du dessin ["Mes Pensées," 1022].

Ancient poetry and letters, like ruins, have become the portals of the imagination. The Golden Age, no longer believed in, has been historicized and poeticized, and the psychological bases for the *retour à l'Antique* set, one generation before the famous voyage of Cochin and Marigny to Italy. Montesquieu himself was, however, still close enough to the values of the *Grand Siècle* and the modern spirit to have doubts about the propriety of this feeling for the antique:

Ayant lu plusieurs critiques faites de nos jours contre les Anciens, j'ai admiré plusieurs de ces critiques; mais j'ai admiré toujours les Anciens. J'ai étudié mon goût et examiné si ce n'était point un de ces goûts malades sur lesquels on ne doit faire aucun fond. Mais, plus j'ai examiné, plus j'ai trouvé que j'avais raison de penser comme j'avais senti [Ibid., 1024].

The ancients survived criticism and the Quarrel of the Ancients and the Moderns, and the taste for the ancients was found to be healthy, eventually noble, and finally the only true taste, so that one may well wonder who won the battle.

It has been assumed by some critics and historians of French literature that the publication of Du Bos' *Réflexions critiques* in 1719 marked the end of the quarrel between the ancients and moderns. It is true that with the appearance of this work certain aspects of the quarrel seemed definitely settled. The *Réflexions critiques* put some issues definitely in the past: they were henceforth looked upon in perspective. Du Bos wrote with detachment, and even today one cannot help but feel that, compared with the work of the critics of the *Grand Siècle*, Du Bos introduced a different attitude in criticism. The days of legislation were over. One finally accepted that progress in the arts and in the sciences were not of that same nature, so that Homer and Hesiod could hardly be degraded because the Ptolemaic system had been discredited. The judgment of taste, implying knowledge of the arts, including also, therefore, the *goût de comparaison* plus sentiment, triumphed over the authority of savants and rules. As for the ancients and their works, they were no longer to be judged on the basis of present taste and fashion, but rather within the context of their own times and conventions. All this, save the last item, looks like a modern victory. But upon closer examination and consideration of the subsequent history of the arts in the eighteenth (and even the nineteenth) century, one wonders. The moderns gained the right to the judgment of taste, and by extension the right to compete for admittance to the Temple of Fame, but antiquity seems to have fascinated men as much after the battle as it ever did before, as the history of the plastic as well as literary arts readily shows. The *retour à l'Antique* (see article "Antique") is the most obvious example, but it is not without its parallels in poetry, drama, novels, and opera. The history of this other eighteenth-century literature still remains to be written. The continuing interest in the antique and the continuing use of classical and mythological themes has been greatly obscured because the light emanating from the Enlightenment has been such as to throw other aspects of the eighteenth century into shadow. The Enlightenment was eminently modern and critical, but the *philosophes*, modern in their psychology, physics, and economics, were not averse to be portrayed *à l'antique*. The pagan gods, and their world of myth and marvels, survived not as motifs alone; but their metamorphosis, first into the amiable and delightful motifs of the rocaille style and decor and later into civic or moral exemplary art and architecture, was further buttressed by archeological and historical interest. One might even argue that the very notion of the *grands siècles* (see article), based upon ancient history, also makes for a victory of the ancients rather than the moderns. All of which is enough to make us doubt of the oft-repeated thesis that the eighteenth century invented and believed in progress. In truth, one need not doubt it, because the men of the eighteenth century, unlike the savants of our own times, were charmingly and humanly inconsistent, and could believe in progress even while they deplored the decadence of their own insipid times.

The idea that the moderns won the battle is not new. It was the view of many contemporaries of Du Bos and of the following generation. Gibbon, in a French essay on the study of letters, thought that this victory signified the triumph of the philosophic and geometric spirit over scholarship and criticism, which he associated with history, erudition, and reason. He was saying, in other words, what many poets also thought at the time, namely (to borrow from Boileau) that philosophy had wrung the neck of poetry. These are interesting views which suggest another result of the quarrel, perhaps the most important, namely the coexistence in the eighteenth century of two literatures: one still founded upon the imitation of ancient or established models and oriented towards the ideal of perfection; the other a literature of enlightenment, which perplexed critics because it did not really fit within the Classical aesthetic which the quarrel did not undermine but merely broadened and historicized. Modern poets and writers of the eighteenth century might be working in both of these literatures without being aware that the literature of Enlightenment implied a new type of literature altogether, based upon a new, if at that time still unstated, aesthetic. One might put it this way: everyone now knew himself to be modern, but went on working and thinking on the basis of an imitative theory of art. Only, the models imitated were no longer uniquely in remote antiquity; they might also be found in the *Grand Siècle* of Louis XIV, while themes and motifs, even from the national and medieval past, would eventually be justified. Thus, all was really for the best, because even the moderns had a chance to become ancients by way of proper imitation of even the most recently established immortal models. There were still, of course, certain doubts in the eighteenth century as to the possibility of perfection, but these very doubts merely showed how right the partisans of the ancients had been. For, if perfection had been attained in the seventeenth century, there was little likelihood of continued perfection in a century that followed a *Grand Siècle*. Thus, there was a feeling of decadence in the eighteenth century, at least among certain poets and critics who persisted in thinking the ancients, their ranks now swelled by the more recent arrival of the former moderns, superior to anything they were presently reading. The purist critics of the eighteenth century may be considered the true successors of the partisans of the ancients.

Thus it is that, the more one ponders the outcome of the quarrel, the more one may doubt the victory of the moderns. It may be that the quarrel never ended. Perhaps it merely changed form to become a false problem, and therefore a thing of the past, only when artistic activity would no longer be thought of in terms of imitation. There already were signs that this would happen in the eighteenth century, but only a new society, with a new public, new pasts, new poets, new dissatisfactions, would bring about change. And the change was slow because the values represented by the imitative theory of art and its supposition of models, craftsmanship, moral value, and universality would continue to survive through institutions such as the academy and various centers of learning, including universities.

* * *

See also: *Art, Critical Theory, Taste*; *Diderot, Voltaire*.
Bibliography: Folkierski; and the following: H. Gillot, *La Querelle des Anciens et des Modernes en France* (Paris, 1914); Philip van Thieghem, *Petite Histoire des Grandes Doctrines Littéraires en France* (Paris, P.U.F., 1954); R. G. Saisselin, "Critical Reflections on the Origins of Modern Aesthetics," *The British Journal of Aesthetics*, IV, 7–21.

ANTIQUE, ANTIQUITY, RETOUR A L'ANTIQUE

THE FIRST TERM refers to specific artistic values, models, and standards of beauty; the second, to a specific past associated with and delimited by those artistic-aesthetic values; and the last, to an artistic, aesthetic, and moral movement which effected a general change in style and taste based on or justified by those standards.

Antiques, or *les antiques*, were simply described by Lacombe, as they had been before by de Piles, as "les morceaux de peinture, d'architecture et de sculpture, des plus célèbres artistes de l'antiquité, et singulièrement les statues et les bas reliefs, ou les médailles et pierres gravées qui ont été conservées jusqu'à nous" (*Dictionnaire portatif*, s.v. "Antique"). These surviving pieces, especially sculptures such as the Apollo Belvedere, the Antinoüs, or the famous Laocoön, came to be accepted as guides to beauty because they were said to embody perfect human proportions and the noblest human expressions. There were, however, partisans or admirers of the ancients who doubted that sculptures were the proper models to be imitated by the painter, so that emulation of the antique was not always of the same intensity, and antiques were not used as the only models by all artists, even artists belonging to the academy. One could be an excellent painter without "imitating" the antique. The beauties which dominated painting in the closing decades of the reign of Louis XIV and during the Régence and the reign of Louis XV were not in the antique manner, even though they were often representations of ancient mythology or history. One could, then, treat antique or ancient motifs in the modern manner, in the *goût moderne*, a taste which would eventually be termed decadent or depraved by the partisans of the *retour à l'Antique* in the later eighteenth century, just as these same partisans would refer to the interior decoration of the Régence and Louis XV styles as "rococo." Thus antiques, in this sense, were destined to become the mainstay of academic or, if you wish, establishment art and its canons of beauty. From objects used by painters and sculptors to attain perfect beauty, antiques gradually became symbolic of a general aesthetic and moral mentality and taste because they were the *artefacts* of a lost ideal, antiquity.

Antiquity exercised a constant charm upon the imagination of poets, painters, and thinkers of the eighteenth century. It is even possible to argue that, if the moderns had been at times uncompromising with the partisans of the ancients in the battles of the previous century and in the early eighteenth, it was because they sought to break that charm. The charm was never broken; for the *retour à l'Antique*, which is characteristic of the closing decades of the eighteenth century, not only in France but all over Europe and even in the new United States, was in preparation long before the new spirit, the new manifestation of the charm of antiquity, was made visible in plastic forms. One may say of it what was said of the French Revolution, that it had been accomplished in men's minds before it was realized visibly. The world of the Greeks and Romans fascinated the minds and imaginations of poets and thinkers even in their Rococo *cabinets d'étude* or salons. Reforms in the Academy of Painting and Sculpture, effected in part through the influence of the antiquarian Comte de Caylus in the decade of the 1740s, and later reforms in Rome gradually prepared artists to accept the standards of the antique as the only true standards of beauty and to reject the manner of Lemoyne and Boucher as mannered and decadent.

But a poetic feeling for antiquity existed before these reforms were effected, before David came back from Rome and independently of artistic developments. The veneration for and the effects of the charm of antiquity may be noted in the works of the more important writers of the early eighteenth century. Fénelon's *Télémaque* is a prose hymn to the antique. Montesquieu's *Temple de Gnide*, inspired by the former work, is in this same antique prose manner, a periodic style which Condillac thought especially suited to description and which we may well consider as the prose poetry of the eighteenth century, based not so much on a direct knowledge of antiquity, but rather on its poetical representation in the work of Poussin, and, in the case of Fénelon, also of Raphael. Du Bos, who was a contemporary of Watteau, considered the taste of his contemporaries petty and thought the Greeks had made of art a national concern where the French merely thought of it as furniture. The aestheticism associated with Winckelmann is already apparent in the generation of Du Bos, and traces of it may also be found in the private notebooks of Montesquieu, whom Madame de Tencin used to call *mon petit Romain.*

As for Fénelon, so for Montesquieu; antiquity represented a lost simplicity and felicity, and when he looked about him he felt the modern world had lost something of that ancient poetry, freshness, charm, and innocence:

Le monde n'a plus cet air riant qu'il avait du temps des Grecs et des Romains. Le Religion était douce et toujours d'accord avec la nature. Une grande gaieté dans le culte était jointe à une indépendence entière du dogme. Les jeux, les danses, les fêtes, les théâtres, tout ce qui peut émouvoir, tout ce qui fait sentir, était du culte religieux [*Oeuvres*, I, 1080–81].

This happy estate was spoiled by Christianity and Islam, both of which emphasize an otherworldly life at the expense of present felicity. Thus antiquity became associated with lost innocence and simplicity, qualities and virtues lost in the course of time among nations which have perhaps become too polished. Wrote Montesquieu,

J'aime à voir dans l'homme lui-même des vertus qu'une certaine éducation ou religion n'ont point inspirées; des vices que la mollesse et le luxe n'ont point faits. J'aime à voir l'innocence rester encore dans les coutumes, lorsque la grandeur du courage, la fierté, la colère, l'ont chassé des coeurs mêmes. J'aime à voir les rois plus forts, plus courageux que les autres hommes, distingués de leurs sujets dans les combats, dans les conseils; hors de là, confondus avec eux [Ibid., 1081].

These sentiments are not far removed from those expressed in the *Premier Discours* of Rousseau, and it is quite obvious that the veneration and love of antiquity has taken a new turn. If one no longer, after the Quarrel of the Ancients and Moderns, accepts the superiority of the works of the ancients without question, one develops on the other hand a nostalgia for the simplicity, innocence, and closeness to nature of the ancients. The ancients were natural, the moderns are tired and artificial: such an attitude typifies the new form taken by the tension between past and present, between the partisans of the ancients and moderns, or, if you will, the poets of greater or lesser imagination and men of a more critical turn of mind. This sense of loss is the reverse effect of accepting the thesis of *perfectionnement* in the arts and sciences: the price paid is a feeling of something lost, a nostalgia of the heart which the mind knows to be hopeless, sentimental perhaps but harmless enough. Eventually, the mind would help work towards a regeneration of mankind based upon the moral virtues thought to be inherent in the world of antiquity. The nostalgia for the classical past engendered love of ruins, but also its reconstruction by a general imitation, the Neoclassic style; and Napoleon, thanks to David, ended by looking remarkably like Augustus, even while his legal advisors devised a code based upon Roman precedents.

✳   ✳   ✳

See also: *Art, Beau Idéal; Diderot, Montesquieu, Rousseau.*
Bibliography: Louis Bertrand, *La Fin du Classicisme et le retour à l'antique* (Paris, Fayard, n. d.); Jean Locquin, *La Peinture d'Histoire en France de 1747 à 1785. Etudes sur l'évolution des idées artistiques dans la seconde moitié du XVIIIe Siècle* (Paris, 1912); Henry Hawley, *Neo-Classicism, Style and Motif* (Cleveland, 1964); Maurice Badolle, *Jean-Jacques Barthélémy (1716–1795) et l'Hellénisme en France dans la seconde Moitié du XVIIIe Siècle* (Paris, 1927).

ART, ARTS, FINE ARTS

> *Arts* (Beaux); il sont distingués des Arts simplement dits, en ce que ceux-ci sont pour l'utilité, ceux-là pour l'agrément. Les *Beaux-Arts* sont enfants du génie; ils ont la nature pour modèle, le goût pour maître, le plaisir pour but. L'aimable simplicité doit former leur principal caractère; ils se corrompent lorsqu'ils donnent dans le luxe, et le clinquant. La véritable règle, pour les juger, est le sentiment. Ils manquent leur effet lorsqu'ils ne parlent qu'à l'esprit; mais ils triomphent lorsqu'ils affectent l'âme, et mettent les passions en mouvement.
>
> *Lacombe*

THE EIGHTEENTH CENTURY belongs to an era of history in which, unlike our own, much of human activity was thought of in terms of art rather than of science. Used in this sense, the word "art" meant a doing, making, or acting according to certain rules, procedures, purposes, standards, and forms. Thus there were the arts of war, fortification, fencing, painting, eloquence, conversation, and seduction. This use of the word "art" still survives, and there are those who have counted some four hundred types and kinds of art, a fact that is enough to make us almost believe that we are still living in the eighteenth century. However, if we look elsewhere we see a significant tendency to relabel many former arts as sciences. Thus, reserve officer trainees no longer learn the art of war but rather military science, librarians are practitioners of library science, and love is subject to scientific investigation rather than to the rules of seduction.

Insofar as the *fine arts* are concerned, however, the term art has acquired a different meaning, inherited from the seventeenth and eighteenth centuries, fully formulated at least in the latter period, and still very much alive today, since it was the questioning of this concept of art that brought on the development of anti-art. Used in this sense, "art" refers not only to a body or collection of individual works of art but to a specifically human activity, a specific kind of world; the eighteenth century posed the preconditions of art and eventually formulated the concept of its autonomy. This autonomous realm of art defined itself as one in rapport with that of nature. Batteux points to this specifically human creation in the introductory chapter of his *Beaux Arts réduits à un même principe*: "Ils [the arts] sont devenus en quelque sorte pour nous un second ordre d'éléments, dont la nature avait réservé la creation à notre industrie" (p. 5). This definition includes all the arts, to be sure, but eventually this position of art as a second order was to become more and more restricted to the fine arts. Batteux thus distinguished between the mechanical and fine arts, and differentiated them in terms of their functions and their relations to nature: the mechanical or useful arts supply the wants of man and use nature as she is found; the fine arts have been devised for the pleasure of mankind and imitate nature in fulfilling this requirement of pleasure. The fine arts may in turn be divided into three broad types: music, poetry, painting, and sculpture; the arts of the mime and the dance; and a third general type that may be termed mixed, for it combines both utility and *agrément*: e.g., eloquence and architecture. Mixed art polishes nature for use and pleasure.

Art is of purely human origin:

Ce sont les hommes qui ont fait les arts; et c'est pour eux-mêmes qu'ils les ont faits. Ennuyés d'une jouissance trop uniforme des objets que leur offrait la nature toute simple, et se trouvant d'ailleurs dans une situation propre à recevoir le plaisir; ils eurent recours à leur génie pour se procurer un nouvel ordre d'idées et de sentiments qui reveillât leur esprit et ranimât leur goût [Ibid., 8].

Art, in this sense, surpassed the world of nature. Men made a certain choice within nature as given and thereby constructed a more perfect whole, which, for all that, did not cease to be "natural." A more perfectly human world was created or elaborated in order to answer human requirements, and, since Batteux alludes to pleasure and enjoyment, he obviously has in mind the fine arts.

Du Bos is more specific about the psychological origins of the arts and insists on ennui even more than Batteux, though he also makes the point that it was only gradually that men came to understand this peculiar necessity of art:

L'âme a ses besoins comme le corps; et l'un des plus grands besoins de l'homme, est celui d'avoir l'esprit occupé. L'ennui qui suit bientôt l'inaction de l'âme est un mal si douloureux pour l'homme, qu'il entreprend souvent les travaux les plus pénibles afin de s'épargner la peine d'en être tourmenté [Réflexions critiques, I, 6].

This view is not far from Pascal's notion of *divertissement* and human nature. Pascal had voiced the same view of man:

Rien n'est si insupportable à l'homme que d'être dans un plain repos, sans passions, sans affaire, sans divertissement, sans application. Il sent alors son néant, son abandon, son insuffisance, sa dépendance, son impuissance, son vide. Incontinent il sortira du fond de son âme l'ennui, la noirceur, la tristesse, le chagrin, le dépit, le désespoir [Pensée 131].

Du Bos elaborates a theory of art upon this desperate need for *divertissement*: what is anathema to the Jansenist and Christian rigorist is a virtue to the worldly, learned, and wise abbé, diplomat, and academician. Du Bos' theory of art resolves the problem posed by Pascal when he writes that "tout le malheur des hommes vient d'une seule chose, qui est de ne savoir pas demeurer en repos dans une chambre" (*Pensée* 139). The hedonistic theory of art turns into a therapeutic of the distressed soul of man in his fallen state, and Du Bos and others formulate, in effect, the classical solution to man's condition. An ideal solution to the problem of the human condition is reached when the passions and the imagination, that source of error, are kept occupied without harm. And it is in the power of art to be able to divert men from themselves, their emptiness, boredom, and fear, and at the same time to satisfy through activity their need for passions without fear that these will cause pain. Thus it is that we may sit alone in our rooms without ennui, fear, and trembling, looking at television. We are diverted from ourselves; the imagination is occupied, fixed upon the screen. We may enjoy violence, fear, joy, cruelty, licentiousness, without ill effects to ourselves or society. The Abbé Du Bos' solution may not be the Christian solution to the problem of man's estate, but it may be significant that the greater degree of secularization of his time also corresponded to a greater interest in the arts. Originally, Du Bos' solution was applicable only to a restricted leisure class, but in time this solution was gradually so widened that it was rejected by some artists and poets of the nineteenth century, while artists and *philosophes* of the eighteenth rejected the hedonistic theory on other grounds.

Du Bos' point of view was not only opposed to Christian rigorism, it was also in conflict with Plato's attitude towards poets and art. Examining Plato's banishment of poets from the Republic, Du Bos admitted that art might be dangerous in some cases, but argued that the risk of this must be taken in order to avoid a greater evil: "Contentons nous de dire que la société qui excluerait de son sein tous les citoyens dont l'art pourrait être nuisible, deviendrait bientôt le séjour de l'ennui" (*Réflexions critiques*, I, 51). Art avoids ennui, the pain of being in a state of boredom, by the creation of artificial passions. The term "artificial," in this case, is obviously not derogatory. The artificial is better than that which is natural but corrupt and unstable. The artificial passions of art correspond to Batteux's *la belle nature* and to Perrault's ideal nature. Perrault, in relation to nature (see article), had opined that it was the task of philosophers to tame savage humanity, and from this point of view we may regard art, in Du Bos' view, either as having the function of supplementing the philosopher's work or else as being necessary because men have been polished and tamed to the point that they are left with nothing to occupy them and are incapable of occupying themselves. For it must be remarked that Du Bos' solution of ennui by way of art represents only one way out of that condition. The other way is study, erudition, curiosity, and meditation. Art is for those incapable of these higher forms of *divertissement*. We are still very much in the aristocratic tradition, since both types of *divertissement* are really considered in nonutilitarian terms. One might thus say that art represents the Jesuit's solution to ennui, and that meditation is more apt to be thought of in connection with Jansenism. As the century "progressed" from the period of the Régence to one dominated more and more by the ideas and values espoused and vulgarized by the *philosophes*, the "Jesuit" solution was abandoned for the more austere way of meditation, instruction, and work. Voltaire's Mondain walks into Candide's garden, a step not so far removed from Du Bos' view of the function of art as it might at first seem. We may think of a widening of the concept of art to include the whole enterprise of civilization.

Also, the shift from a hedonistic concept of art to an instructional or civic view corresponds to the old adage that art ought to please *and instruct*. Du Bos, significantly, hardly discussed this, for, as he put it, men prefer pleasure to instruction. His theory of art was thus addressed to, and a justification of, the attitude of a selected leisure class which had adopted the modern disdain of the pedant. All this gradually changed. Art, partly as the result of a better knowledge of its historical importance, partly because of the renewed interest in the antique and its association with grandeur, noble simplicity, and civic and moral virtue, came to be regarded as an instrument of moral and civic reform. It ceased to be thought of as a necessary form of *divertissement* or as a therapeutic to become instead an instrument to be used for higher purposes.

This more positive view of the function of art, which may be associated with the philosophical movement, was presented quite succinctly by Lacombe in his *Spectacle des Beaux Arts* as early as 1751, and it may be read as a partial answer to Rousseau's attack on the arts and civilization presented in his *Premier Discours*. Where Rousseau had presented a paradox, Lacombe presented the prevalent view of the function of art at this time. The arts, he explained, enlighten the mind, reveal to men the beauties of nature, develop the taste for truth, sharpen perception, and, in terms of historical development, it may be said that the cultivation of the arts has usually preceded the flourishing of the sciences. But the arts do even more than that: they also polish mores and behavior, render society more agreeable, strengthen the bonds between men, and teach individuals humane virtues and feelings. Humanity, progress, and the arts are inseparable. A state not policed by the arts is a state in perpetual danger: the strong oppress the weak, the orders of society are in perpetual ferment, rebellion is always possible, minds are steeped in ignorance, and only bodily exercises are held in honor in such states while those of the mind are despised. Only the arts have raised mankind above this state of rule by force to establish polite and philosophical commerce among nations. Finally, the arts are useful in that they also bring honor to a people and its prince: "Un peuple n'est véritablement grand que par les avantages du génie" (*Spectacle*, p. 55). The victories of arms are limited, but the victories of the mind are not: "Le pouvoir des Grecs et l'empire de Rome furent plus universels, plus absolus, plus grands, lorsqu'ils prescrivirent les lois du beau, qu'ils ne le furent jamais par le succès des armes" (Ibid., 56). Thus the riches of art were the most precious of all, for they alone were universal and lasting.

It is clear that apologies of art were founded upon a concept of human nature, and that the utility and function of art were assessed in terms of this nature. For Du Bos, the arts were useful because they diverted men from themselves; for Lacombe, the arts were useful because they united men in society. The position of the *philosophes* is the same as that of Lacombe. The difference between a Du Bos and the *philosophes* and their generation is one of emphasis and of taste, but in either case the arts are considered useful. The generation of Du Bos thought of the arts in terms of individuals occupied with individual works of art in their salons, reading, looking at pictures or drawings (or simply possessing them), and listening to music; or else they might consider the arts in terms of the greater spaces of the theatre or the opera. From another point of view, recalling Du Bos' view that his contemporaries regarded art as a species of furniture, one might also say, keeping in mind the new financier class of the Régence, that art is luxury and private property: it is riches manifested as beautiful objects. But the *philosophes* generally and the apologists of the *retour à l'Antique* think of art in relation to an entire society, in terms of the nation and of its citizens, and more in connection with action than with private enjoyment. Both types of apologists consider the arts necessary, given the nature of man, but they would use them for different purposes: Du Bos as a cure, the *philosophes* for the instruction of mankind. The difference is one between epicureans and stoics, between sceptics and optimists. Any differences between these generations, despite the vituperations of the partisans of the *retour à l'Antique* in regard to what now was called Rococo art, were as nothing compared to the attitude of Rousseau, who rejected both their views of art as well as human nature. The generation of Du Bos and that of the Encyclopedists differed merely as to whether emphasis should be put on art's potential of pleasure or on its social and moral utility. In either case they still worked and thought within the framework of the Classical aesthetic. But Rousseau went beyond it.

As we have seen, the concept of art in the seventeenth and eighteenth centuries was a function of views of human nature, so that it is possible to understand its significance in terms of human destiny and the psychology of the times, as well as of the more basic economic facts which then obtained. We may also have recourse to metaphor and conjure certain images of specifically human spaces. Thus, a meditation upon art at this time might begin with or in Pascal's room, pass to the salons known to Du Bos and his generation, and end with or in the celebrated garden of Candide. The latter is neither a French nor an English garden: neither *la belle nature*, a tamed, ordered object of contemplation pleasing to the mind (or, to be more accurate, to the reason), as are the *bassins* and parterres of Versailles; nor that artfully simple nature of the picturesque, designed to be pleasing to the imagination. Voltaire's garden is beyond the fine arts: no longer an object of contemplation but of action, even though it is still within the general framework of the Classical aesthetic, supposing a concept of art wide enough to encompass the enterprise of civilization. This was not a novel view at all, but placing it within the general historical context of the second half of the eighteenth century and recalling that it was a garden conceived by a landowner, a rentier, and also a reformist, we may readily perceive that Voltaire has gone beyond a hedonist theory of art to a more utilitarian notion. Candide's garden may thus be considered as one answer to Pascal's view of man in that room he cannot stand, just as Du Bos' is another answer to the same point. Where Du Bos would use *divertissement* to save us from ennui, Voltaire would use labor: the first answers the requirements of a leisure class, the second answers the requirement of humanity. The two are not at odds, but complementary, for we may be sure that it is not the seigneur who will engage in gardening, but those in his pay. The rich have taste and the poor have work to divert themselves from the common human condition. The rich are useful as consumers and the poor are useful as producers, and all is for the best in this natural nonaffluent economy. The Seigneur de Ferney adds to his *Temple du Goût* and to the *Mondain* that he wrote (and was) the *bienfaisance* and utility of the *philosophe* and turns the garden of Candide into a vegetable plot.

In contrast to Voltaire, Rousseau's attitude towards the arts, and therefore also civilization, is that of a poor man who owns no property and has to work for someone else in someone else's garden.

* * *

See also: *Nature, Taste, Truth; Diderot, Du Bos, Rousseau, Voltaire.*

ARTIST

On donne ce nom à ceux qui exercent quel'qu'un des arts libéraux, et singulièrement, aux peintres, sculpteurs et graveurs. Il est assez ordinaire d'ajouter quelque épithète au mot d'*Artiste*, pour caractériser les talents de la personne dont on parle.

THUS, LACOMBE'S definition in his little pocket dictionary of the arts, the *Dictionnaire portatif.* The word was in current usage by 1750 and was included in the *Dictionnaire de l'Académie* in 1762. It had not always been in use. Du Bos still used the term "artisan." Voltaire used the new word on various occasions, as with reference to Du Bos' work on painting and poetry, and also in the article "Critique" which he wrote for his own *Dictionnaire philosophique.* The word was not strictly limited to painters, sculptors, and engravers; the meaning was sometimes broadened to include those who were concerned with the fine arts in general, who cared about beauty, and in this sense the term might also refer to poets. The artist was primarily concerned with beauty, whereas *philosophes* were presumably concerned with truth. There was, we may say, something of the artist in Voltaire when he wrote poetry on the model of the ancients, when he thought of literary values in terms of the Temple of Taste, and when he indulged in purist criticism; but when he wrote a *conte philosophique* he used art without being primarily an artist, but rather a *philosophe.* Diderot too had much of the artist in him, whereas many of the Encyclopedists did not.

By the 1770s *artists*, in the sense of those who practise a plastic art, were expected to lead exemplary lives. This is quite evident from reforms instituted in the French Academy in Rome. The artist was now far removed from the artisan; he had espoused a vocation, whereas the artisan merely exercised a *métier.* The artist was concerned with the universal aesthetic and moral value of beauty as well as with posterity, as witness the long correspondence between Diderot and Falconet on these subjects.

It was not fortuitous that this notion of the vocation of the artist is concomitant with the elaboration of the aesthetic of the *beau idéal*, a concept of beauty inseparable from metaphysical and religious overtones and implying, too, in the artist a near-religious commitment and devotion to his calling and to beauty. It is also worth stressing that the use of the term "artist," rather than that of "artisan," follows the establishment of the salon on a regular basis, and that this institution signifies a changed relation between patron and artist, and between the artist and his art. The artisan, however skilled or endowed with genuis, worked on commission for a patron, and produced works, often, for a specific purpose and place; the *artist* who exposed his work in the salon did something more than that: he submitted his work to the judgment of amateurs and connoisseurs primarily concerned with beauty as exemplified or manifest in the plastic arts. Art was no longer (as Du Bos had characterized it in connection with his contemporaries) a species of furniture used to adorn one's rooms; it had become an institution for the public, supported by the state, and had also become a vocation for the artist. To expose one's works in the salon meant, however, more than merely appealing to the taste of the public; it was also betting on one's own immortality. The artist was much more aware of this aspect of art than was the artisan working for a patron, and he assumed a different attitude towards art as well as towards the public. The same change may be observed among men of letters at about this time, for they also began to think of the art of writing as something more than a social game devised for the amusement and conversation of the leisure class.

*   *   *

See also: *Art, Beau Idéal.*

BEAUTY

> L'esthétique des métaphysiciens exigeait que
> l'on séparât le *Beau* des *belles choses* . . .
>   *Paul Valéry*

IN EIGHTEENTH-CENTURY thought the distinction between beauty in itself and beautiful objects was maintained with considerable difficulty; it survived, but at a price to the meaning of the term "beauty." One began with two fundamental types, to end with almost any number here on earth but with one ideal Beauty somewhere above or beyond the earth; or else — one did not quite know where to look — in certain rapports, not easily visible, between a perceiver and an object and among objects themselves, or else — who knows? — perhaps between an observer and nature, or between an observer and certain well-known and measurable Greek statues. Crouzas, in his *Traité du beau,* had been content to postulate two fundamental types of beauty; Perrault had also accounted for two. Fénelon had evoked Venus and Minerva, but Father André, in his *Essai sur le beau,* found fit to posit a third, while Diderot caused an inflation, and the reader of his article "Beau," written for the *Encyclopédie* and meant to be a summary and resolution of the problem, is exposed to *beauté vraie ou apparente, beau absolu ou relatif, beau dans les moeurs, beau dans les ouvrages d'esprit, beau musical, beau essentiel, artificiel, naturel, arbitraire, beau de génie, beau de pur caprice, beau de goût, beau de création humaine, de sys-*

tème, beau intellectuel, moral, beau réel, beau aperçu, and also, on less exalted ground, *beautés fuyantes ou passagères* and *beautés régulières* and *irrégulières*. Not all of these were of Diderot's making, to be sure, but his attempt to make better sense of the metaphysical problem by dealing with it empirically did not help at all. By the end of the eighteenth century beauty, we may say, was spread rather thin.

The problem of beauty was first raised in the seventeenth century in connection with the beauties of painting and architecture. The painters of the Academy had been asked to elaborate a doctrine of beauty on the basis of the particular beauties of individual paintings. The first critics to write about beauty were thus amateurs and connoisseurs of art such as Fréart de Chambray and Félibien, and later, Roger de Piles. On a purely intuitive, artistic, and non-metaphysical level beauty was thus something associated with visible (but later also with auditive) impressions. "On comprend assez bien," writes Arsène Soreil in his study of eighteenth-century French aesthetics, "que l'dée autonome du beau se soit exprimée tout de suite chez les théoriciens de la peinture, et qu'elle ne l'aît pu, chez les autres, qu'en fonction de la plastique" (p. 19). It may well be that the distinctions concerning beauty drawn by metaphysicians and critics such as Pierre Nicole, who early made one between a true and a false beauty, were based on the effects which visual and auditive beauty made on the passions, for beauty associated with the visible and the audible were founded upon sense impressions, and were consequently associated with pleasure. Nicole, not only a critic but also a moralist, argued that pleasure was no proof of value and that true beauty must be founded in reason. The same type of distinction is excellently portrayed by Fénelon in his prose epic *Télémaque*. Telemachus has a dream in the course of which he perceives Venus: "Elle avait cette éclatante beauté, cette vive jeunesse, ces grâces tendres, qui parurent en elle quand elle sortit de l'écume de l'Océan, et qu'elle éblouit les yeux de Jupiter même" (Book IV, p. 57). At this point Cupid is about to pierce Telemachus with one of his shafts, but Minerva protects and saves him just in time. Now Minerva is also beautiful, but her beauty is of another nature and the effects of these two forms of beauty upon the beholder are quite different:

Le visage de cette déesse n'avait pas cette beauté molle et cette langueur passionnée que j'avais remarquées dans le visage et dans la posture de Vénus. C'était au contraire une beauté simple, négligée, modeste: tout était grave, vigoureux, noble, plein de force et de majesté [Ibid.].

The effects of these beauties upon the soul become apparent during
Telemachus' captivity on Cythera. His will broken, he languishes in
despair and is saved from the poison of love only through the intervention of Minerva in the guise of Mentor. For an instant he is freed
of the charm of Venus and is suddenly able to perceive a purer and
nobler form of love:

Je sentis comme un nuage qui se dissipait de dessus mes yeux et qui me
laissait voir la pure lumière: une joie douce et pleine d'un ferme courage
renaissait dans mon coeur. Cette joie était bien différente de cette autre joie
molle et folâtre dont mes sens avaient d'abord été empoisonnés: l'une est
une joie d'ivresse et de trouble, qui est entrecoupée de passions furieuses et
de cuisans remords; l'autre est une joie de raison, qui a quelque chose de bien
heureux et de céleste; elle est toujours pure et égale, rien ne peut l'épuiser:
plus on s'y plonge, plus elle est douce; elle ravit l'âme sass la troubler [p. 63].

These two beauties and their effects correspond to a constant dualism
of eighteenth-century aesthetics, however demythologized criticism
was to become. The first belongs to those false beauties suspicious to
moralists, critics, and philosophers; the latter is true beauty, accessible
only to those superior spirits willing and able to penetrate dazzling appearances in order to attain the True, the Good, and the Beautiful. The
philosophes assumed the role of Mentor. Amateurs were dismissed as
effeminate, frivolous, and decadent corruptors of true art, true taste,
true beauty; the beau idéal became the plastic manifestation of the
moral qualities associated with the beauty of Minerva, and a supposedly
relativist and materialist century ended by producing and justifying an
art of a highly Platonic nature.

Perrault, contemporary of Fénelon, had used a similar distinction in
a nonmythological context, in order to win his argument with the partisans of the ancients. The President believed beauty to be inherent in
the very nature of certain objects, such as the architectural ornaments
and systems of proportion, that had been invented by the ancients.
The Abbé, partisan of the moderns, argued that these beauties were
purely arbitrary and conventional, and pleased the eyes of men merely
because they were accustomed to these particular ornaments and
proportions. The ornaments or charms of architecture were merely
accidental and properly belonged to fashion. But there were other
beauties of a different order which were not arbitrary, but necessary,
that is to say natural and positive, and which therefore pleased independently of usage and custom. These natural and positive beauties
were, in architecture, smoothness, greatness, correctness, proper dis-

tribution of weight, and so forth, whereas ornaments were merely additions to these fundamental and universal beauties of geometry and technical achievement. The universal beauties may be said to appeal to reason; the arbitrary beauties, to the senses.

The history of the concept of beauty in the eighteenth century is largely that of a rivalry between lovers of Minerva and those of Venus. Philosophers tried to have the best of both beauties: they loved discoursing with Minerva, but one suspects they were not insusceptible to the charms of Venus. The problem was to keep the two beauties at a certain distance from each other, so that faithlessness to one would not be perceived by the other. Put another way, the problem was to reconcile the idea of Beauty with the mounting evidence of particular beauties. In the end, everyone loved Minerva after everyone had slept with Venus.

* * *

Pierre Jean Crousaz' *Traité du Beau, où l'on montre en quoi consiste ce que l'on nomme ainsi, par des Exemples tirés de la plupart des Arts et des Sciences* (Amsterdam, 1715) is one of the first attempts in the eighteenth century to arrive at a metaphysical definition of beauty. Crousaz distinguishes between a beauty relative to our sentiment, causing pleasure to the heart and the senses, and a beauty pleasing to the reason alone. It is the latter he will try to define in a manner reminiscent of Cartesian procedure:

Dans ce dessein, j'éviterai soigneusement de bâtir sur des principes douteux, je me conduirai avec tout l'ordre et toute la précaution qui me sera possible, je ne passerai point à une seconde pensée, sans avoir bien établi la précédente; et j'aime mieux charger mon discours de quelques réflexions superflues, que de hazarder quelques fausses vraisemblances, et de laisser une de mes propositions à demi prouvées [p. 3].

"Beauty" is a relative term, in that it marks a certain rapport between ourselves and some object. Justice and truth are also relative, in this sense, yet they can be agreed upon, so that the task of defining beauty is also possible. Analysis of the usage for the term can be taken as the point of departure of the inquiry:

Tous ceux qui, se piquant de ne pas parler simplement par coutûme, voudront descendre dans eux-mêmes, et faire attention à ce qui se passe chez eux, à ce qu'ils sentent et à la manière dont ils pensent, lorsqu'ils disent *cela est beau*, s'apercevront, qu'ils expriment par ce terme, un certain rapport d'un objet avec des sentiments agréables, ou avec des idées d'approbation, et tombent d'accord que dire, *cela est beau,* c'est dire j'aperçois quelque chose que j'approuve, ou quelque chose qui me fait plaisir. On voit par là que l'idée qu'on attache au mot de Beau est double, et c'est ce qui le rend équivoque [p. 7].

The ambiguity of the word "beauty" comes from its possible association with two different types of perception, ideas and sentiments: the former occupy the mind, the latter the heart. Ideas amuse us, make demands, sometimes tire our attention, according to their degree of complexity; sentiments dominate us, take hold of us, make us happy or unhappy, depending upon their nature. Ideas may be expressed, but it is very difficult to describe one's sentiments, and sometimes it is not possible to give an exact knowledge of these to someone who has not felt the same or similar sentiments. Thus beauty may be defined independently of sentiments and found with the mind alone. Agreement concerning beauty can only be found through the mind, because sentiments are by their very nature imprecise. Once sentiments are kept from interference in the search for the characteristics of beauty pleasing to the mind alone, one can easily agree that beauty is reducible to certain well-defined traits such as variety and unity, regularity, or order and proportion. The foundation of beauty is thus to be found in nature and truth rather than in sentiment.

Crousaz' definition of beauty has something in common with that of Perrault: it is a beauty discernible by the judgment alone. It is not readily perceived, because the senses interfere with judgment, in consequence of the fall of man (see the article "Taste"). Only beauty apprehended by the judgment is the object of good taste. It follows that since beauty is associated with reason it may be found in those areas which occupy the reason, namely science, virtue, and eloquence. There is a beauty of physics, here defined as natural theology which teaches men to admire, love, and serve their Creator, and which, as such, is the science most properly cultivated as the source of those truly agreeable agitations and pleasures of which we are masters, rather than the victims of accident and uncertainty. And, if diversity within unity and irregularity within order are the distinctive signs of beauty, where else but in physics will one find the most beauty?

There is also a beauty proper to history, considered both as a science and as the workings of providence: it is based on fittingness, on the rapports existing between the purposes of history and the means used to achieve these. The beauty of the historian's task lies in the utility of knowledge and the sincerity shown by him in ascertaining his facts.

Moral beauty is also a matter of relation, namely that between virtue in itself and human faculties. Thus virtue is beautiful in itself, but it is also useful and commanded by God: man must therefore think of his interest and his perfection by desiring that which is willed by God, for God gave man his nature. Our conduct should be in conformity with this God-given nature; this is desirable because it is *convenable*. Moral beauty is thus a union of the aesthetic and the ethical, and consists in the proper and fitting use of one's faculties and the achievement of a unity between the ways of man and God's will. Moral beauty makes us approve that which God Himself approves, and it makes us love that which He loves. This is an *essential* rather than a merely relative beauty. It is obvious that Crousaz was not only a metaphysician but also a theologian, and that his views of beauty are inseparable from his natural theology. Yet he did touch on beauty proper in at least one of the arts, that of eloquence.

The beauty of eloquence is founded upon the genius of the language, the fittingness of the means to the end, and the truth to be announced or enunciated. There is, however, also a beauty of fiction, a beauty that is, proper to hypothetical truth, that of the fable and the epic. The beauty of eloquence, however, is inseparable from the beauty of truth and instruction. (There follow certain stylistic requirements which are explained in terms of *convenance*.) Eloquence requires the use of appropriate and familiar terms, approved constructions, a touching and flowing style, brevity without obscurity, and gestures and pronunciation proper (like all the other requirements) to the truth to be propagated. Even the proper length or brevity of discourse may have a beauty of *convenance*, based upon the rapport between the subject matter and the mental capacity of the listener. The idea of *convenance* is also extended to style, which must ever be appropriate to the subject matter. If the aim of a discourse is to please without instruction, then beauty results when the aim is achieved, but this aim must be innocent. Crousaz' last chapter is given to music, but in the second edition he added a final chapter on the beauty of religion.

Crousaz' concept of beauty is primarily intellectual: it escapes sense perception or avoids it. It is a beauty which must be sought behind surface appearance and beneath the deceptions of the senses. One might metaphorically describe it as the beauty of a man meditating in the silence of his study. One is reminded of Kant's reaction to Rousseau:

"I must read Rousseau until his beauty of expression no longer distracts me at all, and only then can I survey him with reason."[1] Only Crousaz surveyed with a reason aglow with veneration the masterpieces of God, nature, providence, truth; and the unity and variety, regularity, order, and proportion he perceived therein he called beauty.

$$* \quad * \quad *$$

Father André's *Essai sur le beau* is a more complex work than Crousaz' *Traité*. There are three fundamental, hierarchically related beauties, each of which in turn may be analyzed into further subdivisions:

Je dis qu'il y a un beau essentiel et indépendant de toute institution, même divine; qu'il y a un beau naturel, et indépendant de l'opinion des hommes: enfin qu'il y a une espèce d'institution humaine, et qui est arbitraire jusqu'à un certain point [p. 5].

Essential beauty corresponds to Perrault's universal beauty, to Crousaz' *beauté de speculation* intelligible to reason, and before these to St. Augustine's identification of beauty with unity. Essential beauty is geometrical beauty and satisfies the requirements of reason, and it may be said to be the ultimate model of architecture: "Vous conviendrez du moins, sans peine, que la similitude, l'égalité, la convenance des parties de votre bâtiment, réduit tout à une espèce d'unité qui contente la raison" (Ibid., 12). This unity cannot be found in nature; it is purely intellectual and may be considered as super-natural, for it is the intimation of an original, sovereign, eternal unity, also identifiable as perfection: and it is this perfection which is the fundamental rule of art, so that each of the arts becomes an approximation of perfection. One might also associate this essential beauty with Batteux's *la belle nature*, which the arts supposedly represent. Essential beauty is independent even of God, who as the supreme architect must conform to its standards.

Natural beauty, unlike essential beauty, depends upon the Creator, but it is independent of human opinion and institutions. Natural beauty may be viewed as the spectacle of nature; it is the world of colors and of diversity. Our opinions about this natural beauty may vary, because it is perceived by the senses, yet there are rules whereby one may judge of the beauties of nature. The eye is the proper judge of natural beauty, and light is the mother of all colors, for God said: "I am the Light." Light is beautiful in itself and embellishes all that it shines

[1] Quoted by Ernst Cassirer, *Rousseau, Kant and Goethe* (New York, 1965), p. 6.

upon, while darkness makes things ugly. Thus light may be considered the standard whereby to judge of natural beauty, or beauties manifesting themselves through color: "Or, de toutes les couleurs, celle qui approche le plus de la lumière, c'est le blanc; celle qui approche le plus des ténèbres, c'est le noir" (Ibid. 17). Father André has recourse to Newton's five primitive colors, yellow, red, green, blue, and violet, to set up a scale of relative merit, within the general order of natural beauty, of the human races in terms of their approximation to light. All races are beautiful, for all are the children of God, yet all are not equally beautiful because all are not equally close to the Light. Since light is inseparable from natural beauty, it stands to reason that it is this beauty which is the object of the painter; however, since natural beauty and natural colors are the work of God, the painter's imitation of this natural beauty must ever be inferior to that of the supreme Artist. Thus, natural beauty is ever superior to man-made beauties. As the work of the architect is but an approximation of the perfection of the unity and beauty of universal order, so the work of the painter can only be an imitation or copy of that incomparably more beautiful work of God, nature.

Below essential beauty, below natural beauty, lie the arbitrary, variable beauties instituted by men. The realm of arbitrary beauty may be described, in relation to those of essential and natural beauty, as a realm of errors, though these errors are usually accepted as strokes of genius, *agrément*, happy irregularities, or mystery. Arbitrary beauty is founded on pleasure: "on passe tout au talent ou bonheur de plaire. C'est la première source de l'erreur" (Ibid., 31). This error, which Father André is at pains to expose and refute, and which he associates with Pyrrhonism and Epicureanism, consists in supposing absolute or essential beauty to be mere fiction and in being content to accept arbitrary beauty as self-sufficient, even though this implies complete relativism, a position which is acceptable only in the arts which are par excellence the domain of arbitrary or artificial beauties.

Now, since the three fundamental types of beauty above outlined may be met with in material as well as mental form, it is possible to make further subdivisions:

Comme le beau se rencontre dans les esprits et dans les corps, on voit assez que pour ne rien confondre, il faut encore le diviser en Beau sensible, et en Beau intelligible. Le Beau sensible, que nous apercevons dans les corps; et le Beau intelligible, que nous apercevons dans les esprits. On conviendra sans doute que l'un et l'autre ne peut être aperçu que par la raison [Ibid., 6].

The tastes of the palate, smell, and touch cannot really perceive beauty because they are but rough and dull senses; the perception of beauty thus remains restricted to sight and hearing. This means two further subdivisions based on the means by which beauty is perceived, namely visible, or optical, beauty and acoustical, or musical, beauty. Father André then takes up these various forms or manifestations of beauty in four chapters: *du beau visible, du beau dans les moeurs, du beau dans les ouvrages de l'esprit, du beau musical*. The three forms or types of beauty, essential, natural, and arbitrary, may be manifested as *intelligible* or *sensible*, and they may be acoustical or visible, if classified as to the manner of perception. Thus essential beauty may be visible, intelligible, acoustical, or sensible, as in geometry, architecture, or harmony. Natural beauty is certainly manifest as sensible and visible beauty, and is intelligible as God's work, while natural sounds fall under the category of acoustical beauty. Finally, arbitrary beauties, as the works of man, are surely made to be apprehended by the senses, so that they are visible or acoustical as well as sensible and intelligible, depending on their specific manifestations as works either of the mind or of craftsmanship in the form of sculpture, painting, etc.

As concerns art and literature and their relation to aesthetics and criticism, the chapter on beauty in works of the mind is surely the most interesting of the *Essai sur le beau*. However, in the view of Father André and of many of his contemporaries, moral beauty took precedence over the merely pleasurable sensations of the arbitrary beauties. Indeed, moral beauty was man's only merit and his highest possible achievement here on earth. It depended on his choice. It alone was capable of surviving old age, sickness, and the accidents of fortune. It was considered man's only merit, because after the Fall he could not know the good and the true without divine grace. Thus moral beauty may be considered as divine grace made manifest in the human and civil order. Moral beauty is therefore unthinkable without the union of the ethical and the aesthetic. Indeed, we may say that in the work of Father André beauty is inseparable from the Christian view of human destiny. Yet, even though one might separate the Christian element from Father André's view of beauty and its relation to the moral order, this would in no wise separate the ethical from the aesthetic, for there is also an echo of stoicism in his view of moral beauty, which consists in a personal conformity to the three basic realms of order:

Le beau moral essentiel, conformité du coeur avec l'ordre essentiel, qui est la loi universelle de toutes les intelligences; le beau moral naturel, conformité du coeur avec l'ordre naturel, qui est la loi générale de toute la nature humaine; le beau moral civil, qui est la loi commune de tous les peuples réunis dans un même corps de cité ou d'Etat [Ibid., 61–62].

Thus moral beauty is, as it were, an ordered construction of the soul, a certain human unity, an accord with the order of reason, nature, and the city. Father André's point of view vis-à-vis man differs from that of the Abbé Du Bos, even though both espoused an essentially Christian view. But, where Du Bos would use the fine arts to divert men from themselves, Father André would use them to inspire men to master themselves and form their souls. (The soul itself, insofar as it is capable of order after the Fall, becomes itself, thanks to the gift of grace, a work of art.) Leave out the allusion to the gift of divine grace, and the kinship between Father André and Descartes's *Traité des passions* becomes clear. Man, victim of his passions, imagination, desires, and fears, possesses a soul which is a field of war, chaos, and revolt unless the will is strong enough to impose order on the passions and thereby attain moral beauty. To order one's soul is to create moral beauty, or better, to imitate the natural order of God. The difference between Du Bos and Father André is akin to that between Pascal and Descartes: Du Bos and Pascal both attributed more power to the disordering capacity of the imagination and its dangers to mankind than did Descartes. Yet Pascal and Father André have similar views of the arts, though for different reasons: both reduce them to the realm of the arbitrary, the first because they are the domain of the imagination rather than the truth; the second because they belong to the realm of pleasure, which is inferior to the moral beauty man is or ought to be capable of attaining. And yet this is not the whole story, for it may also be argued that, just as Pascal was interested in eloquence because it could move men to the truth, so Father André also assumes that in the realm of arbitrary beauty the arts are justified insofar as they conform to higher and nobler aims than mere pleasure. His difference with Du Bos thus turns out to be greater than with Pascal because Father André founded his views of art upon a metaphysical concept of beauty whereas Du Bos did not. The differences are made clear in Father André's description of beauty as manifest in literature.

J'appelle *Beau* dans les ouvrages d'esprit, non pas ce qui plait au premier coup d'oeil de l'imagination dans certaines dispositions particulières des facultés de l'âme, ou des organes du corps; mais ce qui a droit de plaire à la raison et à la réflexion par son excellence propre, par sa lumière, ou par sa justesse, et si l'on me permet ce terme, par son agrément intrinsèque [Ibid., 79].

Now this beauty particular to works of the mind, *beauté spirituelle*, was itself capable of further distinctions into a *beau essentiel*, *naturel*, and *arbitraire*, all of which are manifest in works of the imagination. But in order to know the essential beauty of a work of the mind, be it history, poetry, or eloquence, one must consult and rely on the general taste rather than on the variables of caprice, passions, and humors which are the essence of particular tastes: "Consultons le goût général, fondé sur l'essence même de l'esprit humain, gravé dans tous les coeurs, non par une institution arbitraire, mais par la nécessité de la nature, et par conséquent sûr et infaillible dans ses décisions" (Ibid.). The essential beauty of a work of the imagination, manifest as *beau spirituel*, must consist in the following: "La vérité, l'ordre, l'honnête et le décent" (Ibid.). Truth, because the Word was given to be communicated, to be interpreted, to give light; order, because it exists between various particular truths; respect for religion and decorum, because it is an aspect of moral beauty; decency, because it not only includes respect for religion and decorum but also good sense, human respect, and natural graces.

Natural beauties manifest in works of the mind are less necessary than essential beauty, but they nevertheless play a role because men are not pure minds. Thus the natural beauty of images, sentiments, and pathetic movements were necessary to catch and hold men's attention, fix the imagination, delight the mind and soul.

Arbitrary beauty, unlike essential and natural beauty, depends upon various purely human institutions such as the rules of discourse, the taste of the nation, and the talent of particular persons. Summed up, it is seen as "la beauté qui, dans un ouvrage d'esprit, résulte de l'agrément des paroles" (Ibid., 95). It is a beauty dependent, in turn, upon three elements: "l'expression, qui rend notre pensée; le tour, qui lui donne une certaine forme; le style, qui la développe pour la mettre dans les différents jours qu'elle demande par rapport à notre dessein" (Ibid.). Each of these elements requires its own particular forms of beauty. Expression requires beauty of clarity, variation, and modulation. Turn of mind is a more particular phenomenon, for it serves to distinguish one mind from another, the great mind from the ordinary, the genius from the mind which cannot rise above the level of the national taste or general turn of mind. Yet this *tour d'esprit*, though particular to an individual, cannot be considered as something beyond or without the general order of nature, for it is "une manière de penser ou de sentir les choses, qui n'a rien de commun, et qui n'a rien que de naturel" (Ibid., 101). As for style, put in its simplest terms, it can be reduced to unity.

Father André's last chapter was devoted to musical beauty. Reading it leads one to suppose that music may well have been the Christian metaphysician's preferred art, and indeed that it, more than any other art, characterizes the implications for art and criticism of his concept of beauty. While it is one of the most technical chapters it is also his most enthusiastic, nearly lyrical, indeed, and there is little doubt that Father André perceived in music the intimations of a higher order which his theory of beauty assumes. Consequently the ear, rather than the eye, becomes the most spiritual organ.

Music is at once a mental as well as physical phenomenon. Natural to man, it is also a natural phenomenon within the general order of the universe and nature. There is one page in which Father André evokes the music of nature which might well serve as the program of Beethoven's *Pastoral* Symphony. In another place he draws a parallel between Newton's color scale and the musical scale, concluding that the latter serves to make of music a form of *beauté sensible* even more touching than that of painting. Yet precisely because music may charm us as powerfully as it does, the true idea of music is rarely understood. Most are content to confuse its true beauty with the pleasure of sound, although the ear alone does not suffice to apprehend the true beauty of music. For this, reason must also be called for, for the end of music is twofold:

La fin de la musique est double, comme son objet. Elle veut plaire à l'oreille, qui est son juge naturel. Elle veut plaire à la raison, qui préside essentiellement aux jugements de l'oreille. Et par le plaisir qu'elle cause à l'une et à l'autre, elle veut exciter dans l'âme les mouvements les plus capables de ravir toutes ses facultés. Un ancien auteur, nommé Aristide, fameux par un excellent Traité de musique, lui donne une fin encore plus noble. C'est de nous élever à l'amour du Beau suprême [Ibid., 123–24].

Thus music, for those who use their reason as well as their ear, manifests like the other arts essential, natural, and artificial beauty. Essential beauty resides not in the sounds themselves, but in the idea of harmony, order, proportion, and harmonic progression which as we listen to a concert satisfies, so to say, *un maître de musique intérieur* and does so even after the concert is over and the sounds are no longer audible. As for natural beauty, this is a certain consonance or accord between sounds and our body and soul, for it is beyond question that certain sounds are as in a secret accord with our soul, and that, just as we may speak of a color scale or a musical scale, so too may we think of our sentiments in terms of a scale. Thus natural beauty in music may be described as the harmony of sound and soul. As for the third category of beauty in music, namely artificial or arbitrary beauty, this is founded upon a certain degree of license made necessary because perfect consonance would in the end bring about such harmony as to set us to sleep. Thus harmony must be judiciously broken by dissonance, which adds a certain salt to the sweetness of consonance. But dissonances are also necessary in order to express the irregular passions of mankind such as love, hate, anger, discord, fear, and also to depict the horrors of a battlefield and the dangerous elements of a storm at sea. Music on this third level of beauty thus becomes not so much an intimation of a higher order, but an art of imitation and expression, the preeminent art possessing the *beau sensible*, and manifesting itself as *beau de génie*, the sublime of musical eloquence, as *beau de goût*, to be found in fine and delicate subjects, and finally, as *beau de caprice*, for the lighter subjects still. Thus music turns out to be superior to painting, for it can not only depict the surface of things, it can also express the passions within. One might say then, considering all we have said about Father André's view of and enthusiasm for music, that this was not only an art of imitation and expression, but also, in a sense, the sensible form of the universe and par excellence the most metaphysical of the arts.

Father André's work is more inclusive than that of Crousaz. He was more aware of the fine arts than Crousaz; he sought to define the various beauties of the arts and also to deal with hedonistic theories of beauty. He was still, like Crousaz, in the metaphysical tradition of aesthetics, or rather, to be more precise, in that of aesthetics from above. The existence of beautiful objects, or objects called beautiful, found a place within the range of reason only insofar as they participated in essential beauty so that works of art, in effect, are put on a low rung of a grand scale of values. Objections to a universal and essentialist view of beauty were dismissed as errors due to Pyrrhonism and in the end one may say that, despite the existence of artificial beauty, beauty on the whole was spiritualized. It came to be regarded as a substance, joined in varying degree to bodies or made manifest in certain cases through and as body, but at its highest and most refined state, it was thought to be manifested as unity. In his article on beauty for the *Encyclopédie*, Diderot summed up his critique of the *Essai sur le beau* in these words:

Le P. André distribue avec beaucoup de sagacité et de philosophie le beau en général dans ses différentes espèces; il les définit toutes avec précision; mais on ne trouve la définition du genre, celle du beau en général, dans aucun endroit de son livre, à moins qu'il ne le fasse consister dans l'unité comme saint Augustin. Il parle sans cesse d'ordre, de proportion, d'harmonie, etc., mais il ne dit pas un mot de l'origine de ces idées.[2]

Diderot was not quite right, for in effect Father André implied often enough that the origins of our ideas of order, harmony, proportion, of beauty as unity, in short, came ultimately from God.

Diderot wrote his article on beauty in part to make up for the lack of investigation into the origins of our ideas of beauty. But in doing so, one wonders if he did not spread the idea of beauty even more thinly than did Father André. Metaphysics from above, as news from God, gave way to metaphysics from below, as news from nature. And the beauty of beautiful objects, or of any objects so called, still remained in a relatively unimportant position, ever as part of something greater, never autonomous.

Diderot's contribution to the problem of beauty first took the form of speculations in his "Mémoires sur différents sujets de mathématiques"; later, he made further remarks along the same lines in his *Lettre sur les sourds et muets*. His speculations finally assumed the form of a long article written for the *Encyclopédie* and sometimes referred to as the *Recherches philosophiques sur l'origine et la nature du beau*. The first half of this article consists of summaries of the work of Crousaz, Wolff, Hutcheson, and Father André. In the second half Diderot proposes his own solution to the problem of the origin and nature of our idea of beauty.

Diderot starts his enquiry with sense perception and those objects usually called beautiful, intending to arrive at an idea of beauty encompassing all particular beauties. In short, we may characterize his approach as empirical and from below. However, insofar as Diderot sought to find the one factor which could explain all beauty, we may say that he was still very much inclined to a metaphysical solution of the problem. In opposition or contrast to Father André, Diderot was a

---

[2] "Recherches philosophiques sur l'origine et la nature du beau," in *Oeuvres esthétiques*, p. 407.

materialist who would not be a Pyrrhonist. He tried to reconcile the notions of relative and absolute beauty:

Beau est un terme que nous appliquons à une infinité d'êtres; mais quelque différence qu'il y ait entre ces êtres, il faut ou que nous fassions une fausse application du terme *beau*, ou qu'il y ait dans tous ces êtres une qualité dont le terme *beau* soit le signe [Ibid., 417].

Father André, and Plato before him, had also started there, but they both had ended beyond objects and the perceiver of such objects. Diderot stayed with these and placed beauty in between. The quality which rendered all objects worthy of being called beautiful, even though they differed from each other, was not really a quality or an essence, but the idea of *rapports*. Beauty became a function of relationships: "J'appelle donc *beau* hors de moi, tout ce qui contient en soi de quoi réveiller dans mon entendement l'idée de rapports; et *beau* par rapport à moi, tout ce qui réveille cette idée" (Ibid., p. 418). There were two exceptions to this, namely objects perceived or sensed by taste or smell. The distinction between objects outside the self and objects perceived by it he probably owed to the British empirical school, and particularly to Hutcheson, who, in his *Inquiry into the Original of Our Ideas of Beauty and Virtue*, had distinguished between the idea of beauty and the sentiment thereof, the former being an idea raised in us, the latter referring to a faculty allowing us to perceive or receive this idea. Ideas were interior, sensations were the connection between inside and outside. In Diderot's terms it is the perception of rapports which gives us the idea of beauty rather than, as in the case of Hutcheson, the interior sense of beauty with which men were supposedly endowed and by which they perceived beautiful objects.

Since beauty is a function of perception it stood to reason that it could be called relative. It was, as Hume said, in the eye of the beholder rather than in the object perceived. Diderot avoided this relativism by distinguishing between beauty perceived and beauty without regard to perception, *beau par rapport à moi* and *beau hors de moi*, or beauty relative to me and real beauty, unrelated to me. The world of the three orders of beauty posed by Father André is thus abandoned for an objective natural world perceived and named by man. Unfortunately, as Lichtenberg pointed out in one of his aphorisms, language was invented before philosophers. Diderot was stuck with the word beauty, but objects quite different from each other were all called beautiful, and he had no theology to help him sort out the various beauties in an ascending order from the least perfect to the most. Thus, since objects called beautiful were no longer ordered within a general system of thought which embraced all of creation, they could only be called beautiful in isolation (but on what basis?) or in relation to other objects:

Quand je prononce d'une fleur qu'elle est *belle*, ou d'un poisson qu'il est *beau*, qu'entends-je? Si je considère cette fleur ou ce poisson solitairement, je n'entends pas autre chose, sinon que j'aperçois entre les parties dont ils sont composés, de l'ordre, de l'arrangement, de la symétrie, des rapports (car tous ces mots ne désignent que différentes manières d'envisager les rapports mêmes): en ce sens toute fleur est *belle*, tout poisson est *beau*; mais de quel *beau*? de celui que j'appelle *beau réel* [Ibid., 420].

But if that flower and that fish are considered in relation to other flowers and other fish, more and more rapports are called into being, into view, into mind, and one begins to perceive that some fish and some flowers are less or more beautiful than other fish and other flowers. One thus arrives at the notion of *relative beauty*: "On voit qu'il y a plusieurs *beaux relatifs*, et qu'une tulipe peut être *belle* ou *laide* entre les plantes, *belle* ou *laide* entre les productions de la nature" [Ibid., 421]. All of which takes us far from the world of beauty as manifest in the fine arts and makes us perceive that we live in a world of beautiful or not so beautiful relationships. Which in turn makes us suspect that Diderot's solution to the problem of beauty is more verbal than real and that it merely appears to go beyond the Pyrrhonism of scepticism and the supposed lack of rigor of the dogmatists. Instead of being presented with three types of beauty in well delineated realms, we are now led to perceive beauty, real and relative, nearly everywhere: in the façade and colonnade of the Louvre, in Corneille's *Horace*, in tulips and sturgeons. What all these phenomena have in common are real and relative beauty, because they all have rapports. Beauty in art and beauty in nature are no longer distinct, for obviously there are rapports in art as well as in nature. And the scale of beauty which Diderot devises blurs the differences between the world of art and that of nature, because everything becomes a question of rapports — rapports with the perceiver and rapports between other rapports — and the sharper the eye of the perceiver for the perception of rapports, the better the discernment of beauty:

Selon la nature d'un être, selon qu'il excite en nous la perception d'un plus grand nombre de rapports, et selon la nature des rapports qu'il excite, il est *joli, beau, plus beau, très-beau,* ou *laid; bas, petit, grand, élevé, sublime, outré, burlesque,* ou *plaisant* [Ibid., 422].

The blurring of the lines between art and nature means that Diderot, in effect, naturalized the *belle nature* of Batteux so that it was no longer an order different from what Perrault called pure nature, but merely a choice within it, and what this means in turn is that imitation comes closer and closer to confusion with copying:

Qu'est-ce donc qu'on entend, quand on dit à un artiste: *Imitez la belle nature?* Ou l'on ne sait ce qu'on commande, ou on lui dit: Si vous avez à peindre une fleur, et qu'il vous soit d'ailleurs indifférent laquelle peindre, prenez la plus *belle* d'entre les fleurs [Ibid., 421].

And copy it accurately. Diderot turns out to be a naturalist, and we pass from an aesthetic of art, which derives from an essentialist or idealist metaphysic, to an aesthetic of nature founded upon a materialist metaphysic. The allusion to *la belle nature* in the above passage implies a critique of Batteux, just as certain reservations concerning Father André in the article "Beau" tended to limit the value given the *Essai sur le beau.* Yet one may truly wonder whether Diderot's own contribution to the problem improved upon either. For both Batteux and Father André at least left no doubt in the reader's mind that the word "beauty" referred to very different ideas, depending on whether it was used in the realm of philosophy, science, nature, or art. By thinking in terms of objects, perceivers, and relationships Diderot naturalized the concept of beauty, confused discourse, and spread the phenomenon of beauty so thinly between objects and their perceivers that the term became practically meaningless.

Diderot's excursion into the metaphysics of beauty can be dated about 1751. What can only be called Voltaire's sinking of the same metaphysics appeared in the 1765 edition of his *Dictionnaire philosophique* for which, not to be outdone by the Encyclopedists, he wrote all the articles himself, one of them on beauty. The article is short, witty, eminently readable, much less boring than Diderot's and even less boring than the *Greater Hippias.* It is also quite unfair to disinterested philosophical speculation:

Demandez à un crapaud ce que c'est que la beauté, le grand beau, le *to kalon.* Il vous répondra que c'est sa femelle avec deux gros yeux ronds sortant de sa petite tête, une gueule large et plate, un ventre jaune, un dos brun. Interrogez un nègre de Guinée; le beau est pour lui une peau noire, huileuse, des yeux enfoncés, un nez épaté.

Interrogez le diable; il vous dira que le beau est une paire de cornes, quatre griffes, et une queue. Consultez enfin les philosophes, ils vous répondront par du galimatias; il leur faut quelque chose de conforme à l'archétype du beau en essence, au *to kalon*.

J'assistais un jour à une tragédie auprès d'un philosophe. "Que cela est beau! disait-il. — Que trouvez-vous là de beau? lui dis-je. — C'est, dit-il, que l'auteur a atteint son but." Le lendemain il prit une médecine qui lui fit du bien. "Elle a atteint son but, lui dis-je; voilà une belle médecine!" Il comprit qu'on ne peut pas dire qu'une médecine est belle, et que pour donner à quelque chose le nom de beauté, il faut qu'elle vous cause de l'admiration et du plaisir. Il convint que cette tragédie lui avait inspiré ces deux sentiments, et que c'était là le *to kalon*, le beau.

Nous fîmes un voyage en Angleterre; on y joua la même pièce, parfaitement traduite; elle fit bailler tous les spectateurs. "Oh! oh! dit-il, le *to kalon* n'est pas le même pour les Anglais et pour les Français." Il conclut, après bien des réflexions, que le beau est souvent très relatif, comme ce qui est décent au Japon est indécent à Rome, et ce qui est de mode à Paris ne l'est pas à Pékin; et il s'épargna la peine de composer un long traité sur le beau [p. 50].

It would be erroneous to assume from this nice and pleasant refusal of metaphysics that by 1765 the Pyrrhonists had triumphed over the partisans of absolute beauty. Voltaire was merely being true to himself, and he was quite unrepresentative, for his attitude was that of the *Grand Siècle* which, as was pointed out, was quite content to equate the beautiful with the agreeable and leave the burden of proof or disproof to those who enjoyed metaphysical speculation. It may well be that in neighboring Britain aestheticians were quite discouraged in their search for an objective beauty. In France the enterprise seemed unimportant, not because one had ceased to believe in the existence of absolute beauty, for one can believe in it without being able to define it adequately, but because it needed no precise definition and because, to go back to Valéry's statement about beautiful objects, one hardly needed the evidence of metaphysical reasoning: for beauty could be directly seen. The savant and scholar in his study, writing a learned treatise on beauty one day, when the sky was serene, looked out the window and beheld a Greek statue. He abandoned his treatise, because no verbal proof was needed to demonstrate the existence of ideal beauty, for it was, he learned, not in the suprasensible world but had been and could continue to be in the historical world of flux.

At least, it would until one grew tired of Greek statues and discovered others which one found, first interesting, and then beautiful.

*   *   *

See also: *Beau Idéal, Nature, Taste; Diderot, Du Bos, Voltaire.*
Bibliography: Beardsley, Cassirer, Folkierski, Soreil; and the following:
F. Heidsieck, "La Beauté, aliment de l'âme," *Revue philosophique de la France et de l'Etranger,* Jan.-Mars 1965, No. 1, 71–86; Jerome Stolnitz, "Beauty: Some Stages in the History of an Idea," *Journal of the History of Ideas,* XXII, No. 2, 185–204; Frederic Will, *Flumen Historicum: Victor Cousin's Aesthetic and its Sources* (Chapel Hill, 1965).

BEAU IDEAL

WHILE THE *beau idéal* may be associated with the plastic arts of the closing decades of the eighteenth century and the general taste for the antique and for antiques at that time, the significance of the *beau idéal* is more than artistic. Based upon the antique and on Winckelmann's conception of ideal beauty, the term implies artistic values indissolubly linked with certain moral qualities. The term *beau idéal* refers not only to a model of perfection not found in real nature, in which respect it corresponds to another version of the *belle nature* of Batteux or Perrault, but also to a moral imperative. It supposes the union of the ethical and the aesthetic, and is resonant with Platonic overtones. The *beau idéal* implies nobility, serenity, dignity, noble simplicity, and calm grandeur, to quote from Winckelmann, as well as moral and civic virtue, and controlled and mastered passions. Associated with the artistic and moral values of the Greeks and Romans, it was often contrasted with the false and decadent beauties of French art of the eighteenth century before this was itself reformed along the universalist lines of the *beau idéal*. It may therefore also be associated with the return of a *grande manière* or *grand goût* in opposition to the *petite manière* of the early eighteenth century.

It may be argued that the establishment of the *beau idéal* as the ultimate artistic criterion resolved the opposition of relativist and absolutist views of beauty. For the justification of the *beau idéal* was found in historic examples, such as the Laocoön and the Apollo Belvedere, and thus had a certain empirical foundation. And, since it was the work of the civilization of the ancients, it was also associated with the moral values of that civilization — and these were thought to be universal. But the *beau idéal*, as manifest in the sculpture of the ancients, had the further advantage of being rationally justified on the basis of measurable proportions. Thus relative beauty, based on the customs of the Greeks, and universal beauty, founded upon reason and moral values, were harmoniously united in works found in history, born of history, yet rising above the contingencies of time and change to attain the *beau idéal*. In this realm the good, the true, and the beautiful were one, and in this way it could be argued too that the *beau idéal* also escaped the contingency of taste.

The argument used by the Pyrrhonists and Epicureans to argue against a universal taste and beauty on the basis of human sentiment and sensibility was used against them by Diderot in terms which define the implications of the *beau idéal* rather well. He did not use the term in his argument, but he was acquainted with the work of Winckelmann, and the association of moral and physical beauty is not fortuitous. Whereas the Pyrrhonists and sceptics argued that you could not found universal beauty on sentiment because this was unstable and variable, Diderot argued that men were *sensible* to greatness, moral as well as physical, and thus it is that Pascal's *Dieu sensible au coeur*, rather than mind, was transformed, so to speak, into the *beau idéal sensible au coeur*, and the aesthetic experience became a species of transcendent intimation of a higher truth and beauty:

Si le goût est une chose de caprice, s'il n'y a aucune règle du beau, d'où viennent donc ces émotions délicieuses qui s'élèvent si subitement, si involontairement, si tumultueusement au fond de nos âmes, qui les dilatent ou qui les serrent, et qui forcent de nos yeux les pleurs de la joie, de la douleur, de l'admiration, soit à l'aspect de quelque grand phénomène physique, soit au récit de quelque grand trait moral? *Apage, Sophista!* tu ne persuaderas jamais à mon coeur qu'il a tort de frémir; à mes entrailles, qu'elles ont tort de s'émouvoir. Le vrai, le bon et le beau se tiennent de bien près.[1]

This passage implies a complete reversal of the relations drawn till then between taste, judgment, and sentiment. For the judgment, considered as the controller of sentiment, is practically sacrificed to the power of sensibility: being moved by an object thus comes to be the proof of that object's moral and aesthetic quality. The *beau idéal*, as a moral and aesthetic quality, is capable of touching all men of sensibility in the degree to which they are endowed with such. The man of great sensibility may be so touched as to be unable to express him-

---

[1] "*Essais sur la Peinture*" in *Oeuvres esthétiques*, p. 736.

self clearly: he will be too moved, he will be ravished, like St. Theresa in ecstasy, by the perception of the good, the true, and the beautiful. The *beau idéal* thus affects all the faculties of men: reason, sensibility, and moral sense. The degree of sensibility merely affects the amount of pleasure derived from the perception of the *beau idéal*.

Considered against the historical and cultural background of the closing decades of the eighteenth century the association of a *philosophe* like Diderot with the aesthetic of the *beau idéal* is highly revealing of the latter's significance within the development of art and taste at this time. The *beau idéal* as the union of the true, the good, and the beautiful was especially suited to the taste of philosophers and more specifically of the *philosophes*. One may go even further and, keeping in mind the style of the French Revolution and the Empire, think of the *beau idéal* as the aesthetic of the triumphant bourgeoisie, for it unites instruction with pleasure, luxury with utility, the great nonfeudal past of Greece and Rome with the present, and private taste with public good. Ideal beauty is thus effectively opposed to the corrupt and degenerate art of the effete aristocracy, while the unity of truth, beauty, and goodness, manifest in the styles derived from the antique, insure against the potential of corruption inherent in art. An answer is thereby furnished to the sophistry of Jean-Jacques Rousseau's *Discours sur les sciences et les arts*. Artists are guaranteed from corruption and dissipation. Youth is shielded from the nefarious effects of nudities in the style of Boucher and Fragonard: for it is well known that the nudities of the Greeks and Romans, as manifest in the works of Vien and David, are not such as to corrupt youth, for the nudity is combined with modesty, while the nudity of the heroes of the Romans was of the virile type, befitting men of virtue, vigor, and civic vitality. One may thus say, taking advantage of hindsight, that the *beau idéal* was the aesthetic that answered the requirements of an art conceived for citizens, just as the *je ne sais quoi*, the *agréable*, the *beau de caprice*, and the *beautés fuyantes et passagères* had answered to the taste of the leisure class of the Régence and the financiers of the *ancien régime*. What this also means is that the *beau idéal* answered to the requirements of a public, as against a private, art, and it is of course no accident that the aesthetic of the *beau idéal* may be associated with the artistic policy of the state, whereas the *goût moderne* had been largely a private matter.

*   *   *

See also: *Antique, Beauty; Diderot, Rousseau.*

BIENSEANCE OR DECORUM

DERIVED FROM THE LATIN *decorum*, the concept of *bienséance* was introduced into French criticism by Chapelain, played a role in the quarrel of the *Cid*, and remained an important critical principle at once normative and descriptive. Closely related to *convenance* and to *vraisemblance* it is a rather subtle overall rule, as may be gathered from its discussion by Rapin:

> Outre toutes ces règles prises à la poétique d'Aristote, il y en a encore une dont Horace fait mention, à laquelle toutes les autres règles doivent s'assujétir comme à la plus essentielle, qui est la bienséance. Sans elle les autres règles de la poésie sont fausses, parce qu'elle est le fondement le plus solide de cette vraisemblance qui est si essentielle à cet art. Car ce n'est que par la bienséance que la vraisemblance a son effet: tout devient vraisemblable dès que la bienséance garde son caractère dans toutes les circonstances. . . . Enfin tout ce qui est contre les règles du temps, des moeurs, du sentiment, de l'expression est contraire à la bienséance.[1]

Bienséance here is seen as inseparable from the illusion of truth which is essential to the work of art, and as such is the ruling principle of the arts, though it is still unclear as to what constitutes *bienséance*. Pierre Nicole associated it with *convenance*: "La raison nous apprendra pour règle générale qu'une chose est belle lorsqu'elle a de la convenance avec sa propre nature et avec la nôtre" [Ibid., 216]. *Convenance* thus merges with *bienséance*, which may be interpreted as a certain rapport between an object and its nature, and between the object and our human nature.

René Bray, in his study of the formation of French classical criticism, distinguishes thus between two forms of *bienséance*, internal and external: between an object and its own nature, in which case one may think of *bienséance* in terms of some internal conformity of nature; and between that object and those to whom it is presented. The internal *bienséances* in the case of the drama, for example, imply a theory of character, proper behavior according to that character, ideal types; the external *bienséances*, still with reference to the theatre, imply propriety of representation and satisfaction of the expectations and tastes of the spectators, who in theory participate in or accept the same assumptions as to character and human destiny as does the playwright. The external *bienséances* thus imply conformity between art

---

[1] Quoted in Bray, *Formation de la doctrine classique en France*, p. 215.

and the public. The first is related to verisimilitude, the second to mores; the first is an aesthetic principle, the second is more liable to lead one to ethical considerations. Decorum thus implies more than an artistic principle for the poet, a critical maxim for the critic; it is also a social and moral principle. One might say that it is through the notion of decorum that the aesthetic and the ethical join or meet in the *ancien régime*, and one may say that *bienséance* in the realm of social behavior is nothing less than the principle of imitation outside the realm of art.

The internal *bienséances* led to a certain type of historical realism coupled with the representation of ideal types. Mores of an ancient society ought not to be changed on the stage to suit the spectators of a modern age: historical truth must be observed. Kings ought to be credible, and to be so they must behave as kings ought to behave, just as heroes must act heroically, and lovers like lovers. However, this insistence on conformity to historical truth, and also to a certain concept of man and of ideal types, could easily conflict with the external *bienséances* required of the playwright. This is the case not only as regards his art, for a representation on stage is hardly quite the same thing as a historical event (which is why, indeed, one requires not truth but verisimilitude); it also conflicts with the dramatist's obligations towards the audience. For, as Chapelain puts it, "Tout écrivain qui invente une fable, dont les actions humaines sont le sujet, ne doit pas représenter ses personnages, ni les faire agir que conformément aux moeurs et à la créance de son siècle" (Ibid., 225). Obviously the concept of historical truth implied by the internal *bienséances* was quite different from that of a Peter Weiss and others of our contemporaries who tend to merge art and documentation. It is also quite clear from this that the criticism levelled at the French theatre of the seventeenth century by later eighteenth-century critics, British, French, and German, to the effect that the heroes of Corneille and Racine were hardly Greek or Roman, was founded upon a misunderstanding if not ignorance of the critical assumptions which obtained in the early seventeenth century. Barbarian mores were too crude to be represented on the stage; historical knowledge was not detailed enough; historical understanding and critical assumptions were such that one could very well change the historical past to meet the requirements of the contemporary stage. In effect, themes drawn from the ancients, even by poets who professed admiration for the ancients and took sides against the moderns, really created modern works. But this was something different from the modernization of Homer as practiced by La Motte in the early eighteenth century, even though he did it also in the name of the external *bienséances*.

The problem of the relation of truth to art was avoided in the course of the seventeenth century because one was, in effect, to imitate *la belle nature*, in other words, to conform oneself to a higher truth, and, insofar as art was concerned, what mattered was verisimilitude.

Decorum also implies an art which acts as a veil between the true world of nature in which men live and the spectator, and in the social realm it acts as regulator of the passions. Decorum implies, then, an aesthetic of art and civilized human behavior.

✳ ✳ ✳

See also: *Art, Nature; Aubignac, Chapelain.*
Bibliography: René Bray, *La Formation de la doctrine classique en France* (Paris, 1927).

CONNOISSEUR

THE COMTE DE CAYLUS, antiquarian, engraver, and *amateur* of the arts associated with the Académie Royale de Peinture et de Sculpture, carefully distinguished between *connoisseurs* and *curieux*.

The *connoisseur* was a man of knowledge in the fine arts, especially painting, sculpture, and antiquities. His knowledge was not merely a predilection for a certain master or school, it implied also a general knowledge of the rules and principles of art. Indeed, it might go as far as a knowledge of the practise of the arts. Thus the *connoisseur* might be admitted to the Académie as an *amateur* (see article "Amateur"). Caylus, Mariette, La Live, were *connoisseurs* as was Roger de Piles.

The term, however, had a wider meaning than Caylus' use of it would indicate. One could be a *connoisseur* of letters, poetry, and music, as well as of paintings. One could also be a false *connoisseur*. The *connoisseur*, like the *curieux* (see article "Curieux"), appears in La Bruyère, who is above all interested in him as a social type:

Avec cinq ou six termes de l'art, et rien de plus, l'on se donne pour connoisseur en musique, en tableaux, en bâtiments, et en bonne chère: l'on croit avoir plus de plaisir qu'un autre à entendre, à voir et à manger; l'on impose à ses semblables, et l'on se trompe soi-même.[1]

The term *connoisseur*, La Bruyère notwithstanding, implies enjoyment of the fine arts, knowledge of them, and consciousness of that enjoyment. The *connoisseur* is a man of taste, though the term implies a more restricted area of interest than taste. The man of taste, however, is not necessarily a *connoisseur* (see article "Taste"), but must found his taste, his judgment, in part at least upon the type of knowledge and the judgment expressed by the *connoisseur*. There are, in other words, two different types of knowledge at issue in differentiating the man of taste from the *connoisseur*. The latter has a direct knowledge of works of art, the former might have a knowledge less direct, but one which is supplemented by his feeling and judgment. The *connoisseur*, as the term implies, is a man who knows the arts, or one art: who knows the true from the false, the good from the bad, the original from the copy. He also knows the artists, history, and principles of the various arts he is interested in. In a sense this knowledge is his pleasure, and while he does use a type of judgment which is truly at the origin of the judgment of taste, based upon wide knowledge and perception, intimate knowledge of the arts, and sometimes of the artists and their *métier*, that judgment of taste is restricted to the art he is particularly interested in. The man of taste does something else with the knowledge gained by the *amateur*. The *connoisseur* is closer to the *curieux* in that he has a passion for objets d'art, complemented by knowledge and judgment. He is interested in beauty and artistic quality, rather than in rare objects. The man of taste is interested in something else: where the *connoisseur* gives himself and his interest to art, the man of taste does not; he uses objets d'art, or paintings, or belles lettres, or even knowledge, to make of life an art.

The *connoisseur* is a potential antiquarian, a potential savant, art historian, or art dealer; the man of taste is a more universal type.

$$* \quad * \quad *$$

See also: *Amateur, Curieux.*
Bibliography: Caylus, Cochin, Watelet; and the following: Francis Henry Taylor, *The Taste of Angels* (Boston, 1948); the chapter on

[1] *Les Caractères de Théophraste, traduits du Grec, avec les Caractères ou les Moeurs de ce Siècle*, in *Oeuvres* (Paris: Editions de la Pléiade, 1951), p. 62, No. 82.

French patronage in the seventeenth century in Francis Haskell's first-rate *Patrons and Painters: A Study in the Relations Between Italian Art and Society in the Age of the Baroque* (London, 1963).

CONVENANCE

THIS TERM IS RELATED TO *bienséance*, and also to *costume*; it seems, indeed, to be but a later term for *bienséance* if we are to follow the definition of *convenance* in Lacombe's *Dictionnaire portatif*:

Le sentiment, et le goût indiquent assez ce que ce mot renferme par rapport aux arts. Il y a dans chaque sujet, et dans chaque partie d'un sujet, des égards à observer suivant la scène, les circonstances, et le temps d'une action; suivant les moeurs, l'âge, et le rang des personnages; enfin tout ce qui entre dans la composition d'un sujet, doit concourir à le faire connaître et l'embellir. La *Convenance* exige, par exemple, qu'un Hercule ne soit pas habillé d'étoffes légères, et un Apollon d'une draperie pesante.

Convenance refers not only to rapports within a single work of art, be it a poem, painting, or drama, but also to the rapport of the work to the subject matter and to an entire concept of what is and what is not appropriate among men, heroes, and gods. It supposes, therefore, established models and the conformity of works of art to these established models, be they of the world of art or of history. The term leads us also to *vraisemblance*, for a work lacking in *convenance* will also be lacking in credibility. A king not acting like a king is not credible, given the essential qualities of kingship. If we pursue our thinking further we may also come to the term *harmony*, which is another form of *convenance*. It is obvious that all this rests upon the fundamental concept of unity associated with beauty. The term *convenance* can also be used to refer to what have been termed the *bienséances externes*, in which case it defines a rapport between the work and the public and can thus also be associated with *decorum*.

As used in the definition cited, *convenance* applies best to matters visible to the eye, in painting and on the stage. But it is obvious that it also has social connotations. As LaTour pointed out, as Diderot repeated, as everyone knew, a portraitist supposedly painted his subjects in terms of *convenance*: a king must look like a king, a minister like a minister and not like a king, and so on down to the lower ranks of the social hierarchy. The same rule of *convenance* supposedly had to obtain in architecture: the king must have the most magnificent palace among men. Batteux ends his book on the fine arts with these considerations:

Toute demeure doit être l'image de celui qui l'habite, de sa dignité, de sa fortune, de son goût. C'est la règle qui doit guider les arts dans la construction et dans les ornements des lieux. Ovide ne pouvoit rendre le Palais du Soleil trop brillant, ni Milton le Jardin d'Eden trop délicieux: mais cette magnificence serait condamnable même dans un roi, parce qu'elle est au-dessus de sa condition:

Singula quaeque locum teneant sortita decenter

[Les Beaux-Arts, 291].

It is obvious that while convenance may be defined, its institution is another matter: it depends upon taste. It follows that persons who observe convenance have taste, or judgment; it further follows that they are civilized, and that convenance is a nondemocratic term: it supposes, indeed, a general order of nature, of society, and a hierarchy within that order. The artist reproduces the convenance of that order, and the private man of judgment observes the rule of convenance by knowing his place and his limits within that given order.

COSTUME

WHILE THIS TERM has something to do with costumes, it has much more to do with customs. It refers to a category of phenomena fraught with dangers to the adherents of a metaphysical concept of beauty. To borrow from the language of Father André, it might be called a Pyrrhonist's term. Costume is often used in the discussion of painting, but it is also a term applicable to certain matters concerning the epic, that genre of poetry which corresponds to history painting. The concept of costume leads us from the general and universal to the particular: or, one might say, from the heavenly beauty of the philosophers to the particular beauties of art. As concerns painting the term may be defined as follows:

Terme de peinture, par lequel on entend ce qui est suivant les temps, le génie, les moeurs, les loix, le goût, les richesses, le caractère et les habitudes d'un Pays où l'on place la scène d'un Tableau. Il ne suffit pas que dans la représentation d'un sujet, il n'y ait rien de contraire au Costume, il faut encore, autant qu'il se peut, qu'il y ait quelque signe particulier, pour faire connaître le lieu où l'action se passe, et quels sont les personnages qu'on a voulu représenter. On entend aussi par le *Costume*, tout ce qui regarde la chronologie, l'ordre des temps, et la vérité de certain faits connus de tout le monde; enfin, tout ce qui concerne la qualité, la nature et la propriété essentielle des objets qu'on représente [Lacombe, *Dictionnaire portatif*].

It is quite clear that if *costume* leads us to the particular, it leads us towards variation, towards all the exceptions from an aesthetic of universal beauty. Thus the terms *génie* and *goût* in the above-given definition cease to refer to universal phenomena, and become the genius and the taste particular to a given people. It was admitted by painters and by writers on painting that the various nations and the various schools of painting then known differed from each other (see article "Taste"). *Costume*, then, entered into aesthetic discussion from two sources, the arts and history. It leads us away from universal beauty towards particular beauties, and it also leads us towards the notion of truth, though in this case truth and illusion are joined in art, for correct *costume* is necessary in order to fabricate a proper artistic illusion.

Costume and ideal and universal beauty were reconciled at last towards the end of the eighteenth century, thanks to the influence of men like Winckelmann and Mengs who stated, in effect, that the particular beauty of the Greeks, and therefore by extension the *costume* of the Greeks, was worthy of being regarded as the true and universal beauty. But before this time it would rather seem that universal beauty was something professed by metaphysicians, while poets and painters produced local beauties because of the necessity of observing the rules concerning *costume*.

CRITICAL THEORY AND CRITICISM

> Critiques. Le plus sale roquet peut faire une blessure mortelle; il suffit qu'il ait la *rage*.
> Paul Valéry

CRITICAL THEORY in the period of the *ancien régime* could hardly be separated from what we would now term aesthetic problems. Critics judged and evaluated works of literature, and later of painting and sculpture, on the basis of assumptions which they sometimes expressed and systematized, and sometimes left unformulated, later to be probed by the more philosophically inclined among them. The lines between criticism and aesthetics were thus blurred; most of the time a critic was both critic and aesthetician, though some of the time he might be more one than the other. Even the Abbé Desfontaines, editor of the periodical *Nouvelliste du Parnasse*, sometimes interrupted his news from the republic of letters in order to state his critical premises. Diderot was both an art critic and theorist. Voltaire was not only a man of taste but also a critic who occasionally made excursions into the realm of aesthetic theory. Critical theory proper may thus be discussed under various categories which together make up the aesthetic of Classicism, namely art, beauty, decorum, imitation, nature, taste, and so on. However, critical theory was but one aspect of a rather wide range of critical activity. Other quesions concerning the form, tone, and mores of criticism at this time also have a claim on our interest. We may wonder, in particular, how rather abstract aesthetic considerations were applied by the critical judgment of the Classical period to the perusal and evaluation of works of the imagination.

It is possible to distinguish between a broad prescriptive criticism, a body of rules, and empirical critical practise, though here again the lines of demarcation cannot be sharply drawn. In the first instance we may speak of the exposition and formulation of rules; in the second, of judgments passed on works of literature. In the realm of prescriptive criticism, however, it is possible to distinguish further between general rules and the more particular ones that may also be called advice to authors. One might think of the general rules as aesthetics and of the particular ones as poetics. The problem of imitation belongs to general theory, but the advice given an author on just what imitation means, or how to go about producing a work of literature, belongs to poetics. Both the *Art poétique* of Boileau and Pope's *Essay on Criticism* offer and are examples of the two levels. Consider the following from Boileau:

> Quelque sujet qu'on traite, ou plaisant, ou sublime,
> Que toujours le bon sens s'accorde avec la rime:
> L'un l'autre vainement ils semblent se haïr;
> La rime est une esclave, et ne doit qu'obéir.
>
> . . . .
>
> Aimez-donc la raison: que toujours vos écrits
> Empruntent d'elle seule et leur lustre et leur prix
> [Part I].

This particular advice is based on a general aesthetic principle which has erroneously been associated with Cartesianism because of the rather ambiguous meaning of the word "reason." Presumably the principle makes sense within certain general premises and practises which obtained in the seventeenth century but which no longer do so, even though one might still maintain that, given the circumstances of our day, what present-day artists and poets do is in fact quite reasonable. But aside from this type of general normative advice or body of rules, one may find more particular forms of counsel:

> Hâtez-vous lentement; et, sans perdre courage,
> Vingt fois sur le métier remettez votre ouvrage:
> Polissez-le sans cesse et le repolissez;
> Ajoutez quelquefois, et souvent effacez
>
> [Ibid.].

This exhortation may be fitted into the general imperative of perfection, also an aesthetic principle, but it has little to do with the other rule of reason; and, irrespective of the dominant theory, the advice to work long, hard, and well remains excellent advice, whether one be a Romantic or a Classicist, with one provision, namely, that one has espoused an aesthetic of art rather than of self-expression. In other words, one may envisage that someone in the eighteenth century might well have rethought Boileau as follows:

> Quelque sujet qu'on traite, ou plaisant, ou sublime,
> Que toujours *la nature* s'accorde avec la rime:
> L'une et l'autre vainement semblent se haïr;
> La rime est une esclave, et ne doit qu'obéir.
>
> . . . .
>
> Suivez-donc *la nature:* que toujours vos écrits
> Empruntent d'elle seule et leur lustre et leur prix.

The advice about hard work could still follow, especially if nature is thought of as a general rational order. But if it is thought of in terms of transformation, motion, creative chaos, then one wonders whether the writer would still be asked to polish his work, since to do so would not present what he considered to be a true picture or expression of his perception of truth to nature. In other words, craftsmanship may be deduced from a general aesthetic of art more than from a general aesthetic of nature.

If we turn from the realm of theory to that of critical practise, we do not yet enter into one of empirical criticism, in the modern sense of reading without any prior views as to what a good work of literature ought to be. Critics writing for the *Nouvelliste du Parnasse* or the *Année littéraire* had an a priori idea of what good literature was, though it does not follow that they were therefore regarded as being prejudiced, because everyone else presumably had similar a priori ideas concerning literature. These critics, Desfontaines, Fréron, and others less famous were dogmatic critics, because their opinions and judgments were founded upon a body of general rules or principles. Their views were thus neither objective nor subjective. One may think, rather, in terms of purism and legislation, and it is at times possible to think of certain critics as being rather schoolmasterish and therefore particularly irritating to men of letters. Since these critics presumably knew the rules and principles of literature their attitude was that of judges. They stood at the gate of the Temple of Fame and scrutinized those who would enter. They sought out the errors and breaches of the law, they denounced lack of decorum and pointed to improprieties, and in effect sought to preserve what they thought were true and universal standards of taste. This attitude was reflected in their very style and tone: observers and judges of the literary scene and its production, they took on the tone of men of parts, mind, and sense and also assumed the posture of a certain detachment. This seemed presumptuous to some of the poets of the time, yet there is little doubt that their ideal of a critic was that of a fair judge. This is clearly stated in several letters in the *Nouvelliste du Parnasse*: the critic is to reflect judiciously upon the works which appear in print; he has chosen to write in the epistolary style because it is easy, free, sometimes familiar, and made for vivacity of manner, all of which makes for a better expression of one's reflections. The critic must be bold, but he must remain disinterested and polite. His shafts must not be personal or too strong; he must choose works he can judge well, discuss judiciously and freely; he must not judge works of theology, for these are beyond his competence. His task is very important, because he determines the quality of literature: his task is to control grammar and spelling, watch for neologisms, preciosity, and affectation. For all these tasks he must have good faith, exercise prudence, possess knowledge, and he also must *avoir des lumières*, obviously not the same as those of the *philosophes* in the case of Fréron. The critic must censure without hatred or resentment, must not praise out of friendship for the author but purely on the basis of merit, just as he should not despise a work because of his dislike of or enmity for the author, and while works may be attacked the person of the author must not. Criticism is a noble calling, highly necessary to assure the progress of letters and science. The true writer can never really be discouraged by adverse criticism because it will inspire him to greater efforts and excite him to reestablish his reputation by correcting himself. As for the critic, he need not be a universal, all-knowing man; he need merely possess a superior intelligence as concerns a particular subject. The critic needs but good sense and logic as well as knowledge in the area to be judged.

We may assume that critics did not always live up to this noble ideal, for if they had we should never have heard of them; they are known to us now only because a great many writers thought them unfair, prejudiced, vicious, and ignorant. Critics were generally disliked and disdained. Voltaire compared them to meat inspectors sent to market to see whether the pigs were diseased. He referred to them as toads and called Fréron a wasp, and generally likened them to criminals who, brought before the judge, excused themselves for their crimes by saying that they had to live. Voltaire obviously did not see the necessity of that. (Montesquieu thought it inadvisable for anyone to give himself entirely to criticism.) Voltaire's attitude may be summed up in the two final sentences of the article he wrote on critics in his *Dictionnaire philosophique*: "Un excellent critique serait un artiste qui aurait beaucoup de science et de goût, sans préjugés et sans envie. Cela est difficile à trouver." Voltaire obviously belonged among those who believed that the final arbiters of taste were the poets and artists themselves rather than the professional critics writing reviews in periodicals. This question of the competent judges of works of the imagination was only one of several questions raised in connection with criticism and it is not for nothing that critics were often told:

La critique est aisée, mais l'art difficile,[1]

a verse from Destouches which poses the superiority of the creative over the critical mind.

In short, critics were a nuisance and sometimes also a danger to one's reputation and success. Quite often they were men of learning who knew their humanities rather well, but they were not themselves primarily poets or writers of imagination, and insofar as their learning was concerned this tended to be rather schoolmasterly. The disputes between critics and writers of the eighteenth century may be viewed as a continuation in different forms and on different issues of the old

[1] Quoted in *Dictionnaire philosophique*, p. 159.

quarrels between pedants and poets which had occurred in the seventeenth century. Where one had then argued about rules and authority, one now had disputes concerning taste and genres, purity of language and innovation, and the conflict took on the aspect of a long and acrimonious battle between literary conservatives and literary liberals. Viewed against the general development of letters in the eighteenth century, the critics appear to have opposed the *philosophes* as much on aesthetic as on social and moral grounds: they were mixing genres, introducing jargon and metaphysics into letters; they were lacking in decorum towards religion and morals. It must also be conceded that the critics tended to judge present works in terms of established values, so that the contemporary writer often came out rather badly when compared to the work of those poets who had already stood the test of time. As we have said above, the critics stood at the gate of the Temple of Fame and would not let everyone in; yet writers wrote, presumably, precisely for such admittance.

If some writers thought they were being judged too severely by professional critics in periodicals, others thought they were all too often the victims of the frivolous criticism of the nonprofessional critics of the *beau* or the *grand monde*. There were, in fact, the two broad forms of critical activity in the eighteenth century: a literary-professional type and a worldly type, largely spoken. Paradis de Moncrif, worldly writer and *amuseur*, thus distinguished between the *esprit de critique* and the *esprit critique*. The former may be identified with taste, for he defined it as a justness of discernment in the evaluation of works of the imagination. The *esprit critique*, on the other hand, was a social phenomenon and a trait of character peculiarly evident in his day, and a French character trait to boot. He considered it a penchant for negative criticism, often unjust, generally of little merit, and almost always useless. The *esprit critique* as described by Moncrif is reminiscent of La Bruyère's *décisionnaire*, a social type ready to pass judgment and express his opinion on almost anything, ever talking, ever deciding, a type also to be found in Montesquieu's *Persian letters* and in Voltaire's *Candide*. Sometimes the *esprit critique* was simply referred to as *fausse critique*, criticism founded on opinion and personal prejudice alone rather than on knowledge and thought. Moncrif, again quoting Destouches, was convinced that the writer was the superior of the critic: "La supériorité qu'ordinairement un lecteur croit avoir sur l'auteur qu'il critique, est presque toujours imaginaire. Il entre communément plus d'esprit dans un ouvrage, même médiocre, qu'il n'en faut pour le trouver mauvais" ("De l'esprit critique," in *Oeuvres*, I,

333). In general, thought Moncrif (and with him, many other writers less as well as more exalted than he), critics are most often wrong in their judgment. Most critics, he reminds us, were wrong about the great writers of the seventeenth century; it stands to reason they may well be wrong again in the eighteenth. Nevertheless, they may be quite harmful, and Moncrif is especially interesting in regard to the reasons for the general dislike of both the professional and the mundane critics. The truth is that critics, whether rigorous or frivolous, could ruin a writer, and the frivolous could do it just as easily as the professional critics, with a bon mot, so to speak:

On regarde comme une plaisanterie ordinaire, les traits qu'on lance de gaieté de coeur contre un écrivain qui a bien mérité du public. On sait cependant de quelle importance est la considération. Cet avantage concourt au bonheur de la vie à tel point, que les richesses, et même les grandes places, quand elles en sont séparées, perdent beaucoup de leur prix. Un homme, pour parvenir à cette considération si désirable ou pour la conserver, n'aura que son talent d'écrire, talent que je suppose à un degré très estimable: ses ouvrages sont sa terre, son château, sa fortune, et enfin tout ce qui sert aux autres hommes à représenter avec quelqu'avantage dans la société: et on verra même des gens qui font profession de vertu, travailler à renverser tout cela par une critique souvent aussi amère que peu éclairée, et ne s'en croire pas moins équitables [Ibid., 337].

When one considers that writers were dependent for their livelihood not so much on their actual publications as upon the favors, personal and public, which were the effect of their writings and their reputation as writers, the import of Moncrif's words is clear. Critics were dangerous to one's very livelihood. The writer felt caught among the professional fault-finders, the unprofessional wits, and those who were ever bored. These last were just as dangerous as the others, since they were the type of men and women who found almost any new work a burden to read and a displeasure to evaluate fairly. Superficial criticism of this sort, very much to be found in the world, was harmful and quite useless to literature. It could hardly correct poor writers or stop them from writing; as for the mediocre writers, why not leave them to the delight of mediocre minds?

Opinion about criticism, however, was not wholly negative in the eighteenth century. There were those who thought about the matter with more detachment than a Voltaire or a Moncrif, and reading through Montesquieu's notebooks one may see that there were some who thought that criticism was not as easy as Destouches and those who quoted him believed. The failures of critics could be used to show that critics were usually foolish and wrong, but one could also argue that the criticism had been wrong to begin with, and that if the critics of the *Grand Siècle* had been often wrong it was the fault of their premises and assumptions. A case could be made for a difficult criticism, a new criticism philosophically inclined, more general in its nature, and founded not on authority and ancient poetics, but, on the contrary, upon the examination of the assumptions of critics and of the nature of the arts. In other words, the failure of the old criticism in the seventeenth century led to a new type of philosophical criticism which we may call aesthetic, so that criticism was no longer a matter of judging a given newly published work against the standards and models of the past. This new criticism also supposed lucidity as to the presuppositions of writers and critics as well as reflections upon the relation of art to society, taste, and imagination. Thus Montesquieu noted that "dans les critiques, il faut s'aider, non pas se détruire; chercher le vrai, le bon, le beau; éclairer ou réfléchir (réfléchir et rendre) la lumière par sa nature; n'éclipser que par hasard" (*Oeuvres*, I, 1229). This was, however, a very hard task, and the critic faced something which was sometimes more easily done by time:

Quand on se consacre à l'art de critiquer, et que l'on veut diriger le goût ou le jugement public, il faut examiner si, lorsque le public, après avoir balancé, a une fois décidé, on a été souvent de son avis; car ses jugements scellés par le temps sont presque toujours bons [Ibid.].

Montesquieu in this passage points to an assumption which the dogmatic critics and periodical reviewers did not question, namely that they were the directors and preservers of true taste. To Montesquieu this seemed presumptuous, as criticism was often but a sign of great vanity:

On dédaigne, pour faire paraître de l'esprit. — Pourquoi l'esprit que vous avez est-il une preuve que les autres n'en ont point? Quoi: votre goût sera toujours infaillible, et l'esprit des autres leur manquera toujours? Comment ce partage si différent: que vous jugez toujours bien, et que, sans exception, ils pensent toujours mal? Vous êtes libres. Soyez-le donc de rendre justice aux autres [Ibid., 1230].

* * *

See also: *Art, Beauty, Imitation, Nature, Taste*; *Chapelain, Du Bos, Fontenelle, Voltaire.*
Bibliography: Wellek, Wimsatt and Brooks; and the following: F. Vial and L. Denise, *Idées et doctrines littéraires du XVIIIe Siècle* (Paris, 1909); J. C. Robertson, *Studies in the Genesis of Romantic Theory in the XVIIIth Century* (Cambridge, 1923); Hugh Quigley, *Italy and*

the Rise of a New School of Criticism in the 18th Century (Perth, 1921);
J. Rocafort, *Doctrines littéraires de l'Encyclopédie* (Bordeaux, 1890);
Naomi Hepp, "Esquisse du vocabulaire de la critique littéraire de la
Querelle du Cid à la querelle d'Homère," *Romanische Forschungen*,
Vol. 69 (1957), 332–413; and for the relation of criticism to the novel,
Georges May, *Le Dilèmme du roman au XVIIIe Siècle* (New Haven
and Paris, 1963).

CURIEUX, CURIOSITE

THE CURIEUX, AS A TYPE, and *curiosité*, as a social and psychological
phenomenon, were well established by the end of the seventeenth
century. The term *curieux* at this time was still interchangeable with
that of *connoisseur*. Perrault, in his *Parallèle des Anciens et des Modernes*, uses both without drawing any distinctions between the two.
La Bruyère associates *curiosité* with fashion. In the eighteenth century,
however, the *curieux* was to be distinguished from the *connoisseur* as
well as the *amateur*.

The *curieux* is a person curious about objets d'art, paintings, or,
simply, rare objects. He is, in short, a collector. La Bruyère is rather
hard on this phenomenon:

La curiosité n'est pas un goût pour ce qui est bon ou ce qui est beau, mais
pour ce qui est rare, unique, pour ce qu'on a et ce que les autres n'ont point. Ce
n'est pas un attachement à ce qui est parfait, mais à ce qui est couru, à ce
qui est à la mode. Ce n'est pas un amusement, mais une passion, et souvent
si violente, qu'elle ne cède à l'amour et à l'ambition que par la petitesse de
son objet. Ce n'est pas une passion qu'on a généralement pour les choses
rares et qui ont cours, mais qu'on a seulement pour une certaine chose qui
est rare, et pourtant à la mode.[1]

Curiosité, thus understood, enters the province of the aesthetic as a
psychological phenomenon; it is allied to aesthetic pleasure, even
though what is collected may not belong to the fine arts. La Bruyère,
in his portrait gallery of *curieux*, alludes to those who have manias for
flowers, fruits, medals, prints, travel, books, the sciences, building,
women, birds, insects, sea shells, and so forth. It is perhaps worth
stressing that to La Bruyère *curiosité* is a passion, so that instead of
talking of aesthetic pleasure, one might have to think of a stronger
aesthetic passion. It is also clear that all the objects of *curiosité* are in
fact aesthetic objects *avant la lettre*. If we think more upon the sig-

[1] *Les Caractères de Théophraste, traduits du Grec, avec les Caractères ou Moeurs
de ce Siècle*, in *Oeuvres* (Paris: Editions de la Pléiade, 1951), No. 2, p. 406.

nificance of this passion and its objects, we may also make a further distinction which was in fact drawn by La Bruyère himself, and later by others in the course of the eighteenth century, though it was never clearly formulated: namely, that if *curiosité* is an aspect of the psychology of aesthetics, the latter is not the same thing as the psychology of art. The aesthetic, in other words, is something much wider than the artistic. In practical and historical terms, the *curieux* was not necessarily a *connoisseur*. The difference is clearly brought out by the Comte de Caylus in the eighteenth century. For him the *curieux* was merely a collector with a predilection for a certain type of object, a certain master of painting, or a certain school. He thus followed the direction indicated by La Bruyère, since his restriction of *curiosité* to something rather limited tends to make the *curieux* a mere collector, amassing his objects for purely personal reasons, sentiment, or inclination. A *connoisseur* was something else again.

* * *

See also: *Amateur, Connoisseur.*

DECADENCE, DECLINE

> Le besoin de nouveau est signe de fatigue ou de faiblesse de l'esprit, qui demande ce qui lui manque. Car il n'est rien qui ne soit nouveau.
> *Paul Valéry*

THE IDEAL OF PERFECTION, once reached, was difficult, perhaps impossible, to maintain for long. Decadence inevitably followed. This was deplored by the eighteenth century, but at the same time we may suspect that it must have fascinated many, since the causes of decadence were a frequent subject of investigation, exposition, and reprobation. In a sense, the causes of decadence in the arts were better known than the causes of progress. They could be pointed to and enumerated, while all one found to explain progress or *perfectionnement*, were genius and tautological terms for moral and physical causes. But for decadence one could find even scapegoats, just as one could readily perceive the symptoms of decline.

Decadence was potentially inherent in the very virtues of the Classical tenets of art, taste, and beauty. It is for this reason that decline is explainable in terms of exaggeration: it implies exceeding limits, stepping beyond bounds, upsetting a balance. Decadence also manifests itself in the various aspects of artistic doctrine and practise: in the areas of imitation, creation, patronage, taste, and of conceptions of art's social function and position. In all these areas, decadence turns out to be a form of excess, a departure from the norm.

On the level of imitation decadence sets in as a result of misinterpretation and facility: the term imitation comes to mean the copying of existing models of art rather than the imitation of *la belle nature*. Artists and poets ought never to lose sight of the original model of nature, even though they admire the works of the masters. When the works of the masters are taken as models and the study of nature is neglected, the result is *mannerism*, the production of the merely secondary work of talent rather than that of genius: "On adopte les défauts d'autrui, on dégrade les beautés de l'art en voulant s'approprier celles de l'artiste" (Lacombe, *Spectacle*, 28). One merely produces works in the manner of some master or school, rather than one's own. The true doctrine of imitation also supposes originality, even though the originality is bounded by the proper study of nature. To follow in the footsteps of a school or some master is merely to produce servile imitations, but this is what the majority do out of weakness. "La servile admiration," writes Lacombe, "qui fait négliger l'étude de la Nature, peut donc être regardée comme une des premières causes de la décadence du goût" (Ibid., 30). Imitation supposes a balance between one's own genius and the universal model of nature: to sacrifice one's own self or genius to servile imitation of a master is to upset the balance. On the other hand, to rely too much on one's genius is to upset the balance in the other direction and this consists in the second cause of decadence, the desire for singularity

"L'envie de se signaler qui est un des motifs les plus louables et les plus efficaces pour le progrès des beaux-arts, peut être aussi une des causes qui préjudicient davantage à leur gloire et à leur conservation" (Ibid.). The existence of a great many rivals, of competition, leads everyone to strive to be noticed. And while this is necessary for the perfecting of the arts, it is also a great danger: for those who cannot attain perfection by their own talent and genius tend to compensate for this through singularity, in order to attract the attention of the spectators. These can always be counted on to want the wrong thing; the crowd looks for novelty, and the singular artist will eventually find admirers and patrons. He will have brilliant success, and while such success can never last long, it may manage to survive for a short time, produce a fashion, be talked about, die out, be replaced by another fashion, take new form, die out and so on. Thus singularity is mere fashion, and passing fashions are forms of decadence and false taste.

Singularity, as we have seen, feeds on the public's desire for novelty.

This is an ever-present danger, especially in times like the eighteenth century, in which the public, sufficiently initiated into the fine arts to find fault but not enough to know the true sources of beauty, pretends to judge everything and affects to despise everything that does not astonish it. Decadence is thus often the fault of a public whose taste must be titillated, which seeks the bizarre, unusual, and novel, and leaves well-known, well-established works for new ones. In such circumstances a man of talent may always be found to raise a standard of reform, gather a public, and produce a revolution in the arts. Soon he will have a great number of admirers and servile imitators, and when this happens the true principles of the arts are annihilated: wit replaces sentiment, practise is vitiated, fantasy reigns supreme, and boredom with beauty leads some to prefer the ugly, as J. B. Rousseau put it:

L'ennui du beau nous fait aimer le laid.

Another cause of decline is what Lacombe terms luxury of imagination, or luxurious imagination. The simplicity and nobility of nature are left far behind. A new barbarism results: "Le caractère le moins équivoque de la barbarie est cet amour d'ornements qui chargent et étouffent le goût: par quelle fatalité dans les siècles les plus éclairés cette habitude vicieuse est-elle recherchée? J'en découvre les raisons dans l'amour propre et dans la paresse" (Ibid., 33). The former inclines one towards the caprices of imagination, the latter keeps one from the arduous task of seeking true beauty. Simplicity, the true greatness of art, is thus given up for the easier tastes readily satisfied by ornaments, false beauties, the *clinquant*, brilliance, tinsel.

Often decadence may be attributed to the particular, singular, and capricious taste of patrons and collectors. Here too we may perceive that a cause of decadence is but the vitiation of a virtue. In a society in which perfection has not been attained patronage of the arts is a virtue, and it is then well to help all talents. But in a society enlightened by the arts, in possession of masterpieces, the attention of authorities ought to be fixed upon the maintenance of acquired and established standards. In other words, once perfection has been attained, legislation and patronage must be used to offset the potential of decline. Thus novelty and singularity should be repressed, because they are the source of deviations from the norm and from true standards of beauty. Yet, curiously enough, the contrary happens as if by necessity. Private societies are formed which all have their private patrons, and private academies are created: and all these private bodies vie for success, dominance, and applause. Thus the true works of art, those happy successes of the imitators of genius, are lost in the activity of these private groups and sacrificed to the taste of individual patrons. Unhappy the man of genius who relies on his own talent, who tries to work without the protection of one of these patrons, and attempts to move forward without intrigue. True, his works are always the object of admiration of a small circle of true connoisseurs, and will be admired by posterity, but this man will not have emulators, and artists will take example, rather, from the unjust, opulent, and false amateur or patron. Often artists of merit are forced to sacrifice their genius to the taste of the times in order to survive. Noble simplicity is sacrificed to luxury.

Finally, decadence is a function of changes in the essential characteristics of the state, for the arts and sciences are to the state what the spirit is to the body. The state, national character, and national taste were thought to be inseparable by eighteenth-century critics and aestheticians; they considered the national traits of the various European nations as being founded upon the arts and tastes of their peoples. It followed that a change in the state, in its national taste or even its national character, would affect the other constituent parts. Thus a change of taste could be taken as indicative of changes in the national character, and the state of the arts varied with such changes. In Britain, for example, the state of the arts and sciences was indicative of the national character of the British, a people possessed of a dark but profound genius, a proud, untamed feeling for liberty, and a license which made them confuse the low with the sublime. In France, on the other hand, genius was ever the captive of decorum and was modified by it, and imperial Rome offered the spectacle of the arts gradually dying out under the constraints and fears of despotism.

We may thus associate decadence with mobility, caprice, fashion, instability, and the vagaries of the imagination. This view of decadence derives from a universalist view of beauty, associated with perfection, simplicity, and stability of values. Motion or change in the practise of an art and the creation of beauty is thus possible only as an upward striving for perfection or as a fall away from a perfection attained. In the first of these, the motion is purposeful; in the second, it is mere caprice.

✳　✳　✳

See also: *Gothic, Grands Siècles, Ornament, Perfection.*
Bibliography: Bricaire de la Dixmérie, Dacier, Lacombe (*Spectacle des Beaux-Arts*), Rémond de Saint-Mard.

DRAMATIC POETRY: TRAGEDY AND COMEDY

IN THE SEVENTEENTH CENTURY the discussion of dramatic poetry was still dominated by Aristotle and interpretations of his *Poetics* and by disputes about such matters as the rules of the three unities, verisimilitude, decorum, and the relevance of Greek and Roman drama to the requirements of a modern audience. The discussion of the drama in terms of verisimilitude, argued on the analogy of painting, may be considered an important new dimension, while the development of opera also made for further refinements in theory. To these may also be added the Cartesian psychology of the passions and, so to speak, the awareness of modernity. By the eighteenth century the rules were no longer an issue; they had become part of the conventions of dramatic composition and criticism. It was generally assumed that tragedy and comedy had been perfected as genres; parallels between painters and dramatic poets had become literary exercises; contrasts between Racine and Corneille were readily turned into school exercises; and the differences between tragedy and comedy were summed up as follows by Batteux: "La tragédie imite le beau, le grand; la Comedie imite le ridicule. L'une élève l'âme et forme le coeur: l'autre polit les moeurs, et corrige le dehors" (*Les Beaux-Arts*, p. 218). It was also argued that tragedy was founded on *le vrai* as well as *le beau*, so that an important criterion of validity was its *vraisemblance*, whereas opera, in contrast, was founded on fable and the marvellous, so that it escaped the criterion of verisimilitude. Comedy was divided into high comedy, low comedy, and farce, high comedy being associated with the tone set by good company and the smiles of wit, while low comedy put valets, servants, and ordinary people on the stage. Farce was quite near to burlesque and buffoonery. The basis of ridicule, which was the object of comedy according to Batteux, was defined as "les défauts qui causent la honte, sans causer la douleur. C'est, en général, un mauvais assortiment de choses qui ne sont point faites pour aller ensemble" (Ibid., p. 220). A certain discordance between an individual and social usage and mores, or within an individual's character and his behavior, could be construed and treated in terms of ridicule. Comedy thus lifted masks to show men as they were in society.

Since all this is generally known, and since the eighteenth century added little new to the discussion of this aspect of dramatic poetry, we shall concentrate on questions which remained at the forefront of eighteenth-century preoccupations regarding the theatre. These centered on the passions and the relation of the stage to society. The purgation theory of tragedy was interpreted in terms of the play of the passions as the eighteenth century understood these; at the same time, in a line of thinking related to the passions, one pondered the social role and utility of the theatre. The former was of considerable interest to Du Bos, while the *philosophes* were interested in the relation of the stage to society. Diderot, in addition, occupied himself with the art of acting and once more raised questions concerning the stage and the visual arts. Rousseau posed the problem of the stage within the greater framework of the relation of art to society. But all these questions were no longer discussed with reference to general rules of art, but rather within a more general framework. In the previous century the discussion had been largely limited to savants and playwrights, but that had changed and the vocabulary had changed too: for all the questions relating to the passions and to the social role of theatre were now posed in the new language of philosophy, having reference to nature rather than to rules devised to produce perfect works for the stage.

Du Bos explained tragedy in terms of his *divertissement* theory of the arts. Man was an *être sensible* that had to be continually moved by passions: he had to be diverted, occupied, kept from boredom; he shunned the state of rest. The drama thus entered naturally into the *divertissement* theory of art. But this did not answer the question of why men found pleasure in the spectacle of tragic drama as such: why did we enjoy the pity and the terror? why watch spectacles which in real life would horrify? The point is that even in real life such spectacles did not keep men away: they went in crowds to witness executions as the Romans had swarmed to the games to witness and enjoy gladiatorial combats.

Ainsi nous courons par instinct après les objets qui peuvent exciter nos passions, quoique ces objets fassent sur nous des impressions qui nous coûtent souvent des nuits inquiètes et des journées douloureuses: mais les hommes en général souffrent encore plus à vivre sans passions, que les passions ne les font souffrir [*Réflexions critiques*, I, 11].

This natural disposition could hardly be suppressed by reason, for it answered to a passion too strong for it.

Tragedy as a dramatic spectacle and artistic genre offered a species of substitute excitement to those of real life: it could offer fear, pity, horror, and cruelty without involving the spectator, without those restless nights and painful days. As Lucretius had written, we like to watch a ship's crew battle a storm from the safety of shore just as we enjoy watching the mêlée of a battle from a distant hill. Pleasure in watching dramatic action on the stage differs from being the witnesses of such action in real life, in that one remains a spectator; one can be involved only vicariously. As Marmontel, following Du Bos, put it: "Le vrai plaisir de l'âme, dans ses émotions, est essentiellement le plaisir d'être émue, de l'être vivement, sans aucun des périls dont nous avertit la douleur."[1] The distance between the actions witnessed and the passions felt is greater than in real life. Du Bos did not think that dramatic action really created the illusion that one was witness to a real action: for one knew one was watching a theatrical performance and this very knowledge increased the pleasure of the spectator because he knew himself to be safe from the effects of real passions. Thus the spectator in the theatre remained the master of himself in these occasions, unlike in real life:

Le peintre et le poète ne nous affligent qu'autant que nous le voulons, ils ne nous font aimer leurs héros et leurs héroines qu'autant qu'il nous plaît: au lieu que nous ne serions pas les maîtres de leur vivacité comme de leur durée, si nous avions été frappés par les objets mêmes que ces nobles artisans ont imités. [*Réflexions critiques*, I, 31].

One might refer to the distance which tragedy as a genre creates between a spectator and the action, and also between his reasons and his passions, as a negative virtue. But tragedy also offered something positive, for witnessing the actions and the passions in motion represented on the stage, could also be turned into a lesson. Tragedy not only produced pleasure for the passions, it purged them.

For Du Bos such purgation was associated with what the artificial passions of art revealed about ourselves. Going to see a tragedy was rather like going to confession: it was admitting that we saw ourselves without the mask required by society. The designs, passions, and motives of men were more easily penetrated upon the stage than in real life: "Les personnages de tragédie quittent le masque devant nous. Ils prennent tous les spectateurs pour confidents de leur véritables projets et de leur sentiments les plus cachés" (Ibid., I, 461). (The same holds true of comic action, though the nature of the revelation about ourselves is quite different.) Now, the poets depict these passions and motives as they truly are, and it is through this faithful representation or imitation that we may be instructed as to what we ourselves truly are:

[1] "Tragedie," in *Eléments de littérature*, in *Oeuvres* (Paris, 1818–20), XV, 381.

Enfin, ce qui doit achever de nous convaincre de sa sincérité, nous nous reconnaissons nous-mêmes dans ses tableaux. Or la peinture fidèle des passions suffit seule pour nous les faire craindre, et pour nous engager à prendre la résolution de les éviter avec toute l'attention dont nous sommes capables [Ibid.].

Theatre thus provides a species of knowledge about man. Just as Descartes thought that examining and naming the passions might enable us to control them better, so Du Bos and other critics thought that witnessing them in motion and seeing their effects on stage might serve as a healthy warning. Both Descartes and Du Bos suppose man has the free will necessary to control the passions, and both views or representations of the passions are complementary: Descartes makes them known through a treatise based on introspection; Du Bos supposes that poets make them known directly by offering them to sight. In either case we witness at a certain distance: the Cartesian mind abstracts itself from its machine in order to become conscious of the passions that animate the machine; the poet presents a play which is witnessed at a certain distance by spectators not involved in the actions, so that their passions, though diverted and animated pleasurably, are not strong enough to cloud their vision. The playgoer knows the passions from without as the philosopher knows them through introspection. The philosopher and the novelist analyze the passions, but the dramatic poet represents them. That, in any case, was the theory: Know yourself in order that you may the better master yourself. Du Bos admitted, however, that dramatic poems were not a universal cure for the ills of mankind and that purgation did not always work.

Du Bos discussed the pleasure taken in tragedy in Sections 3, 4, and 5 of his *Réflexions critiques*, but he treated of purgation only in Section 44, hundreds of pages later. One wonders whether the distance between the later and the earlier sections made him miss the contradiction inherent in his doctrine of tragedy and particularly in his view of the purgation of the passions. Jean-Jacques Rousseau was quick to pick it up. He did not think that the theatre could change or correct men. Comedy, for example, was good for good men and evil for evil men, and he did not at all believe in the purgation theory of the passions: "Serait-ce que, pour devenir tempérant et sage, il faut commencer par etre furieux et fou?" [2] Reason alone could purge the passions, and that had no place in the theatre: "J'entends dire que la tragédie mène à la pitié par la terreur, soit. Mais quelle est cette pitié?

---

[2] *Lettre à M. d'Alembert* (Paris: Classiques Garnier, 1954), p. 137.

Une émotion passagère et vaine, qui ne dure pas plus que l'illusion qui l'a produite" (Ibid., 140). Indeed, to take up Du Bos' point of view, if the passions aroused in the theatre were artificial, how could they be an effective purgative of real passions? It is true enough that Du Bos was not unaware of this problem, but he did not try to deal with it in any thorough way; he merely indicated that purgation worked sometimes but not always. One might say that Rousseau, without formulating it, perceived that the hedonistic Du Bosian theory of art was in conflict with a moral view of tragedy. In terms of the *divertissement* theory, tragic spectacle was turned by distance into an agreeable diversion for those refined enough to wish to avoid any real pain. Du Bos knew this, but he did not bring it to bear on the old theory of purgation. Rousseau did:

Si les imitations du théâtre nous arrachent quelquefois plus de pleurs que ne le ferait la présence même des objets imités, c'est moins, comme le pense l'abbé Du Bos, parce que les émotions sont plus faibles et ne vont pas jusqu'à la douleur, que parce qu'elles sont pures et sans mélange d'inquiétude pour nous-mêmes. En donnant des pleurs à ces fictions, nous avons satisfaits à tous les droits de l'humanité, sans avoir plus rien à mettre du nôtre [Ibid., 141].

The spectacles of the stage could not purge the passions and could not instruct or correct mankind, because they were a substitute for the real thing and because men went to the theatre precisely to avoid being involved in and with the real thing.

Rousseau's position, based on a criticism of Du Bos and upon his own assumptions about man, nature, and society, was thorough, logical, and clear, but it led him to reject the entire convention of art as French society of the day knew it. This the *philosophes* were not prepared to do. The theatre was in need of reform, but hardly of rejection. Heedless of Rousseau's thorough criticism of the purgation theory and the didactic view of the stage, the *philosophes* in general continued to believe in the theatre's power to educate mankind. Indeed, their position differs from that of Du Bos only in this respect, that they would use the stage more for purposes of instruction than as a therapeutic for a leisure class in need of diversion.

Diderot's criticism illustrates the new view of the theatre rather well. He treated the same themes which had preoccupied former writers on the theatre: the relation of the stage to society, the theory of imitation and expression, especially in relation to the art of acting, the relation of the stage to painting, the possibilities of the new *drame bourgeois*, and, generally speaking, the relation between the dramatic art and nature, or more specifically, the demarcation between dramatic art and nature, naturalness and convention. Thus Diderot did not think in terms of rejecting the stage altogether, as did Rousseau, but rather envisaged reforms along naturalistic, emotive, moral, and historical lines, so that we sometimes think as much of the theatre of Victor Hugo as of the bourgeois drama of the eighteenth century. Diderot knew that the society he lived in was no longer that of the seventeenth century, and realized that the conventions of the stage would have to change. One might say he realized that Racine was already a classic, and that while he was one of the great dramatic poets it was no longer possible to write for the theatre on the basis of the conventions or rules of the seventeenth century. Diderot's writings are filled with critiques and reflections upon declamation, theatrical conventions, types, and one may say that he criticized the French stage along naturalistic lines much as he did the academic art of his day. This he did within the general conventions of art and with the vocabulary inherited from the past. The result was much less radical than Rousseau's views; it amounted to voicing a need for new subject matter, new acting, and more color and activity, as well as tears, on the stage.

Diderot's critique of the stage of his day may also be understood, as may some of his artistic criticism, within the general context of the return to classical models:

Eschyle, Sophocle, Euripide, ne veillaient pas des années entières pour ne produire que de ces petites impressions passagères qui se dissipent dans la gaieté d'un souper. Ils voulaient profondément attrister sur le sort des malheureux; ils voulaient, non pas amuser seulement leurs concitoyens, mais les rendre meilleurs ["Paradoxe sur le comédien," in *Oeuvres esthétiques*, 344].

Whatever the historical merits of this theory, it was not new, for it had been implicit in the dramatic theories of the *Grand Siècle* and had been explicitly stated by the Abbé d'Aubignac as an effect of the purgation of the passions. Diderot, however, wrote about it in a new context of criticism of society and also of sentiment, so that his views of the theatre strike us as novel: and they are, insofar as he also called for new motifs and themes. The stage was to be used more for moving the spectator to action rather than merely to purge his passions and leave him satisfied with himself. The stage, in effect, ceased to be thought of as simply the mirror of man and as a representation: it could be used as a forum, a call to action and moral reform, and the theatre became, in this sense, a branch of the ancient art of eloquence. As Mercier put it in his essay *Du Théâtre ou nouvel essai sur l'art dramatique* (Amsterdam, 1773),

Le théâtre est fait, je pense, pour suppléer au défaut d'expérience de la jeunesse, pour rectifier ceux qui ont mal vu, pour aider à l'intelligence des esprits médiocres, quelquefois incertains dans leurs idées, ce qu'ils doivent haïr, aimer, estimer [pp. 15–16].

This view differs from the older didactic views of the stage, in that the theatre now is subordinate to moral and social utility, whereas in the older theories the purgation of the passions was thought of as a beneficial effect of art, of the pleasure of illusion. It is not so much the argument which has changed as the historical situation and the explicitness of the utilitarian argument: the stage is no longer a diversion, an amusement which poets have to justify to puritans of one type or another; it is now an instrument of reform. Mercier's program could equally apply to advertising as well as to educational television or Socialist realism, for it supposes that art is no longer an independent convention, but a social instrument. The theatre of the seventeenth and eighteenth centuries had come to be regarded as the amusement of a restricted public; the new theatre, like that of the ancient Greeks and also of Shakespeare, was to be popular, moral, powerful, effective in moving a wider and less corrupt audience to social and moral action. This view amounted to a compromise position between the old *divertissement* theory of the stage and its rejection by Rousseau. The latter had argued that the stage was a symptom as well as a cause of social corruption, and that at most it was merely an unhappy necessity in civilized society. The *philosophes*, unlike Rousseau, accepted the unhappy necessity in order to use it for the benefit of society. Thus art, associated by the thorough Rousseau with social corruption, with deceit and the fall from the state of natural innocence, would become socially useful, and the disinterested pleasure of aristocrats, useless and selfish, would be turned into a moral and useful pleasure, that of a more popular audience watching, for their pleasure and instruction, dramas of interest to them and to society. The tears shed would thus become socially useful, and the audience would no longer be a social gathering of individual observers, distant, disinterested, amused without danger to themselves, but would be united on the level of sentiment along bonds common to all mankind. While the old purgation theory was explained in terms of the representation of an image of man in which he was able to recognize himself, the new effect of tragic drama, or of drama *tout court*, was to unite mankind in a common bath of tears and bathos. All men were no longer heroes with flaws, but brothers with sentiments, senses, and sensibility. The death of Phèdre gave way to the death of a salesman, a bourgeois tragedy, which from the point of view of the eighteenth century might be renamed the failure of the *Philosophe sans le savior*, as written by Jean-Jacques Rousseau, who had seen, two centuries ago, that the philosophy was all wrong to begin with.

* * *

See also: *Perspective*; *Aubignac, Corneille, Diderot, Rousseau*.
Bibliography: Felix Gaiffe, *Le Drame en France au XVIIIe Siècle* (Paris, 1910).

ECLOGUE OR IDYLL

THE ECLOGUE WAS A GENRE of poetry of considerable importance to the men and women of the late seventeenth and early eighteenth centuries. Father Mourgues, in his *Traité de la poésie française*, defined it as

un ouvrage de Poésie, où l'on fait parler des Bergers, ou des gens oisifs avec des termes naturels, et des pensées naïves, comme ont fait Théocrite, Virgile, Vida, Sannazar, et quelques autres, tant anciens que modernes. Son style doit être moins orné qu'élégant; les images riantes; les comparaisons tirées des choses les plus communes; les sentiments tendres et délicats; le tour simple; la cadence modérée [p. 266].

The eclogue, or idyll, was the eighteenth century's mundane dream of a picnic: one thinks of Detroy's hunting pictures depicting a halt for luncheon in the fields, or the modern idylls of Watteau, not to mention the numerous *bergerades* of Boucher. The shepherds involved and depicted in the eclogue or in paintings were obviously witty, clean, and elegant, and the background they played upon was obviously without thorns. As a picture of nature and of the natural life, the eclogue is rather revealing of the ambiguities latent in the word "nature." The eclogue was an imitation of nature, but, as Father Mourgues stipulated, "cette imitation doit toucher une nature choisie, et qui puisse plaire" (Ibid., 267). The shepherds were not to be real ones, because these were rough, common, and usually quite hard-working. The shepherds proper to the eclogue were those who enjoyed an agreeable leisure, were charming to the mind, and ever a source of naïve and fresh sentiments as well as of fine thoughts not usually voiced in polite society. But one must beware of too much metaphysics, of an ornate, pompous, and stylized speech. The shepherds were to be natural, yet not of the nature of real shepherds; they were to be fine, but not overfine.

The eclogue as a genre was the sophisticate's answer to too much sophistication and refinement of sentiment: you feel yourself into half-believing that the happy, easy, and simple nature of the Golden Age can be evoked by stepping from the salon into a French garden, or later, an English garden, and reciting pastoral poetry. It was also the form which nostalgia took among those who knew better than to love the country. In the words of the forgotten poet Roy: "La poésie pastorale retrace l'innocence et la tranquillité des premiers temps: et dans l'agitation du nôtre, ce tableau sait encore nous attacher et nous plaire."[1] The genre was a picture of something lost, and this posed the problem of how best to represent this lost happiness in a world which was obviously very different from a Golden Age of natural simplicity: for the critics of the time were aware that in the eclogue, as in most poetry, artificiality and an insipid taste had spoiled the original purity of the genre; one did not quite believe in its viability in the present, though poets continued to produce a great many eclogues and idylls. (To write an eclogue was to put oneself strictly within the doctrine of the imitation of the ancients, for these provided the best models, though Racan and Segrais were also accepted.) But the poet could do something more to create the illusion of the Golden Age; he could borrow from the painters who included ruins and antique monuments in their scenes of the pastoral life. The poet should animate his work through rustic dances and feasts, and the appearance of divinities. The eclogue thus tended to turn from a narrative poem into something closer to the requirements of the stage, and it is obvious that it is related to the ballet and the opera, and that the *ballet-divertissement* may be considered as a staged or animated eclogue. According to Roy the eclogue was also subject to the rule of perspective; it could not be modern, but must transport the spectator or reader into the past: more precisely, into the Golden Age.

The association of the Golden Age with the fabulous led some critics to ponder the place of the eclogue in the modern world, interpret-

[1] *Oeuvres diverses* (Paris, 1727), p. v.

ing the latter in terms of rationality and science. Fontenelle's *Discours sur la nature de l'églogue* is important in this respect, for his consideration of the genre led him to make pertinent observations upon such subjects as the nature of poetry, the rules of poetry, enthusiasm, and the relation of poetry to reason. Fontenelle recommended a compromise for the eclogue: it should be a middle ground between Theocritus and the *Astrée*, a French pastoral novel of the late sixteenth or early seventeenth centuries filled with Platonic love dialogues. Theocritus was too rough, the *Astrée* too metaphysical. Conversations about sheep and goats tended to be tedious. What really pleased the reader of an eclogue was the idea of tranquillity and leisure:

Voilà proprement ce que l'on imagine dans la vie pastorale. Elle n'admet point l'ambition, ni tout ce qui agite le coeur trop violemment; la paresse a donc lieu d'être contente. Mais cette sorte de vie là, par son oisiveté et sa tranquillité, fait naître l'amour plus facilement que n'importe quelle autre, ou du moins le favorise davantage; et quel amour? Un amour plus simple, parce qu'on a pas l'esprit si dangereusement raffiné; plus appliqué, parce qu'on n'est occupé d'aucune autre passion; plus discret, parce qu'on ne connaît presque pas la vanité; plus fidèle, parce qu'avec une vivacité d'imagination moins exercée, on a aussi moins d'inquiétudes, moins de dégoûts, moins de caprices; c'est-à-dire en un mot, l'amour purgé de tout ce que les excès des fantaisies humaines y ont mêlé d'étranger et de mauvais [*Discours sur la nature de l'églogue*, in *Oeuvres*, III, 98].

Considering the Cartesian author of this view of the eclogue and the type of love which belongs to the genre, we may consider it the only dream he allowed himself. In truth, a pleasant illusion, but hardly more, for after all, the eclogue was centered on a past associated with fictions.

The eclogue thus posed the problem of verisimilitude, and most discourses on it gave some space to this problem. Fontenelle's rather insipid recommendation of a *juste milieu* between the credible and the incredible, the extremes of the rough and true and of the refined and false, was the result of trying to make a dream credible to reason as understood in the salons of his times. But the genre, despite difficulties, lived on even in a mechanistic universe. Cartesians and moderns in general accepted it, either by force of habit or for psychological reasons which they did not illuminate in depth. It appealed to men and women of the court and the town as a form of pleasure, mild, with a touch of reverie and nostalgia: a happy escape which pleased the imagination's dream of repose and rest just as tragedy answered to another craving, that of having one's passions in motion and satisfying the imagination's fascination with disaster.

ENTHUSIASM

ENTHUSIASM WAS AN ATTRIBUTE of genius, a quality thought necessary to the poet, a powerful influence upon the soul, and a matter for suspicion to reason and reasonable men. On the whole, it is a term which the eighteenth century used for what we would now, in all probability, term the creative process. However, enthusiasm was not quite the same as the creative process, if this is thought of as coming from within and as being a good thing; the eighteenth century was of two minds about its origin and about its being a good thing. It could be thought of as coming from within and be associated with bowels, in which case it was not considered a good thing at all; or it could be thought of as coming from above, in which case it was still not thought of as being a good thing by everyone. In short, while there were people enthusiastic about enthusiasm, there were others who were not at all enthusiastic. There were some who tended to think of divine inspiration, ravishment, and the sublime as we tend to think of self-expression and sublimation. Others who were not enthusiastic tended to think of these as unfortunate necessities which must be tamed. On the whole, we may say that in an age of taste enthusiasm was something one had to put up with rather than admire. As the century went on enthusiasm gained favor, and poets, once portrayed as gentlemen, came gradually to be portrayed as beings divinely or naturally inspired.

Fontenelle, La Motte, Voltaire were highly suspicious of enthusiasm; Batteux and Diderot were rather well disposed to it. The suspicious ones associated enthusiasm with instinct, madness, an overheated imagination, entrails, interior agitation, lack of self-control, fury, rage, excessive sensibility, contortions, and sickness. The others thought of it in terms of audacity, intrepidity, genius, inspiration, a noble fire, a vast and creative imagination, profound thought, vision. Those who thought that both enthusiasm and art are necessary for great poetry compromised on something called reasonable enthusiasm, which is likened to wine by Voltaire:

L'enthousiasme est précisément comme le vin; il peut exciter tant de tumulte dans les vaisseaux sanguins, et de si violentes vibrations dans les nerfs, que la raison en est tout-à-fait détruite. Il ne peut causer que de légères secousses, qui ne fassent que donner au cerveau un peu plus d'activité; c'est ce qui arrive dans les grands mouvements d'éloquence, et surtout dans la poésie sublime. L'enthousiasme raisonnable est le partage des grands poètes.

Cet enthousiasme raisonnable est la perfection de leur art; c'est ce qui fit croire autrefois qu'ils étaient inspirés des dieux, et c'est ce qu'on a jamais dit des autres artistes.

Comment le raisonnement peut-il gouverner l'enthousiasme? c'est qu'un poète dessine d'abord l'ordonnance de son tableau; la raison alors tient le crayon. Mais veut-il animer ses personnages et leur donner le caractère des passions, alors l'imagination s'échauffe, l'enthousiasme agit; c'est un coursier qui s'emporte dans sa carrière; mais la carrière est régulièrement tracée. [*Dictionnaire Philosophique*, 182].

Thereby is enthusiasm, a force of nature, reconciled with art, the work of reason.

$$* \quad * \quad *$$

See also: *Genius, Ode, Sublime; Diderot, Fontenelle, La Motte, Voltaire.*

ELOQUENCE

"LA VRAIE ELOQUENCE se moque de l'éloquence": these words of Pascal may stand as the epigraph to any discussion of eloquence in the seventeenth or eighteenth centuries. Treatises and reflections on eloquence often turned out to be variations on the theme set by Pascal. Just as distinctions were made between true and false gentlemen, true and false taste, true and false beauty, one was made with reference to eloquence, which was distinguished from rhetoric. In the eighteenth century, eloquence *tout court* would be associated with nature for the purpose of underlining its ease and facility in contrast to the obviously contrived techniques of rhetoric.

Fénelon distinguished three meanings of the term eloquence:

L'éloquence, si je ne me trompe, peut être prise en trois manières: 1. Comme l'art de persuader la vérité, et de rendre les hommes meilleurs. 2. Comme un art indifférent, dont les méchants peuvent se servir aussi bien que les bons, et qui peut persuader l'erreur, l'injustice, autant que la justice et la vérité. 3. Enfin comme un art qui peut servir aux hommes intéressés à plaire, à s'acquérir de la réputation, et à faire fortune [*Dialogues sur l'Eloquence*, 23].

Eloquence fell into the category of a mixed art. Insofar as it had to please and be agreeable by touching the souls of men, it was a fine art; insofar as it had to persuade and be used in the service of some religious or political cause, it could be considered a useful art, with rules and appropriate use of gestures and images, and it is precisely here that the danger of false eloquence was thought to reside. Fénelon stressed this point in his *Dialogues sur l'Eloquence* by citing Cicero:

Cicéron a eu raison de dire, qu'il ne fallait jamais séparer la philosophie de l'éloquence. Car le talent de persuader sans science et sans sagesse est pernicieux et la sagesse sans art de persuader n'est point capable de gagner les hommes, et de faire entrer la vertu dans les coeurs [Ibid., 88].

It was not enough to convince men; they had to be persuaded to find the truth agreeable and be moved to espouse it. The orator, Fénelon went on, still paraphrasing Cicero, must possess the subtlety of dialecticians, the science of philosophers, nearly as much diction as poets, and the voice and gestures of the greatest actors. The emphasis on moving the spectator was also insisted upon: eloquence addressed itself, not only to the mind, but to the sentiments and passions as well (see article "Expression").

It was this capacity to move the spectator or the listener which associated eloquence with preaching in the *ancien régime*. Writers on eloquence were as concerned with the *éloquence de la chaire*, where the aim was to persuade men of the truth and beauty of doctrine, as they were with the more general subject. The insistence upon touching the layman in order to persuade him of the truth of doctrine may be considered as making *Dieu sensible au coeur*: eloquence was used to supplement the mystical, private, interior knowledge of God which was given only to the few. Political eloquence was a function of the republican form of government; in this case eloquence had to persuade men of the truth of virtue.

In the eighteenth century, eloquence came to be associated more with touching the spectators than with persuasion. D'Alembert, for example, argued that eloquence silenced reason and criticism because it appealed above all to the passions. The shift of emphasis from persuasion to emotion corresponds to the greater value put on the notion of genius, as against taste and judgment, at this time.

Eloquence was discussed in terms of the often unstated dominant aesthetic of the times. With Pascal and Fénelon it may be associated with *le Vrai*; in the eighteenth century it may be associated with the aesthetic of nature. It was thought of in terms of depiction, or of images created in the mind of the listener or spectator with the use of words. It could therefore also be associated with an aesthetic of beauty, of either *la belle* or *la simple nature*. But it could also be associated with poetry, so that one could also speak of proportion, harmony, *rapports*, moderation, diction, and since it was thought to be an inborn talent, whereas rhetoric was something learned, one may also say that eloquence depended upon that *je ne sais quoi* which put true art and beauty beyond the range of verbal definition.

EPIC POETRY

THE EPIC POSED serious problems for eighteenth-century poets: so many, indeed, that only one tried his hand at it, and he is hardly read for that particular accomplishment. If in the ode the requirement of enthusiasm conflicted with the rule of reason, in the epic the requirements of heroism, grandeur, and the marvellous conflicted with an ever more critical view of history and the new vision of the cosmos. All this was further complicated by national pride, for it was felt by the French that they ought to have a national epic, as had the Greeks and Romans and more recently the English, who with Milton had produced a great modern poem which the French could not rival. There had been attempts in the seventeenth century to produce such an epic, but these were hardly thought successful, even by a modern such as Perrault, and Boileau had made short work of the pretensions of Chapelain and Desmarets de Saint-Sorlin. Yet the epic was the great genre, a test case, and its role in literature was similar to that of the painting of history in the plastic arts: it occupied the highest rung in the artistic scale of values inherited from the past.

The rules of the epic were well known. It was a narrative poem telling the story of some great action of interest, not only to an entire nation, but also to humanity. "On peut la définir," wrote Batteux: "Un récit en vers d'une action vraisemblable, héroique, et merveilleuse" (*Les Beaux-Arts*, 193). Part of the difficulties of the epic came from the inability of some minds to reconcile the *vraisemblable* with the *merveilleux*, or, for that matter, to see much heroism in the modern world. The epic was caught up in the doubts raised by those who perceived that the modern world of Newton and Descartes would make the old poetry, based on fable and fiction, well-nigh impossible. Even those who still thought the epic possible in the modern world had to admit that the pagans had an advantage denied the moderns, namely the marvellous. Batteux tried to reconcile verisimilitude and the marvellous as follows: "Le ton d'Oracle m'ébranle, et la vraisemblance des choses me convainc" (Ibid., p. 195). Thus an epic ought to be placed in those times in which belief in the marvellous was still possible, which in effect was to admit that it was a strictly historical genre (see article "Perspective"). Milton alone had succeeded in replacing pagan marvels with Christian truths, but it was not thought possible to use the marvellous in more recent times, as Batteux admitted:

Mais vouloir joindre ce merveilleux de notre Religion avec une histoire toute naturelle, qui est proche de nous: faire descendre des Anges pour opérer des miracles, dans une entreprise dont on fait tous les noeuds et tous les dénouements, qui sont simples et sans mystères; c'est tomber dans le ridicule, qu'on n'évite point, quand on manque le merveilleux [Ibid., 198–99].

But there were other difficulties to be faced. The Abbé Du Bos thought the epic a difficult genre, in part because of the nature of the French language, less proper for images than Latin and more difficult as concerns cadence and harmony of verse. To offset these disadvantages the poet ought to choose a subject capable of holding the reader's attention. Such a subject could be found in the national past. Even here, however, the choice was by no means easy, for men have short memories, and modern society was not given to the celebration of famous feats of history as were, for example, the Romans:

Tous les endroits de l'histoire de France qui sont mémorables, ne nous intéressent pas même également. Nous ne prenons un grand intérêt qu'à ceux dont la mémoire est encore assez récente. Les autres sont presque devenus pour nous les événements d'une histoire étrangère, d'autant plus que nous n'avons pas le soin de perpétuer le souvenir des jours heureux à la Nation par des fêtes et par des jeux anniversaires, ni celui d'éterniser la mémoire de nos héros, ainsi que la pratiquaient les Grecs et les Romains. Combien peu y en a-t'il parmi nous qui s'affectionnent aux événements arrivés sous Clovis et sous la première race de nos Rois? [Réflexions critiques, I, 188].

Thus the epic poet faced the same problem as the tragic poet: he had to choose a time not too distant from the present, yet not too recent: one, in short, which made vraisemblance possible. Voltaire tried to solve this by choosing Henri IV as the subject of his epic. With the Henriade the French at last had an epic poem, though some questions were raised as to whether it really met the definition and rules of the epic. Voltaire, never at a loss for countercriticism, wrote his own rules and argued that the only rules of the epic were that the action be unified, simple, great, interesting, and complete. As for the marvellous and the episodic, these varied in time and place according to custom. He then surveyed various epics to demonstrate that they had not been written according to the rules and were nonetheless great, while the epics written according to the rules had failed: "Le Clovis de *Desmarets*, la Pucelle de *Chapelain*, ces poèmes fameux par leur ridicule, sont, à la honte des règles, conduits avec plus de régularité que l'Iliade, comme le Pirame de *Pradon* est plus exacte que le Cid de *Corneille*."[1] Voltaire had reason to argue as he did, and also reason to be satisfied: for he had managed that *tour de force* which had eluded so many in the previous century and written a *modern* epic poem. The action was more restricted than that of the *Iliad*, there was no quality of the marvellous in the poem, there were no oracles or divinations, and on the whole Henri behaved like a true hero, for he relied upon his own powers to conquer a kingdom while demonstrating the noble virtues of reason and tolerance. As the *Nouvelliste du Parnasse* put it upon the occasion of the 11th edition:

M. de Voltaire, sans l'intervention insipide des Dieux de la Fable, sans le secours frivole des Magiciens des Fées, enfin sans employer ni Anges, ni Démons, est venu à bout de faire un poème de dix chants, qui plaît malgré l'observation peu exacte des règles de l'épopée. Car j'avoue que la Henriade n'est pas absolument conformée à ces règles. Mais puisqu'elle est si goutée dans un siècle éclairé et délicat, n'est-elle pas conforme à la principale de toutes? C'est un poème d'un nouveau genre, et que vous n'appellerez point épique si vous voulez. A la place des Dieux de l'Antiquité, des Anges, des Diables, des Enchanteurs et des Fées, vous y trouverez des êtres moraux ingénieusement personifies, tels que la Religion, la Superstition, la Justice, l'Hypocrisie, la Discorde, la Politique, l'Amour, etc. Tout cela donne lieu à des fictions sublimes, à des portraits brilliants, à des traits sententieux, et à des épisodes heureux et agréables.[2]

Voltaire obviously had managed to create an epic based upon the new history, which he had defined by carefully distinguishing it from all fabulous elements. His poem not only pleased, it also instructed, and it may be likened to the historical painting of the period, in which the same types of personified passions and moral values were used. The

---

[1] *Essai sur la poésie épique*, in *Oeuvres complètes* (Basle, 1791), XII, 340.

[2] Desfontaines, *Le Nouvelliste du Parnasse* (Paris, 1734), I, 257.

Henriade was a huge success: it was translated into English, Italian, German, and Dutch, but it is no longer read. Like so much of the historical painting of the time, the *grandes machines* of art also used to instruct and edify mankind, its interest is now primarily historical, and its lesson is more likely to be the tale of the failure of the epic than the success and grandeur of Henri IV.

*   *   *

See also: *Poetry*; *Le Bossu, Voltaire.*
Bibliography: See the introductory volume of O. R. Taylor's critical edition of the *Henriade* which appeared in Vols. 38, 39, and 40 of the *Studies on Voltaire and the Eighteenth Century* (Geneva, 1966).

EXPRESSION

> L'expression de la pensée, du sentiment, des
> passions, doit être le vrai but de la musique.
> *Rameau*

WHEN CRITICS THOUGHT about subject matter, nature, and beauty, they thought in terms of an aesthetic of imitation; when they considered the public that was to be pleased, touched, or even instructed, they were likely to think in terms of expression. This use of the word is not to be taken in the sense of self-expression, but rather as the expression of emotions common to all mankind within the general aesthetic limits of art. Personal self-expression by the poet or painter did not enter into consideration; the classical notion of expression has nothing to do with expressionism.

If poetry is the language of the gods, expression is the language of human sentiments and passions. For this reason expression may be regarded as a form of nondiscursive communication. Thus music, drama, and historical painting were more apt to raise questions concerning expression than prose and forms relying upon readers. Expression, in short, implied a language without words. This is especially clear in connection with the art of painting, and theories of expression were an important item of discussion in the Académie de Peinture et de Sculpture, in the writings of de Piles, Lebrun, or Testelin much more than among the writings of men of letters. Ultimately the problem goes back to Descartes' treatise on the passions of the soul and to Alberti's discussion of historical painting, but the academy and the amateurs made of these beginnings a rather coherent aesthetic which eventually was extended to cover more than the merely pictorial expression of the pas-

sions. It is possible, indeed, to assume that the Classical aesthetic supposes in fact two complementary parts, a theory of imitation and a
theory of expression.

De Piles treated of expression in several of his works. "Les expressions," he wrote,[1] "sont la pierre de touche de l'esprit du peintre."
And it was through the expressions that the painter communicated
with the spectator. The expressions made up for the silent poetry of
painting (see article "*Ut Pictura Poesis*"). The painting, argued de
Piles, must be considered as the stage of a theatre, as the scene of a
drama in which each of the figures plays a role. Now, while figures
which are well drawn and well colored are admirable in themselves,
many people are sensitive to them only insofar as they are also complemented by vivacity, justness, and delicacy of expression, which make
up for their lack of complete understanding of the art of painting. In
this sense, then, expression in painting corresponds to a literary view of
the art of painting: and this explains readily enough the idea of the
learned painter, acquainted with poetry and ancient history, a fre-
quenter of men of letters and of the world. Expression was not confined
to the face; it was also applied to attitudes. Even inanimate objects,
through color and lighting, could become expressive. (It goes without saying that expression in this sense could also be used in the art of
portraiture, in which case one spoke of a *portrait parlant*. This would
seem to imply that the spectator not only recognized a true likeness,
but in fact also something more, the soul or character of the sitter.)
Thus, in history painting you not only recognized the subject matter,
which might be explained in a label anyway, but you also recognized
the justness of expression of the subject. Paintings could thus be "read."
Du Bos' view of painting was in the tradition of de Piles, and we may
infer from his rejection or questioning of allegory that he thought that
painting might be enriched precisely through expression, an art which
made for better communication and which appealed to a public no
longer interested in the enigmas of fable (see article "Fable"). Expression thus may also be considered as part of the general artistic requirement of clarity. At the same time it answered the desire to be touched
emotionally. Since art had to touch, please, and move the passions of
men, an art of expression became a central concept of speculation, and
it is perhaps no accident that preoccupation with expression arose in
conjunction with the development of opera, which was highly prized
in the later seventeenth century, and during the period of the Régence,

[1] "L'Idée du peintre parfait," in *Abregé de la Vie des Peintres*, p. 43.

in which the insistence was so much more on pleasing than on instructing the public.

By the time Batteux wrote his little treatise on art and imitation the theory of expression was generally accepted, and he formulated it rather clearly on all its levels. "Les hommes ont trois moyens pour exprimer leurs idées et leurs sentiments; la parole, le ton de la voix, et le geste. Nous entendons par geste, les mouvements extérieurs, et les attitudes du corps" (*Les Beaux-Arts*, p. 253). The word was the organ of reason: it instructed and, thought Batteux, convinced. But tone and gesture were the organs of the heart: they moved, won, and persuaded men. The word, the spoken and written language, was a human institution, social and historical; but gestures and tones were the "dictionnaire de la simple nature," the language known to all from birth: short, lively, and energetic. This distinction between words and nonverbal expression corresponds to a frequently used phrase of the times, namely the reference in titles and manuals to *l'esprit et le coeur*. The complete work of art appealed to both; the completely cultivated man possessed both.

The relation of word, tone, and gesture to nature implied three degrees of art: expression of a simple kind for ordinary human needs merely required conversation; if this expression was polished by art for utility as well as *agrément*, one obtained sustained recitation, narration, or oration; if one used expression for pleasure alone, one created various types of art on the basis of measure, movement, modulation, harmony, and obtained versification in the realm of the word, music in the order of tones, and dance in that of gesture. In point of historical fact, as we have seen with de Piles, paintings really represented arrested expressive gestures as well as fixed expressions of the passions as witnessed upon the face. It has been pointed out, indeed, that the connections among dance, music, and painting are especially pronounced in the work of Watteau, while the expression of the passions is sometimes all too obvious in the work of Lebrun or the Coypels.

Music and dance thus imitated the sentiments and passions through an art of expression. All music and dance, according to Batteux, had to have a meaning, a sense, and art increased this sense by rendering expression stronger. Expression thus is inseparable from art, and Batteux uses the term as he would the word "sign" in the arts relying upon verbal communication:

Les expressions, en général, ne sont d'elles-mêmes, ni naturelles, ni artificielles: elles ne sont que des signes. Que l'art les employe, ou la Nature, qu'elles soient liées à la réalité, ou à la fiction, à la vérité, ou au mensonge, elles changent de qualité, mais sans changer de nature ni d'état [Ibid., 261]

From this it would also seem that expressions had become a species of convention, inseparable indeed from stylization. One might put it this way: expressions gave style to natural passions and sentiments. Only passions and sentiments were natural; expression, ruled by art, inseparable from art, transformed these, fortified them, polished them, and sentiments and passions thereby came to express *la belle nature*. This difference between expression and the sentiments and passions, between *la belle nature* and *la nature*, was further underlined by Batteux in distinguishing between sounds from nature and human sounds, between two types of music:

Il y a deux sortes de Musique; une qui n'imite que les sons et les bruits non-passionnés: elle répond au paysage dans la peinture: l'autre qui exprime les sons animés, et qui tiennent aux sentiments: c'est le tableau à personnage [Ibid., p. 266].

Both types of music, like both types of painting, are really of the order of *la belle nature*, as all art is, but the first is founded upon a theory of imitation, the other on one of expression.

Batteux extended the notion of expression beyond its restriction to painting, and with him we come up against a general theory of expression which merges with imitation and with the notion of art as a second order of elements created by men:

Toute expression doit être conforme aux choses qu'elle exprime: c'est l'habit fait pour le corps. Ainsi comme il doit y avoir dans les sujets poétiques ou artificiels de l'unité et de la variété, l'expression doit avoir d'abord ces deux qualités [Ibid., 271].

But expression must also be clear, just, fine, delicate, easy, simple, new, and true to the subject; this is especially important in human passions and sentiments, for it is this which makes for the illusion of truth and recognition:

Il y a pour la musique et pour la danse, de même que pour la peinture, des beautés, que les artistes appellent fuyantes ou passagères; des traits fins, échappés dans la violence des passions, des soupirs, des accents, des airs de tête: ce sont ces traits qui piquent, qui éveillent, et qui raniment l'esprit [Ibid., 274].

Indeed, the *airs de tête* alluded to in this passage were part of the training of the painter, who also was asked to train himself making *têtes d'expressions*. It would also seem from reflection upon Batteux's treatment of expression that it ultimately led to a close scrutiny of nature; expression must bring recognition of the characteristic, of what is natural to men, thus the insistence on sighs, accents, turns of the head.

This inclination towards the expressiveness of nature was highly developed by Diderot, who really leads towards naturalism; one may even say, to the naturalistic fallacy. The distinction between *la belle nature* and *la nature* is more and more blurred, and expression seems to be increasingly linked to an expressive nature rather than to a notion of stylization. This is not true of the *Paradoxe sur le comédien*, but it is more true of his notion of genius (see article "Genius"), and it is also apparent in his view of expression in painting:

> L'expression est en général l'image d'un sentiment.
> Un comédien qui ne se connaît pas en peinture est un pauvre comédien; un peintre qui n'est pas physionomiste est un pauvre peintre.
> Dans chaque partie du monde, chaque contrée; dans une même contrée, chaque province; dans une province, chaque ville; dans une ville, chaque famille; dans une famille, chaque individu; dans un individu, chaque instant à sa physionomie, son expression.[2]

Expression is no longer, as it was for Batteux, something between the natural passion or sentiment and the spectator or listener: it is now part of nature, it is confused with physiognomy. Batteux seems to have been complemented by Lavater, and expression is everywhere, ready to be used by the painter. Indeed, when one reads this chapter on expression one soon perceives that Diderot is not talking about painting any more, but about expression in nature, faces seen in the streets, forces of nature and circumstances that alter facial expressions. He is not writing about a theory of expression for art, but about expressive nature. It may also be supposed that he can do this because he has first learned about expression from looking at a great many paintings, so that nature comes to be conceived in terms of expressive types; the line of demarcation between art, which implies style, and nature has been blurred, and one wanders from one realm to the other without quite knowing where the border is passed. He confuses the pose of the *Antinoüs* with nature; Winckelmann enters the picture. Diderot does

[2] "Essais sur la peinture," in *Oeuvres esthétiques*, p. 699.

not see that the pose of the *Antinoüs* is merely that of another artistic convention, one he confuses with nature and uses to criticize those of the dancing master Marcel, who also creates expressive poses which Diderot associates with the mannerisms of a *petit maître*. In short, with Diderot the theory of expression goes beyond the realm of art to join that of natural phenomena. We have gone beyond *la belle nature*.

* * *

See also: *Imitation, Opera, Pantomime; Chabanon, Diderot, Du Bos, Fénelon.*

FABLE

FABLE REFERRED not only to a poetic genre in which animals and matter were given words in order to express ancient wisdom, but also to mythical or "fabulous" creatures, deities, and so on, associated with the remote past. In this sense fable was opposed to history, which was associated with truth, and came into conflict also with Christian dogma. The term "fable" also brings to mind what was often referred to as the machinery of poetry, by which was meant the miraculous intervention in literary action of angels, demons, gods, dreams, enchantments, and personified moral qualities such as Virtue, Reason, Envy, and so on, especially in epic poetry and opera. Fable and the "machines" obviously conflicted with *vraisemblance*, but it was argued that one ought not to judge machines, fables, and accounts of marvels with an analytical, philosophic spirit. Fable was defended as a harmless amusement of the imagination, useful in that it could easily and agreeably tell a moral. The illusion was never one to seduce the spectators into error, so that the question of verisimilitude was not to the point at all. However, machines, fables, or accounts of marvels were to be used with caution and appropriately, and one had to be careful of not mixing pagan and Christian marvels.

This point was especially stressed by Du Bos in relation to painting. He posed the question: Should a painter of history introduce allegorical elements into his work, mixing thereby truth and fiction? and commented on this, taking as his example the Medici series painted by Rubens, especially the arrival of Marie de Médicis in Marseille and her giving birth to Louis XIII. The issue was to reconcile fiction with history, and was really argued on a psychological level: it is possible that mythical creatures may have been believed in at a certain time in the past, and a painter of history might conceivably include such fabulous creatures in a subject placed in such a remote past, but not in a more recent past in which these were no longer believed in:

Ce n'est point que je dispute aux peintres le droit qui leur est acquis de peindre des Sirènes, des Tritons, des Néréïdes, des faunes et toutes les divinités fabuleuses, nobles chimères dont l'imagination des poètes peupla les eaux et les forêts, et enrichit tant la nature. Ma critique n'est point fondée sur ce qu'il n'y eut jamais de Sirènes et de Néréïdes, mais sur ce qu'il n'y en avait plus, pour ainsi dire, dans le temps où arriva l'événement qui donne lieu à cette discussion [*Réflexions critiques*, I, 199–200].

Rubens, in other words, had mixed mentalities and periods of history; Du Bos' argument was that of a new type of purist, and he argued for a *vraisemblance* based on a psychological view of historical change. Historian that he was, and like Voltaire after him, he separated fable from history. He also seems to have been saying that the moderns were no longer interested in mythical beings, that these belonged to the past. In this respect the painter may depict a subject from antiquity and depict the fabulous, because this was in character with the mentality of the antique:

Le peintre qui représente les aventures d'un héros Grec ou Romain, peut donc y faire intervenir toutes les divinités comme des personnages principaux. Il peut à son gré embellir ses compositions avec les Tritons et les Sirènes. Il ne fait rien contre son système. Je l'ai déjà dit, les livres qui firent l'occupation de notre jeunesse, la vraisemblance qu'on trouve à voir un héros secouru par les Dieux qu'il adorait, nous mettent en disposition de nous prêter sans aucune peine à la fiction [Ibid., 201].

But this is evidently the case only within the system of the ancient mentality. The separation of fable from history meant that the former was reduced to a mere ornament; the insistence on the *vrai* meant that allegory, associated with fabulous elements, was criticized because it often tended to be too obscure. The fabulous past and its various allusions were being lost, and Du Bos did not think painters should indulge in the game of allegory because paintings tended to become enigmas:

Les tableaux ne doivent pas être des énigmes et le but de la peinture n'est pas d'exercer notre imagination en lui donnant des sujets embrouillés à deviner. C'est de nous émouvoir, et par conséquent les sujets de leurs ouvrages ne sauraient être trop faciles à entendre [Ibid., I, 212].

The critique of fable and rejection of allegory are aspects of a modern mentality and represent one point which the ancients lost in the Battle of the Books. It is also evident that, as regards poetry and painting, the scepticism vis-à-vis the fabulous was the gain of history, and what was lost in the realm of the marvellous was compensated for in a feeling of nostalgia for the past. The development of historical painting, the attempt to create a historical drama, Voltaire's *Henriade*, are in part to be explained in terms of this rejection of allegory and the critique of fable, and what painters lost as motifs was made up by greater verisimilitude in history and the expression of the passions. The insistence of Du Bos on clarity, the rejection of allegory as enigma, also implies that fable was lost partly because the public for which he wrote and which he knew was less learned than that of the previous century or of the sixteenth century, if we are to judge on the basis of the highly enigmatic Mannerist paintings.

✳ ✳ ✳

See also: *Epic, Opera, Poetry.*

GENIUS

THE CONCEPT OF GENIUS was a product of theories of taste, art, and the role of the artist or poet in society. The boundaries of the freedom of genius were determined by an imitative doctrine of art and an aesthetic of beauty, or by an expressive theory of art founded upon the concept of nature. The concept of genius was discussed in mythological, naturalistic, artistic, and social terms.

In the seventeenth century genius was often alluded to in mythological terms. It was generally accepted as the sine qua non of artistic creation, but it was hardly discussed at great length. For Poussin it was the golden bough of Virgil, a gift which could hardly be transmitted from master to student; for Boileau it was "du ciel l'influence secrète," without which one might as well not bother trying to be a poet. Its position and function within the Classical doctrine of art and beauty was well delineated by Roger de Piles:

Il est certain que le génie à qui nous devons la naissance des beaux-arts, ne saurait les conduire à leur perfection sans le secours de la culture; que cette culture est impraticable sans la direction du jugement; et que le jugement ne saurait rien faire sans la possession des vrais principes [*Cours de Peinture par Principes*, 385].

In the seventeenth and early eighteenth centuries genius was thus limited by art, which meant not only the principles and tradition of art, but also the artist's own judgment, founded upon the knowledge of the art he practised. Genius was a necessary animating factor; art was associated with a body of rules, procedures, precedents, and techniques, so that one was able to distinguish between those who were excellent mechanics and those who possessed something more than technical mastery and knowledge. The latter, the geniuses, also possessed the faculty of invention. This distinction was often insisted upon by Du Bos for whom "les plus grands versificateurs ne sont pas les plus grands poètes, comme les dessinateurs les plus réguliers ne sont pas les plus grands peintres" (*Réflexions critiques*, II, 2–3).

In the writings of de Piles and Du Bos, genius is accepted as the indispensable quality of a poet or painter, but there is still insistence upon those aspects of art that are subject to the judgment and involve craftsmanship, although Du Bos gives more space and attention to genius than do de Piles and other writers on the arts or poetry at this time. The rules and the beauties of execution are accorded a secondary importance, because they are but the means to a superior end; what really matters in the realm of the arts is that the poet or painter be endowed with a capacity of invention, though even to invent, one must know art well: "Or il faut être né avec du génie pour inventer; et l'on ne parvient même qu'à l'aide d'une longue étude à bien inventer" (*Ibid.*, 3). Thus, what distinguishes genius is its capacity to invent within the general conventions of art and enlarge thereby the horizon of the world of art. Invention insures that an imitative theory of art need not lead to servile copying, need not lead to a fixed style, and, indeed, to an art that does not progress. Obviously invention leads towards the ideal point sought for by the true artist, perfection, and theoretically reaches its limits only when that point is reached. Du Bos brings us to a point beyond the preoccupation with rules and regular beauty, but one still remains within the general aesthetic of art because genius is still expected to work within the conventions accepted by the poets, painters, and men of taste of the times. It is important, however, to note the insistence put on the distinction between the merely mechanical in art and that which belongs to and is the result of genius, between those who merely imitate in a servile mechanical way and those who invent within the general precept of imitation.

The distinction between art and craftsmanship was being drawn at this time, and genius little by little was to become associated with superior mental powers. Genuis was a natural power. Du Bos does not explain this by recourse to the usual mythological metaphors; it has little to do with inspiration from on high, and if it can be called a gift, it is certainly not of the gods, but rather of nature:

On appelle génie, l'aptitude qu'un homme a reçu de la nature, pour faire bien et facilement certaines choses, que les autres ne sauraient faire que très-mal, même en prenant beaucoup de peine. Nous apprenons à faire les choses pour lesquelles nous avons du génie, avec autant de facilité que nous apprenons à parler notre langue naturelle [Ibid., 4].

Du Bos knew very well that this natural power worked and invented in a state of heated imagination or excitement, and that one generally did not compose or sketch in cold blood. He also knew that creation was usually followed by lassitude. However, he did not describe this state of creation, as did Diderot later on, nor did he talk of inspiration. Thus his prosaic treatment of genius and creativity makes it seem less novel than it is. But there is a good reason why his concept of genius is not yet that of the Romantic variety. He also believed that genius alone did not suffice to create or perfect a work of art. Nature must be seconded by study: the work of art was not the result of sudden inspiration, whatever the source, or of flashes of genius and profound insights: it was the result of genius plus knowledge, invention plus study. Du Bos still thinks of genius as working within a general system of the arts, and the genius is not yet the solitary figure of Romantic imagery, though Du Bos did think of genius as contending with certain constraints put on it by society, the conventions of art, or even the poor schooling given a genius by a mediocre master. However, Du Bos believed in the power of genius to overcome these constraints, so that in the end genius formed itself: "La force du génie change en bonne nourriture les préceptes les plus mal digérés" (*Réflexions critiques*, II, 12). Raphael, Annibale Carracci, Rubens, Poussin, all had masters who were mediocre, yet their genius triumphed over the various obstacles they met in their careers. In poetry it was even easier, he thought, to triumph over obstacles, and you did not even need a master to be a poet: "Un homme né avec du génie peut s'instruire lui-même en deux mois de toutes les règles de la poésie française" (Ibid., 13). Du Bos' conception of genius is quite different from the Romantic theory or vision of the genius as a being repressed by a hostile society. There is no question of this for Du Bos, though there are obstacles and mediocrity to contend with. For Du Bos, the genius triumphs; he will assert himself no matter what obstacles he meets because genius, as a force of nature, an impulse, cannot be thwarted: "De toutes les impulsions, celle de la nature, dont il tient son penchant, est la plus forte" (Ibid., 14). Nor must one suppose that geniuses are the product of education; they are born, not made, and parents wishing to direct children born with genius into professions that they approve but the child does not will fail, as witness the cases of Nanteuil, Roberval, Tournefort, Bernouilli. In short, concluded Du Bos, making a distinction which would not be lost upon Rousseau,

la naissance physique l'emporte toujours sur la naissance morale. Je m'explique. L'éducation, laquelle ne saurait donner un certain génie ni de certaines inclinations aux enfants qui ne les ont point, ne saurait aussi priver de ce génie, ni dépouiller de ces inclinations, les enfants qui les ont apportées en naissant [Ibid., 19].

The genius, it would seem, is the natural man, too strong for the moral man created by education, or, to use Rousseau's distinctions, the genius is the natural man who would not, who cannot, because he is too strong, become the *homme de l'homme*, man as society would have him. The history of genius in the eighteenth century is a modern version of Prometheus breaking his chains. In the writings of Du Bos, however, while one may see glimmers of things to come, one might perhaps more justly think of Pygmalion, of the statue animated by genius, and of a statue made within the rules of art and within conventions accepted by society. For despite his natural powers, the genius must perfect his gift with study.

The idea of art, associated with *perfectionnement*, and the idea of nature, still associated with disorder as it is in the work of Perrault, are also made applicable to genius. In short, there are rough and natural geniuses, and there are those that have been perfected: "Le génie le plus heureux ne peut être perfectionné qu'à l'aide d'une longue étude" (Ibid., 24). The type of study involved is that which operates within the area of interest of the genius: "Elle consiste dans une réflexion sérieuse sur les ouvrages des grands maîtres, suivie d'observations sur ce qu'il convient d'imiter, et sur ce qu'il faut tâcher de surpasser" (Ibid., 25). Study is a critical sense exercised by genius upon art, coupled with the power of invention, and it also implies a degree of self-control.

Much the same view of genius and its relation to art and taste was held by Du Bos' contemporary the Comte de Caylus. Reynolds, in his famous *Discourses*, would later echo the same views, especially in connection with imitation. What all these views have in common is the conception of genius as an indispensable force or talent to invent within a general system of the arts, with what might be described as a reciprocal action between given rules and conventions, and the power of invention coupled with critical judgment. Genius as such may be found in various human activities; it is not a phenomenon restricted to the fine arts. It is a quality found in men of letters, poets, painters, soldiers, mathematicians, men of science.

Helvétius, in his work *De l'Esprit* of 1758, also considered the notion of genius and began to distinguish between genius as manifest in the fine arts and genius as manifest in science and philosophy: thus there is *génie de la poésie ou de l'éloquence*, and *génie de réflexion*. However, both types still possess in common the quality of invention. Helvétius, in a certain sense, diminishes the power of genius by shifting emphasis from invention to perfection. Thus the genius in the arts is he who perfects them: "Corneille naît dans un moment où la perfection qu'il ajoute à cet art, doit faire époque; Corneille est un génie" (p. 383).[1] But suppose Corneille had not appeared at the right moment: would he still have been a genius? The genius conceived by Helvétius is perhaps only a limited inventor; he is subject to certain given conditions. There are times in which one cannot invent new forms, new styles, or genres, yet in such periods genius still obtains; it is then called *génie d'expression*, a type of genius eminently possessed by Boileau and La Fontaine, neither of whom invented new forms, though they perfected existing forms within given conventions. The conclusion of Helvétius is worth quoting at length, because it represents, so to speak, a democratization of genius, in that the power of invention is now limited, not so much by the rules, taste, and artistic tradition, as it is by more general factors:

La conclusion de ce chapitre, c'est que, si le génie suppose toujours invention, toute invention, cependant ne suppose pas le génie. Pour obtenir le titre d'homme de génie, il faut que cette invention porte sur des objets généraux et intéressants pour l'humanité; il faut de plus naître dans le moment où, par ses talents et ses découvertes, celui qui cultive les arts ou les sciences, puisse faire époque dans le monde savant. L'homme de génie est donc en partie l'oeuvre du hasard; c'est le hasard qui, toujours en action, prépare les découvertes, rapproche insensiblement les vérités, toujours inutiles lorsqu'elles sont trop éloignées les unes des autres, et qui fait l'homme de génie dans l'instant précis où les vérités, déjà rapprochées, lui donnent des principes

---

[1] The edition cited here is that published in Paris in 1776.

généraux et lumineux: le génie s'en saisit, les présente, et quelque partie de l'empire des arts ou des sciences en est éclairée [Ibid., 389].

The genius is thus merely one part of a more general scheme of progress or development of the arts and sciences which is largely led or pushed by chance: being a genius sounds rather like being in the right profession or art, at the right time, in the right place: a concept which brings to mind Taine's view of the development of the arts in terms of race, milieu, and moment. The individual genius, as inventor in the arts or sciences, is to a certain extent lost within a general scheme. This view conflicts not only with that of Du Bos, more generous to the individual genius, but also with a view put forward by Diderot and Rousseau.

Diderot's view of genius may be gleaned in many of his works, but his conflict with Helvétius is outlined in a refutation of the latter's book *De l'homme*, posthumously printed in 1773. Here again the question of genius and chance was posed, and Diderot readily seized the implications of such a view:

Le hasard cause de l'inégalité de l'esprit; le désir cause de la supériorité d'un homme sur un autre; toute découverte, toute idée neuve, faveurs du hasard. Voilà bien des propositions générales hasardées. . . . Et comme les hasards sont faits également pour tous les hommes communément bien organisés, l'auteur conclut de là l'égalité des esprits; une méthode pour faire des gens de génie. En vérité cela fait pitié. . . . Quel est l'homme qui ne puisse se regarder comme un homme de génie, si le hasard le veut? [2]

Diderot's concept of genius owes more to Du Bos than it did to any materialist scheme of the universe, and it is for this reason that he refused to accept the consequences of Helvétius' rather simple and schematic materialism. However, Diderot went further than Du Bos, in that he individualized the genius even more, so that one generation after the appearance of the *Réflexions critiques* a new concept of genius had been posed: though here again it was not as new as it might seem, for it embodied the old view of genius as the indispensable quality necessary for art or science, although freed of the limitations imposed upon it by the requirements of rules and society.

Rousseau's article on genius, in his *Dictionnaire de musique* of 1764, is indicative, not only of the new concept of genius, but also of the

[2] Réfutation de l'ouvrage d'Helvétius intitulé l'Homme," in *Oeuvres esthétiques*, pp. 613–15.

new style of writing about it; it begins as follows: "Ne cherche point, jeune artiste, ce que c'est que le *génie*. En as-tu, tu le sens en toi-même. N'en as-tu pas, tu ne le connaîtras jamais"[3] following which, genius was described as a devouring fire, a spark, animation, emotion, and the manifestations of genius at work as transports, suffocation, trances. Obviously, genius was a form of inspiration or enthusiasm. If the image of the genius evoked by Du Bos, and even by Helvétius, is one of a man plunged in meditation, or a poet or painter reflecting upon his work, that evoked by Rousseau and by Diderot's Dorval is one of a man inspired. In terms of the art of portraiture, think, for Du Bos' concept of genius, of the Poussin self-portrait at the Louvre; but for Rousseau and Diderot, think of Fragonard's *tête d'expression*, or portrait, called *l'Inspiration*. Not only has the discussion of genius changed, but also its representation.

The best picture in writing of the new type of genius is given by Diderot in his *Entretiens sur le Fils naturel*. We are alluding to a passage which might be entitled, were it a pre-Romantic painting, *Dorval inspired*. The man of genius is warm, sensitive, delirious, animated, ravished by the forces of nature and impatient with the constraints of society and rules of art, but, most interesting, he is a man in direct rapport with the higher powers of nature:

Dorval était arrivé le premier. J'approchais de lui sans qu'il m'aperçut. Il s'était abandonné au spectacle de la nature. Il avait la poitrine élevée. Il respirait avec force. Ses yeux attentifs se portaient sur tous les objets. Je suivais sur son visage les impressions diverses qu'il éprouvait; et je commençais à partager son transport, lorsque je m'écriai, presque sans le vouloir: "Il est sous le charme."[4]

The man of genius is a man of enthusiasm, and it is perhaps not too far off the mark to see in this depiction of Dorval inspired by the contemplation of nature a picture of the same type as that so eloquently painted by Rousseau of himself in his boat on the lake of Bienne, in the "Fifth Promenade" of his *Rêveries d'un promeneur solitaire*. The genius is in union with the powers or being of the universe, and the moment of creation is one of natural enthusiasm:

Le poète sent le moment de l'enthousiasme; c'est après qu'il a médité. Il s'annonce en lui par un frémissement qui part de sa poitrine, et qui passe,

---

[3] "Génie," in *Dictionnaire de musique*, in *Oeuvres complètes*, Vol. XIII.

[4] *Entretiens sur le Fils Naturel*, in *Oeuvres esthétiques*, 97.

d'une manière délicieuse et rapide, jusqu'aux extrémités de son corps. Bientôt ce n'est plus un frémissement; c'est une chaleur forte et permanente qui l'embrase, qui le fait haleter, qui le consume, qui le tue; mais qui donne l'âme, la vie à tout ce qu'il touche [Ibid., 98].

And so on to a state of near-fury which can only be relieved by an outpouring of ideas.

From the descriptions of Diderot we may assume that we have gone from an imitative theory of art to an expressive theory of genius. It is also quite clear that to such a man, such a genius, the rules of art, taste, society, and decorum must seem fetters to be broken. Indeed, the man of genius tends to avoid society and its requirements. He is a man of solitary thought, meditation, and work The reciprocity between genius and judgment, genius and art, has been altered in favor of a genius that knows no bounds. The characteristics usually associated with divine inspiration and illumination have been transferred to nature, and we find ourselves in the muddle of the naturalistic fallacy. We are beyond the Classical doctrine of art: the Romantic, meditating in the midst of nature, hair whipped by the wind, seated on a lonely rock, in the shadow of some pines, deep in melancholy thought, is not far off, and taste will soon be but an attribute of mere gentlemen without power to create, while artists and poets will be hailed as the prophets of a new world.

* * *

See also: *Imagination, Imitation, Nature, Rules, Taste*; *Du Bos, Diderot, Rousseau, Voltaire.*

Bibliography: Helvétius, Marmontel, Mercier, Séran de la Tour; Cassirer, Folkierski; and, for the seventeenth century, Roger Zuber, "La Création littéraire au dix-septième siècle — l'Avis des théoriciens de la traduction," *Revue des Sciences humaines*, 1963, No. 3, 277–94.

GOTHIC

"Un bâtiment d'ordre gothique est une espèce d'énigme pour l'oeil qui le voit; et l'âme est embarassée comme quand on lui présente un poème obscure,"[1] wrote Montesquieu in his essay on taste. It was a sentiment he shared with many. The "Gothick" marked the limits of the artistic understanding of the eighteenth century. In a sense we may say it

[1] "Essai sur le goût dans les choses de la nature et de l'art," in *Oeuvres*, II, 1246.

played for the Classical artistic mentality the role that paganism had played for the Christians of the Middle Ages: as something still very much about and to be feared. The term implied more than it does to us now, for the Gothic was not only associated with the Goths, and therefore with barbarism, not only with the Middle Ages, and therefore with ignorance, superstition, and prejudice; it was also associated with a certain failure of artistic endeavor. As such it could be found in all arts. Montesquieu thought the subject important enough to consider the matter in various of his writings. On his visit to Florence, in the gallery of the Grand Duke, he noticed a figure of Constantine which he termed "Gothic":

On voit un *Constantin* entièrement et totalement gothique. Il a un diadème de perles; ce qui convient bien à ce qu'en dit Julien dans ces *Césars*. On a donné le nom de Gallien à une tête qui est très bonne; ce qui fait manifestement voir que ce n'est pas un *Gallien*.

Cela me fait croire que la manière gothique ne vient point des Goths et autres peuples du Nord: ils ne l'introduisirent point, mais ils la confirmèrent, en faisant régner l'ignorance.[2]

Montesquieu pursued these thoughts in his short essay, "De la manière gothique," in which he states that the Gothic is not particular to any one people, but that it is a general artistic phenomenon, "la manière de la naissance ou de la fin de l'art" (Ibid., p. 966). The Gothic, in short, is an extreme, is exaggeration, either too rough or too *recherché* and affected. Its characteristics are lack of grace, stiffness, hardness, symmetry in the parts of the body but with lack of proportion in these parts. Montesquieu drew a simple schema of artistic development on the basis of his observations of art in the course of his travels through Italy:

Lorsque l'on commence à faire des figures, la première idée est de les dessiner, et on les dessine comme on peut. Dans la suite des temps, on songe à les mettre dans des attitudes convenables. On vient, ensuite, à leur donner du mouvement, et, enfin, de la grâce.

Lorsque l'art commence à décliner, on ne connaît plus ce qu'on appelle *la grâce*. Bientôt, on ne sait plus donner du mouvement aux figures. Ensuite, on ignore la variété des attitudes. On ne songe plus qu'à faire bien ou mal les figures, et on les met dans une position unique. C'est ce qu'on appelle *la manière gothique* [Ibid., I, 967].

[2] "Voyages," in *Oeuvres*, I, 924.

This is precisely what happened to the development of art from the period of the Egyptians through the end of the Roman Empire: the Egyptians remained Gothic, in the sense that their figures remained stiff; the Greeks improved on what they had learned from the Egyptians, gave motion and grace to figures, and all this skill was transmitted to the Romans, who began to lose it even before the Gothic incursions into the Empire. The Christians are in part to blame for this, since they did not purchase as many statues as the pagans had. Thus the arts of design were gradually lost.

The term Gothic was not confined to the plastic arts, for it represented a mentality. Duclos, in one of his novels, calls duels over a woman's honor a Gothic prejudice. There was also Gothic poetry, just as there were eventually new Gothic novels to amuse people who knew better than to take the Gothic seriously. The Gothic was associated with the childish and with lack of reason, judgment, and measure. It was the unclear, confused, and profuse use of ornament. True taste marked a triumph over the Gothic.

GRANDS SIECLES

The grands siecles were the aesthetic moments of history. They might indeed be called the moments of aesthetic revelation, for in a sense they played the same role in artistic thought and doctrine that the revelation and the coming of Christ did in the order of faith. They were the historical manifestations of true and great taste, beacons of civility and beauty in the chaos of temporal events. In these moments mankind managed to rise above the mere contingencies of fashion, fancy, and passion to attain the beautiful and the sublime. The *grands siècles* were those moments in which genius transformed accident into essence: they functioned like the perfect moments Roquentin's former mistress Anny took as models for her private tragedies and scenes, in Sartre's *La Nausée*; Anny was a romantic: she read Michelet. The men and women of the age of Louis XIV and Louis XV fixed upon other perfect moments, on the other hand, in order to avoid tragic drama, preferring rather the ideal of permanence, stability, serenity, noble simplicity, and quiet grandeur.

The theoretician of the *grands siècles* was Abbé Du Bos. He defined them, delimited them, pondered their causes. They were, as he put it, those happy moments in which the arts and sciences had flourished to an extraordinary degree. Such was the times of Alexander, Augustus,

Leo X, and Louis XIV. There were those who, like Voltaire, rather chose Pericles to represent the first of these four ages which were also the four ages of taste. These great moments were brief, but what they lost in duration they made up in intensity, for they were superior to other centuries precisely in their extraordinary flowering. What also gave them a rather special quality was their sudden appearance. One might almost say that for Du Bos and others as well the *grands siècles* were perceived in terms reminiscent of the miraculous, of the sudden appearance of the gods among men. To be sure, they were explained by natural causes, but their manifestation in historical time somehow retained the quality of sudden and almost supernatural inspiration. One spoke neither of miracles nor of fortune; one used the words "causes" and "genius," but for all that one did not quite understand how these perfect moments were produced, fostered, nurtured. Yet there is little doubt that the eighteenth century sought precisely to maintain what had been attained in the last of the *grands siècles*, that of Louis XIV. Du Bos thought that one could distinguish two broad general causes at work in the *grands siècles*, the moral and the physical. The first included patronage, the creation of academies, the distribution of honors and prizes to artists, the existence of leisure, stability, and peace, and a public interested in the fine arts; the physical causes reduced themselves to considerations of moral climate and the existence or nonexistence of genius. There were climates favorable to the arts, there were others that were not; there were times in which the moral causes could be of help, others at which they were of no avail, because ultimately one depended on genius. Pondering the *grands siècles*, the nature of their arts, and the relation of artists to society, patronage, and climate, Du Bos arrived at three general observations:

Ma première réflexion, c'est qu'il est des pays et des temps où les arts et les lettres ne fleurissent pas, quoique les causes morales y travaillent à leur avancement avec activité. La seconde réflexion, c'est que les arts et les lettres ne parviennent pas à leur perfection par un progrès lent et proportionné avec le temps qu'on a employé à leur culture, mais bien par un progrès subit.

Enfin les grands peintres furent toujours contemporains des grands poètes, et les uns et les autres vécurent toujours dans le même temps que les plus grands hommes leurs compatriotes. Il a paru que de leurs jours, je ne sais quel esprit de perfection, se répandait sur le genre humain dans leur patrie. Les professions qui avaient fleuri en même temps que la poésie et que la peinture, sont encore déchues avec elles [*Réflexions critiques*, II, 81–82].

The concept of *grands siècles* implies a theory of civilization as well as a vision of history. The perfect moments of civilization are also the moments of the unity of the various arts. Human activity and thought are interdependent, and a decline of letters implies also a decline of other human activities. We may readily perceive why taste should have been considered a matter of national importance and policy. As for history, the *grands siècles* provide a standard of values with which the worth of historical moments may be evaluated. At the same time history is also thought of in terms of contrasts between *grands siècles* and other periods: the former represent order, the other times are periods of disorder and false or bad taste. It is also possible to view history in terms of a perpetual oscillation between periods of true taste, as represented and manifest in the *grands siècles*, and the all too frequent recurrence of the Gothic.

As concerns artistic doctrine the *grands siècles* are inseparable from the doctrine of imitation. In a sense, one may argue that historical motion and change can be thought of in terms of imitation: princes imitate heroes, painters and poets imitate other painters and poets, patrons imitate other patrons, and the culture of a period may attempt to model itself upon some previous *grand siècle*. History is thus thought of in artistic terms. Metaphors derived from the stage, used in war (the "theatre of operations"), diplomacy, behavior, and art come readily to mind. History is not an impersonal process, but rather a series of acts, of good or bad acting, of poor or successful imitation, and in a sense history still is within the possibilities of human control, though the requirement of genius implies that imitation alone, moral causes alone, do not ensure success. The rules of art, the institution of art, the establishment of academies thus merely provide the means of passing through moments of time between *grands siècles*. Art, rules, imitation, provide continuity; the *grands siècles* are the successes of the doctrine of imitation, the fruit of ceaseless striving for perfection, the rewards of continuity, the consolation of the trials and tribulations of poets and artists who have to work in time and against time to transcend time. For the *grands siècles*, though born of time, attained a supratemporal value: they were the immortal moments of history.

* * *

See also: *Academy, Antique, Gothic, Imitation, Perfection, Taste.*
Bibliography: Du Bos, Montesquieu, Rousseau, Voltaire; Estève, Lacombe (*Spectacle*); Saisselin; and the excellent article by Enzo

Caramaschi, "Du Bos et Voltaire" in *Studies on Voltaire and the Eighteenth Century*, X, 113–236.

HARMONY

THE NOTION OF harmony pervades Classical criticism and aesthetics; it is a concept and a requirement as broad as that of beauty or unity. Harmony, indeed, is hardly to be separated from beauty or unity. Though the use of the term may be more narrowly defined as pertaining to color and music, it can also be applied to poetry and the dance, so that one may also speak of harmony of motion, just as, in painting, we may discuss harmony of line as well as of color. If we look further we may perceive that the entire Classical aesthetic presents a harmonious structure, a body of doctrine founded upon a simple base and a few assumptions uniting poets, painters, philosophers, and public in an illusion of beauty.

Harmony is also related to *convenance* (see article *"Convenance"*), as Abbé Batteux saw:

L'harmonie, en général, est un rapport de convenance, une espèce de concert de deux ou de plusieurs choses. Elle naît de l'ordre, et produit presque tous les plaisirs de l'esprit. Son ressort est d'une étendue infinie; mails elle est surtout l'âme des beaux-arts [*Les Beaux-Arts*, 169].

Regarding poetry (see article "Poetry"), Batteux listed three types of harmony: 1. harmony of style, which meant that style must be in accord with and appropriate to the subject treated; 2. harmony of sound and sense; and 3. artificial harmony, which referred to the art of verse, its motion, meter, melody, and song: "C'est une espèce de chant musical, qui porte le caractère non-seulement du sujet en général, mais de chaque objet en particulier" (Ibid., 175). When Batteux writes that the range of harmony is infinite he must be taken seriously, for in a sense the term was not merely aesthetic; it extended also to metaphysics. The universe was a harmonious structure created by and governed by God through certain natural laws, which is why evil and incidents like earthquakes caused considerable perturbations in the otherwise harmonious mental structure of philosophers. In view of the Lisbon earthquake, then, it may be possible to argue that the differences between optimists and pessimists are basically aesthetic, and also, following the great chain of being, we may say that actual earthquakes perhaps helped to shatter the beautiful and harmonious Classical aesthetic (see article "Nature").

More specifically, however, the term harmony had a precise meaning in painting and music. In the latter, according to Lacombe, harmony results from the union of several sounds heard together. Dissonant sounds, far from stifling or shutting out consonant sounds, serve to render harmony more brilliant by way of a *savant* and wise opposition of contraries. In painting harmony refers to the union and perfect accord of the color tones of painting. But the term also was extended to cover the rapports between the figures themselves and between these and the entire composition. It is obvious that, since the terms accord and tone are musical, harmony is above all a musical concept, used to cover any number of possible relations which strike the eye or the ear as having *convenance*, beauty, and unity.

IMAGINATION

MONTAIGNE, PASCAL, FONTENELLE, and La Motte were all suspicious of the imagination. The last pointed to its relative and ambiguous position within the Classical aesthetic rather well when he termed enthusiasm an overheated imagination. The twentieth-century French philosopher Alain still referred to imagination as *la folle du logis*. It is a characterization which would have been approved by Pascal, and probably was inspired by him. Imagination was associated with instinct, blindness, caprice, rebelliousness, vagueness, divagation, wandering, folly, and if you probed deeper you would see that it could also be considered the source of madness. One may thus consider art as a disciplining of the imagination: rules contained it, pictures might be said to be imagination held within bounds, and decorum regulated its power. The artist's taste or judgment controlled his imagination. There was no question of praising it as we do the creative imagination.

There was, however, another meaning attached to the term. Considered in itself rather than for its effects, the imagination was described in terms of a mechanism of vision and memory. Descartes, in his *Traité des passions*, does not so much write of *the* imagination as of imaginations or imaginings. These he divided into two general types according to their causes, namely those that depend upon the will and those that depend upon the body by way of the nerves. The first are images voluntarily called to the soul by the will; the latter are involuntary imaginings called forth as dreams or reveries due to the movements of the spirits. From the context we may assume that imaginings may be termed false perceptions. Perception is true knowledge of thought or of exterior objects; imagination is fictitious knowledge. We may also say that for the Cartesian the soul has a built-in potential of error, namely its ability to imagine. As Malebranche puts it, the imagination is subject to *dérèglement*. The ghost in the machine is a very, very delicate mechanism within an only slightly less delicate body. The balance between truth and error, perception and imagination, hangs, in a sense, upon the will's power.

Pascal, unlike Descartes, thought the imagination more powerful than the will. It was the source of error, folly, and temptation, inseparable from human nature after the Fall, so that man was most often incapable of distinguishing between truth and error:

> *Imagination.* − C'est cette partie décevante dans l'homme, cette maîtresse d'erreur et de fausseté, et d'autant plus fourbe qu'elle ne l'est pas toujours; car elle serait règle infaillible de vérité, si elle l'était infaillible du mensonge. Mais, étant le plus souvent fausse, elle ne donne aucune marque de sa qualité, marquant du même caractère le vrai et le faux.
>
> Je ne parle pas des fous, je parle des plus sages; et c'est parmi eux que l'imagination a le grand don de persuader les hommes. La raison a beau crier, elle ne peut mettre le prix aux choses [*Pensées*, 95].

One might say, in the light of this view of the imagination, that Descartes could not possibly have given the imagination more space than he did because it would have made his work itself a product of the imagination taking the form of reason. Pascal dismissed Descartes as "inutile et incertain," for it is obvious that if Pascal is right, then imagination, like the folly praised by Erasmus, is the very stuff and life of mankind. Imagination is indeed too strong for the reason, and men, in fact, aspire to be deceived, because this is easier than facing the truth of our own human condition.

In the seventeenth century Bossuet alone saw the creative possibilities of the imagination, in the sense that we have come to think of it. He conceived of the imagination as a species of interior sense creating great passions, capable of idealizing the objects of passions and animating the work of the poets. Thus by the end of the century, with Bossuet and Fontenelle among others, the imagination is no longer thought of exclusively in terms of psychology or the human condition of sin and error, but is also associated with the arts. In the early eighteenth century Vauvenargues defined it as "le don de concevoir les choses d'une manière figurée et de rendre ses pensées par des images. Ainsi, l'imagination parle toujours à nos sens; elle est l'inventrice des arts et l'ornement de l'esprit."[1] This amounts to a considerable reevaluation,

---

[1] *Oeuvres complètes* (Paris, 1929), I, 12.

for imagination is now no longer associated merely with error and folly; it has been freed from Pascal's suspicion and Descartes' association of it with false perception or reverie. The history of the imagination in the course of the eighteenth century is the history of its liberation from such associations. The midpoint between Pascal and Descartes, and the untrammeled imagination of genius as posited, for example, by Diderot was defined by Condillac in his lucid masterpiece, the *Essai sur l'origine des connaissances humaines* of 1746.

Condillac thought of imagination as a power capable of combining ideas and creating fictions. It is still a double edged tool: a help to knowledge and understanding, but also a danger because of its power to deceive. However, imagination is no longer associated with the human condition as Pascal understood it, and the important thing to stress is that the imagination is thought of as a creative power not only in the direction of error but also in that of understanding:

Il n'est rien qui ne puisse prendre, dans notre imagination, une forme nouvelle. Par la liberté avec laquelle elle transporte les qualités d'un sujet dans un autre, elle rassemble dans un seul ce qui suffit à la nature pour en embellir plusieurs. Rien ne paraît d'abord plus contraire à la vérité que cette manière d'ont l'imagination dispose de nos idées. En effet, si nous ne nous rendons pas maîtres de cette opération, elle nous égarera infailliblement: mais elle sera un des principaux ressorts de nos connaissances, si nous savons la régler.[2]

Imagination was thus no longer merely a false perception, a disturbance of vision, a form of folly; it was a power to combine ideas and thus an active mental power which could be dangerous only when it was uncontrolled. Condillac, like Descartes, kept the distinction between the voluntary and involuntary imagination. With the first, you combine ideas at will, in which case you obtain a voluntary and controlled mental activity; with the second, you are the victim of natural impressions stronger than those created by the will and not of your own volition. The first may be interrupted at will; the latter, not. Voluntary imagination is institutional, but the involuntary work of imagination is usually considered to be a natural activity. Both types have their advantages and inconveniencies, but the latter are the more dangerous because of their stronger impact upon the soul. The voluntary use of the imagination is above all evident in language. It may act as an ornament of language, but if one is not careful it can also obfuscate

[2] *Essai sur l'origine des connaissances humaines*, Chapter 18, Number 75.

meaning. The involuntary use of the imagination is useful in that it may preserve us from harm, as when we fear someone or something. But it is also dangerous because it may also fabricate illusions, prejudices, false fears, irrational sympathies and antipathies, and bizarre penchants; and it is here, again, that we may once more link imagination to folly, for the difference between it and folly is merely one of degree:

Il suffit de remarquer que, par le physique, l'imagination et la folie ne peuvent différer que du plus au moins. Tout dépend de la vivacité et de l'abondance avec laquelle les esprits se portent au cerveau. C'est pourquoi, dans les songes, les perceptions se retracent si vivement, qu'au réveil on a quelquefois de la peine à reconnaître son erreur. Voilà certainement un moment de folie [Ibid.].

The same danger lies with reverie. Consider, for example, the seemingly harmless expression *châteaux en Espagne*, castles in Spain. In moments of leisure one may surely dream thus and imagine oneself the hero of a novel without too much harm. Yet, due to unhappy circumstances, one may take refuge in such dreams and never cease to dream. It is for this reason that the reading of novels might prove dangerous especially for young ladies: "Leur esprit, que l'éducation occupe ordinairement trop peu, saisit avec avidité des fictions qui flattent des passions naturelles à leur âge. Elles y trouvent des matériaux pour les beaux châteaux en Espagne" (Ibid.). They live in a world of illusions; they have lost their balance. Madness is thus a disordered imagination. Ideas are associated in an incoherent, disordered manner which influences the judgment. If one reads Condillac carefully one may conclude that even for him, though for other reasons than those of Pascal, we all have a touch of madness in us. Some men are less mad than others, because their particular madness touches on things which are less important for living than the madness of others. There are also various forms of madness: there is madness that is steady and madness that is in perpetual flux, depending upon whether one possesses a cold or a hot imagination. And thus, despite his sensationism, Condillac sounds remarkably like Pascal after all:

Le pouvoir de l'imagination est sans bornes. Elle diminue ou même dissipe nos peines, et peut seule donner au plaisir l'assaisonnement qui en fait tout le prix. Mais quelquefois c'est l'ennemi le plus cruel que nous ayons: elle augmente nos maux, nous en donne que nous n'avions pas, et finit par nous porter le poignard dans le sein [Ibid.].

Voltaire's view of the imagination was unimaginative. It was still quite mechanical and tied to memory: perceptions enter the mind through the senses, were retained by the memory and composed by the imagination. There were two types of imagination, active and passive. The passive imagination was associated with memory, the active imagination was controlled by reflection. Whereas the passive imagination merely stored images, impressions, and perceptions independently of the will, the active imagination was a power to choose, combine, and arrange the images stored in the memory. It was the passive memory which was subject to error and passions. Voltaire's concept of the imagination was a simplified version of Descartes and Condillac, with emphasis on memory rather than on the power of the imagination to create fictions capable of changing one's visions of the world.

Diderot judged imagination to be of prime importance in the arts, but important also for men in general. Indeed, imagination was a distinguishing trait between men and beasts, and among men themselves, and the indispensable faculty of all human endeavor. Without imagination one would not be a poet, a philosopher, a man of wit and reason, or, simply, a man. It was, however, also indispensable to possess sensibility and memory, for imagination was dependent upon one's sensibility and the vivacity of one's sensations. While Diderot thought imagination dependent upon memory, he did not reduce it to either voluntary or involuntary memory. Memory may be a faithful copyist of the exterior world, but the imagination gave color and movement to the images of memory. Nevertheless, because the imagination was a function of one's memory, sensibility, and body organization (or organ, as Diderot was fond of saying), the imagination remained limited by the world of nature. One might say that it was nontranscendent and that Diderot did not posit a Romantic imagination which aspired to and in the end created a world beyond that of nature. Indeed, for Diderot the world of nature itself was more creative than any man's imagination, for even fictitious creatures, or, if you will, monsters, were imitated from nature by the combinatory power of man's imagination. They were not inventions, properly, but alterations. Diderot did not conceive of a fully creative imagination. What the imagination could do was to combine, alter, perceive, and change relationships, but it did all this within the bounds of nature.

Marmontel's article on imagination in his *Eléments de littérature* summarizes eighteenth-century thought on this subject. Significantly, the term "creative" is now used in connection with imagination, and the established distinction between voluntary and involuntary imagination, connected with memory, is somewhat altered because creativity is also associated with genius:

Imagination. On appelle ainsi cette faculté de l'âme qui rend les objets présents à la pensée; elle suppose dans l'entendement une appréhension vive et forte, et la facilité la plus prompte à reproduire ce qu'il a reçu. Quand l'imagination ne fait que retracer les objets qui frappent les sens, elle ne diffère de la mémoire que par la vivacité des couleurs. Quand de l'assemblage des traits que la mémoire a recueillis l'imagination compose elle-même des tableaux dont l'ensemble n'a point de modèle dans la nature, elle devient créatrice; c'est alors qu'elle appartient au génie.[3]

The association of imagination with sensibility, nature, and genius rather than with folly and error marks an important development in the concept of artistic creation. It heralds the passage from an aesthetic built on the notion of imitation to one based on imagination or, to put it another way, we pass from an aesthetic of art to an aesthetic of nature. Batteux had argued that man could not go beyond nature and that he could therefore not really create, for even monsters were but nature unnaturally rearranged (see article "Imitation"). An aesthetic of imitation may thus be said to answer to the first part of Marmontel's definition of imagination: it is a species of memory *en beau*; the second part, however, dealing with creative genius implies a new aesthetic in which the role of imagination is put in first place. In the first case imagination retraces what is perceived to produce something which is more or less *vraisemblable*; in the second instance genius goes beyond this particular type of *vraisemblance* towards a view of art which is also beyond imitation. It must be stressed, however, that the implications of putting imagination in the forefront of creation were not worked out in the eighteenth century itself, for even the concept of the creative as against the merely imitative genius remained within the bounds of nature. Even Chabanon, who perceived the limits of an imitative theory of art, could not fully break with it (see article "Chabanon"). Thus, in the eighteenth century the passage from an aesthetic of art to one of nature merely meant that one abandoned established models of perfection, once held to be worthy of emulation, in order to imitate other models thought to be closer to nature (see article "Antique") or else models in the natural world which were still subject to imitation *en beau*. The ambiguous nature of the eighteenth century's view of imagination is made clear in the Marmontel article.

[3] *Eléments de littérature*, in *Oeuvres* (Paris, 1818–20), XIV, pp. 124–41.

The first and most common form of imagination, namely the faculty of retracing memory images in the mind, is possessed by all mankind, even children:

Il est peu d'hommes en qui la réminiscence des objets sensibles ne devienne, par la réflexion, par la contention de l'esprit, assez vive, assez détaillée pour servir de modèle à la poésie. Les enfants mêmes ont la faculté de se faire une image frappante, non-seulement de ce qu'ils ont vu, mais de ce qu'ils ont ouï dire d'intéressant, de pathétique [Ibid.].

One thinks not only of "emotion recollected in tranquillity" but also of a species of democratization of poetry: the philosopher's view of the mind leads one to conclude that all men are potential poets because all men are *sensibles* and all men are capable of memory pictures. The difference between good and bad poetry is a matter of degree and dependent upon the attention and care given the images recalled. The allusion to children is not without interest when one considers that the Gothic style, for example, with its rough and ready works, could be considered as that of an art in its infancy. If we turn to the second part of Marmontel's view of imagination we soon see that *creative* does not mean exactly what we tend to associate with the word. Marmontel does not even evoke in us the thought of the fantastic and really imaginative world of Fuseli. Instead we find ourselves on the stage and are reminded of Diderot's *Paradoxe sur le comédien*:

On confond souvent avec *l'imagination* un don plus précieux encore, celui de s'oublier soi-même; de se mettre à la place du personnage que l'on veut peindre; d'en revêtir le caractère; d'en prendre les inclinations, les intérêts, les sentiments; de le faire agir comme il agirait, et de s'exprimer sous son nom comme il s'exprimerait lui-même [Ibid.].

This is the imagination of the artist and the poet, and it is to be nurtured by the experience of life and the study of the arts, and is, in the last analysis, a life-long exercise. It may require imagination, but it must not be confused with imagination proper. This is something not given to all; it borders on enthusiasm and may indeed be exactly that, should one feel as if possessed by another or as if one had become the character portrayed. But this enthusiasm does not wait for inspiration; it is the result of a profound study of the human heart: "Ce que Platon appelle *manie*, suppose donc beaucoup de sagesse; et je doute que Locke et Pascal fussent plus philosophes que Racine et Molière" (Ibid.). This particular form of imagination or enthusiasm, stripped of its associations with the supernatural, is perhaps best described as a species of empathy, a capacity to apprehend the reality of a moment or of a passion and, so to speak, enter into it. In this sense, then, the imagination is not only capable of being struck by an image and of reproducing it; it can also animate it, because the entire soul of the poet is moved as if in communion with the forces of nature. It is obvious that this second type of imagination, creative, allied to enthusiasm, supposes a genius similar to that conceived by Diderot (see article "Genius"). But Marmontel is in fact less enthusiastic than Diderot. As if afraid of the word "creative" that he used in connection with imagination and genius, he limits it by quoting Voltaire on enthusiasm in order to explain what he really means:

L'homme du monde qui pouvait le mieux parler de l'enthousiasme, M. de Voltaire, nous dit que l'enthousiasme raisonnable est le partage des grands poètes. Mais comment l'enthousiasme peut-il être gouverné par le raisonnement? Voici sa réponse: "Un poète dessine d'abord l'ordonnance de son tableau; la raison alors tient le crayon. Mais veut-il animer ses personnages et leur donner le caractère des passions: alors l'imagination s'échauffe, l'enthousiasme agit; c'est un coursier qui s'emporte dans la carrière, mais sa carrière est régulièrement tracée." Il le compare au grand Condé, qui méditait avec sagesse, et combattait avec fureur [Ibid.].

One is tempted to say that imagination, in the course of the eighteenth century, became enthusiasm naturalized.

Upon reflection, then, it would seem that opinion concerning the imagination shifted, in the course of the seventeenth and eighteenth centuries, from associations with folly and madness to ones with creativity and nature. This perhaps marks less a liberalization of the imagination, as we had initially thought, than its taming. In the seventeenth century one feared the creativity of the imagination because it affected true perception and judgment, and was thus a source of error. In the eighteenth century one feared imagination less, or not at all, because one knew in advance that its creations were either fictions or combinations of ideas taken from the world of nature. It could thus be a source of pleasant illusions as well as harmless delusions, while imagination associated with genius was a nature-given gift to embrace a wide range of ideas.

* * *

See also *Genius*; *Condillac, Diderot, Pascal, Rousseau.*
Bibliography: Beardsley, Wimsatt and Brooks; and, for a thorough and

philosophical discussion of the theories of the imagination in the seventeenth and eighteenth centuries, R. G. Collingwood, *The Principles of Art*, Book II (Oxford, 1938).

IMITATION

THE CLASSICAL DOCTRINE OF ART is reducible to a very short formula: art is an imitation of nature. There are ways of saying much the same thing in different ways and of placing emphasis now on one, now on another term, but no matter what one does to elaborate on this definition, one will have to have recourse to the word "imitation" or to some other word meaning the same thing. A work of art was an imitation, in one sense of the term; but the term also referred to a process, to the making of a work of art. The association of art with imitation was accepted so widely that few bothered defining the word. There is no entry for it in Lacombe's *Dictionnaire portatif des beaux-arts*, though significantly enough there is one for invention. Yet imitation is central: it pervades Classical aesthetics; it turns up in discussions of beauty, the ancients, models, masters, and nature. One thing was certain to all, namely that artists and poets imitated, the only question left open being whom and what to imitate. One reason for this lack of concern with a precise meaning of imitation lay perhaps in the fact that the arts could flourish even without a clear and precise definition; it may also be that, since the very process of imitation was the object of all the rules and reflections upon art, to write about any of the fine arts in effect meant that one indirectly wrote about imitation.

It is only because of the rival notion of genius that, little by little, the notion of imitation came to be defined and clarified. Reynolds, in Britain, had to devote an entire Discourse to imitation in order to distinguish it from the false notion of servile copying and also to defend it against the equally false notion of the sufficiency of inspiration without knowledge of the art. Batteux also saw fit to define the term in his *Les Beaux-Arts réduits à un même principe*, since the one principle which lay behind all the arts was the imitation of *la belle nature*. But there are other sources, among amateurs, in the counsels offered to painters and poets as to which nature they ought to imitate.

To Batteux imitation was a function of genius, but was limited by the notion of nature: "Le génie, qui est le père des arts, doit imiter la belle nature" (*Les Beaux-Arts*, p. 9). The premise of the doctrine of imitation supposes the linkage of beauty and truth, and also the assumption that the universe, or if you will, nature, is the masterpiece of God.

Thus man cannot really create; he can only imitate. As Batteux put it: "L'esprit humain ne peut créer qu'improprement: toutes ses productions portent l'empreinte d'un modèle" (Ibid., 10). Imitation limits the range of genius and imagination. Even monsters cannot be invented; they can only be unnatural rearrangements of parts taken from nature. The implication is that nothing can come from nothing; that man is part of nature and cannot go beyond it; that certain limits cannot be passed. To go beyond nature, or try to do so, merely causes horror and chaos: "Les limites sont marquées, dès qu'on les passe on se perd. On fait un chaos plutôt qu'un monde, et on cause de l'horreur plutôt que du plaisir" (Ibid.). The genius therefore need not attempt to go beyond the limits of nature, for his function is not to imagine what might be, but to find what is: "Inventer dans les arts, n'est point donner l'être à un objet, c'est le reconnaître où il est, et comme il est (Ibid., 11). Thus imitation is also the limit of invention, and the doctrine of imitation supposes a closed system of the arts, unless of course one alters the definition of nature. But because Batteux thought art to be an imitation of la belle nature, rather than the nature one might see in looking out of a window in the country, imitation was not to be confused with merely copying what one saw. What the genius found and imitated was the perfection behind the actuality, so that imitation supposes a prototype and the copying of that prototype. Nature, la belle nature in the case of Batteux, is the prototype, and the work of art is the copy or imitation. One might think of imitation also in terms of transposition, and of the artist as a diviner of a higher and more perfect order and beauty which he transposes from the realm of the ideal into the material world. It is easy to see how and why the eighteenth-century aestheticians ended by being philosophical idealists, and why a line of descent may be established from Crousaz, Father André, and Batteux to the beau idéal, and later to Victor Cousin. On the other hand, if you consider that the artist is not supposed to copy nature as she is in the sublunar world, then obviously one may also argue that imitation is a species of creation in spite of the assumptions of the philosophers, a creation of an ideal order and world which they supposed to be real or more real than the material, sublunar world of disorder and chaos. Imitation in this sense was a species of invention. It is obvious that the most important term in the formula, "Art is an imitation of nature" is the last, for upon the definition and evaluation of nature depends the value put on imitation, whether the lesser value associated with copying or the greater value associated with invention.

There was, however, another accepted meaning for the term "imitation." Batteux used it in a very wide sense in reference to the instruction of humanity and the innate natural disposition toward mimicry. Man he considered an imitative animal; imitation was a source of pleasure, and by extension the arts were, so to speak, a natural result of this human activity. Man not only loved imitating, he also enjoyed comparing imitations with originals, especially when the imitations were the result of intelligence and intellectual penetration. But even considered as a natural disposition outside the realm of the fine arts, imitation raised questions regarding what and how to imitate.

Batteux realized that imitation was often confused with copying, and he guarded against this confusion by insisting upon intelligence. Art is not trompe-l'oeil, and, as may be readily gleaned from contemporary discussions of nature, this type of imitation was not highly regarded. Imitation, according to Batteux, must raise the soul above the realm of the commonplace to the level of the perfect, which means that an imitation must possess two qualities: exactitude and liberty. These two requirements seem self-contradictory, and Batteux was aware of it, though he did not seem to realize that the contradiction derived from the very ambiguity of the doctrine of imitation. He tried to reconcile exactitude and liberty by associating exactitude with the actions of the mind rather than with external conformity to the object imitated. For him, exactitude was fidelity to the perfect model formed in the mind which, once perfectly apprehended or clearly conceived, could be easily rendered on canvas. At this point he quoted Boileau:

> Ce que l'on conçoit bien s'énonce clairement,
> Et les mots pour le dire, arrivent aisément.

The ideal of perfection regulated the choice of nature, objects, and thoughts, while liberty animated the imitation so that it would end up being an illusion of truth, *vraisemblable*. To better illustrate his meaning he had recourse to the practises of certain painters:

C'est pour atteindre à cette liberté que les grands peintres laissent quelquefois jouer leur pinceau sur la toile: tantôt, c'est une symmétrie rompue; tantôt, un désordre affecté dans quelque petite partie; ici, c'est un ornement négligé; là, un défaut même, laissé à dessein: c'est la loi de l'imitation qui le veut:

> A ces petits défauts marqués dans la peinture,
> L'esprit avec plaisir reconnaît la nature

[Ibid., 91–92].

But even this qualification of imitation and the conciliation of exactitude and liberty did not prevent another problem from presenting itself quite naturally: why is it that things which are unpleasant in nature are nevertheless pleasant as imitations? This problem is treated elsewhere (see article "Dramatic Poetry"). The question of liberty itself leads us to an older term, namely the *je ne sais quoi* (see article). In truth, imitation cannot be treated or understood in isolation.

Imitation was an unfortunate term: it could be assimilated to or reconciled with invention, but it also could be interpreted as a type of copying. Interpretations of the term's meaning varied between the strict and the loose, especially as regards the art of painting, which lends itself most readily and obviously to definition as an art of imitation. But even here the concept of nature, models, and masters tended to affect the meaning of the term, since painters were often told to imitate nature as well as study the masters. But since the conception of nature was much more vague than references to known masters, one could easily make distinctions among *la belle*, *la simple*, and *la vraie nature*, so that those who urged painters to imitate nature tended to loosen the term imitation, while those who advocated the imitation of the masters tended to espouse a stricter interpretation. Yet there remained a way towards greater liberty, no matter what the degree of strictness or indulgence towards imitation, for one could always say that one ought to do what the ancients had done, for they had imitated nature by being original.

✳ ✳ ✳

See also: *Art, Genius, Imagination, Nature, Rules, Truth*; *Diderot.*
Bibliography: Marmontel; Wimsatt and Brooks.

INTEREST

"THE ONLY RULE THERE IS," wrote Voltaire in his *Essay on Epic Poetry*, "is that an action be one, interesting, and complete." This seems a truism, and I had decided to pay little attention to the term "interesting" until I attended a John Cage concert. I then understood that the word *intérêt*, which is treated by Marmontel in his *Eléments de littérature* might be illuminating even today, and that it had a value and meaning in the eighteenth century which it has lost today. For what struck me at the John Cage concert was that obviously sounds did not have enough interest in themselves to quiet, captivate, or discipline the audience, and that once curiosity was satisfied, interest could hardly be maintained. Thus it is that in a time like ours, in which everything is called interesting at some time or another, and in which interest is therefore rapidly lost, it might be interesting to find out just what the term meant in the Classical aesthetic.

Marmontel defined interest as an affection of the soul:

Affection de l'âme qui lui est chère et qui l'attache à son objet. Dans un récit, dans une peinture, dans une scène, dans un ouvrage d'esprit en général, c'est l'attrait de l'émotion qu'il nous cause ou le plaisir que nous éprouvons à en être ému de curiosité, d'inquiétude, de crainte, de pitié, d'admiration, etc.[1]

There are two types of interest: you take interest in the work of art as such, or in the virtuosity it required, and you also take interest in the subject matter. Both are necessary to maintain full interest:

Le poète aura donc soin de choisir des sujets qui, par leur agrément ou leur utilité, soient dignes d'exercer son génie; sans quoi l'abus du talent changerait en un froid dédain ce premier mouvement de surprise et d'admiration que la difficulté vaincue aurait causé [Ibid.].

Interest is caused by the relation which a work of art has to us, and this relation or *rapport* may be one either of resemblance or of influence: in the first case the object reminds us of our condition; in the second, it pertains to the moral realm and brings to mind ideas of good and evil, desire or fear. Interest is an effect of imagination, of the spectator's capacity for empathy:

Lorsque la peinture d'un paysage riant et paisible vous cause une douce émotion, une rêverie agréable, consultez-vous, et vous trouverez que, dans ce moment, vous vous supposez assis au pied de cet hêtre, au bord de ce ruisseau, sur cette herbe tendre et fleurie, au milieu de ces troupeaux, qui, de retour le soir au village, vos donneront un lait délicieux [Ibid.].

Interest is a function of the possibility of identifying with a work of art. It is also a function of pleasure, the ability to touch the reader or spectator. Interest is thus intimately tied to the human function of art and its role of being a second nature, exempt from pain. Marmontel is merely saying what Du Bos said in other words: that a successful work of art is one which pleases; such a work maintains interest, and this is further proof that one has properly imitated *la belle nature*, "car la beauté poétique n'est autre chose que l'*intérêt*; et pour lui la belle nature est

[1] *Eléments de littérature*, in *Oeuvres* (Paris, 1818–20), XIV, 143–53.

celle dont l'imitation nous émeut comme nous voulons être émus"
(Ibid.). The merit of a work of art or a poem lies in this capacity to
arouse and maintain interest, and we begin to see why criticism in
the eighteenth century was concerned above all with the question: Can
this or that work maintain our interest? It was another way of asking:
Does this work move me, touch me, please me? The insistence on interest thus also supposes a certain relation between the poet or artist
and the reader or spectator: interest forms a bridge between them.

The greatest interest is associated with the pathetic. Marmontel
makes his point by choosing two paintings, one of a magnificent palace
and one of ruins. The latter will be the more touching, the more interesting, because it is the more pathetic of the subjects:

En général la nature qui ne dit rien à l'âme, qui n'y excite aucun sentiment, ou
qui la rébute et la révolte par des impressions qu'elle fuit, va contre l'intention
du poète, et doit être bannie de la poésie. Celle au contraire dont nous sommes
émus, comme il veut que nous le soyons et comme nous aimons à l'être, est
celle qu'il doit imiter. Si donc il veut inspirer la crainte ou le désir, l'envie
ou la pitié, la joie ou la mélancolie, qu'il interroge son âme: il est certain
que pour se bien conduire, il n'a qu'à se bien consulter [Ibid.].

This is especially true for the mental realm, for "rien n'est si près de
l'homme que l'homme même." In a sense then, interest also supposes
self-interest: the poet or the artist must speak to us about ourselves.
Man is the central subject of art, and it is for this reason that the dramatic art represents also the greatest interest. John Cage aroused interest and curiosity, but because his sounds did not really speak to us,
or all of us, but merely that part of the brain which happened to be
curious, his concert was not sufficiently interesting to maintain serious
attention for long.

JE NE SAIS QUOI

THE JE NE SAIS QUOI lay beyond the boundaries of discourse, the rules,
and such established aesthetic categories as *le vrai, le beau, le naturel,*
and *le sublime.* For its distinguishing trait was precisely that it could
not be explained or understood in terms of such known categories. One
may, indeed, wonder whether it can at all be classified as a phenomenon
belonging to the aesthetic realm since its essence, so to speak, is the
indefinable. We shall see, however, that it may be so classified. The
je ne sais quoi was a certain something which pleased, one knew not

quite why, and this pleasure might be aroused by natural as well as man-made objects or, for that matter, by qualities possessed by human beings.

Pascal used the term to describe the attraction between lovers; Vaugelas, author of the *Remarques sur la langue française* of 1647, called it an 'élément insaisissable" which was essential to gallantry and refinement; Guez de Balzac, his contemporary, thought of it in terms of humility before the inexpressible; Rapin thought it highly important for eloquence; Boileau referred to it as a spell or charm upon the eyes of a beholder of some object; Voiture, an early seventeenth-century man of letters and wit, used its Spanish version, *el no se que*, and called it graces which are touching, but "si petites que même on ne sait ce que c'est"; the Chevalier de Méré, author of several seventeenth-century treatises on the social and moral qualities of gentlemen, used it in connection with social qualities. The *je ne sais quoi* obviously obsessed, though not unduly, the seventeenth century. It was Father Bouhours who, in his *Entretiens d'Ariste et d'Eugène*, did most to define or describe its qualities or effects insofar as its nature permitted. Thus the *je ne sais quoi* is an element of the friendship between Eugène and Ariste, and also part of the pleasure they have in each other's company. But precisely what it is that pleases they cannot define, which is why it is called the *je ne sais quoi*: "Sa nature est d'être incompréhensible, et inexplicable." One can only say what it is not, thus:

Ce n'est précisément ni la beauté, ni la bonne mine, ni la bonne grâce, ni l'enjouement de l'humeur, ni le brillant de l'esprit; puisque l'on voit tous les jours des personnes qui ont toutes ces qualités sans avoir ce qui plaît.[2]

The *je ne sais quoi* is something which may please some, displease others. It seems to be a cause known through its effects only and closely connected with subjectivity of taste and perception. One might say that, in a world of rationalism and universality, and within an aesthetic founded on *le vrai*, or *le grand beau* and *le grand goût*, the *je ne sais quoi* is the intimate, the highly personal; one might call it the equivalent of grace in the realm of secular pleasures and graces. One may also think of it as evidence that the seventeenth century did not elaborate a monolithic, rationalistic world view, that its philosophy cannot be reduced to or be thought of solely in terms of mechanism, or its aesthetic associated with Descartes. The *je ne sais quoi* is a certain mystery within a world all too readily explained by metaphysicians as

[2] *Entretiens d'Ariste et d'Eugène* (Paris: Edition de Cluny), pp. 140–41.

being made up of spirit plus matter or of only one or the other. The
je ne sais quoi is an effect or a perception of the "esprit de finesse, qui
ne peut s'exprimer, et dont on ferait bien de se taire." Or, in the words
of Wittgenstein, "Whereof one cannot speak, thereof one must be silent." But of course one went on thinking and even writing about the
je ne sais quoi.

Eventually it came to be associated with certain qualities in works
of art which pleased the spectator of such works. The transfer is made
by Marivaux in a fantasy in one of his early periodical ventures, the
Cabinet du philosophe. The point of his argument is that beauty and
the *je ne sais quoi* are rarely found together; each is an aesthetic category of its own. The question is treated allegorically: a man muses
about some forms of beauty he has known and wanders till he finds
himself between two gardens, one which houses beauty and the other
the *je ne sais quoi*; he visits both and finds that beauty is easily defined
and recognized, for beauty is grand, magnificent, superb, and of exact
symmetry. But the garden of the *je ne sais quoi* is completely different:
it seems the work of happy chance, disorderly and yet quite charming
and delightful; but the *je ne sais quoi*, supposedly housed in the garden,
can never be found or seen, because unlike beauty it cannot be personified. It takes rather the form of a voice defining itself and the garden at
the same time:

Dans tout ce que vous apercevez ici de simple, de négligé, d'irrégulier même,
d'orné ou de non orné, j'y suis, je m'y montre, j'en fais tout le charme;
je vous entoure. Sous la figure de ces grâces, je suis le *Je ne sais quoi*
qui plaît en peinture; là, le *Je ne sais quoi* qui plaît en architecture, en
ameublements, en jardins, en tout ce qui peut faire l'objet du goût. Ne me
cherchez point sous une forme fixe; j'en ai mille, et pas une de fixe. Voilà
pourquoi l'on me voit sans me connaître, sans pouvoir ni me saisir ni me
définir. On me perd de vue en me voyant; il faut me sentir et non me démêler
["Le Cabinet du philosophe," *Oeuvres complètes*, IX, 386].

It would seem then that by the early eighteenth century the *je ne sais
quoi* took on characteristics remarkably like those usually associated
with the aesthetic. It marked the limit of the Classical doctrine of art
and beauty; it could, from the above description, be associated with the
charm of the rocaille style and the *petits genres* of the eighteenth century. But because it is a pleasure and a something which can be associated with objects of art and nature, the *je ne sais quoi* also marks the
point or area where the aesthetic of art joined an aesthetic of nature, a

union implying a psychological link which we might name aesthetic delight.

As far as we know the Marivaux piece on the *je ne sais quoi* is the last one worthy of great interest. Montesquieu discussed the term in his *Essai sur le goût*, but his views do not add to those of Marivaux. Montesquieu associated it with surprise and limited his discussion of it to human beauty as manifest in nature, poetry, and painting. It may be that the eighteenth century was too avid for universal explanations, precepts, and utility to be long interested in a term which might have seemed rather frivolous to those who would reduce most phenomena to a rational explanation.

*   *   *

Bibliography: Montesquieu; Bouhours, Marivaux; and, for a recent study, "Le *Je ne sais quoi* de Trissotin," in *Revue des Sciences humaines*, July-Sept., 1961, 367–78.

MACHINES, GRANDES MACHINES

"MACHINES," IN DISCOURSES concerning poetry, or in treatises on the epic or opera, pertain to supernatural machinations, interventions, or operations. More precisely, the term implies that the intervening being must make itself manifest and visible. In this sense, machines were part of the visible marvels the amateurs of opera were so fond of. The gods, however, might operate in other ways, namely through oracles, dreams, and extraordinary inspiration. The term was not limited to gods; it could also be used to refer to the intervention or apparitions of demons or personified moral virtues or vices. While such apparitions or interventions were obviously supernatural, or at least extranatural, they were nevertheless subject to the general rule of verisimilitude. Certain machines were allowed in the epic which were not allowed on stage. Horace, for example, would allow a metamorphosis in narrative poetry but he would not allow it to be seen on the stage. (The tricks necessary to bring across the metamorphosis of a man into a rhinoceros in Ionesco's play of that name may, in the view of some, demonstrate the judiciousness of this classical restriction.) As for entirely absurd machines, such as retrieving a child alive from a monster which had swallowed it, these should be banished from poetry as well as stage. On the whole, machines should be used with care and discretion: the audience must not be offended, and verisimilitude in the use of machines must be founded upon the taste of the public. In the epic machines may be used freely, because the essence of such poetry is fable. Thus almost the entire action of an epic may be determined by machines, that is by divine intervention. As Le Bossu put it: "Quiconque donc veut être poète, doit laisser écrire aux historiens: qu'une flotte fut écartée par la tempête, et jettée sur des bords étrangers; et doit dire avec Virgile, que Junon alla trouver Eole, et que ce Dieu, à sa prière, envoya les vents contre les Troyens."[1] Machines are the manifestation of supernatural causes, permissible in fable and in epic poetry, permissible too in a world still associated with fable, as in Fénelon's prose epic the *Telemachus*, but banished from history, in which only natural causation is allowed. Voltaire's *Henriade* could be considered a modern epic, based on recent history, if only because one type of machine was excluded from it, the intervention of divinities. With the spread of the philosophic spirit the supposition that machines and verisimilitude could be reconciled came to be questioned. Machines made the difference between fable and history, and they were, in the end, accepted mostly in opera, which as everyone knew was a world of pure fantasy having nothing whatsoever to do with credibility.

The term "machine" was also used in the art of painting. It referred to the assemblage of the several parts of a painting, which concurred to form a perfect whole, and as such the term was more or less the equivalent of "composition." The term *grande machine*, which one also meets with often in the discussion of the art of painting, meant specifically a painting of vast or rich composition. These were mostly histories whose matter was taken either from fable or antiquity, but later also from more recent history. They corresponded to the epic in poetry. The Medici cycle by Rubens, now in the Louvre, the various historical paintings of David are *grandes machines*. The problem of verisimilitude was posed in painting as in poetry. The questions of whether pagan elements might be mixed with a Christian motif, or whether mythological creatures might be introduced into a historical painting, as Rubens did in his Medici cycle, were also judged in terms of verisimilitude, and as in the art of poetry, so in painting the *grandes machines* of history gradually replaced those of mythology, and the interventions of the gods gave way to the historical actions of men.

✶   ✶   ✶

See also: *Epic Poetry, Truth; Le Bossu.*

[1] Quoted in René Bray, *La Formation de la doctrine classique en France* (Paris, 1927).

METHOD

"Pour moi," wrote Houdar de la Motte in an essay on poetry, "je crois indépendamment des exemples, qu'il faut de la méthode dans toutes sortes d'ouvrages" ("Discours sur la poésie"). Method was something the eighteenth century prided itself upon very much. We may say that it became, in a sense, an aesthetic category which appealed to certain minds.

Condillac defined it as "l'art de concilier la plus grande clarté et la plus grande précision avec toutes les beautés dont un sujet est susceptible."[1] It must not be associated with being methodical, as we understand this today, but rather with composition, order, clarity. One spoke of a methodical work, a methodical writer, and, following La Motte, one could conceivably also expect methodical poets. Boileau's *Art poétique* possessed method, it was clearly organized. Pope's *Essay on Criticism*, on the other hand, lacked method because it was poorly composed. Method made for clarity of communication between writer and reader; it spared the latter effort and left him in no uncertainty as to what was being presented to his mind. The *Nouvelliste du Parnasse* found Pope's *Essay on Criticism* somewhat boring, precisely because it lacked method: "Quoiqu'il y ait dans la traduction de ce poème un grand nombre de très beaux vers, rien cependant n'y attache l'esprit, parce qu'on n'y trouve aucun ordre, aucune liaison, aucune analogie dans les pensées; voilà la source de l'ennui qu'il cause."[2] It might be objected that Pope's poem is as it is because it was inspired by Horace's *Epistle to the Pisons*, so that its lack of method can hardly be blamed on Pope. In that case, all one can say is that the fault must also be ascribed to Horace. Indeed the ancients often lacked method, and it is precisely method which serves to distinguish the modern from the ancient writers.

Method was associated with the triumph of the philosophic spirit and its extension even into belles lettres, with consequent effects upon the imagination. One need not associate it with the mechanical, as the Romantics might do, for something else is involved. It would be fairer to define it as organized perception and sustained attention as far as the reader is concerned, while from the point of view of the writer it is an art which assures his work unity. In psychological terms method implies the triumph of reason over the materials furnished by sensation

---

[1] "Traité de l'Art d'Ecrire," in *Oeuvres complètes*, V, 452.

[2] Desfontaines, *Le Nouvelliste du Parnasse* (Paris, 1734), I, 36–37.

and imagination. In terms of style and prose it may further be described
as perfect discourse: "Dans tout discours," writes Condillac in his *Art
d'écrire,*

il y a une idée par où l'on doit commencer, une par où l'on doit finir, et
d'autres par où l'on doit passer. La ligne est tracée, tout ce qui s'en écarte
est superflu. Or on s'en écarte en insérant des choses étrangères, en répétant
ce qui a déjà été dit, en s'arrêtant sur des détails inutiles [p. 422].

Method was ideally suited for the perfection of discourse and for making reading as effortless as possible, and while it was thought most appropriate to philosophical discourse, the ideal was extended to other
works as well.

La méthode qui apprend à faire un tout est commune à tous les genres. Elle
est surtout nécessaire dans les ouvrages de raisonnement: car l'attention
diminue à proportion qu'on la partage, et l'esprit ne saisit plus rien lorsqu'il
est distrait par un trop grand nombre d'objets [Ibid., 436].

Thus method implies sustained attention, continuous interest, concen-
tration. The opposite is *fatras, désordre, délire, distraction,* faults found
all too often in the literature of the ancients, the medieval writers, and
generally before the seventeenth century. More than a mechanical term,
it is one which is inseparable from psychology, for in fact it defines a
certain relation or attitude towards the imagination. An unmethodical
book is one made by a writer who has not mastered his imagination.
Thus method is after all inseparable from an aesthetic of art as well,
and is perhaps the philosopher's importation into his own concerns of
the old classical artistic ideal of unity of action. But the philosopher
makes of it unity of thought achieved by the most perfect liaison of
ideas.

Si l'ouvrage entier a un sujet et une fin, chaque chapitre a également l'un
et l'autre, chaque article, chaque phrase. Il faut donc tenir la même conduite
dans les détails. Par là l'ouvrage sera un dans son tout, un dans chaque partie, et tout y sera dans la plus grande liaison possible [Ibid., 439].

If La Motte could hold that method was also necessary in poetry it was
because in his day both poetry and prose were governed by an ideal
of representation, namely clarity. Method insured for the poet a perfect picture, just as it offered the prose writer a means of perfectly

organizing his thoughts with the use of conventional signs, also called words, which were not used as in the case of poetry to present pictures, but rather abstract reasoning.

While method gave unity to a work, it must not be confused with unity itself as an aesthetic ideal. Unity was an attribute of art and beauty long before the concept of method, which more properly belongs to the Cartesian ideal of clarity of perception followed by the greatest possible liaison of ideas, came into existence. Method belongs to that Cartesian aesthetic which Descartes himself never elaborated but which nevertheless exists in the writings of men like Fontenelle, La Motte, Terrasson, d'Alembert, and Condillac.

NATURE, BELLE NATURE

> On parle beaucoup de la belle nature; il n'y a pas même de peuple poli qui ne se pique de l'imiter; mais chacun croit en trouver le modèle dans sa manière de sentir. Qu'on ne s'étonne pas si on a tant de peine à la reconnaître; elle change trop souvent de visage ou du moins elle prend trop l'air de chaque pays. Je ne sais même si la façon dont j'en parle actuellement ne se sent pas du ton qu'elle prend, depuis quelque temps, en France.
>
> *Condillac*

LOOKING BACK UPON the eighteenth century, we may say that the term "nature" was what might be called an open one: indeed, one could even go so far as to call it wide open. Nature may even be to blame for the French Revolution and all that followed; it was the Pandora's box of the *philosophes*. The end-all and be-all of philosophical enterprise, it justified *philosophes* and *anti-philosophes*, painters and poets, and atheists, deists, and theists as well as Christians. To some it was a source of goodness, to others a source of evil. In all probability it was the central concept of the age, manifesting itself also as subconcepts when used with adjectives, so that subnatures proliferated: philosophers postulated a natural man, endowed with natural rights, enjoying the possession of natural taste, recalling to mind in the prison of society a lost natural state in which he had enjoyed a natural innocence, natural pleasures, and natural goodness, and had joined with others in a natural religion. Towards the end of the eighteenth century people came to suppose that there was no truth but nature and that Rousseau had been its prophet; and behold! lords, ladies, and gentlemen took walks in the country, there was much talk of nature, and many tears were shed as men, women, and children naturally loved being natural. To be in the midst of nature was once more to be close to God: and thus the itinerary of aesthetic thought in the eighteenth century seems, as far as nature was concerned, to have gone full circle, from spirit to matter, and from matter back to spirit.

From our vantage point we can see that "nature" proved to be the catalyst which dissolved one aesthetic and permitted the elaboration of a new one. It could be rather difficult to know just what was meant by nature, because everything was contained within it (so that, as the Marquis de Sade did not fail to see, it justified everything). In time, though, thanks to Rousseau, the eighteenth century came to know what nature was not: clearly, its opposite was art. It is possible, therefore, to say that part of the confusion in the aesthetics of the eighteenth century came from the mixture of two antithetical systems, one founded upon the concept of nature and the other upon the institution of art: though few, if any, were aware of this confusion, which involved contradictions in thought concerning art, beauty, and nature, and their relation to each other. The ambiguities of aesthetic thought were not clarified either by the fact that both aesthetics were conceived with the same vocabulary, and it is of course for this reason that, if one wishes to know just what was meant in certain instances by such terms as beauty, nature, imitation, the sublime, and so on, it is well to know the works of art and literature to which they refer. Changes of form changed the meaning of words, although the words remained the same. It is undeniable, however, that despite the limitations of language there were those who, in the early eighteenth century at least, sensed the danger of founding not only moral but also aesthetic values on the concept of nature. This is evident in the question of taste (see article "Taste"). It is for this reason that theorists usually attempted to limit the concept of nature by modifying the word itself: *la nature* was not at all the same thing as *la belle nature*. It is thus possible to think of eighteenth-century aesthetics in terms of an oscillation between two poles which determine the limit of nature; the first is beauty, which engenders *la belle nature* and an aesthetic of art, the second is a new version of truth, *le vrai* (now confused with nature), which engenders a naturalistic aesthetic.

In the late seventeenth and early eighteenth centuries the concept of nature was often elucidated by citing the art of painting. Painters imitated nature, so that one could actually see in their works various types of nature which corresponded to different concepts. Painting proved especially useful because of a philosophical dualism, founded upon a theological view of man, which informed much thought of this time, a dualism between essence and accident, the general and the particular, and spirit and matter. Nature was not what one might see outside one's window, not the countryside alone, but that and something else as well. This dualism is well defined by Roger de Piles in his *L'Idée du peintre parfait*, a treatise on painting which is also an excellent illustration of the aesthetic-metaphysical presuppositions of the late seventeenth century:

> La Nature doit être considérée de deux manières, ou dans des objets particuliers, ou dans des objets en général, et en elle-même. La Nature est ordinairement défectueuse dans les objets particuliers, dans la formation desquels elle est, comme nous venons de dire, détournée par quelques accidents contre son intention, qui est toujours de faire un ouvrage parfait. Mais si on la considère en elle-même dans son intention et dans le général de ses productions, on la trouvera parfaite [p. 21].

It is from this general nature, considered in herself, that the principles of art were derived, and it is in this general nature, expressed in man, that the ancient sculptors found the true proportions of human beauty. The painter, like the sculptor, founded his rules upon this general nature, and de Piles made an important distinction concerning the relative position of art to nature:

> Si l'on compare l'art du peintre, qui a été formé sur la nature en général, avec une production particulière de cette même nature, il sera vrai de dire que l'art est au-dessus de la nature; mais si on le compare avec la nature en elle-même, qui est son modèle, cette proposition se trouvera fausse [Ibid., 22].

Painters are not merely to copy nature on the level of individual objects, which are usually imperfect, in a servile fashion but are to keep in mind general nature, which is perfect. Art is superior to nature in particular but not to nature in general. We may say that it occupies a middle position between the particular and the general, between the perfection of the general and the imperfections of the particular, between pure mind and pure matter. The assumption is that God is the supreme artist and architect, and it is clear that de Piles, like his contemporary Leibniz, supposed a harmonious and perfect universe of which the arts were but one part of a greater chain of being, and which as forms of representation were but intimations of a higher and more perfect order. As he says, there is always room for greater perfection in the artist's work when it is considered in terms of general nature.

The same view expressed for a different purpose and in a different context was put forth by Perrault in his *Parallèle des anciens et des modernes*. He distinguished between *la belle* and *la pure nature*, the latter being not pure at all, but on the contrary wild, savage, disorderly, and thereby unfit for art, which must imitate *la belle nature* —which obviously corresponds to de Piles' general nature. Pure nature, untamed, unspoiled, is not without its attractions; woods and streams, torrents or deserts may be admirable, if you think of admiration as a Cartesian passion, but it has no place in art, just as it has no place in a garden where, left to its own devices, it would soon spoil everything. This same notion of pure nature is applied to the moral realm and criticized in the same way: Man is by nature brutal; it is therefore the philosopher's task to tame that nature, just as it is the gardener's task to weed his garden and the artist's to imitate *la belle nature*. Perrault was not one to commit the naturalistic fallacy: pure nature was the norm neither of art nor of ethics, and therefore obviously not of aesthetics either. The Chevalier who in these dialogues represents the point of view of a man of the world and a *bel esprit*, very similar to that in Voltaire's *Mondain*, puts the matter succinctly, though nonphilosophically, by saying: "Ceux qui aiment tant la pure nature devraient manger du gland comme on faisait au siècle d'or, et manger aussi leur viande toute crue et sans sel" (*Parallèle*, III, 213). This is the remark of a true modern, for whom pure or accidental nature is the opposite, not only of *la belle nature*, but also of the values of art and civilization. Within the context of the late seventeenth century there was little doubt in the minds of most poets, painters, and philosophers that civilization was preferable to pure nature. The argument was used against partisans of the ancients who claimed that one ought to imitate the ancients because they had been closer to nature than the moderns were. Since both moderns and ancients were agreed that art was an imitation of nature, it was essential to distinguish between natures. If the ancients had imitated pure nature, in Perrault's use of the term, their works could hardly be perfect, because pure nature was accidental. If the moderns imitated *la belle nature*, then they could improve upon the ancients. Thus nature, already at this early date, was in effect a way of modifying and loosening the meaning and precept of imitation. Here

again paintings could be useful to illustrate rather metaphysical concepts. Perrault made his point by referring to the Flemish school of
painting:

C'est un talent peu envié aux peintres flamands, qui la représentent si bien
qu'on y est trompé [that is, represent pure nature]. Ils représentent une
cuisine, on croit la voir. La plus grande difficulté ne consiste pas à bien représenter des objets, mais à représenter de beaux objets, et par les endroits
où ils sont les plus beaux. Je vais encore plus loin et je dis que ce n'est pas
assez au peintre, d'imiter la plus belle nature telle que ses yeux la voient, il
faut qu'il aille au delà, et qu'il tâche à attraper l'idée du beau, à laquelle
non seulement la pure nature, mais la belle nature même ne sont jamais
arrivées; c'est d'après cette idée qu'il faut qu'il travaille, et qu'il ne se serve
de la nature que pour y parvenir [Ibid., 214].

Perrault, in fact, has posed three different natures rather than two:
pure nature, which may be seen outside the window and which is wild,
common, vulgar, sometimes even ugly; *la belle nature*, which is visible in
art and which ought to be a selective abstraction from pure nature; and
beyond *belle nature*, making it possible, the *idea* of nature, which not
only guides the choice of the artist but even allows him to improve on
the best chosen from pure nature. This third realm, that of the idea of
nature, may also be called that of *le vrai*, as is evident from the distinctions drawn by Roger de Piles in his *Cours de Peinture par Principes*,
a work in which the distinctions of Perrault, or similar ones, result in
three types of truth rather than of nature: *le vrai simple, le vrai idéal*,
and *le vrai parfait*, terms which from the context of the times and also
the book may be readily exchanged with nature. The same identification of *le vrai* and nature was also assumed by Father Bouhours in his
De la Manière de bien penser dans les ouvrages de l'esprit, in which he
advises writers to model themselves upon the painters:

Concluons enfin de tout ce que nous avons dit, que la raison est d'elle-même
ennemie du faux, et que ceux qui veulent penser juste, doivent imiter les
grands peintres qui donnent la vérité à tous leurs ouvrages, ou plutôt suivre
la nature sur laquelle les peintres se règlent [p. 72].

Quite obviously, at the end of the seventeenth century and well into
the eighteenth the concept of nature was merging with those of beauty
and the true. When it was associated with the true, however, the term
"nature" did not refer to empirical nature, but rather to an order beyond
the realm of sense perception, accessible to the mind but also repre-

sented in art, in the form of painting, poetry, gardens, or sculpture and thus rendered visible or made apprehensible to those who did not divine it beyond the realm of sense perception. It may seem paradoxical that the partisans of this ideal nature were the moderns, since this notion of an ideal realm or order beyond sense perception is Platonic in inspiration: "Avec Perrault," writes Jean Ehrard in his monumental study of nature in the eighteenth century, "Platon l'emporte sur Aristote, et le *beau idéal* sur l'observation fidèle de la réalité."[1] But what Perrault's Platonism turns out to be is an ideal of perfection in the arts with the point of perfection placed, as we have said, in modern times rather than antiquity. This altered not so much the meaning of imitation as the models to be imitated, since these were no longer specific works of the ancients, but, rather, ideal types existing in the mind; doing this, in turn, meant that to imitate could also mean to perfect rather than to copy.

The most thorough formulation of the aesthetic of *la belle nature*, which may be associated with an aesthetic of art, was that of Abbé Batteux. His *belle nature*, like Perrault's general nature, is also ideal, and like de Piles he stresses that its reality has nothing to do with what we see about us in the world we live in: "Ce n'est pas le vrai qui est; mais le vrai qui peut être, le beau vrai, qui est représenté comme s'il existait réellement, et avec toutes les perfections qu'il peut recevoir." To this definition of *la belle nature* he appends an important note to the effect that the quality or nature of the object imitated is of no importance, a remark which is an echo of Boileau's

> Il n'est point de serpent, ni de monstre odieux,
> Qui, par l'art imité, ne puisse plaire aux yeux;
> D'un pinceau délicat l'artifice agréable
> Du plus affreux objet fait un objet aimable.

Historical and empirical truth may both serve as bases upon which art may build its more perfect order, and what Boileau and Batteux both say, in effect, is that art transforms the given nature into *la belle nature*, which is another way of saying that the latter is a product of or is inseparable from art. And since Batteux also thought that art was wholly man-made, a purely human institution, we may also suppose that *la belle nature* was an elaborate fiction or an artificial world. What seemed to be latent Platonism with Perrault, de Piles, and Fénelon,

[1] L'Idée de nature en France dans la première moitié du XVIIIe Siècle (Paris, 1963), I, 260.

becomes with Batteux a doctrine of art with a built-in contradiction or, if you will, tension between the suppositions that art is wholly manmade, and that it is an imitation of some preexisting order. The contradiction can be resolved only if the term "imitation" is taken to mean construction or if it is assumed that the ideal order to be imitated is not preexistent at all, but constructed by the human mind, imagined. It is perhaps worth stressing that in his definition of *la belle nature* Batteux uses the conditional tense, *comme si elle existait réellement*. In this case all art becomes an "as if" proposition, a game of make-believe at least insofar as the agreeable arts are concerned. But contradictions notwithstanding, from Perrault to Batteux there is little doubt that when one speaks of imitation of nature one does not mean to say an artist should copy what he sees, a dramatic poet represent men as they are in real life, but rather that they should transform, transpose, embellish, select, and in effect build another order of nature.

The concept of nature was thus built upon a dualism: there was the nature of the everyday world, visible, imperfect, unstable, changing, accidental, banal; and there was an invisible nature, a presumably rational and harmonious order of the universe. As long as this dualism was accepted as an assumption in aesthetic theory and artistic doctrine, it was possible to imitate perfect nature in order to try to produce perfect works of art, and in so doing one posed a difference between the everyday world and that of art. The realm of art was that of imitated nature, *la belle nature*, of conventions, created by man, suggesting an ideal order, although the perfect order of the universe was beyond his sense perceptions and pure or brute nature was all too close to him. The world of art was the mean between de Piles' *vrai parfait* and *vrai simple*; we might also refer to it as the area where civilization was possible, given the limitations of man and his fall from grace.

As stated above, accidental nature was considered by some to be brutishness; from the theological point of view, it was corrupt. The dualism we alluded to thus supposes a theological view of man as a fallen creature, and we can readily see why in ethics he must imitate Christ and follow the laws of God, and why in the realm of art he must imitate the perfect or ideal nature rather than the given. As Ehrard puts it:

En réalité l'étude des premières théories esthétiques du XVIIIe Siècle fait ressortir clairement un fait capital. La ligne de partage n'est pas entre les rationalistes et les défenseurs du sentiment, mais entre deux conceptions de la nature humaine, dont l'une est encore théologique, l'autre déjà "philoso-phique" [Op. cit., I, 286].

Attention in artistic work was thus fixed upon the ideal if you espoused the theological view of man. But if nature was no longer thought of in terms of corruption and man no longer considered a fallen creature, then the attitude towards imitation, nature, and art would obviously change too. Such a revaluation occurred with Diderot and Rousseau, but its consequences were not fully worked out in the eighteenth century as far as the fine arts are concerned, though Rousseau went as far as he could in the direction indicated.

Diderot perceived that what had been termed accidental nature was a rich source of literary and artistic motifs, and that there were beauties of pure nature more expressive and moving than those of *la belle nature*. He also knew that pure nature was neither beautiful nor ugly, and that genius involved much more than taste and imitation. Consequently his attitude towards the relation of art to nature, taste and genius was con-siderably broader than the doctrines of Batteux, André, Crousaz—though this does not mean he was right or that the idealist doctrines of the former were irrelevant to the art of their times because they were founded upon metaphysical assumptions. What occurred between Bat-teux and Diderot was merely a change in metaphysical assumptions: dualism gave way to monism, and nature ceased being the subject of Platonic distinctions to become not only a model to be imitated, but also a source of creative power and inspiration and a realm of experi-mentation. One could still tell artists to imitate nature, but it no longer meant the same thing, because the dualism between pure and *belle nature* had been abolished: though this does not mean that one always judged or worked in consequence of this revaluation of nature. Indeed, one must take care not to attribute changes in taste and art at the end of the eighteenth century merely to revaluations of the concept of nature. The end of distinctions did not bring about a revolution in artistic pro-duction, but it did bring considerable confusion in the realm of aesthetics.

Rousseau was less confused than Diderot, though one would be hard put to know just what he meant by nature. What is certain is that he opposed nature to art, which he associated quite rightly with civiliza-tion; civilization, in turn, he attributed to a fall, not from grace, but from nature, which he associated with a lost state of innocence. Rous-seau revaluated the pure nature of Perrault. His form of reasoning may be described as theological naturalism. Dualism still obtains, but it has been changed: it is no longer a question of pure versus universal nature, but of nature versus art, a dualism made possible because nature has become an awareness within man of his fall from natural innocence, an awareness frustrated, hidden, hampered by society and its rules and conventions. This position is extremely important for art because it affects the theory of genius, just as Diderot's views of nature imply a different view of imitation.

However, despite the intuitions of Diderot and Rousseau and the critique of the aesthetic of *la belle nature*, it must not be thought that the last decades of the eighteenth century produced a new art and a new literature as a consequence: what was new was so in spite of aesthetic theories, and what changes were brought about on the level of theory served not to elaborate a new aesthetic founded upon the new view of nature, monistic and materialistic, but on the contrary served to elaborate an idealist aesthetic. One may wonder about the differences between the idealist aesthetic of the late eighteenth century and that of Perrault, de Piles, Fénelon, and Batteux or Father André and conclude that the late eighteenth-century idealism in art supposed that it should be morally useful, instructive, but above all, able to be coupled with sentiment. In truth, the differences are ones of nuance, of style, of attitude, one might even say of tonality. One may also suspect that, whereas in the early eighteenth century metaphysical doctrines of beauty and truth were used in order to be able rationally to discuss works of art, in the late eighteenth century such doctrines preceded the creation of works of art. Thus new rules, founded on the concept of nature, triumphed in the form of academic standards of beauty and taste. It may even be argued that this triumph of nature was a species of disguised and belated triumph of the ancients over the moderns; for indeed, never before had the moderns tried as hard to be close to the Greeks as did the poets and painters of the closing decades of the eighteenth century. Thus it was not empirical, given nature, which triumphed at the end of the eighteenth century: it was the nature of the Greeks, manifested through Homer, Phidias, and Praxiteles.

Another result of this transvaluation of nature, or perhaps to be more precise, the new confidence in nature, was that one did what no Perrault or Batteux, or even Voltaire would ever have done, idealize nature herself. This took the form of dithyrambic meditations or studies of nature, a fashion for children, landscapes, and tears. A religious enthusiasm was thus transferred to nature and the foundations of Romanticism were thereby set.

There was, it is true, one brief moment at which it was recognized that *la belle nature* was after all only a convention. Presumably the arts could be constructed on other conventions. But this glimmer, this perception by Condillac, came to nothing, for even he opted for a moral-utilitarian view of art and letters which was in accord with the reforming spirit of the *philosophes*, that which, in the realm of the fine arts and literature, really led to academicism and also, we might add, to an educational view of letters and arts.

In retrospect, and viewing not only theory but the arts and the public, we may say that the artist or the poet enjoyed more autonomy as concerns his *métier* in the first half of the eighteenth century than he did in the second, because the doctrine that art is an imitation of *la belle nature* rather than of nature itself served to distinguish between art and pure nature, whereas in the later eighteenth century this distinction became blurred by moral and utilitarian considerations and a monistic view of nature. The result was that the artist and the poet came to be expected to be moral, useful to society, and natural. It is also worth noting that the surviving works of the French eighteenth century, in letters as well as in the arts, were largely done outside the conventions of art espoused by the *philosophes* or, if within those conventions, despite them.

✳   ✳   ✳

See also: *Art, Beauty, Beau Idéal, Genius, Imitation, Taste, Truth.*
Bibliography: Diderot, Fénelon, Perrault, Rousseau; Batteux, De Piles, Lacombe, Marmontel, Watelet; Beardsley, Folkierski, Wimsatt and Brooks; and the following: Geoffrey Atkinson, *Le Sentiment de la nature et le retour à la vie simple* (Geneva, 1960), a reedition of an older standard work; Jean Ehrard, *L'Idée de Nature en France dans la première moitié du XVIIIe Siècle* (Paris, 1963), a major recent monumental work; and the still-excellent work of Arthur O. Lovejoy, *Essays in the History of Ideas* (2nd edition, N.Y., 1955), especially the essay "*Nature* as an Aesthetic Norm."

NOVEL

THE NOVEL as a literary genre posed several problems intimately connected with the aesthetic and moral assumptions of the Classical period, and it is with these in mind that I have decided to write this entry.

Though novels had been widely read before, and many had been written, the novel form had no theoretical justification until the second half of the eighteenth century. Critics pondered its nature, rejected, accepted, or tolerated it; theologian-critics thundered against novels and warned youth of their ill effects, while novelists attempted to justify themselves. What has been termed the dilemma of the novel in the eighteenth century shows rather well how it was difficult in those days to distinguish the aesthetic from the ethical.

The aesthetic problem of the novel revolved about the question of verisimilitude. In the seventeenth century the novel as a genre had been satirized by Boileau in the name of *le vrai*; in the eighteenth century it was thought dangerous because the pictures it presented were too true. What had occurred between Boileau's time and about 1740 was a marked improvement in the genre, which was no longer lightly to be dismissed as fantasy. As Crébillon *fils* explained in the preface to his masterpiece, *Les Egarements du coeur et de l'esprit*:

Le Roman, si méprisé des personnes sensées, et souvent avec justice, serait peut être celui de tous les genres qu'on pourrait rendre le plus utile, s'il était bien manié, si, au lieu de le remplir de situations ténébreuses et forcés, de Héros dont les caractères et les aventures sont toujours hors du vraisemblable, on le rendait, comme la Comédie, le tableau de la vie humaine, et qu'on y censurât les vices et les ridicules.[1]

In the new type of novel envisaged by Crebillon *fils*, "le sentiment ne serait point outré; l'homme enfin verrait l'homme tel qu'il est; on l'éblouirait moins, mais on l'instruirait davantage" (Ibid.). And such a novel would be constructed on the principle of the imitation of nature, but obviously not so much the kind of nature fit for a fantastic tale as that most accessible to all men, the (so to speak) natural nature of every day. Once dismissed as frivolous in the name of verisimilitude, it was later suspected because of its verisimilitude.

But the novel also posed a problem because, given the aesthetic principles of the critics, it had no reason for existence. The novel had no prestige. Though its origin was sometimes fixed in Greek antiquity, it was more likely to be traced to the Middle Ages: the word *roman* being adduced as proof enough that it was really a medieval (and therefore barbarous) genre. It was a tale narrated in *roman*, or old French, and could therefore easily be associated with the irrational and superstitious Middle Ages. At best one might consider it a degenerate form of the epic, written in prose. In any case it was not a high art; it was not an established genre; it had no rules; it was an intruder in the world of *belles lettres*. In this sense it was rather like

[1] Quoted in *Romanciers du XVIIIe Siècle* (Paris, 1963), II, 9.

opera, also considered by some to be a frivolous, amusing, but bastard genre; and, as with opera, which many attended, so with novels. Almost everyone read them, but hardly anyone talked about doing so. Insofar as its prestige among critics was concerned, the novel was rather like television today. Although the cinema was at length accepted as an art worthy of esteem and study (as opera was at last accepted in the eighteenth century), television is still considered as not quite established by most academics, whose teaching of the humanities is founded upon what remains of *belles lettres* in the universities. The novel was obviously alive, unfortunately, and was therefore discussed in the journals, but it remained under suspicion for a long time.

The criticism of the novel, however, took a different form from that of opera. Opera, like the novel, could be criticized on aesthetic grounds as a mixed genre or as being frivolous, but could not be accounted a danger to morality, precisely because it was closer to fable and fantasy than to the real world that was supposedly the province of the new novel. The novel *was* a danger, because it was a fiction founded upon *vraisemblance*, dealing with men and women rather than gods and heroes.

The ethical case for and against the novel was argued on the basis of didactic utility versus moral danger. One could argue that it was a useless genre, which could instruct no one, or one could say that it was a useful genre because it could be employed for moral instruction. If one believed the latter, one believed that the novel could warn the reader of the dangers of the world and the flesh in an especially effective way, because the message could be made pleasing as well as instructive. Other genres claimed the same thing, but the novel was more obviously a form of *divertissement* than were the established genres for the moral instruction of mankind. Still, moralists speculated as to whether the novel was or was not dangerous to the salvation of the reader. One may wonder why this question seemed so acute in regard to the novel. The same question had been posed in the seventeenth century concerning the theatre (and Rousseau would pose it again in the eighteenth), but with less urgency. It may well be that the theatre, despite the theologians, was too well established an institution to be vulnerable, being frequented by the powerful, and besides affected only a rather limited public. The novel, on the other hand, was accessible to more persons; it could easily be carried about, be read anywhere, and thus be much more of a common danger than a stage representation, which was fixed in one spot and seen by a restricted number. People read more novels than were good for their souls, many believed. Thus the problem of the danger of the novel may be viewed as an especially acute aspect of the much broader problems of the moral use of art and, as Diderot, especially in his *Neveu de Rameau*, stated, of the ambiguity of art and the discontinuity between the ethical and the aesthetic realm.

But how could a novel be thought dangerous to the soul? The potential danger was pointed to by Abbé Jacquin in his *Entretiens sur les romans* (Paris, 1755). Jacquin began by drawing certain distinctions between the novel and other established genres with which it was usually compared, namely history, epic poetry, and fable. Where an historian sought truth, the novelist created a fiction; where the epic poet sought to attain the sublime, noble, and elevated, the novelist confined himself to the low and the simple; and, whereas the epic transported the reader into the realm of the sublime and the heroic, the novelist sought rather to "touch and soften the heart." As for the novel's relation to fable, the novelist replaced the gods and heroes of the fabulous past with ordinary men and women and thus founded his work upon the notion of *vraisemblance*. The novel, as it existed in 1755, was described as follows by Abbé Jacquin: "Présentement on entend par un roman une fiction morale, amoureuse ou guerrière, imaginée pour amuser un lecteur. Il y a des romans qui renferment quelquefois ces trois parties, quoiqu'à présent l'amour y tienne ordinairement le premier rang" (p. 14). This opinion did not significantly differ from the views expressed by the Chevalier de Jaucourt, who wrote the article "Roman" in the *Encyclopédie*. Jaucourt thought little of the novels of the seventeenth century, but he did think well of the *Télémaque*, "le plus beau roman du monde," and he saw no reason for praising the novels of his own times as much better than those of the previous century:

La plupart des romans qui leur ont succédé dans ce siècle, sont ou des productions dénuées d'imagination, ou des ouvrages propres à gâter le goût, ou ce qui est pis encore, des peintures obscènes dont les honnêtes gens sont révoltés. Enfin, les Anglais ont heureusement imaginé depuis peu de tourner ce genre de fictions à des choses utiles, et de les employer pour inspirer en amusant l'amour des bonnes moeurs et de la vertu, par des tableaux simples, naturels et ingénieux, des événements de la vie. C'est ce qu'ont exécuté avec beaucoup de gloire et d'esprit, MM. Richardson et Fielding.[2]

Crébillon *fils* had claimed he was doing the same thing, and Rousseau also attempted to write a virtuous novel with his *Nouvelle Héloïse*; he

[2] In the third edition (Geneva, 1779), Vol. XXVI, pp. 370–73.

succeeded only too well. Indeed, everyone, including the Marquis de Sade, claimed to be writing virtuous, moral, instructive novels, and Abbé Jacquin's arguments proved of little effect against the production of novels: his argument was not faulty in its assumptions, but one could just as well use them to defend the novel as attack it. The real issue was not so much that of a new art form which existed independently of accepted rules, but rather the question of who was to do the pleasing and instructing, secular moralists or priests. The *philosophes* were just as moral about the novel as Abbé Jacquin, and the following by Marmontel, referring to the novels of the eighteenth century, could have been written by the Abbé:

Dans la foule des romans qui depuis ont eu tant de vogue, c'est tantôt le vice coloré en vertu, tantôt le vice au naturel, mais peint avec tous ses attraits. . . . c'est un libertinage éffronté, qui se joue de tout ce qu'il y a de plus saint, et qui, dans sa légèreté, a toutes les grâces de l'esprit, tout le piquant du badinage, tout l'agrément des airs et des manières; c'est, en un mot, le vice armé de tous les moyens de séduire, et il faut avouer que si ces peintures n'avaient pas le mérite d'être morales, elles avaient celui d'être fidèles et ressemblantes.[3]

It was precisely in this faithful representation of the passions in motion, of the effects of love and its charms, that the danger of the novel was seen by the moralists. It was considered dangerous because one still feared the imagination, and the reading of novels might induce those "égarements du coeur et de l'esprit" in the reader which were the object of Crébillon's novel, which Abbé Jacquin thought dangerous. The novelists argued they presented a moral by depicting with truthfulness the effects of passion. The scenes represented supposedly constituted a warning. But the opponents of the novel of *divertissement* (or of all novels) answered that the very depiction of these passions sufficed to set them in motion in the reader, so that the novel could become what Abbé Jacquin called an *occasion prochaine* for sin, crime, and perdition. Marmontel would undoubtedly have agreed with the substance of this, if not with the language used, for he thought even the *Princesse de Clèves* a dangerous novel because of the princess' fall. The moral must not be lost on the reader, and the greater the artistic quality of the novel, the greater its danger to morals, because it was all the more attractive and pleasing. The power of the novel, in short, was a power of seduction: "De tous les poisons, celui qu'on présente dans une coupe dorée

[3] Essai sur les romans considérées du côté moral," in *Oeuvres complètes* (Paris, 1818–20), Vol. X, 312.

et sous des dehors pleins de charmes, est souvent le plus dangereux" (Jacquin, op. cit., 289). Novels of love were especially dangerous because the reader sinned by empathy, by identifying with the characters of the novel, thus becoming infected by passion and desire. The power of illusion possessed by fiction, set in the world of the reader, made it more immediate for the reader than the ideal realm of fable, the noble world of history, or the obviously unreal world of comedy, which had aesthetic distance, perspective. The novel was too close to life, to the self, to the passions and desires of men rather than gods or heroes. In claiming this the critics were perhaps unwittingly credulous, for authors did not fail to put in their novels characters, both men and women, who learned the art of seduction and the screening of the passions of their victims by reading novels, thus engendering in the critics the fear that the *vraisemblance* might cease to be merely that and turn into the *vrai*. The novel's danger was its potential, not only as *divertissement*, but also as school for scandal. In the novel, life and art met, and, given the possibilities of imitation, one can see why the lesson of the novel, or rather *in* the novel, had to be clear and moral.

The questions raised in the seventeenth and eighteenth centuries by the novel point to the ambiguities inherent in the Classical aesthetic and to the rapports between the aesthetic and ethical realms. As long as the doctrine of imitation was founded upon *la belle nature* there was little danger to morals, even in the novel. However, given such an aesthetic, it may well be that the only type of novel that could be written would be of the *Telemachus* type, noble, elevated, didactic, safe for any young prince, noble, or gentleman to imitate. But if one writes a novel in terms of the aesthetic of the imitation of sublunar nature, of human nature not universally conceived, of the human nature of passions in motion, human nature after the Fall, one immediately poses certain moral problems. One presents a mixture of vice and virtue, evil and good, and, since the passions are involved, one can no longer be sure of the effects of the fiction, or the art, on the reader. In the case of the imitation of *la belle nature* the effect of art was to be morally useful and elevating; in the case of the imitation of human nature as passions in motion, the effect of art was ambiguous, uncertain, fraught with danger. The assumption in both cases is the same, that art is a species of picture which may instruct, so that art is also a species of knowledge. Thus the novel was thought a potential danger because in it the lines between truth and fiction were blurred. This was not the case for opera, or even for certain dramas which effectively established perspective or aesthetic distance between the play and the spectator.

Thus in certain cases or genres the lines of demarcation between art and life were clearly drawn, but they were not clear in the novel. The genre suffered in effect from its very newness, for it is undeniable that eighteenth-century novelists did attempt to modernize the genre by writing of modern love and placing their characters in contemporary settings. But this very novelty made a fair criticism of the genre difficult, because the critical assumptions of the time were derived from art forms and metaphysical assumptions which had not taken the novel for granted at all. The novel therefore also points to the problem of the acceptance of new genres in Classical aesthetics and the discussion of such with the critical terms and values proper to established genres. Essentially the novel belonged to another literature than that which could be associated with the aesthetics of art and of *la belle nature*. And it may be for this reason that the *philosphes* did not differ from the priests as to the merit of the novel, though they did not agree for quite the same reasons. Thus the novel in the eighteenth century might be called an open genre faced by a criticism devised for closed genres.

* * *

See also: *Art, Perspective.*
Bibliography: Diderot; Marmontel; and also, in the eighteenth century, Lenglet Dufresnoy [Gordon de Percel], *De l'Usage des romans* (Amsterdam, 1734), an apology for the novel and a long bibliography and classification of novels; Abbé Jacquin, *Entretiens sur les romans* (Paris, 1755), a series of dialogues; and for contemporary works, see Georges May, *Le Dilèmme du roman au XVIIIe Siècle* (Paris and New Haven, 1963), a thorough study of the aesthetic problem of the novel; also Vivienne Mylne, *The Eighteenth Century French Novel; techniques of illusion* (Manchester, 1965).

ODE

"L'ODE," WROTE THE POET ROY,

sans être un ouvrage de longue haleine est le plus susceptible de poésie. Elle est caracterisée par le désordre apparent, par la hardiesse des pensées, la vivacité des images, la force des expressions, l'adresse des transitions. C'est cet Enthousiasme, plus facile à sentir qu'à définir, qui ne dépend pas d'un trait, qui n'est pas renfermé dans une strophe, qui circule dans l'ouvrage entier, qui lui donne la chaleur et la vie.[1]

[1] *Oeuvres diverses* (Paris, 1727), II, ii–iii.

We may readily see from this succinct description of the ode why this genre prompted almost as much reflection as the *Eclogue*. But where the pastoral genre posed problems concerning the credibility of shepherds, the ode raised questions concerning the proper degree of enthusiasm, the nature of the sublime, and the relation of imagination to reason. The reason these genres posed problems for the poets was pointed to by Roy: "Je sais bien qu'il faut dans nos ecarts même conserver à la Raison tous ses droits" (Ibid., iii). But more than this, no one really believed in the pagan divinities any more. It is therefore no wonder that reflections upon the ode also turned into reflections upon poetry in general and more particularly upon the relation of imagination and enthusiasm to art and taste. All this did not prevent the composition of numerous odes and Father Mourgues gave five rules for the ode, even though the genre was founded on enthusiasm and imagination.

La première règle de l'ode est, que le début soit frappant dans l'un et l'autre genre. Traitez-vous un sujet naïf? entrez d'abord en matière par quelque tour naturel et agréable. . . . Votre sujet est-il grand? que l'entrée soit magnifique et pompeuse [*Traité*, 277–78].

The beginning must sometimes be like a sudden flight, such as the eagle's first to the clouds and then down, in a plunge upon its prey. The second rule was to keep up this flight for the rest of the poem, to increase the beauties of the poem continuously in order to create a sharp and durable impression on the reader. This, as Father Mourgues admitted, was the most difficult of the rules. Too often, poets lost their breath. The third rule governed the use of the gracious and the sublime. The fourth rule was derived from Boileau and was contained in this verse:

Souvent un beau désordre est un effet de l'art.

This was in turn defined as a happy medium between too much disorder and a too uniform movement: grammatical transitions may be neglected, transitions need not be too scrupulously observed, thoughts may suddenly change, one must be enchanted, wish to go right but feel pulled to the left, be lost as in a labyrinth, yet follow a thread out, without seeing it too clearly. Art must simulate the disorder and fire of the imagination. But in effect what was wanted was a French garden. The fifth rule touched on expression and required a more lively, imaged, precise, and chosen expression than in the other poems. The ode ought to be an elixir of poetic qualities. Naturally all this referred only to the more general precepts. There were, as Father Mourgues put it, infinite finesses and nuances which could hardly be put into precepts but which could be learned with practise and knowledge of the correct and accepted models.

These were of two general types, the Pindaric and the Anacreontic. The first was to be in the sublime and noble style; the other in the gracious style mentioned by Mourgues. If enthusiasm and the sublime were associated primarily with the Pindaric ode, imagination and ingenuity, playfulness and sentiment, dominated the ode in the manner of Anacreon. These two types of ode corresponded to two overall tendencies of the art of the time, one towards the noble, elevated, and spiritual, the other towards the natural, playful, and mundane: a division which is reflected also in taste and in beauty, and which may be associated with those inclined to a Platonic view of art in the first instance, and an epicurean attitude in the second case. The first type was used to celebrate gods and heroes, the second drinkers and lovers. But to this original function the eighteenth century added new ones, or variations thereon, though ever in the line of the original division. Thus Roy writes odes to various heroes and poets, upon various subjects of a moral, aesthetic, mythological, religious nature, addressed to poets as well as nobles.

OPERA

> La vraie musique est le langage du coeur.
>
> *Rameau*

> La musique de Rameau est un des exemples de beautés neuves toujours regrettées par quelques-uns. C'est le Newtonisme de la Musique, qui essuie les mêmes contradictions, et qui remportera peut-être la même victoire.
>
> *Terrasson*

OPERA, PERHAPS MORE than any other art form of the *ancien régime*, answered to most of the referents and requirements of the Classical aesthetic: it combined all the arts and appealed to all the senses. It thus occupied an important place in the pleasures and aesthetic speculations of the seventeenth and eighteenth centuries, despite Boileau's dislike of Quinault and Voltaire's disdain of Lulli's music, and even though opera was, in point of historical time, a modern genre which did not fit the rules of established art forms and was sometimes dismissed as mixed and therefore inferior. When, in the first decades of the eighteenth century, opera began to be discussed on the level of theory this was done with the vocabulary used to speculate upon and explain the other arts, so that it, like them, was thought of in terms of nature, beauty, verisimilitude, truth, fable, imitation, and expression: though, to be sure, for opera the rules were relaxed, so that it was free of the requirements of the established genres. For savants like Madame Dacier and poets and critics like Boileau the opera must have seemed as cinema and television do to the purists of the twentieth century who, until a decade or so ago, would not consider either as serious arts; but little by little opera came to be accepted as worthy of serious attention and productive of legitimate delight. The place of opera within the Classical aesthetic was very well described by Montesquieu in one of his notebooks:

Nos moderns sont inventeurs d'un certain spectacle qui, uniquement fait pour ravir les sens et enchanter l'imagination, a eu besoin des ces ressorts étrangers que la tragédie rejette. Dans ce spectacle fait pour être admiré, et non pour être examiné, on s'est servi si heureusement des ressorts de la Fable, ancienne et moderne, que la raison s'est indignée en vain, que ceux qui ont échoué à la simple tragédie, où rien ne les aidait à agiter le coeur, ont excellé dans ce nouveau spectacle, où tout semblait leur servir; et tel en a été le succès que l'esprit même y a gagné. Car tout ce que nous avons de plus exquis et de plus délicat, tout ce que le coeur a de plus tendre se trouve dans les opéras de Quinault, Fontenelle, La Motte, Danchet, Roi, etc.[1]

This sympathetic view of the new genre is indicative of the first half of the eighteenth century and differs, as we shall see, from the attitude of the *philosophes* who engaged in the famous Quarrel of the Buffoons of the years 1752–54 and from that of the later partisans of Piccini or Glück. Montesquieu was not assessing opera in terms of rules. He took delight in it despite established genres.

His contemporary Du Bos was also fascinated by the new genre, but unlike Montesquieu he set out to examine it within the framework of his psychology of art and historical approach to the arts. The genre was bound to interest him, since it obviously was an answer to his notion of *divertissement*, but he also thought there was a relation between the music of the ancient Greeks and the modern opera. Du Bos praised the genre because of its expressiveness: opera imitated the passions, or at least expressed them more naturally than those arts which relied on words or pictures alone:

[1] "Mes Pensées," in *Oeuvres complètes*, I, 1021.

Les signes naturels des passions que la musique rassemble, et qu'elle employe
avec art pour augmenter l'énergie des paroles qu'elle met en chant, doivent
donc les rendre plus capables de nous toucher, parce que ces signes naturels
ont une force merveilleuse pour nous émouvoir. Ils tiennent de la nature
même. . . . C'est ainsi que le plaisir de l'oreille devient le plaisir du coeur
[*Réflexions critiques*, I, 471].

Opera thus has its own truth or *vraisemblance*, even though it is often
the *mise en scène* of fable, and this truth lies in the imitation of natural
passions and sentiments:

Cette vérité consiste dans l'imitation des tons, des accents, des soupirs, et des
sons qui sont propres naturellement aux sentiments contenus dans les paroles.
La même vérité peut se trouver dans l'harmonie et dans le rithme de toute
la composition [Ibid., 472].

This strength attributed to music is founded upon an important distinction made by Du Bos, in his consideration of poetry, between natural
and artificial signs. Words are artificial signs; sound and images are
natural. And since art is also construed as an imitation of nature, that
imitation which relies on natural signs must be more effective (see
article "Imitation"). Music went even further than merely to imitate
the passions or nature and sentiments of men; it could also imitate the
inarticulate sounds of nature, this being left to the symphonic part of
opera, that of the instruments alone. Thus even instrumental music may
be a true imitation of nature: "Telle est la symphonie qui imite une
tempête dans l'Opéra d'Alcione de M. Marais" (Ibid., 473). Inarticulate sound could heighten the interest in the action of the opera and
thereby increase the degree of illusion and the impressions made on
the spectators. Music and sound are used to supplement the limited
evocative power of words.

While Du Bos argued that music was more effective than simple
declamation and that it gave more affective strength to verse, it did not
however follow that all verse was fit to be put to music. Opera, like all
the other arts, was subject to the law of *convenance*. As there were subjects proper for painting but not poetry, or proper for poetry but
not painting, so opera and its music were necessarily appropriate
to certain subjects, which would suffer from being imitated in other
media. Concerning verse proper to be put into music, Du Bos concluded
that only verse containing sentiments was proper for opera, not that
which contained images. In other words, verse susceptible of being sub-

sumed under the rule of *ut pictura poesis* could not be put to music. And verse susceptible of musical treatment revealed itself quite naturally: "Nous ne saurions même prononcer avec affection les vers qui contiennent des sentiments tendres et touchants, sans faire des soupirs, sans employer des accents et des ports de voix qu'un homme de génie de la musique, réduit facilement en un chant continu" (Ibid., 509). The reason is that each sentiment had its proper tones, sighs, and accents. Du Bos, we must not forget, was a contemporary of Couperin and Rameau. His reasoning on this matter may be illuminated by recourse to the theory of expression (see article "Expression"), and the realization, moreover, that this contemporary of Couperin was also a contemporary of Lebrun, who had elaborated a theory of expression of the passions which applied to painting.

If Du Bos was both favorable to opera and almost obsessed with the music of the ancients, it was partly because much of his thinking about art was founded upon a hedonistic concept of its function; he insisted much more on being touched and pleased than on being instructed. To such a person opera would always be a delight and, under the Classical aesthetic, fable and poetry, criticized by the Cartesians and banished as ancient and foolish prejudices by reason, found refuge in opera as fiction. For Batteux, opera was a lyrical spectacle, distinguished from tragedy in that its matter was the marvellous rather than the heroic: "Un Opéra est donc la représentation d'une action merveilleuse. C'est le divin de l'Epopée mis en spectacle" (*Les Beaux-Arts*, 211–12). And since the heroes of opera are not men but gods, they must act accordingly and announce themselves to mortals through actions, inflections of voice, and a language surpassing the verisimilitude expected of ordinary men and events. The existence of opera thus posed two types of *vraisemblance*, one which was based upon the imitation of nature and was linked to *le vrai*, one which was based upon the imitation of the world of fable, and which, were it not for the term's associations with the unconscious, we might well label the *surréel*. Opera allowed fancy and fantasy a degree of free play not allowed the accepted genres, and one can easily see how it could appeal to men and women tired of their regularity, decorum, and moral intent. The opera escaped the requirements of reason: the sky opened and brought the luminosity of a celestial being; enchanted palaces appeared and disappeared upon a sign. The language of the gods was lyrical, expressive of enthusiasm and ecstasy of sentiment, while the music and words touched the feelings through their modulation, cadence, inflections.

Du Bos, Montesquieu, Batteux, Père André, and others who wrote about music and opera (and it must be understood that music *was* opera in the early eighteenth century), were acquainted with *opera seria*, or what the French called lyrical tragedy. Disputes concerning the relative merits of French or Italian music existed but may be described as family quarrels, since the opera was then an international courtly art form, and such differences of opinion concerned technical matters within the genre. French and Italian opera or music differed in libretto, the number of acts, the mixing of serious and comic elements, and, quite important, the relation of recitative to declamation and to song, as well as in the inclusion or exclusion of ballet and chorus. Despite national rivalries there were reciprocal influences, and French opera in the first half of the eighteenth century was no longer purely French: it was opera as played in Paris, formed by Lully, an Italian, for the French taste of the court of Louis XIV and reformed by Rameau in the early eighteenth century, but informed still by Italian elements. As may be seen from the work of Rameau, the differences between French and Italian opera concerned especially the role of recitative, that is the spoken or declamatory part of the libretto and action, the airs or sung parts, and the symphonic or instrumental part. The French public thought recitative essential; the Italians did not: they considered it an accessory to the more important part of opera, namely song. Rameau caused an innovation by accompanying recitative with the orchestra rather than the harpsichord, and he also composed airs closer to declamation in style than those of the Italians. Thus, if French airs were closer to declamation because the public wished to listen attentively in order to follow the action, Italian airs were much more melodious and generally followed the rhythms of musical instruments. Strangers used to Italian opera who came to Paris found it sometimes hard to distinguish the airs of French opera from the recitatives, especially in the dramatic *airs de scène*. These were parts of the action and were distinguished from the *airs de divertissement*, which were sung dances, such as minuets and gavottes, and also from the *ariettes*, which were also part of the *divertissement* rather than being part of the drama, as was the case in Italian opera. Finally, the stranger who knew only Italian opera would also note that the French in general, and Rameau especially, assigned the chorus an important part in opera, that symphonies were used to heighten dramatic effect and for the purposes of choreography, and furthermore, as another innovation, that the overture itself was a dramatic symphony. On the whole then, Rameau — and we insist upon him as the greatest representative of French opera in the early eighteenth century and as perhaps the greatest classical com-

poser of opera — used symphony more than his predecessor Lully had
to give opera psychological, dramatic, and descriptive coloring and relief: thunder, storms, earthquakes, floods, the rising of the sun, the song
of birds, and moving waters were evoked by instrumental music. These
innovations were by no means short-lived. They were, indeed, perfected
by Glück. Glück tightened dramatic action and plot by reducing the
opera from five to three acts; he concentrated on stronger passions, grand
images, and tragic situations; he also insisted upon a good libretto, something neglected by Rameau, and emphasized what he referred to as
the language of the heart, an expression then current and that was also
used by Rameau. In short, Glück, the inspirator of Berlioz as well as
Wagner, simplified; he cut out the *trilles, passages, cadences*, and other
superfluous ornaments, and did this, significantly, in the name of nature.
In a sense we may suppose that he synthesized the best of French and
Italian music.

One more thing must be stressed concerning Italian and French
opera before we move to a new phase of thought concerning this art
form. The subjects in both French and Italian opera were the same as
regards serious opera: they were either taken from fable, history, or
dramatic poetry; opera was a noble genre, for nobles, about nobles or
about gods and heroes. This does not imply that other types of opera did
not exist. In Italy the *opera bouffa* developed along with the *opera
seria*; in France the *opéra comique en vaudeville* developed in opposition to the *opera seria*, although no one wrote about these genres. If
the *opera seria* corresponded, in dramatic terms, to tragedy, the *opera
bouffa* or *opéra comique* corresponded to farce and comedy.

We have dwelled on these matters to show how wrong the men of
letters could be when they wrote about arts which were not their spe-
cialties, which were basically discursive, narrative, critical, and dramatic
prose or poetry. One might even go so far as to say that they often
showed their weaknesses whenever they had to deal with genres that
were, in a sense, pure play.

In the year 1752 a Neapolitan troupe came to Paris to perform *La
Serva Padrona*. It was a success. A literary-journalistic battle ensued
which has come to be known as the *Querelle des Bouffons*. Fought
mostly by obscure writers and hacks, it nevertheless involved some
notables of the literary establishment of the times, namely d'Alembert, Rousseau, and Marmontel. This battle, like that of the books, was
a very confused affair, for as Eugène Borel, writer of the chapter on the
Querelle in the *Histoire de la musique* of the *Encyclopédie de la Pléiade*,
remarked:

OPERA   145

Il convient de noter ce fait remarquable que, pendant toute la durée de la
querelle des bouffons, personne, ou presque, ne remarqua qu'il ne s'agissait
de l'opéra bouffe italien et de l'opéra comique, mais, d'une comparaison
entre l'opéra bouffe et l'*opera seria* française de Rameau et de Mondonville.
L' opéra comique semble avoir été considérée trop vulgaire pour mériter l'attention.

In short, the writers and journalists concerned in the quarrel were
fighting about a comparison which ought not have been made. It
amounted to justifying *opéra comique* at the expense of a highly original modern art form. But the mistake is quite interesting for the light
it sheds upon what we have called the aesthetic of nature, an aesthetic
which may be said to have been that of the *philosophes*. It is thus possible to view the *Querelle des Bouffons* as an aspect of the great shift
from an aesthetic of art to one of nature. This comes out very well in
Rousseau's article on opera, which he wrote for his *Dictionnaire de
musique*: a work we have preferred to consult rather than the polemical
Lettre sur la musique française, which M. Borel scathingly described
as an "extraordinaire mélange d'incompétence, d'incompréhension, et
de parti-pris."

Rousseau begins with a clear and concise definition of opera: "Spectacle dramatique et lyrique où l'on s'efforce de réunir tous les charmes
des beaux-arts dans la représentation d'une action passionnée, pour exciter, à l'aide des sensations agréables, l'intérêt et l'illusion."[2] He then
distinguishes the various parts of this lyrical drama: poetry, music, decoration. "Par la poésie on parle à l'esprit; par la musique, à l'oreille; par
la peinture, aux yeux: et le tout doit se réunir pour émouvoir le coeur,
et y porter à la fois la même impression par divers organes." After which
he goes back to consider opera with relation to the Greeks. Quite clearly,
there is nothing new here, for Du Bos and Batteux had both preceded
Rousseau. But Rousseau made more of Greek lyric drama (which no
one really knew, directly or even indirectly, but about which there was
a great deal of speculation) than Du Bos ever did. If for Rousseau the
origins of modern lyrical drama may be traced to the Greeks, such a
belief may be explained in terms of his own peculiar and personal view
of nature. Among the Greeks the union of poetry and music was natural
because it was intimately and harmoniously tied to their language:
poetry, music, and language merged. The Greeks, therefore, did not
need opera because their language was naturally beautiful, harmonious,

[2] Article "Opéra" in Rousseau's *Dictionnaire de musique*, in *Oeuvres complètes*, Vol. 13.

poetic, expressive, and touching. This harmony having been lost, language in modern times had to be supplemented by art in order to touch the heart:

En écoutant un langage hypothétique et contraint, nous avons peine à concevoir ce qu'on veut nous dire; avec beaucoup de bruit on nous donne peu d'émotion: de là naît la nécéssité d'amener le plaisir physique au secours du moral, et de suppléer par l'attrait de l'harmonie à l'énergie de l'expression. Ainsi moins on sait toucher le coeur, plus il faut flatter l'oreille; et nous sommes forcés de chercher dans la sensation le plaisir que le sentiment nous refuse [Ibid.].

The origins of airs, choruses, symphonies, melodies are to be found in this loss of poetry and the inability of language to touch directly through its own expressive and poetic power. This union of music and discourse, however, was not natural, and it was precisely for this reason that the inventors of the genre placed the action in heaven or hell: "faute de savior faire parler les hommes, ils aimèrent mieux faire chanter des dieux et des diables que les héros et les bergers" (Ibid.). The marvellous thus became the foundation of the new genre, admired for a long time and defended on the grounds that it went beyond the rules of Aristotle since it added admiration to pity and terror. But to Rousseau this new genre (the delight of epicureans and of those who dared enjoy themselves outside the realm approved by the *philosophes*, with its machines, elaborate decor, enchantments, marvels, gods and heroes) was but a sign of sterility, the art form of a decadent and corrupt society in which man was alienated from his fellows: "C'était faute de savoir toucher qu'ils voulaient surprendre, et cette admiration prétendue n'était en effet qu'un étonnement puéril dont ils auraient dû rougir" (Ibid.).

Nevertheless, little by little the opera was reformed; one began to see that music could touch the heart and that it need not be limited in its effect to a titillation of the senses. Movement, harmony, and song were united as expressions of the passions, and music became more and more the central part of dramatic lyric poetry: "C'est alors que, commençant à se dégoûter de tout le clinquant de la féerie, du puéril fracas des machines, et de la fantasque image des choses qu'on n'a jamais vues, on chercha dans l'imitation de la nature des tableaux plus intéressants et plus vrais" (Ibid.). It was the expressive and evocative power of music which led to the reform of opera, and all that opera had taken from tragedy, the discourses, explanations, deliberations, all those aspects which appealed to the mind — and which appealed also, let us not forget, to the French public — were banished, so that the energy of the passions and sentiments became the dominant trait. Thus, if for Batteux the fabulous was what distinguished opera from tragedy, for Rousseau it was above all the predominance of sentiment. Batteux's view was not only literary and musical, it was also visual. Opera was a marvellous spectacle. Rousseau's view, however, while admitting a degree of spectacle, was dominated by sentiment. Marmontel, in his article on opera, expressed similar views but for a different reason, namely, the greater effectiveness of the marvellous. Rousseau would banish this and all other elements derived from tragedy for the sake of greater truth to nature. The old problem of verisimilitude was now argued on the basis not of theatrical effectiveness so much as of truth to human sentiments and feelings. Rousseau was a partisan of Italian opera on naturalistic grounds: the Italians were better singers than the French, not because the French were poor singers who enjoyed a monopoly and thus did not greatly feel the need to reform, but because the divorce of poetry and music was less pronounced in the Italian language than in the French — which is another way of saying that the Italians had never become as corrupted or modernized as the French, or, put even more simply, that they were closer to the original true, pure, harmonious union of music and poetry, namely that found in ancient Greek! Thus, in opposition to those who accepted *opera seria* as a universe of marvels and fantasy made for the delight of all the senses and also of the mind, Rousseau posed a theory of opera based on the conventionalization of simple nature. Obviously, since the opera in Paris was largely dominated by Rameau, it hardly fitted his aesthetic of simple nature. And the whole battle really turned, not so much on the French misuse of the expressive power of music, as on the subject matter; for obviously *opera bouffa*, better sung but also putting onstage ordinary people in ordinary situations, came closer to simple nature than the world of marvels and enchantments of *opera seria*. The aesthetic of simple nature may thus be described as that of a democrat, while the aesthetic of art was undeniably aristocratic. Rousseau did not at all differ from the views of Rameau as concerns the expressive power of music. What Rousseau advocated was also an integral and original part of Rameau's art, even though the latter was an art used to stage the ways of gods and heroes rather than of the simple men and women that Rousseau identified with simple nature. Rousseau's vicious attack on French opera at the time of the *Querelle des Bouffons* was not so much an aesthetic-critical pronouncement as part of a personal fight with Paris.

Marmontel, though a *philosophe* too, was more judicious about the opera as a genre, even though he took the wrong side during the disputes between the Piccinists and the Glückists. He realized that the strength of the genre lay in the fact that it could not be compared to any other; it had to be judged on its own terms. It may be that the *Querelle* and the advent of Glück taught him something, namely the autonomy of opera, which escaped the strictures of a narrow view of the doctrine of imitation, since it was the art of perfect and complete illusion:

> Dans ce composé tout est mensonge, mais tout est d'accord; et cet accord en fait la vérité. La musique y fait le charme du merveilleux, le merveilleux y fait la vraisemblance de la musique: on est dans un monde nouveau; c'est la nature dans l'enchantement et visiblement animée par une foule d'intelligences, dont les volontés sont ses lois.[3]

The advantage of French opera lay precisely in this power of enchantment; to associate opera with a *vraisemblance* derived from *la simple nature* would mean losing the freedom gained by the need to enchant the spectator. One would turn good tragedy into bad opera: for the historical subjects of tragedy, the political intrigues, and machinery of fate had to be convincing in terms of nature, whereas the world of the marvellous did not have to be convincing in the same manner at all. Truth, associated with tragic action, was in conflict with the convention of poetry and music. Spectators thus divided their attention between song and action, music and scenery, and readily perceived that the heroes they associated with tragic drama did not conform to operatic singers. It was thus in bad taste to change Oedipus into a character in an opera. Finally, opera had another advantage in the direction away from simple nature; it could be used for noble and gallant subjects, pastoral or *bergeries*, while the comic genre and *genre bouffon* also had a right to exist on a basis other than the verisimilitude associated with simple nature.

In the Quarrel of the Buffoons d'Alembert played the role Fontenelle had played in the first phase of the Quarrel of the Ancients and the Moderns: he clarified the issues and pointed to the possibility of a combination of the virtues of both French and Italian opera. His essay *De*

---

[3] Article "Opéra," in Marmontel's *Eléments de littérature*, in *Oeuvres* (Paris, 1818–20), XIV, 407–55.

la liberté de la musique is the best of the numerous works written on
the occasion of the famous dispute. He saw the merits of French opera,
but it is quite possible that he did not think much of the genre as a
whole, because for him verisimilitude was founded upon nature and
truth rather than fable. As he put it, "Au reste . . . il sera toujours
incontestable que la tragédie *parlée* est préférable à la tragédie *chan-
tée*; la première est une action, dont la vérité ne dépend que de ceux
qui l'exécutent, la seconde ne sera jamais qu'un spectacle."[4] The
philosophe's prejudice vis-à-vis an art form directed above all to the
senses shows all too readily. He did not dismiss opera, but thought
it should be reformed along more naturalistic lines so as to combine
the best of both French and Italian opera, especially as concerned song:
Italian music should be adapted to French opera. Three things should
thus be reformed: recitative, *airs chantants*, and symphonies. He makes
a rather detailed criticism of these three aspects: he did not think much
of the French recitative; he thought Italian airs should be simplified;
and he thought symphonies the best parts of French opera. Recitative,
in d'Alembert's opinion, ought to be a midpoint between ordinary
declamation and song. The airs ought to have interest through their
subjects. The libretto in French opera should be improved, and its words
be in accord with the airs and vice versa: "Le chant français a le défaut
le plus contraire à l'expression; c'est *de se ressembler toujours à lui-
même*" (Ibid., 559). On the whole his views are along the lines pro-
posed by Rousseau, though they are devoid of polemics and are not
founded upon Rousseau's assumptions about language. One might also
describe his attitude as literary, a trait he shared with all the *philosophes*
and also perhaps with the French public in general at that time. Nevertheless he did recognize the merits of French opera and put the matter
succinctly: "Nous avons, ce me semble, mieux connu qu'aucun autre
peuple le vrai caractère de chaque théâtre; chez nous *la comédie est
le spectacle de l'esprit, la tragédie celui de l'âme, l'opéra celui des sens*;
voilà tout ce qu'il est et ce qu'il peut être" (Ibid., 523). However, he
was also convinced that this genre, uniquely directed to the pleasure
of the senses, was destined to pass. What did happen, in fact, is that
the *tragédie lyrique* gradually lost its position of dominance and gave
way to a new type of comic opera which combined both French and
Italian elements.

In an age in which the arts were often scrutinized too closely and
were expected to conform to the requirements of reason and truth, to

⁴ "De la liberté de la musique," in *Oeuvres complètes*, I, 524.

be useful as well as pleasing, the opera appears as a form of play and as a genre which, like the novel, escaped to a certain degree the general laws governing the arts. But both the opera and the novel paid a price for this, because neither was taken quite seriously by all. The opera found sympathy and understanding in the first half of the century, but it pleased the *philosophes* and a public perhaps unduly influenced by the new philosophical approach to the fine arts only by the sacrifice of what had delighted a former audience, namely fantasy and fable. Nevertheless opera must be considered one of the major arts of the Classical period, for it may well have been the place of refuge of poetry and the compensation for the failure of tragedy in an age more and more convinced of the possibility of progress and happiness.

* * *

See also: *Expression, Poetry, Pantomime, Truth.*
Bibliography: Alembert, Du Bos, Rousseau; Chastellux, Lacombe, Marmontel, Morellet, Rémond de Saint-Mard; and also the following secondary works: Jules Ecorcheville, *De Lulli à Rameau, L'Esthétique musicale,* 1690–1730 (Paris, 1906) — not only a work on music, but also on the aesthetics of the period since musical aesthetics derived from a general aesthetic; Cuthbert Girdlestone, *Jean-Philippe Rameau, His Life and Work* (London, 1957); Donald Jay Grout, *A Short History of Opera,* Vol. I (New York and London, 1965), excellent for background; A. Jullien, *La Musique et les philosophes du XVIIIe Siècle* (Paris, 1873), to be supplemented by Richard Oliver, *The Encyclopedists as Critics of Music* (New York, 1947); see also the excellent and classic work of Paul Marie Masson, *L'Opéra de Rameau* (Paris, 1930).

ORNAMENT

"IF A BUILDING had neither columns nor pilasters, architraves, friezes, or cornices, and were all of a piece, could one call it a fine piece of architecture?" (*Parallèle,* I, 127–28.) Thus spoke Perrault's *Président* in the course of his visit to Versailles with the Abbé and the Chevalier. The Abbé, protagonist of the moderns, replied that one could not — from which the *Président* deduced that the beauty of architecture was invented by the ancients because they had invented its ornaments. It is obvious that ornament was an important factor in the Classical idea of beauty. It might even be possible to elaborate a theory of art for the seventeenth and eighteenth centuries centered on the notion and role of ornament. A visit to an *hôtel particulier* in the Régence or Louis XV styles, or studies in the *Musée des Arts decoratifs*, would provide ample material for the illustration of such a theory. In such a view art might be defined as the ornament of life, and one might, within the same general aesthetic, distinguish between various types of beauty on the basis of their respective relation to and use of ornament. Furthermore, the attitude towards ornamentation, and the degree of it allowed, might serve as indications of artistic development and taste within a given general style. In the Classical period of the seventeenth and eighteenth centuries one might say that the concept of art, insofar as it related to ornament, oscillated between the ideal of natural simplicity and its antithesis, the *clinquant*: by their ornaments shall ye know them. Too much ornamentation spoils beauty; too little fails to attract the eye and hold one's interest. In the words of Fénelon, "on gagne beaucoup en perdant tous les ornements superflus, pour se borner aux beautés simples, faciles, claires et négligées en apparence. Pour la poésie, comme pour l'architecture, il faut que tous les morceaux nécessaires se tournent en ornements naturels." [1] Ornament turned the merely utilitarian into art and *agrément*; it separated art from pure nature, though too much of it might spoil the ideal of simple nature which was the object of artistic imitation. Ornament also made of architecture an art, turned furniture into objets d'art, and interiors into delightful artificial worlds which evoked the *belle nature* that was not, in fact, to be found in the sublunar world. Regarding the mind, that interior space within the body of man, ornament may also be said to have made the difference between the man still gross, rough, and natural, endowed with a clean slate of a mind, and the man of taste, refinement, and knowledge, whose slate had obviously been written upon. A man of learning and wit was, indeed, sometimes referred to as a man in possession of an ornate mind. And the degree of ornateness was as important for the mind as it was for architecture or interiors, for a mind too ornate might be as burdensome as a surface spoiled by too much ornamentation. Ornament was thus an index of refinement and judgment: its proper use indicated that one knew how to reconcile a sense of play with the soundness of reason.

Condillac, in his considerations of written style, developed a view of ornament which defines its place in the Enlightenment quite clearly. Ornament belongs properly to periods of civilization, for it is what is

---

[1] *Lettre écrite à l'Académie Française sur l'éloquence, la poésie, l'histoire, etc.,* in *Dialogues sur l'Eloquence,* p. 322.

left over from periods of history in which men still believed in the fabulous and mythical. In writing, ornaments are figures, metaphors, images
whose original meanings have been forgotten through time. It stands
to reason that the more philosophical and modern a style the less ornate
it will become, so that the history of language is one of progress from
poetry towards a greater degree of clarity and abstraction, though not
wholly devoid of ornament appropriate to the matter. Condillac seems
to be saying, in effect, that each age must find its own ornaments:

A mesure que l'écriture devint plus simple, le style le devint également. En
oubliant la signification des hiéroglyphes, on perdit peu à peu l'usage de bien
des figures et de bien des métaphores; mais il fallut des siècles pour rendre
ce changement sensible. Le style des anciens asiatiques était prodigieusement
figuré. . . . Enfin les figures, après toutes ces révolutions, furent employées
pour l'ornement du discours, quand les hommes eurent acquis des connaissances assez exactes et assez étendues des arts et des sciences pour en tirer
des images qui, sans jamais nuire à la clarté, étaient aussi riantes, aussi nobles,
aussi sublimes, que la matière demandait. . . . C'est ainsi que les figures et
les métaphores, d'abord inventées par nécéssité, ensuite choisies pour servir
au mystère, sont devenues l'ornement du discours, lorsqu'elles ont pu être
employées avec discernement; et c'est ainsi que, dans la décadence des
langues, elles ont porté les premiers coups par l'abus qu'on en a fait.[2]

Ornament became a point of aesthetic dispute in the course of the
eighteenth century: it divided artists, architects, and moralists. Purists
tended to play ornament down, epicures to delight in it. When Jean-
Jacques Rousseau gave up gold braid, watch and chain, sword and
three-cornered hat for his simple broadcloth or Armenian garb, he
gave up the ornaments of civility for the simplicities of an uncorrupted
nature. When Charles Nicholas Cochin parodied a decree to the gold-
smiths he satirized those who indulged in a profusion of ornament in
architecture. Thus attitudes to ornament opposed partisans of the *goût
moderne* to those who founded taste upon the *goût antique*. Partisans
of this taste associated profusion of ornament with decadence, frivolity,
chicorée, and, eventually, the Rococo. But, as we have seen with Condillac, the same association could be made in language. Profusion of
ornament was also blamed for the decline of historical painting, since
such profusion took up space which could have been used for paintings, just as profusion of ornament in poetry was associated with frivolous play and frivolous minds, and was blamed for the decline of great,
noble, and moving poetry. Thus ornament differentiated tastes and men

[2] *Essai sur l'origine des connaissances humaines*, Ch. 14, no. 140.

of taste from others, for the degree of ornament to be used was subject
to the judgment of taste.

* * *

See also: *Antique, Gothic, Grands Siècles, Nature, Taste.*

PANTOMIME

"C'EST LE LANGAGE DE L'ACTION, l'art de parler aux yeux, l'expression
muette" ("Pantomime," in *Oeuvres*, XIV, 484–94). Thus did Marmontel
define an art which usually came up in various discussions concerning
dance, opera, and, generally speaking, those arts concerned with the
expression of the passions. Pantomime was an art of pure expression
which especially interested those concerned with moving spectators by
direct visual effect. As in painting (to argue along Du Bosian lines) the
advantage of pantomime was that it affected the public without recourse
to the artificial signs of the written or spoken language: it communicated without words. It was especially suited to the expression of strong
passions and could be used to supplement or even supplant the spoken
word. This consideration gained importance because not everyone was
happy with stage declamation, since this did not accord with a general
ideal of naturalness which gradually gained the minds of critics and
philosophes in the second half of the eighteenth century. Diderot en-
visioned dramatic action executed in mimed tableaux, because he
thought there was too much talk on the stage. Indeed, in his essay on
dramatic poetry he devoted an entire section to pantomime. He thought
that the Italian actors of comedies acted with much more liberty than
the French, precisely because they were closer to pantomime; they
improvised, and did not act according to a theory of imitation, but rather
to one of expression. Pantomime, for Diderot, was thus part of dramatic
action:

> J'ai dit que la pantomime est une portion du drame; que l'auteur s'en
> doit occuper sérieusement; que si elle ne lui est pas familière et présente, il
> ne saura ni commencer, ni conduire, ni terminer sa scène avec quelque vérité;
> et que le geste doit s'écrire souvent à la place du discours.
> J'ajoute qu'il y a des scènes entières où il est infiniment plus naturel aux
> personnages de se mouvoir que de parler.[1]

The importance attributed to pantomime was connected with the
broad assumptions which can be subsumed under the general heading

[1] "De la poésie dramatique," in *Oeuvres esthétiques*, p. 269.

of the *ut pictura poesis* rule. It was a moving, acted, picture: "Appliquez les lois de la composition pittoresque à la pantomime," writes Diderot, "et vous verrez que ce sont les mêmes" (Ibid.)

As tragedy was connected with Greece, so pantomime was associated with Rome. This was of considerable importance for its evaluation. The Romans were less refined than the Greeks and preferred pantomime because it appealed to the eyes above all other senses. It was an art more vehement than eloquence itself: all was action, attention did not lag, and the public gave itself completely over to the pleasure of being moved by visible action without the trouble of thinking, for even where ideas were supposedly being exposed on the stage they were necessarily so vague as to be almost dreamlike. "La *pantomime*," writes Marmontel,

est tout à l'expression du geste; ses mouvements ne lui sont point tracés; la passion seule est son guide. L'acteur est continuellement le copiste du poète; le *pantomime* est original: l'un est asservi au sentiment et à la pensée d'autrui, l'autre se livre et s'abandonne aux mouvements de son âme [Op. cit.].

Acting in a drama involving the spoken language was an art of imitation; pantomime was an art of direct expression, and was therefore closer to that new ideal, nature. From there it was easy to go further and confuse pantomime with true nature, and acting within a play with art. Diderot's famous *Paradoxe sur le comédien* treats this very theme, indirectly, but without making the point that there is a difference between the dramatic action of the actor and that of the mime. One could argue, however, on the basis of the naturalistic assumptions concerning pantomime, that the man of sensibility, who would be a poor actor in a drama because he could not control his passions, might on the other hand be an excellent mime because there was no model to imitate, so that he could be himself. The *philosophes* made the naturalistic assumption, and Marmontel thought pantomime so much a part of nature that he was forced to reject it as dangerous.

The mime, however, was not occupied with the expression of the passions alone, but also with the graceful carriage and movement of the body, so that pantomime could also express the beauty of the human form. So regarded, pantomime leads to the development of dance as an autonomous art form, a development which took place precisely at this period, thanks to the work of the ballet master Noverre. We may thus consider pantomime as the natural base of both drama and dance: drama is pantomime with words, while dance is pantomime stylized with music, both departures from pure pantomime thus becoming independent arts. The dancer, however, unlike the actor, who had to use words, still retained the original advantage of the mime in that he also acted through a purely visual medium; it is precisely this directness of expression which made pantomime a danger to all the other arts. If pantomime were once more to develop to the point it had reached in Rome, thought Marmontel, it might well replace tragedy and comedy, for it avoided all the difficulties of comic and dramatic action. Since the mind is hardly involved when one watches pantomime, and since the attention is ever fixed upon the action, there is no problem of theatrical verisimilitude, rules, or unities. One might put it this way: natural expression avoids the difficulties of an art of imitation precisely because there is no imitation in the artistic sense at all: the mime proceeds instinctively. There is no translation of truth or nature from itself into another medium of expression. In a certain sense, to draw an example from contemporary art or at least from art that was contemporary a few years ago, the action of the mime, as understood by Marmontel, resembles the supposed action of the Abstract Expressionist painter in his studio, the difference being that the gestures of the mime were a silent language which did communicate, sometimes all too clearly, whereas paint, no matter how expressively used, produced a much vaguer message, requiring critical exegesis in art magazines. One could also think of mime, as conceived by Marmontel, in terms of the happening. Now the *philosophes*, like the critics of today, were convinced that the arts had to be interpreted and that they ought to serve society, and while one could argue that mimes did communicate messages, these were, as we have seen, very vague indeed. This hardly suited philosophic purposes. Thus pantomime, though a natural expressive art (or non-art if you will) was nevertheless thought dangerous because it did not exactly express the nature the *philosophes* had in mind. It was dangerous too because it made all the other arts, which could be useful, seem insipid. It made for a very agreeable and absorbing spectacle, but it was useless. The *philosophe* Marmontel, author of moral tales and the civic novel *Belisarius*, thus shrank from the possible consequences of pantomime: "De la *pantomime*, rien ne reste que des impressions quelquefois dangereuses; on sait qu'elle acheva de corrompre les moeurs de Rome; au lieu que de la bonne tragédie et de la saine comédie, il reste d'utiles leçons. Au spectacle de la *pantomime* on n'est qu'ému; aux deux autres on est instruit" (Op. cit.). Pantomime, being merely attractive to the senses, necessarily drew the crowd; it neither corrected mores nor tamed passions, so that governments would be well advised to withhold from citizens this type of spectacle and expose them rather to sane, enlightening, and instructive theatre. After all, the end of dramatic action was not merely sensual pleasure or *divertissement*, nor was it pure spectacle like opera, but rather instruction, the education of mankind. "On ne forme point les esprits avec des tableaux et des coups de théâtre" (Ibid.). Such things appealed to the crowd, which sought strong effects and sharp emotions, but to make of them the end of art was to pervert its purpose, "et à la place de la poésie et de l'eloquence, on n'aura plus que la *pantomime*: de temps en temps encore on fera crier la nature, mais on ne la fera plus parler" (Ibid.). Pantomime, we are tempted to say, did not bring the right messages across because it was an unclear expressive art. The *philosophes* wanted to telegraph their punches. Pantomime was a commercial without a message, dangerous like a cigarette ad.

$$* \quad * \quad *$$

See also: *Expression, Nature, Ut Pictura Poesis.*
Bibliography: Diderot; Marmontel, Noverre.

PERFECTION, PERFECTIONNEMENT

> Il y a de belles choses qui ont plus d'éclat
> quand elles demeurent imparfaites que quand
> elles sont trop achevées.
>
> *La Rochefoucauld*

LA ROCHEFOUCAULD'S ATTITUDE concerning things that are too perfect strikes a modern note; it was certainly not usual for his times. He was, we must assume, less pedantic than the critics for whom "*perfectionnement*" referred to historical evidence of progress in the arts and sciences while "perfection" suggested an aesthetic-moral obligation put upon poets and painters to produce perfect works. Perfection, indeed, can hardly be separated as an idea from the doctrine of imitation and from classical periods of art. It implies a certain relation between the artist and his models, his work, his public, and also himself. It also has important implications for criticism because it allows critics to think in terms of a standard of purity or perfection to be maintained or attained, and of new works in terms of established or imagined models of perfection. The ideal of perfection was one of the central issues of the Quarrel of the Ancients and the Moderns: for the partisans of the ancients the perfect models had been created in the past and could not be improved upon, only emulated; for the moderns the perfect models were ideals still to be attained and worked for. When an artist or poet settled down to work, however, it may well be that he had in mind both types of models, for it was generally admitted that imitation allowed one at least to try to surpass the accepted perfect models. But in addition to this, the ideal of perfection and the process of *perfectionnement* also referred to the special care to be given the *métier* of letters and art:

> Hâtez-vous lentement; et, sans perdre courage,
> Vingt fois sur le métier remettez votre ouvrage:
> Polissez-le sans cesse et le repolissez;
> Ajoutez quelquefois, et souvent effacez
>   (Boileau, *Art poétique*, Part I).

This is not only a matter of personal discipline and pride, and of an artistic requirement posed by the rules of art; it is in a sense an ethical aspect of artistic work as well as a social obligation. For perfection is a good; it is not only an aesthetic, but also a moral value. More than that, it satisfies the requirements of reason: a perfect work is one which cannot be improved upon, one in which the possibilities have been exhausted, so that there is nothing left to be done. Thus Poussin, who was said to work with his mind, was quoted as saying upon the completion of a work, *"Je n'ai rien négligé."* In a perfect work reason and the resources of art have been fully employed, a thing that satisfies the requirements of the spectator's reason too; he is spared the labor of completing the work with his imagination, he is left in no uncertainty and no doubt: the work of art presents him with the perfect work which his reason requires but knows cannot be obtained in the world of everyday nature. Like Vinteuil's sonata the perfect work of the Classical artist was an intimation of a higher order of beauty, value, and truth, the only one possible to man in his fallen state.

The ideal of perfection implies also that the imagination is not held to be a particularly positive virtue; indeed, it is seen as a source of error, and for this reason one does not find in the late seventeenth and the early eighteenth century an aesthetic based upon the creative power of the imagination which would allow a certain degree of incompleteness in a work of art and thereby require the imagination of the spectator or reader to complete what the artist had failed to depict or the poet had left unsaid. The idea of perfection answers the requirements of the *grand goût* and *grand beau*; it supposes a beauty quite different in essence from that *je ne sais quoi* which sets the imagination in motion. A consideration of the *je ne sais quoi*, however, allows a certain insight into La Rochefoucauld's observation. For the term "imperfect," in fact, does not here refer to the incomplete or the unfinished; it must be understood in contrast, not so much to the perfect as to the too-perfect. Indeed, the point of perfection, precisely because of the power of the imagination, is perhaps difficult to fix, and one is thus tempted to improve upon something which had better be left as it is. As Boileau put it in the *Art poétique*:

> Tout ce qu'on dit de trop est fade et rebutant;
> L'esprit rassasié le rejette à l'instant.
> Qui ne sait se borner ne sut jamais écrire.

> Souvent la peur d'un mal nous conduit dans un pire.
> Un vers était trop faible, et vous le rendez dure;
> J'évite d'être long, et je deviens obscur;
> L'un n'est point trop fardé, mais sa muse est trop nue;
> L'autre a peur de ramper, il se perd dans la nue.

Perfection is thus a point reached in a process of artistic activity that is judged to be attained by taste; it is an effect of true judgment and may therefore be associated with the rules of art or with an aesthetic of art rather than with genius and an aesthetic of nature. Indeed, the argument of the greater perfection of modern over ancient works was founded on the idea that rules could insure perfection. And since rules were forms of knowledge and control over matter, associated with rationality, we may see how the ideal of perfection in the arts gradually came to be extended into the more ambiguous notion of progress in the arts and sciences.

See also: *Decadence.*

* * *

PERSPECTIVE

THIS ARTISTIC TERM, originally confined to vision and the art of painting, was extended in the Classical period to cover a phenomenon that we might call aesthetic distance. We are treating this phenomenon as perspective because it had no adequate term in the seventeenth or eighteenth centuries. In the aesthetic realm, as distinct from that of painting, perspective has to do with time rather than space. But like aerial perspective it is concerned with the illusion of truth, and if the perspective of the painter creates an illusion of space, that of the poet creates an illusion of time. The gist of a theory of perspective is that some phenomena, pictures, and actions ought not to be looked at very

closely, but from a distance. As regards poetry or drama the principle
is quite clearly stated in Racine's second preface to *Bajazet*:

Quelques lecteurs pourront s'étonner qu'on aît osé mettre sur la scène une
histoire si récente. Mais je n'ai rien vu dans les règles du poème dramatique
qui dût me détourner de mon entreprise. A la vérité, je ne conseillerais pas
à un auteur de prendre pour sujet d'une tragédie une action aussi moderne
que celle-ci, si elle s'était passée dans le pays où il veut faire représenter sa
tragédie, ni de mettre des héros sur le théâtre qui auraient été connus de
la plupart des spectateurs. Les personnages tragiques doivent être regardés
d'un autre oeil que nous ne regardons d'ordinaire les personnages que
nous avons vus de si près. On peut dire que le respect que l'on a pour les
héros augmente à mesure qu'ils s'éloignent de nous: *major e longuinquo re-
verentia.* L'éloignement des pays répare en quelque sorte la trop grande
proximité des temps: car le peuple ne met guère de différence entre ce qui
est, si j'ose ainsi parler, à mille ans de lui, et ce qui est à mille lieues.[1]

Perspective, in this sense, is what renders something near in time or
space credible as art. Distance in time as well as space often transforms
the true into the beautiful, and makes for verisimilitude. "Perspective,"
used in relation to time, also implies that art is most certainly not a
copy of reality, but rather its transformation into a world of illusion,
self-contained because distance in time makes the subject matter of
art nonverifiable. Art is not history, art is not truth, but something belonging to another realm. For the man of the theatre or the poet, we
may say, perspective in time played the same role that the frame did
for the painter. As the frame separated the painting from everyday
reality, so remoteness in time separated the art work's subject matter
from present truth. Perspective told the reader of an epic that what he
was reading was a particular type of tale, not subject to verifiability. In
the theatre the distance was reinforced by the convention of the pro-
scenium which, as in painting, framed the action. Since perspective
supposedly heightened the illusion by removing the subject or object
from the present and its reality, the insistence on *costume* (see article)
implied a certain contradiction, since it was supposed to be founded
on historical truth. There was, we might say, a mixture of truths involved here: *costume* was supposedly founded on historical truth and
geographic variation, while the whole notion of perspective in time
implied that historical truth, in Racine's case the true story of Bajazet,
was unfit for artistic representation because it was too near in time, or

[1] In *Théâtre Classique Français* (Paris: Club Français du Livre, 1960), XII, 8–9.

that historical truth as such was quite different from what we would call aesthetic truth: *Le Vrai n'est quelquefois pas vraisemblable.*

Perspective in historical time also implied that the modern world was different from the ancient, and from an even more remote past associated with the fabulous (see article "Fable"). This difference posed problems as to the possibility of keeping the old ornaments of poetry, and mythological figures and characters (see article "Poetry"), just as it also posed problems as to the possibility of epic poetry and the mixing of Christian and pagan ornaments in poetry and painting. But more was involved. The essential difference drawn between the modern world and that which drew upon certain resources of tragic and epic motifs, implied that the present had no resources of beauty and grandeur. Thus beauty and the heroic, the sublime and the marvellous, like poetry in its most general sense, were seen as belonging to the past. Perspective was thus obviously more necessary for certain forms than for others: it was more essential to tragedy and the epic than to comedy and satire. It is therefore possible to argue that certain genres were susceptible of further development and that others were not, insofar as these genres required perspective of time. On this basis, tragedy was not capable of development, but comedy was; epic poetry was not, but satire was. Both the opera and the novel were, though opera did need perspective, not to create an illusion of truth, but rather a quality of fantasy, while the novel did not need quite the same perspective because it was not primarily concerned with tragic heroes.

PLEASE AND INSTRUCT: PLAIRE ET INSTRUIRE

THE INJUNCTION THAT WRITERS ought to please and instruct the public is frequently found in the prefaces of plays and novels throughout the Classical period. It was, indeed, an axiom which was inseparable from the worldly ethics of the time, and might in this respect be considered merely as an affair of manners extended into the world of letters. Pleasure was something more than amusement; it was a moral imperative associated with civility and a species of enlightened self-interest. As Paradis de Moncrif put it in the conclusion of his *Essais sur la necéssité et sur les moyens de plaire*:

C'est dès la première année de notre vie que doit commencer notre éducation; et après les principes de la Religion, qui est elle-même la source de toutes les vertus sociales, rien n'est plus important que de bien établir en nous le désir et les moyens de disposer en notre faveur les esprits, afin de parvenir à nous concilier les coeurs; parce que dans le commerce ordinaire de la vie, pour être heureux, il faut être aimé; que pour être aimé, il faut plaire; et qu'on ne plaît qu'autant qu'on sait contribuer au bonheur des autres [*Oeuvres*, I, 137].

The arts play a role in this scheme of education; they are not only an ornament of the mind but also a pleasure. It is also possible to see how one could easily move from the notion of pleasure to that of instruction, for Paradis de Moncrif's treatise was not concerned with aesthetic pleasure alone but also with education, with pleasure as a social phenomenon, as an aspect of sociability. Thus, while the imperative to please and instruct the public is to be found frequently at this time, equal weight and importance was not always given the two terms of the injunction. According to Arsène Soreil, the seventeenth century was on the whole content to emphasize pleasure alone as far as the arts were concerned:

Plus on fréquente les théoriciens classiques, plus on se rend compte que, débarrassée de toute fin morale ou didactique, l'art leur apparaît comme un instrument de plaisir choisi, et la beauté comme un autre nom de l'agréable. Autrement dit, l'essence du beau est de plaire, bien que ce plaisir puisse être utilisé en vue de fins morales ou pratiques [*Introduction*, 37].

Pleasure in this sense, as an effect of the *agréable*, played perhaps a more prominent role in the seventeenth century than in the following one, when it tended to become the means whereby men might be instructed. Thus the role assigned pleasure in the arts can differ considerably, and its function within the general Classical aesthetic is not constant.

In the *Grand Siècle* pleasure played an important part in limiting the normative power of the rules. The pleasure of the spectator was adduced as proof that rules did not make for necessarily successful plays. Pleasure was posed as the highest rule of all, so that it was used to cancel the rules and criticisms of the pedants. The pleasures of the soul were the censors of the rule of reason. Thus, within the aesthetic of rules, pleasure may be considered as a factor of indeterminacy or of freedom for the artist, though a freedom that was limited by the necessity of pleasing another set of spectators or readers, for no one was free to be displeasing. The type of pleasure required therefore depended upon the public one addressed or sought to woo. Insofar as pleasure was used as a defense against critics, it took the form of a positive obligation towards the public of the court at one time; in another time, perhaps, one might wish to use the same argument of pleasure to woo the town. The poet often had to choose, for he could not always please everyone: a public which wished to be pleased irrespective of the rules, and a body of critics which would be pleased only according to the rules. In the course of the second half of the seventeenth century the critics lost this particular battle, but the poets or writers did not thereby gain the right to be displeasing and write what they wished. There was no question of this at all. They could continue to please, indeed they must, but now they could do so without paying as much heed to rules as they had done in the former century: for it was accepted that rules could not determine the quality of a play, this being the prerogative of taste, which was itself a form of pleasure. Yet, poets and writers ought not only to please, but also to instruct. The shift in emphasis took place as early as the first half of the eighteenth century. The Abbé Du Bos was not greatly affected by this, for it may be reasonably demonstrated that he had advocated a hedonistic aesthetic which, in a negative way, kept men's passions from doing more harm than they would if they were left unoccupied. Better the artificial pleasures induced by art than the real but destructive passions of nature. But within one generation the emphasis changed, and the injunction to please was invariably followed by the imperative of instruction. It was even perceived, in the course of the century, that the pleasure taking the form of malice, interest, and laughter could become a powerful instrument. The philosophical movement thus exploited a certain type of pleasure for the purpose of enlightenment and instruction. The new meaning of the phrase was succinctly put by Condillac:

La fin de tout écrivain est d'instruire ou de plaire, ou de plaire et d'instruire tout à la fois. Il plaît en parlant aux sens, en frappant l'imagination, en remuant les passions; il instruit en donnant des connaissances, en dissipant des préjugés, en détruisant des erreurs, en combattant des vices et des ridicules ["Art d'Ecrire," in *Oeuvres complètes*, V, 461].

The first half of the second sentence would have been accepted by the *Grand Siècle*; the second half might well have seemed incomprehensible to it; the entire passage is an excellent résumé of the aesthetics of the Enlightenment.

*　　*　　*

See also: *Art, Public, Rules*; *Du Bos*.

POETRY AND POETIC THEORY

A GREAT DEAL OF POETRY was produced in the course of the seventeenth and eighteenth centuries. Most of it has survived only as rows of calf bindings. Some is still read, thanks to anthologies, explications, and seminars; Boileau is still quoted, La Fontaine translated, Corneille, Racine, and Molière staged. Surveying both centuries from our point of view, we may say that the poetry of the *Grand Siècle* was undeniably greater than that of the eighteenth century, which was rather deficient in poetry. J. B. Rousseau, the greatest lyric poet of the eighteenth century, is no longer read; neither are La Motte, Gresset, Gentil Bernard, Colardeau, Malfilâtre, Piron, Delille, or Parny, save perhaps in preparation for examinations — a form of survival which we may term artificial. Two poets alone are read for their own sake. Voltaire was another great poet of the eighteenth century; his poetry is still read, as a contribution to the history of ideas. André Chénier has survived, thanks to a few harmonious verses and the poetry of his life and death. But if the eighteenth century failed generally to produce great or moving poetry, it compensated by producing a great many treatises on poetry in general and odes in particular. (It may perhaps be argued that there is a connection between the poverty of poetry and the plenitude of criticism.) The criticism of poetry and elaboration of theory was an activity of poets, philosophers, scholarly abbés, poetic cardinals, and amateurs. If the seventeenth century sought to determine the rules of poetry, delineate its genres, and establish the primacy of reason over rhyme, the eighteenth century concerned itself with problems of greater range and of more fruitful implication for the future of poetic theory. Eighteenth-century critics and poets wondered about the nature or essence of poetry, its relation to genius and enthusiasm, nature and history, taste and society, and sought to understand why the poetic production of their own times was poor: for it was indeed generally felt that something was wrong. Remedies were sought, but not found — in part because the way one thought about poetry determined where or how one sought the remedies. While one knew with precision what literary forms the term "poetry" referred to, one ceased to be sure of its meaning when one wondered about its essence.

It is possible to examine the notion of poetry in terms of a dualism: poetry in the sense of certain accepted literary forms, and poetry considered as something difficult to define, something rather vague associated with the feelings, the conflict with modern philosophical trends, and taste. It is with the second problem that we shall be primarily concerned here.

It is not difficult to find eighteenth-century definitions of poetry. These may be reduced to two general categories: those which associate poetry with verse, and those which do not. If we read eighteenth-century literature and look for poetry with the first category of definition in mind, then we may say that it was a century of immense poetic production; if we take time to read the poetry itself we may add that much of this poetry leaves us quite indifferent, and if we read even more eighteenth-century literature, including criticism, we will find it left a great many people cold in the eighteenth century as well. That is why there were critics and philosophers, and even poets, who thought that there was more to poetry than form associated with verse, so that the second type of definition of poetry usually tended to associate it with enthusiasm, imagination, nostalgia.

Father Mourgues provides concise definitions of poetry as versification. His *Traité de la poésie française* begins as follows: "Le terme de *Poésie Française*, qui pourrait avoir une signification plus étendue, est pris ici pour *l'art qui comprend la construction, et l'arrangement de nos vers*. C'est ce que l'on nomme aussi *versification*" (p. 3). Most of his treatise is concerned with the rules governing what may and what may not be done in versification, these rules being derived from existing models and the nature of the language. His observations of a more general nature which are appended to his treatise are little different from his initial definition, though he does tell us a few more things about poetry: "La Poésie est un langage mesuré exactement, orné de fictions, et de figures hardies. . . . Il suffit . . . de savoir que c'est en cela précisément que la poésie diffère du langage ordinare, qui n'a ni mesure exacte, ni fictions, ni figures outrées" (p. 260). It is obvious that this is merely an elaboration of the identification of poetry with versification. However, other notions are involved: ornament is all-important and, bearing in mind the general concept of art at the time we see that poetry differs from ordinary language in the same way that architecture differs from ordinary shelter and utility: precisely through ornament. Thus, poetry is something added to language. The assumption is brought forth by Batteux: art is the imitation of *la belle nature*. Ordinary language is unimproved nature; ornament, when added, transforms this nature into *la belle nature*.

But poetry is not ornament for the sake of ornament: its purpose is to please and instruct, and ornament plays a subordinate role. It attracts the mind of a reader and fixes his attention, so that the mind may be instructed in addition to being pleased. Poetry thus is a species of instrument which may be used to good or ill effect, according to the choice of the poet: "C'est aux poètes," writes Father Mourgues, "à la faire servir à la vertu, et non pas au vice; puisqu'elle est d'ailleurs, aussi bien que la peinture, *un art indifférent*" (italics mine) (Ibid.). This same instrumental view of poetry is also exposed by La Motte in his *Discours sur la poésie en général, et sur l'ode en particulier*, in which the notion of the neutrality of verse or poetry is also extended to painting:

Le Carache n'est pas moins peintre dans ses tableaux cyniques, que dans ses tableaux chrétiens; et de même, pour revenir à la poésie, La Fontaine n'est pas moins poète dans ses Contes que dans des Fables; quoique les uns soient dangereux et que les autres soient utiles [*Oeuvres*, I, 22].

This neutrality of verse forms implies, in effect, that definitions of poetry as verse also suppose the possible separation of form and content.

This view may be described as analytical; it is reminiscent of the Cartesian approach to an object, calculated to obtain a clear and distinct idea of it. Thus the elements of poetry are separated: it is distinguished from other genres, and in the end what is obtained is a clear idea of a verse form, itself susceptible of being further analyzed into language, rhyme, rhythm, measure, ornament, figures, and ideas. Since painting, music, and architecture also possess ornament, since both poetry and painting may represent ideas in different ways, since both music and poetry have *agrément*, but only poetry and painting can please *and* instruct, it follows by analysis that the essence of poetry is measured language or verse, while the essence of painting is color and space. The effect of this view was to confine poetry to what was already accepted as poetry. It also made possible the elaboration of a body of rules governing the making of poetry and the delimitation of genres. It followed that if poetry was identified with versification, the knowledge of the rules of this art should suffice to produce poetry. The poet became a technician. However, few critics accepted this inference, though La Motte came close to it at times. Mourgues himself did not:

Les talents qu'exige la poésie sont une imagination vive et belle, un jugement sûr, un goût exquis.
    L'imagination est le principe de l'enthousiasme; c'est-à-dire, de ce feu divin qui rend l'esprit fécond et inventif, source de beautés et de défauts.
    Le jugement sert à régler ce feu, qui ne doit pas ressembler à une ivresse, ou à un incendie, mais à une chaleur modérée, à une flamme pure et légère. . . .

Le goût est un sentiment fin et délicat, non seulement du beau, mais du gracieux [*Traité de la poésie française*, 261].

This would indicate a dualism, and we may say, borrowing from a contemporary British philosopher, that the versification or mechanical theory of poetry implied a *ghost in the machine*. The ghost, indeed, continued to haunt critics as well as poets, despite reason, geometry, and philosophy. For it could well be that the center of poetry was not at all to be found in versification.

Within the vast machinery of art in general, or of poetry in particular, the ghost was genius or enthusiasm, and in poetry we should not be surprised to find that the identification of poetry and enthusiasm was posed by the apologist of Quietism, Fénelon. "Toute l'Ecriture," he wrote in his *Lettre écrite à l'Académie Française*, "est pleine de poésie dans les endroit même où l'on ne trouve aucune trace de versification." [1] The origins of the world, religious beliefs, the beginnings of societies were inseparable from poetry, which recorded divine truths from the earliest times. It was the instrument of revelation and also of the enunciation of laws:

D'ailleurs la poésie a donné au monde les premières lois. C'est elle qui a adouci les hommes farouches et sauvages, qui les a rassemblés des forêts où ils étaient épars et errants, qui les a policés, qui a réglé les moeurs, qui a formé les familles et les nations, qui a fait sentir les douceurs de la société, qui a rappelé l'usage de la raison, cultivé la vertu, et inventé les beaux-arts. C'est elle qui a élevé les courages pour la guerre, et qui les a modérés pour la paix [Ibid.].

Fénelon takes us far from the versification theory of poetry. We may even say that he had a poetic imagination in a world given to versifiers. It is obvious that poetry is something more than poems. It was a power, a spirit which moved men, a state of mind, a certain state of society too, and in this particular context, something associated with the beginnings of society. This was brought out more forcefully by Diderot in his *De la poésie dramatique*: "La poésie veut quelque chose d'énorme, de barbare et de sauvage. . . . Quand verra-t-on naître des poètes? Ce sera après les temps de désastres et de grands malheurs; lorsque les peuples harassés commencent à respirer." [2] Poetry could

---

[1] *Lettre écrite à l'Académie Française sur l'éloquence, la poésie, l'histoire, etc.*, in *Dialogues sur l'Eloquence*, p. 307.

[2] In *Oeuvres esthétiques*, pp. 261, 262.

thus be associated with the imagination in primitive conditions and stages of society, with peoples who had strong and powerful imaginations and great passion. This, in effect, historicized poetry, and like fable fixed it to a certain time in the past or in some hypothetical future which might reproduce conditions similar to those which had obtained in the beginnings of society. Thus it was sometimes called the language of the gods:

La parole animée par les vives images, par les grandes figures, par le transport des passions, et par le charme de l'harmonie fut nommé le langage des dieux. Les peuples les plus barbares mêmes n'y ont pas été insensibles. Autant qu'on doit mépriser les mauvais poètes, autant doit-on admirer et chérir un grand poète, qui ne fait point de la poésie un jeu d'esprit, pour s'attirer une vaine gloire, mais qui l'emploie à transporter les hommes en faveur de la sagesse, de la vertu, et de la religion [Fénelon, op. cit., 308].

Clearly, even a view associating poetry with enthusiasm and a primitive imagination does not cancel the idea of its instrumentality. It makes it a more effective tool because it is more moving. However, associating poetry with imagination, religion, passion, and a fabulous past raised a very important problem, namely the possibility of great poetry in the eighteenth century in general, and, given its nature, in the French language. Thus the values of reason, science, society, taste were brought into conflict with the requirements of great poetry.

Saint-Evremond, Fontenelle, Trublet, d'Alembert, Montesquieu, Voltaire and others all knew that the cosmos of Newton or Descartes, conceived in terms of general laws and principles as a giant mechanism of forces that could be mathematically described, radically affected a poetry still founded upon the imitation of models formed and invented in a remote pre-Cartesian past. Gods and heroes could no longer be used with any credibility in poetry, and the entire stock of metaphors, figures, images, themes, and ornaments inherited from that remote past was about to be abandoned, in theory if not in practise. If it was not abandoned, it was because there were poets who did not make the connection between their versification and the new cosmos. These continued to write poetry of a traditional and rather insipid type, irrespective of the revolutions which had occurred in the heavens, just as painters continued to decorate ceilings with the ancient creatures of myth and fable. To these, science was one thing, poetry another; truth pertained to the sciences, while fiction was the province of poetry, and since there was a body of motifs ready to hand, why not use them even if they were a bit old-fashioned and paradoxical? Poetry thus became a harmless social game for the leisured and a somewhat less pleasant one for the poets, who depended upon poetry to amuse those who could give them pensions. The history of philosophy and science, indeed, are one thing (or two sometimes), and the history of poetry is another, and syntheses of all three do not always happen. One would certainly be hard put to make an eighteenth-century synthesis of this kind. Critics of a philosophical turn of mind considered the poetic game rather silly, while others thought that philosophy would eventually replace poetry and that this was to the good, since it was in line with the general progress of the human mind. Other critics deplored such a thing and thought philosophy the scourge of poetry. Montesquieu, Gibbon, and Saint-Evremond thought of the problem in historical terms and tended to associate the past with poetry and the present with rationality and a certain greyness.

Those who chose to ignore the new science in order to continue writing poetry with the use of inherited motifs did not escape criticism or difficulties, for more than science seemed to inhibit the creation of poetry in the eighteenth century. There were those who thought that the French language was not proper for great poetry, that it had been refined to excess and thereby impoverished, and that this process had gone so far that it could hardly be changed now. Taste had developed to a point which made poetry, as formerly understood and loved, wellnigh impossible: not only because of the rejection of violence and passion, the fantastic and fabulous, but also because taste required the poet to write a pure, correct, clear French. This problem particularly occupied Fénelon, who questioned French rhyme although he did not suggest abolishing it. He thought that it made for monotony, and that its rules tended to make the poet lose the advantage of variety, harmony, and ease:

Souvent la rime, qu'un poète va chercher bien loin, le réduit à allonger, et à faire languir son discours. Il lui faut deux ou trois vers postiches, pour en amener un dont il a besoin. On est scrupuleux pour n'employer que des rimes riches, et on ne l'est ni sur le fonds des pensées et des sentiments, ni sur la clarté des termes, ni sur les tours naturels, ni sur la noblesse des expressions. La rime ne nous donne que l'uniformité de finales, qui est ennuyeuse, et qu'on évite dans la prose, tant elle est loin de flatter l'oreille. Cette répétition de finales lasse même dans les grands vers héroïques, où deux masculins sont toujours suivis de deux féminins [Ibid., 310–11].

Rhyme should be relaxed in order to perfect reason, and Fénelon recommended the Latins as examples in this matter. He also found fault with the rule against inversion: "On s'est mis en pure perte dans une espèce de torture pour faire un ouvrage. Nous serions tentés de croire qu'on a cherché le difficile, plutôt que le beau" (Ibid., 314).

Yet despite all his reservations about language, inversion, rhyme, Fénelon could hardly point to a remedy. Indeed, when one ponders his reflections on poetry, one must conclude that what he finally recommends is an ideal befitting prose rather than poetry; for he too felt that the poet was obligated to write a clear poetry which would save the reader effort: "Le goût exquis craint le trop en tout, sans en excepter l'esprit même" (Ibid., 321). His ideal was simplicity. He would rid poetry of superfluous ornament: "On gagne beaucoup en perdant tous les ornements superflus, pour se borner aux beautés simples, faciles, claires et négligées en apparence. Pour la poésie, comme pour l'architecture, il faut que tous les morceaux nécessaires se tournent en ornements naturels" (Ibid., 322-23). Fénelon's ideal of beauty is reminiscent of that which would triumph universally in the closing decades of the eighteenth century, and he pointed the way towards the *beau idéal*, confused with natural simplicity in an age still dominated by Baroque ornament. In a sense his poetic ideal is to be found in the prose of his *Telemachus*. What he did understand very well, and what the versifiers did not, was that poetry was an evocation of an ideal world, something which must take us away from the present through the imagination; and this other world which Fénelon posited as the object of poetry was the Golden Age, which he associated, much as would Winckelmann later on, with *le beau simple, aimable, et commode* (the terminology is not Winckelmann's but the spirit is). However, the term "poetry" has now, in effect, merged into a general concept of beauty which is universal: "Le Beau ne perdrait rien de son prix, quand il serait commun à tout le genre humain; il en serait plus estimable. La rareté est un défaut, et une pauvreté de la nature" (Ibid., 327-28). Fénelon was an admirer of Raphael and Poussin, and it is in the world which these painters represented that he found poetry. But it was precisely this world of antiquity and poetry which to some seemed forever lost. Yet it was this sense of loss which in the end would prove to be the source of a new, or at least renewed, poetry: for from this sense of loss and the nostalgia for and sense of the past there arose a new poetic feeling. But before this could triumph, poetry would have to cease being associated with the Classical ideal of *la belle nature* altogether, for it was precisely this association which limited its potential and restricted it to the forms and aesthetic of art. This is made clear by Batteux, who subsumes poetry under a general system of imitation which merges poetry with the concept of art as he and his contemporaries understood it: "L'art poétique est renfermé dans l'imitation de la belle nature" (*Les Beaux-Arts*, 134). Batteux's view may be seen as a systematic presentation of the intimations of Fénelon; for after all, where but in the Golden Age could *la belle nature* be located? Even if one argued the Golden Age was a fiction, then *la belle nature* could still be thought of as an ideal realm: in which case poetry came once more to be regarded either as a representation of that realm or else as the embellishment of given language. Dissatisfaction with poetry in the eighteenth century thus also meant doubts concerning *la belle nature* and the whole aesthetic of art. Batteux's treatment of poetry can hardly be considered as of much help.

The rejuvenation of poetry in the eighteenth century did not come from criticism, even from the best, such as that of Diderot. Rather, it came from the prose writings of Jean-Jacques Rousseau, who unlike his contemporaries had a feeling, not for *la belle nature*, but for his own and that of his youth. And eventually this feeling for nature, however vaguely understood, fixed not only on the Greek and Roman past but also upon a more immediate nature accessible to all, or at least to those who could travel to meditate upon the lakes or the Alps, created a new poetic feeling. This feeling did not always take the form of verse, which remained for a long time dominated by the Classical canons of taste, but it is undeniable that the *Rêveries* of Rousseau and the later long novel of Sénancour, *Oberman*, represent the new poetry, precisely because this was no longer founded upon the aesthetic of *la belle nature*, but was rather associated with feeling and with ideas of time and infinity. But until these appeared it may well be that, for those who found the verse of the eighteenth century insipid or frivolous, tedious, repetitious, and banal, the opera was the true refuge of poetry — even though, significantly enough, poetry was but one part of that great art form.

*   *   *

See also: *Beauty, Nature, Opera*.
Bibliography: Diderot, Du Bos, Fénelon, Fontenelle, La Motte, Montesquieu; Voltaire; Du Cerceau, Rémond de Saint-Mard; and also, for a thorough treatment of the program, Margaret Gilman, *The Idea of*

Poetry in France; from Houdar de la Motte to Baudelaire (Cambridge, Mass., 1958). See also the best book on the subject, Robert Finch, *The Sixth Sense: Individualism in French Poetry, 1686–1760* (Toronto, 1966).

PUBLIC

THE JUDGMENT OF TASTE, discussed and defined by philosophers, ultimately rested upon a public which played the role of a final court of appeal. The public and its judgment put an end to all vain and endless discussion as to the merits of a work of poetry or painting. This role of the public seems to have been accepted by Boileau, Du Bos, and Voltaire, though it was no longer accepted without question after the reforms effected in the Academy of Painting and Sculpture and in the period of the *retour à l'Antique*.

Du Bos was very much concerned with the public in connection with the judgment of taste and the establishment of value in art and poetry, and was careful to define the public — or rather publics, for it was clear that when works first appeared they were judged by two publics rather than one, namely *les gens du métier* and *le public*. The first result of the appearance of a new work was to leave the public undecided as to its real merits: "Le public demeure indécis sur la question, s'il est bon ou mauvais à tout prendre, et il en croit même quelquefois les gens du métier qui le trompent, mais il ne les croit que durant un temps assez court" (*Réflexions critiques*, II, 337). But once a certain time had elapsed, the public appreciated the new work at its true value and either gave it the rank it deserved or forgot it. And the public did not usually err: "Il ne se trompe point dans cette décision, parce qu'il en juge avec désinteressement, et parce qu'il en juge par sentiment" (Ibid.). What Du Bos meant by *désinteressement* was not exactly the same thing that Kant later meant. Du Bos defined it in terms prompted by what seems to have been his knowledge of the literary and artistic milieu of his own day. There is no attempt on his part to define this disinterestedness in metaphysical terms: there is no question of the relation of the aesthetic judgment to beauty, its autonomy and so on.

The public judges disinterestedly, because its vanity is not involved, because it bases its judgment upon sentiment, the impression which the work presented makes on it, and finally, because it is not a public made up of individualistic experts. Poets, opined Du Bos, are of such temperament as to believe that when they present a new work the entire town is interested in this work and its author and is divided into factions which are either for him or against him, and that the work will be judged in the interested manner of personal involvement. But, as Du Bos put it, there will not be fifty persons who will take a part for or against the poet himself. "La plupart de ceux en qui il suppose des sentiments de haine ou d'amitié très-décidés, sont dans l'indifférence, et disposés à juger de l'auteur par sa comédie, et non de la comédie par son auteur" (Ibid., 338). Du Bos was above all concerned to distinguish the judgment of the public from that of the artisans and poets themselves on the one hand, and the critics and pedants on the other. The public has better sense than the experts: "Les professeurs qui toute leur vie ont enseigné la logique, sont-ils ceux qui connaissent le mieux quand un homme parle de bons sens, et quand il raisonne avec justesse?" (Ibid., 347.) But it must not be assumed that by the public Du Bos meant what we tend to mean. The public was not expert in matters of artistic production, it judged only on the basis of the impression which the work made on it; but it was not a passive mass audience. It is indeed referred to as "les esprits du premier ordre," and may be identified as that same public to which Boileau had already appealed, and which Molière had counted on to oppose the pedants. This public could judge very well without knowing the rules of poetry or painting: "Tous les hommes, à l'aide du sentiment intérieur qui est en eux, connaissent, sans savoir les règles, si les productions des arts sont des bons ou des mauvais ouvrages, et si le raisonnement qu'ils entendent, conclut bien" (Ibid., 398). And more specifically, in the theatre: "Le parterre, sans savoir les règles, juge d'une pièce de théâtre aussi bien que les gens du métier" (Ibid., 379). He was, however, very careful to limit this public to those who had a certain degree of education, knowledge of the world, and some acquaintance with the arts:

C'est que je ne comprends point le bas peuple dans le public capable de prononcer sur les poèmes ou sur les tableaux, comme de décider à quel degré ils sont excellents. Le mot de public ne renferme ici que les personnes qui ont acquis des lumières, soit par la lecture, soit par le commerce du monde. Elles sont les seules qui puissent marquer le rang des poèmes et des tableaux, quoiqu'il se rencontre dans les ouvrages excellents des beautés capables de se faire sentir au peuple du plus bas étage, et de l'obliger de se récrier. Mais comme il est sans connaissance des autres ouvrages du même genre, il n'est pas en état de discerner à quel point le poème qui le fait pleurer, est excellent, ni quel rang il doit tenir parmi les autres poèmes. Le public, dont il s'agit ici, est donc borné aux personnes qui lisent, qui connaisent les spectacles, qui voient et qui entendent parler de tableaux, ou qui ont acquis de quelque manière que ce soit, ce discernement qu'on appelle *goût de comparaison* [Ibid., 352].

It is quite clear that the sentiment on which Du Bos bases his judgment is complemented by knowledge of the entire convention of art, acquaintance with works of art of one type or another. It is not pure sensation. It is, indeed, precisely this knowledge of the arts which distinguishes his public from the *bas peuple*. As men, all are capable of being touched, *bas peuple* as well as *honnêtes gens*, but only the latter are capable of judging of the merits of works of art because only the latter are acquainted with the arts. It will also be noted that this particular type of knowledge and discernment referred to as *goût de comparaison* differentiates *les esprits du premier ordre* from the experts, from the artisans as well as the critics; for the knowledge involved is quite different from that possessed by experts. Also, this *goût de comparaison* was itself limited. Not everyone was a universal judge. Those well acquainted with French tragedy were not ipso facto proper judges of the works of Homer or Virgil. Thus the public itself was a final court of appeals only within limited areas of competence. Thus, the Italians, Du Bos thought, were generally better judges of painting than the French, who, on the whole or at least in Paris, were good judges of dramatic production. The reason for this was the difference in artistic environment of the two populations.

Turning his attention to the judgment of the *gens du métier*, Du Bos found reason to distrust it for three reasons:

La sensibilité des gens du métier est usée. Ils jugent de tout par voie de discussion. Enfin ils sont prévenus en faveur de quelque partie de l'art, et ils la comptent dans les jugements généraux qu'ils portent pour plus qu'elle ne vaut. Sous le nom de gens du métier, je comprends ici, non seulement les personnes, qui composent ou qui peignent; mais encore un grand nombre de ceux qui écrivent sur les poèmes et sur les tableaux [Ibid., II, 383–84].

There was only one exception to this rule: artists of genius were obviously men worth listening to. But these were very rare; on the whole, the *gens du métier* were artisans who painted and wrote, not out of conviction, but because they earned their living by it. These were more likely to be interested in technical questions than in the overall effect of a poem or painting. Their judgment was also often false because they were liable to be jealous of each other. Their judgment, in short, was interested rather than disinterested. But in the end the limited public of connoisseurs did not suffice either; for a work of art had to appeal to all men and it was only the ability of a work of art to touch all men which assured its survival for posterity. But it is doubtful that "all men" here meant all men as we mean it: it was again the restricted public, but that of all ages of history than of merely one. In short, what pleased the Roman gentleman, if worthy at all, ought also still to be able to please the *honnête homme* of the early eighteenth century and the centuries to come.

Du Bos' view of the role of the public in the judgment of taste and the establishment of artistic values was the result of the failure of criticism founded on the rules, the fruitless disputes about color and drawing in the Academy of Painting, for instance, or the criticism of the pedantic dogmatists directed at Molière and others, but also probably resulted from an acquaintance with and knowledge of the cabals, jealousies, and rivalries among men of letters and painters of his own times. In addition to this we must not forget that men of letters in his day still had not won the respect they obtained in the second half of the eighteenth century. They depended upon the public of *honnêtes gens* for their livelihood, and it seemed that they must also depend upon its taste. However, Du Bos' view of the public is also a function of the judgment upon taste as founded upon sentiment rather than expertise. The question of genius is also involved, as witness his exemptions of genius from the strictures put upon the opinions of the *gens du métier*. Indeed, as the century progressed, or if you will, regressed towards an aesthetic of nature and an expression theory of genius, the role of the public and the value put on its taste changed accordingly. The judgment of the *philosophes* as critics, and of the artist as a genius, took precedence over what now appeared to be the mere taste of the amateurs.

In truth, the views of Du Bos represent an ideal model of the relation between art, taste, and the public. In historical terms neither poets nor public trusted the judgment of the public, however restricted, completely. One wrote as if one did; one professed that the town and the court knew best. Poets and writers rewrote in order to please this public. But in practise one sometimes made sure, by highly nonaesthetic means, that the public was pleased by the right works by insuring the success of such works. This was true especially in the theatre, for success there was sometimes sought through the use of paid claques, trained to applaud at certain times. The use of the gazettes for criticism could also be of some help, not to mention the protection of powerful lords and men of letters, who could put in a good word here and there.

All this means that the public was indeed highly important, but not for the reasons described by Du Bos — not, that is, because of some inborn or at least preexisting true aesthetic judgment possessed by the ladies and gentlemen of the court and the town. On the contrary, the public was important because its taste had to be formed, its judgment inclined in one or another direction. In the course of the century the relation between artists, the poets and painters, and public was to change, and on the eve of the French Revolution the former were much less dependent on the public than they had been. Or at least they were so in a different and much more subtle way; the public was broader, therefore less personalized, less clearly defined, and it may be that the notion of a disinterested judgment of taste, acting, so to speak, independently of historical conditions, classes, and the necessity to please in order to eat reflects this change of relation. When patrons were well known, when artists painted for specific connoisseurs and amateurs who knew what they wanted, then obviously the artist's taste reflected that of the patron; the same may be said in regard to certain types of poetry that can hardly be thought of without reference to a certain social milieu. But the painters who began to think of glory, of being exhibited and made famous through the Salons, thought of something much vaguer, more abstract and ideal, than the taste of such and such a lord; the same holds in letters for those writers who wrote for a general public interested in the new topics of the day, progress, humanity, nature, and also in personal experience and vision. In short, Du Bos could set up the public, as he defined and restricted it, as the ultimate judge, given the public of his day, but in other periods the public could not be accepted as the ultimate judge. In the second half of the eighteenth century there were, in truth, two publics rather than one, and neither had much disinterestedness, because the arts in question were inseparable from social considerations. Disinterestedness is perhaps possible only after the issues of a time are resolved or forgotten so that the arts with which they are associated can be separated from them. In the case of the eighteenth century, as Tocqueville saw, there were two literatures in the making, one aristocratic in nature, the other tending towards a democratic society. After 1789 it became possible to be disinterested about some works; it was perhaps less possible before that time.

* * *

See also: *Amateur, Connoisseur, Critical Theory, Curieux, Genius, Please and Instruct, Rules, Taste.*
Bibliography: Du Bos, Voltaire; Moncrif; as for secondary sources,

much remains to be done in the area of the public of the eighteenth century, but see John Lough, *Paris Theatre Audiences in the 17th and 18th Centuries* (Oxford, 1957); Daniel Mornet, "Les Enseignements des bibliothèques privées (1750–1780)," in the *Revue d'Histoire littéraire de la France*, XVII, 1910, is more on taste than on judgment, but is indirectly pertinent; also, for a broader view of the question brought up to the present, Levin L. Schücking, *The Sociology of Literary Taste* (Chicago, 1966).

RULES

FRENCH LITERATURE of the seventeenth century has long been associated with rules, and students of that literature are familiar with the celebrated rule of the three unities of time, place, and action. If one thinks of the term "legislator of Parnassus," sometimes given erroneously to Boileau, one may be forgiven the tendency to imagine poets and painters at their desks or easels, working with the rules in the back of their minds and constrained, against their natural inclinations, to confine themselves and their geniuses within artificial limits. What we may term this mythical image of the rules as so many fetters may be traced back even to the seventeenth century, and is even lent some credence by Fontenelle, who knew better than to believe in myths: "Alors M. Corneille," he writes in his "Vie de Corneille,"

par l'étude d'*Aristote* et d'*Horace*, par son expérience, par ses réflexions, et plus encore par son génie, trouva les véritables règles du poème dramatique, et découvrit les sources du beau, qu'il a depuis ouvertes à tout le monde dans les discours qui sont à la tête de ses comédies.[1]

In point of fact, despite the appearance of Aristotle and Horace at the beginning of this statement, ideas and attitudes on the rules were much more subtle and uncertain than we might suspect from innumerable manuals of literature and even from the statements of seventeenth-century critics. The term "rules," *règles*, was ambiguous and was used in two broad ways, to prescribe certain values and to describe certain practises; the rules were at once normative and empirical, and it is well to keep this double nature in mind. Also, as is the case in most Classical aesthetics, the rules were subject to various types of distinctions which tended to give them flexibility. Corneille himself was among the first to make such distinctions and thereby modify attitudes concerning

[1] "Vie de Corneille l'aîné," in *Le Théâtre de P. Corneille* (Paris, 1738), II, lxxx.

rules. He insisted that the rules of the drama, for example, had been elaborated, not by playwrights, but by philosophers and savants; by men, in other words, who had no experience in the theatre. While it was very well to know these rules, and though they might make a man more learned, they could hardly help to produce better plays. Thus, already in the time of Corneille it was agreed, by some at least, that the rules were one thing and practise another. Indeed, upon close examination the passage from Fontenelle cited above supports this attitude, for while Aristotle and Horace are given first place in order of credit, they are not given the most weight, that being accorded to genius ("et plus encore par son génie"). The rules presupposed genius; they did *not* mean: When you sit down to write a play or an epic, reread Aristotle, Horace, or Boileau, not to mention Le Bossu or d'Aubignac. As Fontenelle also wrote, concerning his own *Eglogues*: I wrote first and then made the rules, and just because rules exist it does not follow one must follow them. And, as Voltaire aptly wrote of Le Bossu: "Son *Traité sur le poème épique* a beaucoup de réputation, mais il ne fera jamais de poètes" (Cf. *Siècle de Louis XIV*). In our own times Professor Adam, in his history of seventeenth-century French literature, has underlined the same points concerning the relation of the rules to the new theatre:

Ce n'est ni directement d'Aristote, ni même des théoriciens italiens qu'est venue la première impulsion. Ce ne sont pas des raisons de doctrine qui ont été d'abord alléguées. Ce n'est même pas le mouvement général des esprits vers l'ordre et la discipline qui a imposé aux écrivains une formule nouvelle. Il s'agit d'abord d'une entreprise étroitement limitée, menée par un jeune auteur, sur les indications de deux amateurs éclairés, inspirée par l'exemple de la pastorale italienne, et qui s'appuie sur l'heureux succès de l'*Aminta* et du *Pastor Fido*.[2]

Thus, when Corneille reformed the theatre by the example of his own pieces, he did not do it in order to observe the laws set down by or derived from Aristotle, but because little by little dramatists had come to learn the value of a concentrated dramatic action. The rules, in this sense, were arrived at empirically and artistically on the example of specific Italian artistic models. Later, practise was pondered upon and rules were elaborated and discussed, and even before the Academy imposed the principle of rules, there had been a ten-year polemic about

[2] Antoine Adam, *Histoire de la littérature française au XVIIe Siècle* (Paris, 1948–62), I, 435–36.

them. In 1637 they were simply established in principle by decree of the Academy, and almost everyone admitted their existence. Savants elaborated them in detail, but poets and men of letters found ways of justifying departures from them — which really means that for any set of rules which a poet found distasteful he could always invent another set to counteract or to justify a departure from them. Thus, to the rules of the three unities and of *bienséance*, strictly interpreted, Molière and others opposed the rule of pleasure, to wit that the first rule of all theatre was to please the audience rather than, by implication, the critics or savants who had elaborated a complex body of rules.

Apropos of the rules another observation may be made: not only was the term "rule" ambiguous, but discussion of the rules also implied different points of view and positions from which to discuss the arts. The rules imply a division between the poets and the critics, and the dislike and discredit of the critics dates from the seventeenth century. Perrault puts them on the lowest level of the literary hierarchy: they are those men who cannot themselves write poetry. Moreover, the fact that the rules could be used to defend various artistic positions implied a gap between artistic practise and reflection upon the arts. One may say that modern aesthetic theory began with the elaboration of the rules, and that in this there may already be perceived the ambiguities of such an enterprise. One can make a case for Chapelain as one of the first modern aestheticians, for it was he who sought to establish dramatic practise upon general, universally valid, principles. Now, the problem for anyone attempting to subsume artistic practise and genius under certain universal and rationally established rules lies in the fact that artists and poets tend to go beyond such rules, to escape them, to contradict them, or simply to work outside their system. The result in the Classical period was that the body of rules increased for those who attempted to bring artistic and poetic production under the authority of reason and principle, while the poets tended to gradually reduce them to a matter of generally accepted practise and common sense. Examples of the former tendency will be found in Father Mourgues' *Traité de la poésie française*, which is a detailed elaboration of the rules governing versification, and the latter in Voltaire's *Essay on dramatic poetry*, in which he argues that in the last analysis the rules of epic poetry can be reduced to the following: that an action must be one, simple, great, interesting, and complete. If we examine Father Mourgues' treatise it is not difficult to understand why the poets disregarded the rules and reduced them to a few tautologies. For Mourgues' work cannot really be accepted as prescriptive: it is above all descriptive of practise. Opening his book at any page will demonstrate this: "La voyelle *i*, et la diphtongue *ui* peuvent rimer ensemble se trouvant à l'endroit de l'appui devant les mêmes consonnes: Exemples.

(vivre) (captive) (quitte) (évite   )
(suivre) (suive) (fuitte) (poursuite)" (p. 103).

And so on. One thinks of present-day linguistic studies which are of great interest to linguists but which are of doubtful utility to newspaper men, editors, writers, poets, playwrights (except perhaps Ionesco), and novelists. In short, to refer to the gap alluded to above between rules and artistic practise, we may describe it as the distance between the classroom or *cabinet d'étude* and the poet's writing table and play-wright's stage.

What was one to do about the rules? Were they false, were they true, were they useful, or were they useless? As in beauty and taste, so in rules: the seventeenth and eighteenth centuries compromised by drawing distinctions. The matter was put rather well by Montesquieu in his "Essai sur le goût dans les choses de la nature et de l'art":

Tous les ouvrages de l'art ont des règles générales qui sont des guides qu'il ne faut jamais perdre de vue.

Mais comme les lois sont toujours justes dans leur être général, mais presque toujours injustes dans l'application; de même les règles, toujours vraies dans la théorie, peuvent devenir fausses dans l'hypothèse (*Oeuvres complètes*, II, 1260).

Reason and its requirements were thus reconciled with practise and its demands, and as was so often the case in the post-Renaissance society of the *ancien régime*, one knew what was right and true, but one often did only what one could or had to. In the arts this did not create a very serious or even a very wide discrepancy. Indeed, one may even say that the distance between general and valid rules and particular applications was necessary to the poet and the artist: the distance was the area of his freedom of choice. It was here that he exercised his genius or his judgment. As Montesquieu further refined this notion of general and particular rules:

Quoique chaque effet dépende d'une cause générale, il s'y mêle tant d'autres causes particulières, que chaque effet a, en quelque façon, une cause à part. Ainsi l'art donne les règles, et le goût les exceptions; le goût nous découvre en quelles occasions l'art doit soumettre, et en quelles occasions il doit être soumis [Ibid.].

It is clear from this passage that the rules were derived from the practise of the arts and from established models; an aesthetic of art supposes rules, tradition, usages, genres within which artists and poets
worked and thought. But within this artistic-aesthetic milieu or establishment a considerable degree of latitude was left the poet, painter,
or amateur because of the function of taste as a control upon the rules,
a basis for judgment as to their true power, limits, and worth. Within
a system of rules, taste allowed for flexibility, innovation, and questioning of the rules themselves. It was understood that within the Classical aesthetic rules had to be broken, exceptions found, escapes devised,
so that the arts could continue to live. This was clear enough to a poet
like Voltaire, who wrote that rules did not make poets, but it was sometimes less clear to critics and savants. The point of complete freedom
vis-à-vis the rules was perhaps best put by Condillac:

On demande, par exemple, quelle est l'essence des poèmes dramatiques qu'on
appelle *comédies*; et si certaines pièces auxquelles on donne ce nom méritent
de le porter.

Je remarque que le premier qui a imaginé des comédies, n'a point eu de
modèle: par conséquent, l'essence de cette sorte de poème était uniquement
dans la notion qu'il s'en est faite. Ceux qui sont venus après lui ont succes-
sivement ajouté quelque chose à cette première notion, et ont par là changé
l'essence de la comédie. Nous avons le droit d'en faire autant; mais, au lieu
d'en user, nous consultons les modèles que nous avons aujourd'hui, et nous
formons notre idée d'après ceux qui nous plaisent davantage. En conséquence,
nous n'admettons dans la classe des comédies, que certaines pièces, et nous
en excluons toutes les autres. Qu'on demande ensuite si tel poème est une
comédie, ou non; nous répondrons chacun selon les notions que nous nous
sommes faites; et, comme elles ne sont pas les mêmes, nous paraîtrons prendre
des partis différents. Si nous voulions substituer les idées à la place des noms,
nous connaîtrions bientôt que nous ne différons que par la manière de nous
exprimer. Au lieu de borner ainsi la notion d'une chose, il serait bien plus
raisonnable de l'étendre à mesure qu'on trouve de nouveaux genres qui peuvent lui être subordonnés. Ce serait ensuite une recherche curieuse et solide
que d'examiner quel genre est supérieur aux autres [*Essai sur l'Origine des
Connaissances Humaines*, 1746].

In this passage the rules have not been done away with, but they have
been opened to such an extent that they are hardly binding any more:
they follow imagination and invention, they no longer limit it. In effect
this point of view is not too different from the position of a Fontenelle
or a Montesquieu. The point is that one began at this point to think

about the rules no longer with reference solely to established artistic models to be imitated and the judgment of taste, but also with reference to nature.

Within the general development of aesthetics the rules hold an important part and represent a salient aspect of aesthetic theory. One might say that the initial philosophical reflection upon works of art brought on the idea of rules and that further reflection upon rules led to the notion of taste and genius. We are thus tempted to formulate the following *rule* of aesthetic speculation: that the history of aesthetics since the seventeenth century has gone through three entire stages: in the first, rules of art were elaborated; in the second, philosophers speculated about beauty, taste, genius, and nature; in the third, they elaborated the naturalistic fallacy; and in a final stage, that in which we now find ourselves, they are at last questioning their own assumptions, wondering about perception and language, and seeking a language appropriate to the discussion of the arts — which means, in effect, that we are back in the seventeenth century, or in a similar position, though this time less sure, perhaps, of the prerogatives of philosophy to subsume everything under itself. Aesthetic speculation tends, indeed, to become more and more autonomous, more distinct from philosophy itself.

* * *

See also: *Art, Critical Theory, Genius, Taste.*
Bibliography: Aubignac, Boileau, Chapelain, Corneille, Fontenelle, Montesquieu, Terrasson.

SATIRE

SATIRE, IF WE ARE to believe Boileau, is the tool of truth:

> L'ardeur de se montrer, et non pas de médire,
> Arma la vérité du vers de la satire.
> Lucile le premier osa la faire voir,
> Aux vices des Romains présenta le miroir,
> Vengea l'humble vertu, de la richesse altière,
> Et l'honnête homme à pied, du faquin en litière.
> Horace à cette aigreur mêla son enjoûment;
> On ne fut plus ni fat ni sot impunément;
> Et malheur à tout nom, qui, propre à la censure,
> Put entrer dans un vers sans rompre la mesure!
> [*Art poétique,* II]

The task of satire is to show men their vices. The allusion to it as a mirror implies a certain distance between the poet and his objects, but it also means that men are capable of assuming a certain distance vis-à-vis themselves, or in short that they will look at themselves. Satire supposes a certain standard of civility, and if the mirror is held up at all it is because to those to whom it is held up do not live up to this standard. It is related to comedy in that it also acts as a corrective to human nature, though its effect is hardly to make men laugh or smile at themselves because it is sharper than comedy and is not so much a spectacle as a sometimes cruel revelation. Satire assumes right judgment, but hardly pity or charity; it is not a Christian art form, and it is probably not democratic either. It is significant that in the eighteenth century it changed form; that moralistic age tended to deplore satire, so that it gradually tended to change its nature and in its new form came to be directed against institutions, beliefs, and modes of behavior rather than against supposedly universal human traits of character.

Satire could be playful as well as serious; it could prick, or it could wound, and it was considered a dangerous genre for all concerned. Victims of satire sometimes owed their immortality to it, as witness the numerous victims of Pope, Molière, Voltaire, and Boileau. It could be in verse or in prose form, and in the latter its range was considerably widened in the course of the eighteenth century. Voltaire's *fusées volantes* may be regarded as new forms of satire, as may some of his moral tales or novels. Diderot's *Neveu de Rameau* was also considered a satire by its author. Rousseau, significantly enough, was not satirical; he was perhaps too moral, not sceptical enough about human folly, too inclined to believe in the goodness of men, too involved in himself, to be a satirist; and while he was obviously very intelligent, he was not malignant enough for satire. Satire is the tool of a particular type of intelligence, one not free of malice but also impatient with injustice, stupidity, or, to use a word made famous by Pope, dullness. Indeed, we may say that the satirist supposes dullness to be an ever-present danger, and that the values and virtues of civility are, in effect, victories over dullness, which is associated with chaos and darkness. The whole enterprise of the Enlightenment can be seen as the triumph of various forms of satire over the darkness attributed to certain institutions and forms of fanaticism. It is also possible, indeed, to associate satire with an aesthetic of art rather than of nature, because within that aesthetic, on the supposition of satire, chaos, darkness, and dullness are extensions or forms of the nature, the vicious nature, of man. Assume man is fundamentally good, and you abandon satire in favor of education.

Because it is often directed against dullness in various forms, satire can also be associated with criticism, or rather with a special form of it that we may term counter-criticism. Voltaire is an example of this, as is Pope, for both were masters in dealing with their critics. Thus satire could be a weapon dangerous to men of letters, critics, or pedants who dared to attack or censure certain powers of the Republic of Letters. The satirical vein, indeed, sometimes sufficed to establish such powers: it was a species of terrorism within that Republic. Satire as counter-criticism made it possible to meet the critics on ground other than their own. There was no intention of refutation, but solely of destroying the critic's reputation; he was made ridiculous, and the laughter directed at him diverted attention from whatever truth there might have been in his criticism. Satire could thus be used as a defense against purism, against rules and the strictures of those who presumed to legislate to poets.

Though regarded as a dangerous tool and sometimes questioned as to its nobility as a genre, satire was perhaps a necessary escape valve for bile in a world supposedly governed by decorum. Within the closed system of Classical aesthetic-moral values, it allowed the writer a certain free play. Through it, he might give vent to his humors and could come closest to self-expression, even though it was self-expression channeled in certain directions and given an accepted form. In this respect the *Satires* of Boileau deserve special attention, for close reading may well give invaluable insight into the mentality of the author and the *métier* of the writer of the time. There is little doubt that the ability to write excellent satire must have been an invaluable help to a writer; it guaranteed his security; like the Prince of Machiavelli, the able satirist ruled alone and undisputed, possessing his own arms, thanks to a healthy fear about him. Can it be doubted that Boileau, Pope, and Voltaire attained their eminence in part because they were dangerous to attack? If we look to the satirist himself, we also see that this capacity for satire was a built-in system of defense, for it was recognized by men like Boileau and Voltaire, and later by Stendhal, that intelligence is really an insult to the rest of mankind. As Boileau put it in his Seventh Satire:

> Un éloge ennuyeux, un froid panégyrique,
> Peut pourrir à son aise au fond d'une boutique,
> Ne craint point du public les jugements divers,
> Et n'a pour ennemis que la poudre et les vers:
> Mais un auteur malin, qui rit et qui fait rire,

> Qu'on blâme en le lisant, et pourtant qu'on veut lire,
> Dans ses plaisants accès qui se croit tout permis,
> De ses propres rieurs se fait des ennemis.
> Un discours trop sincère aisément nous outrage:
> Chacun dans ce miroir pense voir son visage:
> Et tel, en vous lisant admire chaque trait,
> Qui dans le fond de l'âme et vous craint et vous hait.

Given this fact, unhappy the writer who, like Pope, Boileau, or Voltaire, cannot stand stupidity. Unhappy too the writer, born with a sharp critical mind, and who, like Flaubert or Valéry, seems to see through everything, as Boileau put it:

> Tout ce qui s'offre à moi passe par l'étamine.
> Le mérite pourtant m'est toujours précieux:
> Mais tout fat me déplaît, et me blesse les yeux;
> Je le poursuis partout, comme un chien fait sa proie,
> Et ne le sens jamais qu'aussitôt je n'aboie.

It is also noteworthy that in this same satire Boileau admits that despite the dangers inherent in the art of satire and in the position occupied by the satirist, he cannot help himself, for he must write:

> Dût ma muse par là choquer tout l'univers,
> Riche, gueux, triste ou gai, je veux faire des vers.

It is a matter of humors and bile, and satirists are obviously thus not by election, but by birth:

> Enfin c'est mon plaisir; je veux me satisfaire.
> Je ne puis bien parler, et ne saurais me taire;
> Et, dès qu'un mot plaisant vient luire à mon esprit
> Je n'ai point de repos qu'il ne soit en écrit:
> Je ne résiste point au torrent qui m'entraine.

It must not be supposed, however, that satire was always a matter of bilious reactions against writers and writings of a mediocre nature. It can also be considered in terms of play, and as such it is indicative of the entire game of literature, of a sense of play not necessarily fair about life and letters. Thus letters flourished along with laughter; they were connected with the pleasures of the mind, and literature supposedly lived independently of the *esprit de sérieux*, heavy scholarship, and the secular pieties of pedants. Satiric bile was directed against those who would spoil the game, and these were often dullards or very moral critics. The game too was supposed to be played well so that satire was used to put the presumptuous in their place, keep them away from the game. It is precisely this sense of play which makes these satires still readable, however closely they were bound to contemporary issues and events.

Insofar as satire is indicative of this play concerning letters and the life of letters, its novel use in the eighteenth century, especially in France, marks an important change in literature itself and in the uses to which literature is put. For satire, as used by Boileau and Pope, primarily concerned with the foibles of men of letters, supposes that the game of literature is its own end and that the rules of the game are above all aesthetic. But once literature is used for utilitarian purposes, for the betterment of mankind and the improvement of society, satire can no longer function in the same way. It may still exist, but its form, function, and purpose will change. Thus, in the eighteenth century, the sense of play ceased and gave way to a serious purpose, and humor gave way to malicious and destructive wit. The power of wit in both Voltaire and Pope was remarkably strong, but the form, tone, and objects of that wit were quite different, though neither author could suffer fools. Thus one may say that, little by little in the course of the eighteenth century, and thanks mostly to Voltaire, satire was transformed and mobilized; a literary form and weapon came to be used for extraliterary purposes, and it might well be said that the satirical spirit simply reincarnated itself in the *esprit voltairien*. It might conceivably be argued that the genre died with Voltaire and could not be revived, because some writers espoused the idea of progress, while those who did not sought flight into ideal realms of the imagination — attitudes which might be objects of satire, but which hardly admitted it as part of the rules of the new game.

STYLE

"LE STYLE, C'EST L'HOMME MEME," said Buffon in a celebrated *Discours sur le style*, and this particular definition of style has been cited ever since. One is tempted to associate it with an expressive theory of art, but this would be an error. One must not forget Pascal's *moi haïssable*; one ought not to take Buffon's *l'homme même* for the *moi* of the writer.

The concept of style in the eighteenth century was quite complex and was not associated with an expressive theory of art. It was affected by assumptions concerning art, nature, taste, genius, and beauty. On the whole, one could associate it with a certain rapport between art and nature which did not remain fixed, but varied with one's assumptions concerning the relation of art to nature. The eccentric Cartaud de la Vilatte saw style as an expression of the soul, which means that he saw it as closely connected to human nature: "Le style est une empreinte de l'âme, où l'on voit les divers caractères des passions."[1] One could analyze style to find the passions of an author: "La passion d'un homme dont l'esprit est plein de vues fines et délicates, est élégante et réflechie" (Ibid., 261). Marivaux also saw a rapport between style and a man's mind and character, and had some things to say about Montaigne's style which were certainly not in accord with the view of style in the *Grand Siècle*. When Rousseau considered writing his *Confessions* he realized that complete sincerity implied a new style of writing. Diderot thought that the style of a painter was an expression of his character. It was generally accepted that the style was often inseparable from the *tour d'esprit* of a writer. Geniuses were allowed more personal style than men without genius who also wrote. As Montesquieu put it: "Un homme qui écrit bien n'écrit pas comme on a écrit, mais comme il écrit, et c'est souvent en parlant mal qu'il parle bien" ("Mes Pensées," in *Oeuvres*, I, 1261). Such remarks, however, are more the exception than the rule in eighteenth-century writings on style. More often one finds opinions, though usually less well turned, like that of Voltaire in his *Dictionnaire philosophique*: "Sans le style, il est impossible qu'il y ait un seul bon ouvrage en aucun genre d'éloquence et de poésie." One is more likely to find that the eighteenth century thought of style in terms of artistic necessity rather than of personal expression. The ideal of style is different for those who conceive of it in general terms, implying an almost impersonal style, and those who think of style in terms of the expression of genius. It may be that the majority held to the former ideal, because thought and representation were one.

In fact, there were various meanings given the word "style" in the eighteenth century, just as there were many styles. If style was associated with art or eloquence, then style varied with subject matter, genre, object of discourse; if style was associated with nature, it varied from one writer, language, or nation, to another. As an instance of style in-

[1] *Essai historiqe et philosophique sur le goût* (London, 1751), p. 258.

separable from an aesthetic of art and beauty, we may cite Father
André's definition:

J'appelle style une certaine suite d'expressions et de tours tellement soutenue
dans le cours d'un ouvrage, que toutes parties ne semblent être que les traits
d'un même pinceau: ou si nous considérons le discours comme une espèce
de musique naturelle, un certain arrangement de paroles, qui forment ensemble des accords, d'où il résulte à l'oreille une harmonie agréable [*Essai*,
101].

Or, as Voltaire put it — with more style: "Il est bon que chaque chose
soit à sa place." Both these statements really suppose as an ideal the
belle nature of Batteux, the *beauté essentielle* of Father André, the artistic values of the *grand goût*. This view of style is inseparable from
other values such as order, unity, clarity, reason, nature, and harmony.
It is style associated with art, with specific genres and their requirements, and such a view supposes that the *moi* of the writer will subordinate itself to the laws of genre, reason, and decorum. The style will thus
be in a sense completely impersonal, almost objective. Style and content will be one and the same, because the soul of the poet will act as if
it were not a prisoner in a body. Yet it is apparent that even this view
of style was not incompatible with the *tour d'esprit* of the poet. A
dualism was implied which obtained as well in matters of taste and
beauty generally: a universal ideal of perfection and style was posed;
the poet or artist strove to attain it but, human nature being what it
is, could only hope to approximate the perfect. Style possessed both
universal and particular characteristics; it was impersonal as well as
personal. One could conceivably argue in favor of personality, as did
Marivaux, because a personal style could be more lively, charming,
piquant, than the universal. The notion of the *je ne sais quoi* would play
an important role in such a definition or view of style since it could
be associated with the *tour d'esprit* of the author while the qualities
of style were supposedly universal. Style thought of in universal and
rational terms was thus the *manière de bien penser dans les ouvrages
de l'esprit*, to use the title, quite appropriate, of Father Bouhours' book.
The *je ne sais quoi* would be but the personal element in this striving
for universality founded upon *le vrai*.

Style as an impersonal ideal could not only be associated with the
universal values of *le vrai et le beau*, but also with the particular genres
of literary tradition. The *Encyclopédie* still treated the concept of style
in this rather conservative manner. The article on style defined it as

a "manière d'exprimer ses pensées de vive voix, ou par écrit: les mots étant choisis et arrangés selon les loix de l'harmonie et du nombre, relativement à l'élévation ou à la simplicité du sujet qu'on traite, il en résulte ce qu'on appelle *style*." In terms of this elevation or simplicity of subject matter, style could be either simple, middling, or sublime. But there were further subdivisions as to prose: *style périodique, coupé, oratoire, historique, épistolaire,* and *naïf.* All these styles were to have the general qualities of all style, namely, clarity, sentiment, naturalness. The vices of style were obscurity, sterility, excess uniformity, and excess elevation, *style empoulé.* The best way to acquire or form a style was to read the best writers, write oneself, imitate the best models, and pick a judicious critic. Voltaire was less confident than the writer of the *Encyclopédie* article: "Il est très difficile de se faire des idées nettes sur dieu et sur la nature; il est peut-être aussi difficile de se faire un bon style." Everyone knew how to define a *bon style,* but to acquire one was something else again.

As one became more and more interested in nature and less and less in rules, the notion of style changed accordingly. One did not abandon what one had said, but added more to what had already been said and written. This is quite apparent from Marmontel's discussion of the subject. One might say that he naturalized style by associating it with the national language as well as with the aesthetic of art; an imitation theory of style was coupled with an expression theory:

C'est [style], dans la langue écrite, le caractère de la diction: et ce caractère est modifié par le génie de la langue, par les qualités de l'esprit et de l'âme de l'écrivain, par le genre dans lequel il s'exerce, par le sujet qu'il traite, par les moeurs ou la situation du personnage qu'il fait parler, ou de celui qu'il revêt lui-même, enfin par la nature des choses qu'il exprime.

On a dit que le style d'un écrivain portait toujours l'empreinte du génie national. Cela doit être; et cela vient de ce que le génie national imprime lui-même son caractère à la langue [In "Style," in *Eléments,* in *Oeuvres,* XV].

If in the first half of the eighteenth century style could still be defined in terms of the rapport between a writer and a literary tradition, it now became apparent that a third term had been added, namely, an awareness of language, and through this something called the national genius. The writer was no longer constrained to deal with the rules of art, but rather with the force of the national character and language. The writer thus defined or formed his style in relation to his national language; he submitted to it completely, or he mastered it, or else both yielded, in which case he achieved what Marmontel called a middling style, formed partly by the genius of the writer, partly by the genius of the language. Style thus became a species of natural extension of the language, modified by the writer to the degree of the writer's own strength of genius. Art alone no longer imposed the sole boundaries of the artist's or writer's possibilities; now nature, in the form of language or national genius, set the limits. The less pronounced the national character, the more susceptible of different styles was the language itself, and the best language was one which is both supple and energetic, such as ancient Greek, the richest and most expressive of languages. Thus, if for Cartaud de la Vilatte and Marivaux the style of a writer was expressive of his passions and thought, for Marmontel style was, in addition, expressive of the national genius. Style was the result of a reciprocal action between the writer and the national language: nature was language, style was art, and the degree of art in a written language was dependent in part upon the richness of the language itself, for some languages are naturally so rich as to require little art. But the natural richness of the language not only determined the degree of style, but also the content of its literature. Thus a very musical language, for example, would be more for the ear than for the mind:

Dans une langue qui n'a rien de séduisant par elle-même, ni du côté de la couleur, ni du côté de l'harmonie, le besoin d'intéresser par la pensée et par le sentiment, et de captiver l'esprit et l'âme en dépit de l'oreille et sans le prestige de l'imagination, force l'écrivain à serrer son style, à lui donner du poids, de la solidité, et une plénitude d'idées qui ne laisse pas le temps de regretter ce qui lui manque d'agrément. Au contraire, dans une langue naturellement flatteuse et séduisante par l'abondance, la richesse, la beauté de l'expression, l'écrivain ressemble souvent aux habitants d'un heureux climat, que la fertilité naturelle de leurs campagnes rend à la fois indolents et prodigues . . . son style est une symphonie qui peut flatter l'oreille, mais qui ne dit presque rien à l'âme, et ne laisse rien à l'esprit [Ibid.].

In view of this one may define style in terms of a counterweight to nature; it is as if Marmontel perceived that you could not found style on nature itself but only in rapport with it, so that style as expression of the national character became modified to include style as modification of the national language. Style was the corrective of nature when the latter is too bountiful, too luxurious, and not rational enough. There is little doubt that these views of language and national genius reflected certain aspects of the quarrel over the merits of Italian versus French music, and also a growing awareness of the importance of the nation and its language in the elaboration of the institution of art.

* * *

See also: *Art, Beauty, Expression, Perfection, Truth.*
Bibliography: Cartaud de la Vilatte, Condillac, Fénelon, Montesquieu, Terrasson, Voltaire.

SUBLIME

THE SUBLIME was an important aesthetic category of the eighteenth century, though it was never as important to the French as it was to the British aestheticians. Boileau introduced the concept into the critical vocabulary in his preface to the *Traité du Sublime* of Longinus and defined it as follows:

Il faut donc savoir que par Sublime Longin n'entend pas ce que les orateurs appellent le style sublime: mais cet extraordinaire et ce merveilleux qui frappe dans le discours, et qui fait qu'un ouvrage enlève, ravit, transporte. Le style sublime veut toujours de grands mots; mais le sublime se peut trouver dans une seule pensée, dans une seule figure, dans un seul tour de paroles. Une chose peut être dans le style sublime, et pourtant n'être pas sublime, c'est-à-dire n'avoir rien d'extraordinaire ni de surprenant. . . . Il faut donc entendre par sublime dans Longin, l'extraordinaire, le surprenant, et, comme je l'ai traduit, le merveilleux dans le discours.[1]

The distinction between the sublime style and the sublime itself is quite important: the former belongs to the art of rhetoric and may be associated with the *clinquant*, in contrast to the real sublime, which may refer to actions, sentiments, thoughts, and passions capable of striking the imagination of readers as well as spectators. The Chevalier de Jaucourt, in an article on the sublime written for the *Encyclopédie*, distinguishes between the *sublime des images* and the *sublime des sentiments*. The former is again within the domain of rhetoric, for it means merely the description of noble things in a noble manner, but the second concerns the affective power of the sublime to move the emotions and strike the imagination and mind of spectators and readers. The sublime is that which elevates the mind and ravishes the soul, and while Boileau was inclined to think of it in connection with literature, the concept tended gradually to be extended to objects and phenomena

[1] In *Oeuvres* (Paris, 1859), pp. 417–18.

of nature as well as of art. The effect of the sublime may be thought of as either an upward or an arresting motion and as producing a stronger emotion than the perception of beauty. Thus the sublime may be associated with expression as well as with enthusiasm. And one may say that while beauty pleases and the *je ne sais quoi* charms and fascinates, the sublime strikes, elevates, and ravishes the soul. It is connected not only with certain actions and sentiments, but also with the perceptions, thought of in terms suggesting sudden revelation of sublime truths. The *fiat lux* of Genesis was a sublime action; Horace the elder was sublime when he pronounced those simple words involving the death of his own son, "Qu'il mourût!," itself a sublime expression, and we may also surmise that in the period of the classical revival of the later eighteenth century the David *Oath of the Horatii* must have struck the public as sublime. In the sublime, then, man surpasses himself and nearly touches on the divine, or at least has intimations thereof. According to Longinus, the sublime could be effected either through ornamental or simple language. Boileau preferred the simple, as did La Motte, who even thought the sublime could be associated with the elegant.

For Diderot enthusiasm was the indispensable quality needed for the sublime. He distinguished between *l'enthousiasme d'âme* and that of the *métier* and thought that a union of the two made for sublime works. Dorval, in his moments of profound reverie and meditation, may be said to have been sublime and also perhaps in touch with the sublime. Marmontel distinguished between a sublime tone, which might dominate an occasional poem, and sublime moments, which were more readily encountered. In a sublime moment the sublime resided more in what was not said than in what was written or spoken; it was something intimated, understood, so to speak, without explicit statements, without words written or spoken. Marmontel also pointed to the thin line which separated the sublime from the ridiculous. Indeed, if the sublime style is not far from the *clinquant*, the sublime in sentiment, action, and the quality of the moment is not far from what is sometimes called "ham." In a sense, we may think of the sublime as being at the very limit of taste and sublime only when it is associated with the marvellous, with power, with grandeur: terms which all tend to associate it with expression, genius, and nature rather than with taste, imitation, and art.

* * *

See also: *Enthusiasm, Expression, Genius; Diderot.*
Bibliography: *Boileau, La Motte, Marmontel.*

TASTE

SINCE BEAUTY WAS DISCERNED by taste, the problems faced by the numerous writers of essays on taste were much the same as those posed by the subject of beauty. Considering taste, one first had to draw certain preliminary distinctions, since the word itself could be used in various senses: the taste of the palate, taste as exercised in connoisseurship, and taste as revealed in the approved and established models of propriety and greatness in art. These distinctions having been drawn, certain questions invariably followed: was taste universal or relative? was it innate in an individual or was it an acquired quality? was it formed by natural dispositions, society, education, or knowledge of the arts? were all men capable of it or only a few privileged individuals? precisely what happened in the mind when someone made a judgment of taste? what is good taste? bad taste? true taste? false taste?

To answer these questions philosophers reasoned, analyzed, and made distinctions; critics gave opinions and proceeded to maintain standards of true taste against the inroads of the ever-present danger of the victory of false taste; historians perceived relativity or chaos as well as unity in variety; but on the whole everyone kept his wits about him, for it was generally known that the taste of Europe was the true taste, that the Gothic taste was barbaric and poor, that the Chinese might be amusing and playful but was hardly to be taken seriously, and that on the whole one did well to maintain the standards set by the universal Greeks.

The problems posed by taste produced the same divisions among philosophers which we have seen in regard to beauty: though everyone agreed there was a good and a bad taste, there were divisions between relativists and absolutists, sceptics and dogmatists, epicureans and puritans, differences of opinion which one sometimes sought to explain in terms of the inadequacy of language, errors of judgment, and even original sin. One may say there existed a will to believe in a universal taste but that the evidence continually forced thinkers and critics to deal with variables, and that the whole problem of the definition of taste revolved precisely on one problem: how to conciliate the desired universality with the evidence of particular variations. The problem was not resolved logically, but rather in terms of history and will. The early eighteenth century tended to be rather sceptical and epicurean, therefore somewhat relativistic, with regard to taste, while the later decades of the century tended more and more to insist upon the invariable and universal in taste; or, put in another way, the taste of the early eighteenth century was more inclusive than exclusive, while the period of the triumph of the *philosophes* tended to be much more rationalistic and utilitarian. This change of attitude corresponds to the gradual depreciation of what was termed the *goût moderne* in the fine arts and the greater emphasis put on the imitation of the antique. But it also corresponds to the shift from an aesthetic founded on the institution of art to one more and more justified in terms of nature.

In the early eighteenth century Cartaud de la Vilatte defined taste in terms of a delicacy of sentiment: "Le goût délicat est un discernement exquis, que la nature a mis dans certains organes, pour démêler les différentes vertus des objets qui relèvent du sentiment."[1] His contemporaries of the Régence period thought much the same, though they might use different words. Madame de Lambert, for example, associated taste with instinct: "Le goût est le premier mouvement et une espèce d'instinct qui nous entraîne, et qui nous conduit plus sûrement que tous les raisonnements."[2] Whereas the savants and critics of the *Grand Siècle*, at least up to Boileau, had sought to found taste on rules, the men and women of the Régence salons relied on what they called delicacy, instinct, or sentiment to judge of the merit of works of the imagination. There is little doubt that coupling taste with sentiment, instinct, delicate organs and so on, implies relativism. Montesquieu perceived this readily enough: "Un organe de plus ou de moins dans notre machine nous aurait fait une autre éloquence, une autre poésie."[3] And the same type of relativism was also perceived by Formey, who attributed it to the corruption of human nature:

Quoique le Beau puisse être déterminé par le jugement, il est pourtant vrai que nos sentiments sur la beauté préviennent pour l'ordinaire nos réflexions. L'homme est capable d'idées et de sentiments; c'est un principe d'expérience: et par un effet de la sagesse admirable aussi bien que de l'infinie bonté du Souverain Etre, ce qui mérite d'être approuvé, doit en même temps exciter des sensations agréables, comme réciproquement ce qui fait des impressions agréables sur les organes de nos sens quand ils ne sont point dérangés, agit d'une manière dont l'idée nous plairait déjà par elle-même, si nous en avions la connaissance. Cet accord aurait été d'une constance parfaite, sans la dépravation de la Nature humaine, altérée par la chute qui a attiré la malédiction de Dieu sur la Terre, et causé du désordre dans les organes de

---

[1] *Essai historique et philosophique sur le goût* (London, 1751), p. 253.

[2] "Reflexions sur le goût," in *Oeuvres* (Paris, 1764), p. 215.

[3] "Essai sur le goût dans les choses de la nature et de l'art," in *Oeuvres complètes*, II, 1241.

nos sens; leur dérangement est encore souvent l'effet du dérèglement de nos
pères, de l'éducation, et de l'intempérance qui gâte les sensations naturelles.[4]

It is evident, then, that association of taste with feeling and instinct,
and therefore with human nature, implies relativity and uncertainty
of judgment. There were three ways of dealing with this problem:
(1) one could limit taste to a certain public; (2) one could draw
certain face-saving distinctions; (3) one could also tie taste to art and
redefine nature. All three were used at various times with greater or
lesser insistence upon one or another point. Amateurs and connoisseurs tended to associate taste with themselves and with knowledge of
the arts; philosophers sought to found taste on human nature, *la belle
nature*, or historical evidence; painters sought to fix it on certain artistic models and precedents. What it all means is that the concept of
taste was gradually extended to cover not only a twofold relation
between a man and an object, but also taste as a social and moral
phenomenon.

Indeed, it is quite clear from historical evidence that, despite certain
definitions of taste founded upon human nature, taste as defined by
Du Bos, Cartaud de la Vilatte, Montesquieu, and others during the period of the Régence and the early years of the reign of Louis XV is best
understood in terms of certain social classes. It is an attribute of the
beau monde, of the leisure class, noble as well as *financier*, and as such
taste marks the victory of the man who enjoys the arts, owns objects of
beauty, and attends the theatre, over the savants and critics and also
over the *hommes de métier*. The doctrine of taste as thus elaborated
and explained supposes an *art de plaire et de luxe*, and if superiority
of judgment is attributed to the man who owns and enjoys, rather than
to the one who produces, works of beauty and luxury, it is because
taste is founded on a sentiment possessed only by the discriminating
few rather than by all, and because the production of art was still regarded somewhat as a mechanical rather than as a mental activity.
This view of taste was probably a direct result of the Quarrel of the
Ancients and Moderns: those involved fought each other to a draw and
left the field to a third force, the amused spectators of the vain battle;
and, significantly enough, the man of taste, as conceived in the early
eighteenth century, was a species of detached or, if you will, disinterested spectator. The man who won was not the Abbé or the *Président*, to allude to Perrault's three characters in his *Parallèle des Anciens*

[4] Formey, "Discours préliminaire" to the 1760 edition of André's *Essai sur le
beau*, p. xxii.

et des Modernes, it was the Chevalier, the man about town, hardly a savant and little given to reasoning. The association of taste with a restricted public is evident also from Du Bos' writings, especially in his discussion of the public. And even when taste was associated with instinct, one found ways to limit the potential sway of relativity. Thus Madame de Lambert, despite her definition of taste in terms of instinct, insisted upon the existence of a just and true taste and fixed her notion of taste by founding it upon established values: "Jusqu'à présent on a défini le bon goût, *un usage établi par les personnes du grand monde, poli, et spirituel.* Je crois qu'il dépend de deux choses: d'un sentiment très-délicat dans le coeur, et d'une grande justesse dans l'esprit" (Op. cit., 218). There are three distinct elements in this short statement: a social element, one pertaining to sentiment, a third pertaining to mind. In short, taste refers to a form of judgment applied to certain objects, to values, to an establishment or social class, *personnes du grand monde, poli, et spirituel.* And if one concentrated on any one of these aspects, one could always draw more distinctions. Montesquieu distinguished between a natural taste and an acquired taste, the former being not theoretical knowledge, but rather "une application prompte et exquise des règles mêmes que l'on ne connaît pas" (Op. cit., 1242). Eventually the notion of taste would be widened to include the understanding of the rules too, that is to say, the knowledge of why one was or was not pleased by certain works. Du Bos had argued that the judgment of taste preceded reflection and that this sufficed to judge of the merit of a work of art, but that this did not mean that once this was accomplished one did not go on to reflect upon the causes of pleasure or displeasure; it meant merely that one did not judge by rules given by critics. The distinction between sentiment and reasoning was also stated in other terms. Formey, for example, distinguished between the *goût corporel,* or *goût matériel,* and the *goût de l'âme*: the former carries mere sensations to the soul, which then considers the causes or reasons for the pleasure or displeasure felt. This analysis produced by the *goût de l'âme* increased the pleasure, purified it, perfected it, though such analysis might of course be deranged by false impressions or prejudices, and it is precisely here that variations as well as depravations of taste occurred. Everyone had sensations, *goût matériel,* but not everyone had the same degree of *goût de l'âme.*

Formey, significantly, extended his notion of taste to cover beauties of nature as well as art, but on the whole it is fair to say that French writers tended to associate the judgment of taste more with the beauties of works of the imagination than they did the beauties of nature, or at least the written evidence points that way. (We may include too, in addition to the beauties of art, those of the social graces.) This being so, it was not adequate to define taste solely in terms of sentiment; one had to know why certain works pleased and others did not, so that considerations on taste tended to merge with those concerning beauty and other artistic qualities. Montesquieu's essay on taste is thus really an essay on beauty in the arts, in contrast to Diderot's article "Beau," which is an essay on a metaphysical concept of beauty.

Montesquieu associated taste with the pleasures of the soul. Indeed he termed taste "l'avantage de découvrir avec finesse et avec promptitude la mesure du plaisir que chaque chose doit donner aux hommes" (Ibid., 1240). Obviously such things could include works of nature as well as of man, and pleasures could be separated into the natural and the acquired, but also into innate pleasures, which the soul possesses independently of its union with the body, and those which the soul knows through the senses. However, Montesquieu admitted that it was quite difficult to know whether certain pleasures derived from the soul alone or from the soul united to the body. He consequently confused the two (and, we may add, the reader too) by referring to all the pleasures of the soul as natural, though he kept the distinction between natural and acquired pleasures and a corresponding distinction between natural and acquired taste. The difference amounts to this: natural taste and natural pleasure are more or less the same thing, whereas acquired pleasure and taste are the knowledge one has of this natural pleasure and taste: you can have the former without the latter, but if you do have the latter they will influence the former:

On croit d'abord qu'il suffirait de connaître les diverses sources de nos plaisirs pour avoir le goût, et que, quand on a lu ce que la philosophie nous dit là-dessus, on a du goût, et que l'on peut hardiment juger des ouvrages. Mais le goût naturel n'est pas une connaissance de théorie; c'est une application prompte et exquise des règles mêmes que l'on ne connaît pas. Il n'est pas nécessaire de savoir que le plaisir que nous donne une certaine chose que nous trouvons belle, vient de la surprise; il suffit qu'elle nous surprenne, et qu'elle nous surprenne autant qu'elle le doit, ni plus ni moins. Ainsi ce que nous pourrions dire ici, et tous les préceptes que nous pourrions donner pour former le goût, ne peuvent regarder que le goût acquis, c'est-à-dire ne peuvent regarder directement que ce goût acquis, quoiqu'ils regardent encore indirectement le goût naturel; car le goût acquis affecte, change, augmente et diminue le goût naturel, comme le goût naturel affecte, change, augmente et diminue le goût acquis [Ibid., 1242].

The pleasures of the soul, in other words, are due to the natural disposition and taste of an individual, interacting with the acquired taste of that individual, as well as to the institutions of art and society, which contribute also to acquired taste. And the pleasures of the soul are not solely due to sentiment but also to the mind, the two being dependent upon each other. The soul must possess one quality in order to have pleasure, that of curiosity: "Notre âme est faite pour penser, c'est-à-dire pour apercevoir: or un tel être doit avoir de la curiosité" (Ibid., 1243), for without it there would indeed be no motion, no thought, no quest, in a sense no soul or pleasure, because the soul by its essence is restless and seeks ever to perceive, to see something new, something different, in order to acquire more pleasure.

Ainsi, quand on nous montre une partie d'un tableau, nous souhaitons de voir la partie que l'on nous cache, à proportion du plaisir que nous a fait celle que nous avons vue.

C'est donc le plaisir que nous donne un objet qui nous porte vers un autre; c'est pour cela que l'âme cherche toujours des choses nouvelles, et ne se repose jamais [Ibid.].

This view of the soul and its function is rather close to Pascal's view of man's restless imagination, and is also reminiscent of Du Bos' view that man needs and seeks *divertissement*. Now the arts, like certain natural phenomena, possessed the qualities which could satisfy this curiosity, which in its turn caused pleasure. Montesquieu therefore considered various artistic-aesthetic categories such as order, variety, diversity, symmetry, contrast, and the *je ne sais quoi*, all of which rather abstract concepts he also illustrated with examples from architecture, decoration, poetry, gardening, and views of nature. It is quite possible to see in his attitude towards architecture and interior decoration, and in his insistence upon the pleasure caused by surprise, a partial reflection of the Régence and early Louis XV styles, which combined symmetry and variety, a just play between order and surprise, simplicity and variety:

L'âme aime la variété; mais elle ne l'aime, avons nous dit, que parce qu'elle est faite pour connaître et pour voir: il faut donc qu'elle puisse voir, et que la variété le lui permette; c'est-à-dire, il faut qu'une chose soit assez simple pour être aperçue, et assez variée pour être aperçue avec plaisir [Ibid., 1246].

The Gothic had variety, to be sure, but so much of it that the eye was lost in it. The same ideas could be applied to gardens:

Nous aimons mieux voir un jardin bien arrangé qu'une confusion d'arbres:
(1) parce que notre vue, qui serait arrêtée, ne l'est pas; (2) chaque allée
est une, et forme une grande chose, au lieu que dans la confusion chaque
arbre est une chose, et une petite chose; (3) nous voyons un arrangement que
nous n'avons pas coûtume de voir; (4) nous savons bon gré de la peine que
l'on a prise; (5) nous admirons le soin que l'on a de combattre sans cesse la
nature, qui, par des productions qu'on ne lui demande pas, cherche à tout
confondre: ce qui est si vrai, qu'un jardin négligé nous est insupportable
[Ibid., 1251].

Montesquieu's concept of taste, which represents rather well the period of the first half of the eighteenth century, was built, so to speak,
on the analogy of the French garden and was symbolic of the relation
of art to nature, taste and genius, and of civilization to nature, at this
time. Change these relations and you change the concept of taste; and
such changes were accomplished in the second half of the eighteenth
century. Indications of the broadening of the concept of taste, tending
to dissociate it from pleasure and raising its social and educational
importance, may be discerned already in Rollin's introduction to his
work on the teaching of literature, *De la Manière d'enseigner et d'étudier
les belles lettres par rapport à l'esprit et au coeur* (Paris, 1741), a title
which bespeaks the twofold nature of taste, but which, being at the
head of a manual for the teaching of literature, also testifies to the importance of taste for something else besides pleasure. Indeed, taste
becomes a form of judgment, which covers not only the arts but also
social relations, which in turn are seen as determined by the study of
letters:

Le bon goût dont nous parlons ici, qui est celui de la littérature, ne se borne
pas à ce qu'on appelle sciences; il influe comme imperceptiblement sur les
autres arts, tels que sont l'architecture, la peinture, la sculpture, la musique.
C'est un même discernment qui introduit partout la même élégance, la
même symmétrie, le même ordre dans la disposition des parties: qui rend
attentif à une noble simplicité, aux beautés naturelles, au choix judicieux des
ornements. Au contraire la dépravation du goût dans les arts, a toujours été
un indice et une suite de celle de la littérature. Les ornements chargés, confus,
grossiers des anciens édifices gothiques, et placés pour l'ordinaire sans choix,
contre les bonnes règles, et hors des plus belles proportions, étaient l'image
des écrits des auteurs du même siècle [I, 400].

Rollin's view of good taste — and it must be stressed that he is above
all concerned with that rather than with taste as such — and his association of it with literature, are quite important. It is indicative of the

meaning attached to taste in the second half of the eighteenth century, a period in which accepted taste and the arts generally became more and more academic. Good taste became a norm which regulated all the arts — one might even speak of a general style — and one which implied certain moral and social norms. There is a significant shift away from considerations of pleasure to supposedly more serious moral, social, and utilitarian concerns, and with this came a gradual diminution of the importance attributed to the particular taste of individuals, to taste founded on pleasure, and a greater consideration given to genius.

This shift in emphasis is discernible even in the work of Batteux, who was hardly a revolutionary thinker. In his writings, genius is assigned an active role, taste a passive one, and both are tied to the institution of art: "Le Génie et le Goût ont le même objet dans les Arts. L'un le crée, l'autre en juge" (Les Beaux-Arts, p. 52). Taste and genius are but two complementary faces of the institution of art, and it is precisely because taste was increasingly associated with certain works of art that the distinction between good and bad taste became more fixed than it ever had been before. The association of taste with pleasure had made for a great deal of variety and for a theory of taste largely founded upon psychology; but the association of taste with art, with la belle nature, and eventually with the normative concept of nature, tended at length to associate taste with the good, the useful, and the universal; and the old distinctions between the natural and the acquired, the universal and the particular, tended to be blurred by the new value put on good taste, now associated with a certain style of art. The proofs of good taste were now found in history, as witness the examples of Du Bos, Batteux, Voltaire, Lacombe, Duclos, Marmontel, and others too numerous to mention.

Batteux sketched out a short history of the beginnings of civilization and the arts in his Les Beaux-Arts réduits à un même principe. He divided this history into three stages. In the first of these men live in a state of nature and merely think of surviving: there are no arts; men work out a living as best as they can. In the second stage they devise laws, arrive at the idea of justice and virtue, and express their joy through song and dance; again, there are as yet no works of art, only rough and ready imitations, though in a later development of this second stage there may be a few advanced works. The third period is the most important and explains why the first two did not produce proper works of art, for it is only in the course of this third stage that man contemplates nature and perceives its harmony. Nature thus becomes the universal model, distinctions are drawn, laws divined, the arts made possible and behold! the Greek miracle which marks the first triumph of the arts:

Ils [les Grecs] jugèrent que l'unité, la variété, la proportion, devaient être le fondement de tous les arts; et sur ce fonds si beau, si juste, si conforme aux lois du goût et du sentiment, on vit chez eux la toile prendre le relief et les couleurs de la Nature, le bronze et le marbre s'animer sous le ciseau [Ibid., 72].

From the Greeks onward the history of art and civilization became the familiar story of true beauty and true nature lost and found, lost in the Middle Ages, found in the Renaissance, after which the antique became the nature of the moderns: "L'Antique fut pour nous, ce que la Nature avait été pour les Anciens" (Ibid., p. 74). Obviously nature was still *la belle nature* and hardly the state of nature as Rousseau, for example, understood it. This is made quite clear by Voltaire, who discusses much the same process of artistic development in his article on taste written for his *Philosophical Dictionary*. He thinks in terms of progress from natural beauties, still imperfect but appealing to sentiment, to more perfect and polished beauties which appeal to the mind and to a more refined and delicate taste. The vantage point for judging of the quality of past arts is perfection, not a value put on some natural state in which men were supposedly better off and more innocent than they are in civilized times.

In such a view of the development of the arts, the relation of taste to art is thought of in terms of reciprocal actions: the arts form taste, but taste in turn corrects, polishes, refines the arts. This process is made possible by what was sometimes called le *goût de comparaison*, which is the aesthetic judgment as it is exercised within the convention and tradition of the various arts: for discernment, which is the essence of taste, supposes comparison, and it is of course the existence of a tradition, a body of works of art, which makes possible this type of comparison and judgment. The *goût de comparaison* is thus taste in a late development of civilization, and for this reason, because it presupposes knowledge, taste becomes something more than the discernment of beauties among faults, or of faults among beauties, to follow Voltaire; it is also the discernment of characteristics which differentiate civilizations and works of art in time and space, so that in the eighteenth century the development of taste and the writing of histories of civilization are part of the same process of thought and discernment.

The implications of this were quite important, because they tended to create a social and educational view of the function of the arts and of taste. It is no accident that one begins to discuss the relation of taste, art and society, to reform the Academy, and to elaborate the aesthetic of the *beau idéal* concurrently. Connoisseurs and amateurs, the men of taste of the late seventeenth and early eighteenth centuries, are downgraded in favor of the new arbiters of taste, the *philosophes* and antiquarians, and the men and women of the world, the *beaux esprits* and the *amateurs* and *curieux*, are blamed for the decline of true taste and true beauty: "Ce fut toujours par ceux qu'on appelle beaux esprits que la décadence commença," writes Batteux,

Ils furent plus funestes aux arts que les Goths, qui ne firent qu'achever ce qui avait été commencé par les Plines et les Sénèques, et tous ceux qui voulurent les imiter. Les Français sont arrivés au plus haut point: auront-ils des préservatifs assez puissants pour les empêcher de descendre? L'exemple du bel esprit est brillant, et contagieux d'autant plus, qu'il est peut-être moins difficile à suivre [Ibid., 76].

One may conjecture that the various essays on taste and beauty which appeared in the course of the century, the reforms of the Academy, the elaboration of the *beau idéal*, were in fact attempts to stave off decadence. Philosophy was also called upon for help, though Duclos admitted its effects in the arts might be ambiguous: it might enlighten the taste of some, but it could also dry up that of others. But some thought of another way to maintain true taste: state interference in the arts. Duclos took Athens as an example of the proper use of luxury: this, he admitted, had given birth to art and letters, but such luxury was public rather than private as it was in modern times:

Les Athéniens ne disputaient pas entre eux du faste extérieur. Ils voulaient que leur ville fût l'ornement de la Grèce. L'ambition de ce luxe national opérait sur tout un peuple ce qu'on voit parmi nous chez des particuliers, avec cette différence que le luxe public fait naître des chefs-d'oeuvre en tout genre, au lieu que le luxe privé est rarement en état de traiter les arts en grand, et en corrompt quelquefois le goût par des fantaisies bizarres et des caprices de mode ["Essai," in *Oeuvres*, I, 562].

This statement outlines clearly enough the reasons for the *retour à l'Antique* as formulated by the critics and the philosophic party. The arts and taste were to be justified on utilitarian grounds: luxury was reconciled with utility on the national level; decadence was attributed to fashion and private luxury; grandeur in art was supposed to be possible through enlightened state patronage; and the dream of Arcadia and the nostalgia for the antique were about to become the active principles of artistic production and taste. Diderot was very enthusiastic about these ideas and wrote to Falconet:

Le bon goût est un être abstrait qui ne meurt point: sa voix se fait entendre sans discontinuer par des organes successifs qui se succèdent les uns aux autres: cette voix se taira sans doute pour nous, quand nous ne serons plus: mais c'est elle que nous entendons à présent; elle est immortelle: elle s'en va et s'en ira disant toujours: Homère! Homère! [5]

Man was mortal, but art and true taste were immortal. In the late eighteenth century one thought rather that it was possible to resolve the evidence of variations of taste by an act of faith in the beauty of the antique. And we might say that with such noble thoughts and great sentiments were laid the foundations of future kitsch.

* * *

See also: *Antique, Art, Beau Idéal, Beauty, Decadence, Genius, Grands Siècles, Nature, Public.*
Bibliography: Alembert, Cartaud de la Vilatte, Condillac, Diderot, Du Bos, Montesquieu, Terrasson, Voltaire; Batteux, Formey, Gédoyn; Séran de la Tour; Beardsley, Cassirer, Folkierski, Mustoxidi, Soreil.

TRUTH AND VERISIMILITUDE

> La vérité est le fondement et la raison de la perfection de la beauté. Une chose, de quelque nature qu'elle soit, ne saurait être belle et parfaite, si elle n'est véritablement tout ce qu'elle doit être, et si elle n'a tout ce qu'elle doit avoir.
> *La Rochefoucauld*

IN HIS ESSAY on Cartesianism and Classicism, Lanson opined that a Cartesian aesthetic was impossible because the doctrine of Descartes confused the Beautiful with the True. The thinkers of the seventeenth century might have replied that an aesthetic could only be possible if it were constructed on the True, and one may add that the seven-

[5] Diderot et Falconet, *Le Pour et le Contre, Correspondence polémique sur le Respect de la Posterité, Pline et les Anciens.* Introduction and notes by Yves Benot (Paris: Editeurs Français Réunis, 1958), p. 49.

teenth century produced a considerable body of writings concerned precisely with what might be described an aesthetic of the True. It is also possible to argue that one ought to search for a Cartesian aesthetic in this concern with *le Vrai* rather than in such notions as rationality, geometry, and progress. *Le Vrai* would thus be to the critic what certainty was to Descartes, and with both, *le Vrai* as well as certainty, proper presentation and the clear and distinct recognition of an object, thought, or action were important. The role of the Beautiful was merely to attract men's attention and fix it upon the True. Thus if, as has been argued by Arsène Soreil, it was the amateurs of painting such as Fréart de Chambray and Félibien who introduced the notion of the Beautiful into aesthetic speculation, the concern with the True was more likely introduced by philosophers and theologians. From these it then passed to the critics and the poets and also, most importantly, to those concerned with eloquence, the art of persuading men of the truth.

If Descartes did not bother with aesthetics it was because he refused to elaborate on eloquence, which he regarded as a gift rather than as a technique to be acquired. As Soreil has shown, beauty at this time was associated with the agreeable, and it was precisely because the agreeable could, in turn, be associated with the instability of human passions that Pascal, for example, did not think it possible to make much sense of definitions of the Beautiful, the agreeable, and so on. But the True could be presented: the gift of eloquence could be artfully used to present the truth, just as painters might use their art to make the True evident to the eye. *Le Vrai* thus supposes a cognitive theory of art, and discussion of it necessarily affects the concepts of beauty and nature, and also the function and evaluation of art. Indeed, by the end of the century the True and the Beautiful were closely allied, and we may assume that the aesthetic which had by then been evolved was constructed upon the True as manifest in works of the imagination. This is well brought out by Boileau in the preface to the 1701 edition of his works:

Un ouvrage a beau être approuvé d'un petit nombre de connoisseurs; s'il n'est plein d'un certain agrément et d'un certain sel propre à piquer le goût général des hommes, il ne passera jamais pour un bon ouvrage, et il faudra à la fin que les connoisseurs eux-mêmes avouent qu'ils se sont trompés en lui donnant leur approbation. Que si on me demande ce que c'est que cet agrément et ce sel, je répondrai que c'est un je ne sais quoi, qu'on peut beaucoup mieux sentir que dire. A mon avis néanmoins, il consiste principalement à ne jamais présenter au lecteur que des pensées vraies et des expressions justes. L'esprit de l'homme est naturellement plein d'un nombre infini d'idées confuses du vrai, que souvent il n'entrevoit qu'à demi; et rien ne lui est plus agréable que lorsqu'on lui offre quelqu'une de ces idées bien éclaircie et mise dans un beau jour.[1]

The poet, like the philosopher, is thus concerned with the True, and he too clears up those confused ideas of it that men in general possess, but he differs from the philosopher in that he does not use the same method to get at the True, and in that his domain is not the same as that of the philosopher. There is little doubt that in this passage Boileau subscribes to or outlines an aesthetic of the True without, for all that, being a Cartesian. He is, indeed, more likely to be a Platonist. What both kinds of philosophers have in common is an intuition of the True as being beyond the confused ideas that all men have. But the emphasis on the True also affected the value put on the rules and one could argue, for example, that the moderns thought they were more effective in presenting the True because they knew and had evolved more perfect rules of art. Thus concern with *le Vrai* brings us to the moderns, who were as much its partisans as were the ancients. This may seem paradoxical, for one is tempted to associate the aesthetics of the True with Platonism, in which case it would be better to associate it with the ancients. But little was clear among partisans of the ancients and moderns; and, as we have seen, Lanson associated the ideal of the True with the moderns, whom he blamed for the end of Classicism. Part of the confusion surely comes from the association of Cartesianism with science, that is, with progress, and this in turn with the decline of Classicism. But one may associate the aesthetics of the True with Descartes too, as Lanson did, without drawing the same conclusions. It was not the same truth as that of science, as we have come to understand it since the nineteenth century, but rather a True conceived in metaphysical terms, founded upon God and also upon certain general truths concerning the nature of man and the workings of the universe, and in any case beyond immediate sense perception—the object of intuition much more than of experimental science. One thing is certain, that *le Vrai* was thought to be the object of philosophical enquiry and the foundation of representation in the arts. It was so much the latter, indeed, that one did not even bother to mention it, for as de Piles put it in his *Cours de Peinture par Principes*: "L'homme tout menteur qu'il est ne hait rien tant que le mensonge, et le moyen le plus puissant pour

---

[1] In *Oeuvres* (Paris: Classiques Garnier, 1952), p. 9.

attirer sa confiance, c'est la sincérité. Ainsi il est inutile ici de faire
l'éloge du Vrai" (p. 30). Nevertheless, because the True was, in a sense,
beyond the immediate, hidden by confused ideas, and because men
were sinners with inadequate senses and often with false judgment,
the True alone did not suffice to attract men and hold their attention;
it had to appeal not only to the intellect but also their senses, not only
to the reason but also the heart.

"Il faut de l'agréable et du réel," wrote Pascal in his *Pensées*, "mais il
faut que cet agréable soit lui-même pris du vrai" (*Pensée* 25). This as
concerns eloquence, a subject of major interest to Pascal and his contemporaries. But much the same thought was repeated by Father
Bouhours for prose alone, just as de Piles concerned himself with the
same problem in regard to painting. "Les pensées," wrote Bouhours in
his *De la Manière de bien penser dans les ouvrages de l'esprit,*

sont les images des choses, comme les paroles sont les images des pensées;
et penser, à parler en général, c'est former en soi la peinture d'un objet, ou
spirituel, ou sensible. Or, les images et les peintures ne sont véritables qu'autant qu'elles sont ressemblantes: ainsi une pensée est vraie, lorsqu'elle représente les choses fidèlement; et elle est fausse, quand elle les fait voir autrement
qu'elles ne sont en elles-mêmes.[2]

This view of thought and mind poses an objective order, of which
thoughts and pictures are to be the faithful representations; the mind,
we may say, is a painter's studio much more than a ghost in the machine: or if it is a ghost, it is one that paints. The True is something
beyond the immediately perceived, and the problem is to lead one's
thought in such wise that the True may be apprehended: thus, the
title of Bouhours' book. It is, in a sense, a literary critic's *Discourse on
Method,* and the implication is that the ghost in the machine is not
always a faithful painter because he has to rely on an imperfect machine. *Le Vrai,* as the foundation of an aesthetic, thus implies dualisms
between appearance and truth, in the order of nature between objects and spectators, and in the world of the arts, that is of representation of objects, between artists depicting or representing these in various
media and spectators not so much observing as judging these representations or imitations. The model of the aesthetic of *le Vrai* is painting. Pascal had recourse to the same art to make a point about truth
and eloquence, and significantly he chose an art that was supposedly
concerned only with a true likeness of a person depicted, the portrait:

[2] Pp. 9–10 in the Paris edition of 1771.

"L'éloquence est une peinture de la pensée; et ainsi, ceux qui, après avoir peint, ajoutent encore, font un tableau au lieu d'un portrait" (*Pensée 26*). The tableau is something more than a likeness or copy of the True; it is, because of additions, alterations, agreeableness, and so forth, an alteration of the True, a work of art. We can see why Lanson could have been led to suppose that the True was incompatible with art and beauty. In effect, the aesthetic of the True represents only one possible base of art among others justified on other assumptions, and requires a special attitude of the artist, be he poet or painter. His art must not show his personality; his self must not intrude between the object perceived and to be represented faithfully and its representation. In short, the aesthetic of *le Vrai* supposes a Jansenist art of the portrait, truth without ornamentation, art as a *manière de bien penser et de bien voir*, not art as an autonomous activity or an *agrément* to make reality somewhat more likeable than it is. Fénelon's view of style derived from the same aesthetic of the True: "Afin qu'un ouvrage soit véritablement beau, il faut que l'Auteur s'y oublie, et me permette de l'oublier."[3]

Fénelon thought very highly of Raphael, partly because of this virtue of self-effacement: Loin de vouloir que l'art saute aux yeux, il ne songe qu'à le cacher" [Ibid., 328]. One may readily see why mannerism was considered a vice and also why decadence was thought of as a falling away from the perfect or the True. However, because thoughts and works of art were but imitations or representations of the True rather than the True itself, it is obvious that such works would pose questions concerning not only their relation to the True, but also their relation to their judges and perceivers. Thus one of Bouhours' interlocutors did not quite accept the idea that literary works and thoughts were always founded on the True:

Je ne comprends point votre doctrine . . . et j'ai peine à me persuader qu'une pensée ingénieuse soit toujours fondée sur le vrai: je crois, au contraire, avec un fameux critique, que le faux en fait souvent toute la grâce, et en est comme l'âme. En effet, ne voyons-nous pas que ce qui pique davantage dans les épigrammes et dans d'autres pièces où brille l'esprit, roule d'ordinaire sur la fiction, sur l'équivoque et sur l'hyperbole, qui sont autant de mensonges [Bouhours, op. cit., 10]?

To answer this objection one was forced to create two orders of truth, one associated with the original truth, or truth itself, and one associated

[3] "Lettre écrite à l'Académie Française sur l'éloquence, la poésie, l'histoire, etc.," in *Dialogues sur l'Eloquence*, pp. 325–26.

with the arts. The simple opposition of the True and the False was altered by introducing the notion of fiction, a third order, so to speak, between truth and falsehood: "Tout ce qui paraît faux, ne l'est pas, et il y a bien de la différence entre la fiction et la fausseté: l'une imite et perfectionne, en quelque façon, la nature; l'autre la gâte et la détruit entièrement" (Ibid.). If the world of art is thus not a copy of the True, or its likeness, it may, as an imitation, be something different from nature, a world of fiction.

The creation of a third order between the True and the False allowed for the coexistence of a Christian as well as a pagan literature and art. Fable has nothing to do with truth, but it does suppose a certain type of truth or verisimilitude: "A la vérité," writes Bouhours,

le monde fabuleux, qui est le monde des poètes, n'a rien en soi de réel: c'est l'ouvrage tout pur de l'imagination; et le Parnasse, Apollon, les Muses avec le cheval Pégase, ne sont que d'agréables chimères. Mais ce système étant une fois supposé, tout ce qu'on feint dans l'étendue du même système ne passe point pour faux parmi les savants, surtout quand la fiction est vraisemblable et qu'elle cache quelque vérité [Ibid., 10–11].

There is the True, and there are truths that belong to artistic conventions which no longer imply a simple relation between the True and its copy. The arts suppose, rather, a system of rapports based on *vraisemblance*, a concept derived from the True but applicable above all to the arts and particularly to fiction. Bouhours has in effect posed two worlds, that of the True, which may at times be called nature or *la belle nature*, and the world of art, which is, it is true, built upon the other but not completely dependent on it. The existence of fiction and the delight allowed imagination also make possible the portrait *en beau* as well as the portrait *en vrai*, but it must be understood that beauty, the arts, are but additions to the basis of the True:

La vérité est à la pensée ce que les fondements sont aux édifices; elle la soutient et la rend solide. Mais un bâtiment qui ne serait que solide, n'aurait pas de quoi plaire à ceux qui se connaissent en architecture. Outre la solidité, on veut de la grandeur, de l'agrément, et même de la délicatesse dans les maisons bien bâties; et c'est aussi ce que je voudrais dans les pensées dont nous parlons [Ibid., 79].

To have recourse to an analogy from mathematics, let us say that the solution to a problem must be not only correct but also elegant. Thus style, elegance, the great, the noble, the sublime, beauty, were additions to or ornaments of the True, or else forms of the True.

As we have seen, however, one of the characters used by Bouhours to illustrate his thoughts concerning literary discernment called *le faux* the very essence or soul of an ingenious thought. Indeed the union of *agrément*, beauty, and truth in works of the imagination posed problems as difficult to resolve as that of the mind-body relationship in Cartesian philosophy. Father Bouhours' criticism may be called a criticism of discernment, precisely because it was concerned with this union and because one had to be very careful to distinguish between true and false beauties, true and false thoughts. Works of the imagination produced *agrément* only insofar as the True was manifest rather than being hidden by false beauties. Attitudes towards the *clinquant*, towards affectations of various types, lack of measure, profusion of ornament, overrefinement, and bathos were determined by the relation of the True to the Beautiful, a relation which, Bouhours thought, was to be founded on nature, and which could be arrived at by proceeding as did painters: "Ceux qui veulent penser juste, doivent imiter les grands peintres, qui donnent de la vérité à tous leurs ouvrages, ou plutôt suivre la nature sur laquelle les peintres se règlent" (Ibid., 72). Only this type of imitation could produce what he called *une pensée naturelle*:

J'entends . . . quelque chose qui n'est point recherché, ni tiré de loin, que la nature du sujet présente, et qui naît pour ainsi dire du sujet même. J'entends je ne sais quelle beauté simple sans fard et sans artifice, telle qu'un Ancien dépeint la vraie éloquence. On dirait qu'une pensée naturelle devrait venir à tout le monde; on l'avait, ce semble, dans la tête avant que de la lire: elle paraît aisée à trouver, et ne coûte rien dès qu'on la rencontre; elle vient moins en quelque façon de l'esprit de celui qui pense que de la chose dont on parle [Ibid., 231]

One is tempted to say that a natural thought is an intuition of a clear and distinct idea immediately presented and leaving no doubt as to its truth in the mind of a reader or perceiver, so that he has an impression of recognition, familiarity, and ease. It implies that clarity is the primary quality of style and discourse. Indeed, all the *agréments* of style are nothing if the discourse or thought be not clear: "Rien ne me plaît, rien ne me pique que je n'entende parfaitement" (Ibid., 362). Pleasure in this context is obviously intellectual, a thing of the understanding, of the inner rather than the outer eye; it is not a delight in sensuous qualities, but in the perception of internal coherence.

The True, considered as the foundation of the arts, thus determines its qualities and virtues and makes criticism possible on the basis of propriety, coherence, clarity, justness, and judgment rather than on various forms of subjective, personal pleasures. It is also possible to argue, however, that the True does not make for a general theory of art so much as it does for the autonomy of various different arts and activities. For *le Vrai* is an aesthetic category *avant la lettre* and may be used to evaluate the worth of various aspects of human activities as well as natural qualities. Thus the essence of a work of art, an action, or a man is associated not so much with the general concept of beauty as it is with the True, and it is therefore possible to say that the general aesthetic category of the seventeenth century was the True rather than the Beautiful. Father André sought in the eighteenth century to explain the presence and form of beauty in various aspects of art and nature, but La Rochefoucauld sought rather to explain in similar terms the pervasiveness of the True:

Le vrai, dans quelque sujet qu'il se trouve, ne peut être effacé par aucune comparaison d'un autre vrai, et quelque différence qui puisse être entre deux sujets, ce qui est vrai dans l'un n'efface point ce qui est vrai dans l'autre: ils peuvent avoir plus ou moins d'étendue et être plus ou moins éclatants, mais ils sont toujours égaux par leur vérité, qui n'est pas plus vérité dans le plus grand que dans le plus petit. L'art de la guerre est plus étendu, plus noble et plus brillant que celui de la poésie: mais le poète et le conquérant sont comparables l'un à l'autre; comme aussi, tant qu'ils sont véritablement ce qu'ils sont, le législateur, le peintre, etc., etc.[4]

To borrow from Father André, one may say that La Rochefoucauld poses a *Vrai essentiel* as the fundamental aesthetic, or if you will, metaphysical category, of certain arts, actions, and objects, and it is this *Vrai*, this truth of an action, art, or object, which is the object of perception and judgment of the thinker, reader, critic, observer, or spectator. Beauty is merely an adjunct, an added quality of the True; it does not play a determining role as far as the judgment is concerned, for the True is considered the overall determining quality, and as such it assigns the role given beauty within the whole:

Quelque proportion qu'il y ait entre deux maisons qui ont les beautés qui leur conviennent, elles ne s'effacent point l'une par l'autre: ce qui fait que Chantilly n'efface point Liancourt, bien qu'il ait infiniment plus de diverses

---

[4] "Réflexions diverses," in *Oeuvres complètes* (Paris: Editions de la Pléiade, 1950), p. 357.

beautés, et que Liancourt n'efface pas aussi Chantilly, c'est que Chantilly a les beautés qui conviennent à la grandeur de Monsieur le Prince, et que Liancourt a les beautés qui conviennent à un particulier, et qu'ils ont chacun de vraies beautés [Ibid., 358].

In short, the universal quality is not so much beauty as it is the True, and it is for this reason that the seventeenth century did not found a universal standard of beauty, as did the eighteenth century, but rather a universal standard of the True upon the notions of internal coherence, hierarchy, fittingness, and propriety of rapports, all of which allowed for the conciliation of variety and universality, unity and variety and, in the order of the arts, the coexistence of various styles, genres, and tastes. It was because the eighteenth century sought to establish a universal standard of beauty, irrespective of variations in taste, that the art of the closing decades of the eighteenth century took on a uniformity which had not obtained in the *Grand Siècle*. Other factors were involved, of course, but we may surmise this "universal" standard to have been, so to speak, the intellectual cause or, if not a cause, its philosophical justification.

Taste also had not been institutionalized in the seventeenth century to the degree that it was to be by the end of the following century. La Rochefoucauld still thought of taste in terms of an uncertain discernment, subject to personal prejudices and caprices precisely because its object was beauty rather than the True; the latter is discerned by the mind, and "il y a plus de variété et de caprice dans le goût que dans l'esprit" (Ibid., 371). Thus his view of taste, put forth in a short essay, was more relativistic than any such views held in the eighteenth century. Given human nature as it is, we are more often wrong than right when asked to exercise our taste in matters which directly affect our person. We can discern the True only in matters which do not affect us personally. This is a view which seems to be founded upon the mind-body duality, for taste errs more than the mind because it is obviously more closely tied to the senses than the mind is; the mind is occupied with the perception of relationships, whereas taste is concerned with the various *agréments* connected with beauty. The conflict between the capriciousness of taste and the mind's concern with right or true judgment was resolved in the eighteenth century by institutionalizing taste, by attempting to found a true or right taste on generally accepted artistic models which supposedly represented universal beauty: something which became possible because works of art induced artificial passions, less touching, less affecting than real ones, so that taste was less disturbed than it was when concerned with objects in the world of passions in motion.

What may be called the aesthetic of the True made for a criticism of discernment. The task of the critic or judge was to discern the true nature of a work or object perceived. In the art which was the favorite model of those who founded value in the arts on the True, namely painting, it was supposedly possible to discern a veritable hierarchy of truth, founded upon a base called nature. Roger de Piles applied to the art of painting the aesthetic of the True and the criticism of discernment which Father Bouhours had exercised in the realm of *belles lettres.* The result was not a distinction between the True, fiction, and the false, but rather between three types of truth, all visible to the eye of the spectator but attained by various degrees of mental activity and abstraction on the part of the painter.

De Piles, in his *Cours de Peinture par Principes,* distinguishes between the *vrai simple, vrai idéal,* and *vrai parfait.* In the first case nature is simply and faithfully imitated; in the second a choice is made within this imitation so that only the most perfect forms and models are used in order to form an ideal whole; and in the last both simple and ideal nature or truth are combined to form a perfect whole. The Roman school of painting is associated with the *vrai idéal* and the Venetian with the *vrai simple.* The *vrai simple* plays in the scheme of de Piles the role assigned *le Vrai* in the thought of Bouhours: it is the basis of the other types, the foundation of the art, and it is described as the

imitation simple et fidèle des mouvements expressifs de la Nature, et des objets tels que le peintre les a choisis pour modèle, et qu'ils se présentent d'abord à nos yeux, en sorte que les carnations paraissent de véritables chairs, et les draperies de véritables étoffes selon leur diversité, et que chaque objet en détail conserve le véritable caractère de sa nature; que par l'intelligence du clair-obscur et de l'union des couleurs, les objets qui sont peints paraissent de relief, et le tout ensemble harmonieux [p. 300 ff.].

Needless to say, this *vrai simple* is in no wise a copy of nature, a mechanical imitation, for it does imply a choice, an artful imitation, and is therefore a work of art. It is the first degree of abstraction from the rough-and-ready nature of the sublunar, imperfect world. The second truth, the *vrai idéal,* represents a greater degree of intellection still, though it is founded upon this first *vrai simple.* The *vrai idéal* is founded upon choice models; it implies the painter has used more invention and set himself a higher task than that of simple imitation, and demands more mental activity on the part of both spectator and painter. The *vrai simple* often pleases because the object imitated is pleasing to begin with, so that it gives a good rendering of the expressive movements and truth of nature without all the nobility, grace, and exactitude the motif is capable of possessing. The *vrai idéal* leads, not away from the truth of simple nature, but rather to its essence, which the world of infinite appearances has fragmented. The *vrai parfait* is a composite of the two and the ultimate achievement of art, the perfect imitation — or shall we say its perfect intimation? — of *la belle nature*, the representation of an order and truth beyond the senses and yet recognized when seen:

Tout est alors vraisemblable parce que tout est vrai; mais tout est surprenant, parce que tout est rare. Tout fait impression, parce que l'on a observé tout ce qui est capable d'en faire; mais rien ne paraît affecté, parce qu'on a choisi le naturel en choisissant le merveilleux et le parfait [Ibid.].

This description of the effects of the perception of this *vrai parfait* in painting is reminiscent of what Bouhours described as *pensées naturelles*, the recognition of those higher truths beyond the gross and corrupted senses of man discerned by the inner eye of the poet and the painter.

There is an important word in the passage we have just cited from de Piles: *vraisemblable*. The relation between truth and verisimilitude might at first sight appear to be simply stated as one between the original object and its imitation. If in the *vrai parfait* of de Piles everything is *vraisemblable*, it is because we are looking at a picture, an illusion of *le vrai* produced by art. *Vraisemblance* in this sense would be for painting what fictions were in the thought of Bouhours. And we might add that whereas the artist's object was to imitate *le Vrai*, whether simple, ideal, or perfect, the connoisseur's task was to judge of the degree of *vraisemblance* achieved by the painter. It is thus possible to have an aesthetic founded on *le Vrai* and a criticism based upon the *vraisemblable*. However, all was not as simple as that in the seventeenth and eighteenth centuries, for one cannot assume that truth, transferred to the stage, represented on a flat surface with color and line, or narrated in prose or poetic discourse, thereby became an *objet vraisemblant* in relation to the original model, and was thus subject to a criticism founded upon this type of comparison. For *vraisemblance* was not the same thing as perfect resemblance, as it would be in something copied.

D'Aubignac, in his *Pratique du théâtre* (Paris, 1657), is most illuminating on this matter. *Vraisemblance*, he wrote, is the essence of dramatic poetry, without which nothing reasonable may be done on the stage; the word to emphasize is "reasonable." The object of dramatic representation is thus not *le Vrai*, but *le vraisemblable*. No objective truth or historical fact is to be represented on the stage by virtue of its truth, for too many true events are absurd, trivial, and of little interest; and many things which are true ought not to be represented because they would be unbearable: "Il est vrai," writes d'Aubignac,

que Néron fit étrangler sa mère, et lui ouvrir le sein pour voir en quel endroit il avait été porté neuf mois avant que de naître; mais cette barbarie, bien qu'agréable à celui qui l'exécuta, serait non seulement horrible à ceux qui la verraient, mais même *incroyable, à cause que cela ne devait point arriver*.

We underline the last words because they point indirectly to what is involved in the notion of verisimilitude. The only true and possible subjects for the stage are those fit for the stage, fit that is for a certain art, for the eye, for the reason; *vraisemblance* is an artistic concept and requirement, whereas *le Vrai* is more apt to be associated with metaphysical suppositions. *Vraisemblance* is truth in the great domain of fiction, it is truth within the man-made world of art and in the representations possible in that world. It is noteworthy that d'Aubignac built his argument for *vraisemblance* on the stage on its analogy to painting. In both cases, painting as well as dramatic representation, ideal types, pictures, thoughts and actions were to be represented — images of the world that ought to be rather than of what it was in fact. The concept of *vraisemblance* thus acted as a regulative principle:

Le vrai n'est quelquefois pas vraisemblable.

It is not, however, a principle which excludes all unpleasant truths from the arts, for it is of the essence of art to transform what it touches:

Il n'est point de serpent ni de monstre odieux,
Qui, par l'art imité, ne puisse plaire aux yeux:
D'un pinceau délicat l'artifice agréable
Du plus affreux objet fait un objet aimable.
Ainsi, pour nous charmer, la Tragédie en pleurs
D'Oedipe tout sanglant fit parler les douleurs,
D'Oreste parricide exprima les alarmes,
Et, pour nous divertir, nous arracha des larmes.

There is no contradiction between d'Aubignac's limitations of *vraisemblance* and Boileau's remarks about the transforming power of art, for in the French theatre subject matter hideous to sight was kept off-stage, and imitation as understood by Boileau is quite similar to what d'Aubignac meant by *vraisemblance*. In both instances the True is defined by the requirements of art, of the genre: some things may be said, others may be shown. It is not so much the subject matter which is affected as its credible presentation to a spectator or reader who is not directly involved but who nevertheless wishes to be moved. But the relationships among truth, verisimilitude, horror, and pleasure, taken in the representation of what would in real life frighten or disgust, were to be explained only in the eighteenth century through the speculations of Du Bos.

The question of verisimilitude was not a major preoccupation of eighteenth-century thinkers. Still, it was not ignored, and Marmontel wrote a rather complicated article on it for his *Eléments de littérature*. His views seem to be based on those of d'Aubignac, though the relation of verisimilitude to truth had by then become more complex because of the emphasis put on nature in the second half of the eighteenth century and also because of the sentimental-moral concerns of the times. Nor does Marmontel restrict his notion of *vraisemblance* to the stage or found it on the analogy of thought to images, and thinking and representation to the art of painting. His view seems to be closer to the concerns of eloquence than theatrical-pictorial representation:

Le but que se propose immediatement la fiction, c'est de persuader; or elle ne peut persuader qu'en ressemblant à l'idée que nous avons de ce qu'elle imite. Ainsi la *vraisemblance* consiste dans la manière de teindre [*sic*; did he mean to write *peindre*?] conforme à notre manière de concevoir; et tout ce que l'esprit humain peut concevoir, il peut le croire, pourvu qu'il y soit amené [*Oeuvres*, XV, 533–64].

This would seem to make for a rather strict doctrine of imitation, limited to *le vrai simple*, even perhaps to the copying of nature rather than its imitation, for verisimilitude is based on the resemblance between an idea and an object rather than on the transposition of the True into the realm of fiction. We may say also that Marmontel, unlike Bouhours and Boileau, pays as little attention to the difficulty of discerning the True in the midst of confused ideas of it as he does to its faithful reproduction. In other words, his view of verisimilitude is more philosophical than it is artistic; it seems to be derived from considerations of human nature and perception rather than artistic representation and truth of fiction. The old distinctions between ordinary and extraordinary *vraisemblance*, alluded to by d'Aubignac and based upon the representation of natural events or supernatural ones, are replaced by considerations upon the relation of nature to art; miracles were no longer believed in. In the seventeenth century, naturally impossible events could become possible and credible through divine intervention, and it is this which made for the *vraisemblance extraordinaire*. Marmontel is not interested in this type of distinction but rather in the relation between *ressemblance* and *vraisemblance*. *Ressemblance* refers to a relation between an exterior object perceived and the memory image of that object in the perceiver's mind; or it can refer to a conformity of our own feelings and those of others. *Ressemblance* is thus a psychological, natural category. *Vraisemblance*, on the other hand, is an artistic term, limited to fiction or to things which have no objective existence in nature, or else to events which are purely imaginary. Marmontel becomes quite muddled on this point, and it is not easy to follow his train of thought, partly because, like so many of his contemporaries, he did not clearly distinguish between the realm of art and that of nature.

D'Aubignac had written that the object of the drama was verisimilitude rather than the True itself. Marmontel states that verisimilitude is the object of fictions — which is fine as far as it goes; but he adds that verisimilitude is a reflected truth, and it is here that difficulties begin. He distinguishes between, not only truth and verisimilitude, but also between *vérité directe* and *vérité réfléchie*, which are in turn subject to two further subdivisions as to their manner of perception. For is truth perceived or is it felt? Both, for there is a truth of perception and a truth of sentiment.

The concept of the True and its relation to verisimilitude became complicated because of the introduction of the feelings, of sentiment, in the manner of perceiving or discerning truth, and we may suppose that this was in part because of the greater emphasis put on nature and beauty in matters of aesthetic and artistic concern. The perception of truth in the seventeenth century had supposed the elimination of sentiment, feeling, taste, because these were all subject to caprice; but the introduction of the feelings into questions of aesthetic judgment changed this rather simple relation between an object whose true nature was to be known and an observer who would be pleased only once that true nature was clear to him. For it had been accepted since Du Bos that the merit of works of the imagination appeared through sentiment rather than through conformity with rules devised by the mind. Consequently verisimilitude ceased to be a matter merely of sight and reason; it also became a matter of concern to feelings and sentiments. Thus there is a *vraisemblance* for sight based on the analogy of thought to pictures used in the preceding age and a *vraisemblance* based on something much more vague, the supposition of a common humanity founded in sentiment and feeling, in which case "la vraisemblance, dans les choses de sentiment, n'est donc que l'accord parfait du génie du poète avec l'âme du spectateur" (Ibid.). The eighteenth century sensibilized *le Vrai*, and it is quite clear that from the seventeenth century to the late eighteenth we have moved from a truth associated with the clear or clarifying perception of the perfect aesthetic observer, *qua* artist or poet, to the man of taste, who discerns various aspects of manifestations of the true and its various forms which also make for *agrément*, to the man of genius, conceived as the man of universal feelings. The analogy to painting is now blurred; there is less concern with mind, with ideal types and discernment, and more with universal sentiment, universal beauty and universal morality. By the end of the eighteenth century the True, the Good, the Beautiful, apprehended by mind, sentiment, and sensibility merged in a common bath of tears of happiness in a general communion with Nature.

✳ ✳ ✳

See also: *Beauty, Dramatic Poetry, Imitation, Taste, Ut Pictura Poesis.* Bibliography: Aubignac, Du Bos; Boileau, Bouhours, de Piles, Marmontel.

UT PICTURA POESIS

> On retrouve les poètes dans les peintres, et les peintres dans poètes. La vue des tableaux des grands maîtres est aussi utile à un auteur, que la lecture des grands ouvrages à un artiste.
>
> *Diderot*

IN THE SEVENTEENTH and eighteenth centuries it was often said that poets and painters depicted actions, delineated character, or sketched out scenes, and it was also assumed that all the arts joined hands. Poetry and painting were considered sister arts. Painter and poet both used a common fund of motifs. Du Bos used Horace's *Ut pictura, poesis erit* as the epigraph of his *Réflexions critiques*, which may be described as a series of essays on the aesthetic implied by this phrase, taken from Horace. In the seventeenth century d'Aubignac, Le Bossu, and Bouhours had used painting as a model whereon to base certain rules of epic, dramatic, and lyric poetry, while others wrote literary portraits with painted portraits in mind. The conventions of French Classical tragedy are not solely to be explained in terms of pedants elaborating rules against nature and reason, but on the contrary may be seen as making excellent sense on the basis of certain assumptions concerning the visible and the imagined. The rules of the three unities and the requirements of *bienséance* were determined by considerations on the power of images: some things might be seen, others had better be imagined rather than represented on the stage.

The seventeenth and eighteenth centuries tended to think in pictures, or as Michel Foucault put it: "Le centre du savoir, au XVIIe et au XVIIIe siècle, c'est le tableau" (*Les Mots et les Choses* [Paris, 1966], 89). The known can be represented. Knowledge took the form of tableaux or pictures which could be seen or which could be imagined on the basis of the signs which represented knowledge. By extension we may say that the various arts were all arts of representation and that the entire realm of the arts was in effect the representation of another nature, *la belle nature*. Each single art, whether poetry, painting, or music, represented pictures of an ideal order or nature, of course within the limits of its medium, which could represent only certain aspects of that total world of beauty and higher order of nature constituted by art. Poetry represented through artificial signs, painting through natural signs, music through sounds, the dance by way of movement; and all the arts had meaning because they were all pictures or representations of *la belle nature*.

Thus not only poetry but the stage as well was often thought of as a tableau in which characters moved and spoke. And Voltaire thought of his *Essai sur les moeurs* as a *tableau* of history, so that even that discipline was itself an art of representation. The parallel of painting and poetry was so well established that Batteux's chapter on painting in his *Beaux-Arts réduits à un même principe* is one of the shortest in the book. There was, indeed, little reason to write a chapter on painting, for all one had to do was to apply to painting what had already been said about poetry. It was assumed, obviously, that the painter knew his technique, the mechanical part of the art, as well as the poet did his, and that the really important matter lay in the subject matter represented. It is also quite obvious that from the point of view of representation Batteux's book is a treatise on what to represent in the fine arts, so that the term "representation" differs little, in the context of art, from the term "imitation." We can also see why the Classical aesthetic was inseparable from a moral and didactic point of view of the function of art: representation being a form of knowledge, the arts could be used for didactic purposes. Pictures in the form of prose, poetry, or painting might be thought of as good, bad, or indifferent in terms of the effects they might produce upon the reader or spectator's imagination and passions. These general considerations aside, the *ut pictura poesis* doctrine also implied certain limits applicable to the various arts: it defined their role and range within the general aesthetic of imitation, or if you will, of representation, and it also defined, as we stated above, their role vis-à-vis the imagination. The *ut pictura poesis* acted as a species of regulator of the division of labor within the general convention of art. The poet did one thing, the painter another, the dancer and musician others still, but all together made for a magnificent concert. It is for this reason that opera strikes us as the ultimate expression of the Classical doctrine of art; it combines not only *ut pictura poesis* but also *ut pictura musica*, combines imitation, expression, and representation. It was only towards the end of the eighteenth century, however, that this extension of the principle was fully grasped, and even then it was often based on the notion of nature; but it is obvious in such works as Noverre's *Lettres sur la danse*, in which the principle is fully applied. Before this time, though, the *ut pictura poesis* principle was discussed only in relation to the two original sister arts, painting and poetry.

The doctrine was summed up quite clearly by Perrault in his *Parallèle des anciens et des modernes*: "Un tableau est un poème muet, où l'unité de lieu, de temps et d'action doit être encore plus religieusement observée que dans un poème véritable, parce que le lieu y est immuable, le temps indivisible, et l'action momentanée" (I, 223). The poet narrates an action in time; the painter depicts an action restricted to an instant. If one could insist on unity of place in dramatic representation it was because the stage acted as a frame for a picture, but also because sight acted as a control of truth, so that the *ut pictura poesis* doctrine was also a regulating factor of verisimilitude. Du Bos explored the implications of the doctrine at length. He discussed not only the similarities between the two arts, but also their significant differences. Painting and poetry were both arts of imitation, and poet and painter might both treat the same motifs taken from fable, history, or nature, but they could not depict or imitate, or if you will, represent the motifs in the same manner, or in quite the same aspects. The painter could do some things the poet could not, and vice versa; the sister arts were complementary rather than interchangeable. There was one aspect of painting, however, which inclined Du Bos to suppose it to be an art superior in its effects to poetry. Painting appealed to the more refined organ of sight; it thus used natural rather than artificial signs, colors rather than abstract words, and was therefore more immediately effective and touching than poetry. This was another way of saying something rather ambiguous, namely that painting was closer to nature, or less ambiguously, that it gave a direct picture or imitation rather than something which was a picture at one remove from the True. Consequently, painting operated much more effectively and powerfully on the soul and was more capable of moving the passions than literature, and since Du Bos' aesthetic rests on the necessity of keeping one's passions occupied one can readily see why the visual occupied an important place in his considerations of the arts:

La vue a plus d'empire sur l'âme que les autres sens. La vue est celui des sens en qui l'âme, par un instinct que l'expérience fortifie, a le plus de confiance. C'est au sens de la vue que l'âme appelle du rapport des autres sens, lorsqu'elle soupçonne ce rapport d'être infidele. Ainsi les bruits et même les sons naturels ne nous affectent pas à proportion des objets visibles. Par exemple, les cris d'un homme blessé que nous ne voyons point, ne nous affectent pas, bien que nous ayons connaissance du sujet qui lui fait jetter les cris que nous entendons, comme nous affecterait la vue de son sang et de sa blessure. On peut dire, métaphoriquement parlant, que l'oeil est plus près de l'âme que l'oreille [*Réflexions critiques*, I, 416].

As an art form painting can also present a greater degree of illusion of truth than can poetry. Poetry is at two removes from direct perception. The brain must intervene in order to compose images in the mind whereas sight gives that image directly:

Les vers les plus touchants ne sauraient nous émouvoir que par degrés, et en faisant jouer plusieurs ressorts de notre machine les uns après les autres. Les mots doivent d'abord réveiller les idées dont ils ne sont que des signes arbitraires. Il faut ensuite que ces idées s'arrangent dans l'imagination, et qu'elles y forment ces tableaux qui nous touchent, et ces peintures qui nous intéressent [Ibid., 417–18].

This view of reading, contrasted with direct sight perception, follows from his premises concerning the human soul as being avid for *divertissement*. Pictures act on the perceptions immediately, without the effort and mechanical operation required by reading. At the same time this psychology of perception, direct and indirect, visual and mental, also explains why certain acts were banished from the stage and were left to the spectator's imagination. For, curiously enough, this analysis of perception and reading supposes that the spectator does not possess an active imagination, but merely a species of mental camera which can take in pictures directly and so be diverted and occupied, whereas in fact reading requires a more active imagination, the composing of mental pictures within the mind. This implies that pictures presented to the mind directly, rather than through reading, can control the spectator, whereas mental pictures which he has to form himself as he reads are more prone to error, to the vagaries of the imagination, thence the danger of novels. There is a certain ambiguity in Du Bos' view of the power of sight and the lesser power of reading. It is as if two different psychologies were involved and with this, two different views of man. The art of reading is analyzed in mechanical terms: you see words, arbitrary signs, which evoke certain ideas in the mind, which are in turn composed into images — a view of perception and thought which makes us rather think of the *homme machine* of the Cartesian mechanical model. But sight is something else. Here man is directly touched, moved, by the sight of what is presented to him, and the psychology involved is more closely that associated with the sublime, with revelation, than with modern mechanical perception founded on a faculties view of the mind, and the image of man presented here is not so much *l'homme machine* as *l'homme sensible*. This view of the power of sight was indeed associated with a more ancient psychology, sometimes referred to as the *effet de prime regard* insofar as it concerned the art of painting or the rhetorical power to move men to action. What it means is most succinctly stated in the Chinese proverb: A picture is worth a thousand words. This was perhaps a valid view of perception until television, though it is doubtful that we can still accept it without serious modification. In any case, it depends upon one's view of the imagination, and given that of Du Bos, which was based on that of Pascal, the greater power attributed to sight makes sense. It is best to view the two types of perception, reading as an indirect form of perception and visual perception as a direct form, as complementary. Let us not forget what we said above about representation: the mind, to know with certainty, needs a tableau, a visual aid, a picture which in effect completes the arbitrary signs and which also serves to fix the imagination; for men are prone to err when they try to represent to themselves the True on the basis of purely verbal descriptions:

Il faut des figures pour faire entendre sûrement et distinctement les livres les plus méthodiques qui traitent de ces sortes de choses [i.e. descriptions of certain animals, siege dispositions, orders of battle, certain pieces of architecture]. L'imagination la plus sage forge souvent des fantômes, lorsqu'elle veut réduire en tableau les descriptions; principalement quand l'homme qui prétend imaginer, n'a jamais vu des choses pareilles à celles dont il lit ou dont il entend la description [Ibid., 421].

We can readily see why poets were sometimes told to look at paintings, but can we readily understand why painters were told to read poets? Indeed, though they were referred to motifs in Homer and other poets, they knew that painting proceeded from painting, so that while they might find inspiration in poetry or fable they studied other paintings and painters in order to paint pictures. Noverre the dancer recommended that ballet masters study painters; Talma studied the paintings of David; and David, when he thought of the Horatii, thought better than to inspire himself from a specific scene of Corneille's drama. He reimagined the subject for the purposes of his art. Indeed, there were certain things which could not be visually represented, even though sight was the more refined of the senses. The painter could depict emotion, the movement of the passions, only insofar as these made themselves manifest visually. Thus Poussin was able to convey the feelings aroused by the death of Germanicus in his friends and admirers indirectly through their expressions and gestures, but he could not let the spectator know visually the last thoughts and sentiments of the dying Germanicus; for that, one had to rely on history, on prose, on narration, on words which could be used to analyze the passions. Though it must be stressed that even here the boundary between what could be represented visually and what could be said was not as rigid as it might seem, for to each passion there corresponded, as Lebrun and other painters knew, certain postures, gestures, and expressions. Interiority, so to speak, was the domain of prose, and a memoir, a portrait in time, not in two dimensions, was something different from a painted portrait.

In description, however, painting triumphed over poetry. What would be a tediously long description in words could in painting be a delight for the eyes and be taken in at one glance. As Diderot put it: "Un coup d'oeil supplée à cent pages de raisonnement." Or, one might add, a hundred lines of description. That all this was not merely doctrine, but actual practise, may be gleaned from the poetry and prose of the times. To use the language of the *ut pictura poesis*, novelists sketched char-

acters in a few words in either the noble or picturesque style, and indications as to setting were usually vague and left to the imagination.

However, while Du Bos, and sometimes even Diderot, argued for
the superiority of the sense of sight over the others and thereby implied the superiority of painting to poetry, there was one art in which
the limitations of sight were perceived and also, it would seem, by
implication, the limits of art and the psychology based upon vision.
We refer to the art of portraiture with regard to the knowledge of men.
This was quite clearly seen by the great moralists of the seventeenth
century, Corneille among others:

> Les visages souvent sont de doux imposteurs:
> Que de défauts d'esprits se couvrent de leurs grâces,
> Et que de beaux semblants cachent des âmes basses!
> Les yeux en ce grand choix ont la première part;
> Mais leur déférer tout, c'est tout mettre au hasard.

Thus, Clarice in Act II, Scene II, of Corneille's appropriately named
play *Le Menteur*. While the words refer to real faces rather than portraits, perceived by real eyes in real life, it is obvious that the eyes
are not to be trusted, that this distrust has certain implications for the
art of portraiture, and that what the moralist is saying is that there is
more to man than his exterior. Du Bos had made this point in connection with the depiction of sentiments in history painting. Moralists
made the point in connection with portraiture and thereby belittled
the power of the eye, at least insofar as it touched upon human character. But at the same time they also stressed the difference between
art and life, so that even the painted portrait turned out to be a work
of art, that is to say, an illusion.

The first requirement of a painted portrait was that it be a good likeness of the original. This was generally accepted as a point of departure
for the discussion of portraiture. But it was also taken for granted that
the original might be improved upon, put in a favorable light, while
the portrait itself could be more or less striking and imposing in ac-
cordance with the social prestige, power, rank, and dress of the sitter.
Portraits might thus be painted *en vrai* or *en beau*, a distinction which
corresponds to de Piles' distinctions of the various degrees of *vrai* (see
article "Truth and Verisimilitude"), and since they could also be full-
length, middle-length, bust, or head portraits, with or without various
accessories, so as to be also historical, mythological, modern or in the

antique manner, it can be readily seen that a portrait was most often more than merely a likeness. It presented a sitter, man or woman, girl or boy, with or without animals, inside or outside, as a work of art. The portrait constructed a personality in terms of an ideal nature, beauty, and truth. Like many other works of art of the times, it was an image not of what was but of what ought to be.

It thus followed that one must not judge a person as one might a portrait or a painting. In the latter cases the eye sufficed, but in real life it was limited. La Bruyère put it as follows:

Il ne faut pas juger des hommes comme d'un tableau ou d'une figure, sur une seule et première vue, il y a un intérieur, et un coeur qu'il faut approfondir: le voile de la modestie couvre le mérite, et le masque de l'hypocrisie cache la malignité; il n'y a qu'un très petit nombre de connaisseurs qui discerne, et qui soit en droit de prononcer; ce n'est que peu à peu, et forcés même par le temps et les occasions, que la vertu parfaite et le vice consommé viennent enfin à se déclarer.[1]

In real life the *effet de prime regard* does not suffice to know men by. Time, affording long acquaintance with and ample chance for study of the man, must second the eye if one is to know the heart. The portrait, painted or written, unlike an impression of a man one casually knows, is the result of the artist's or moralist's considered study of the man, of the original. The painted portrait is thus, according to the *ut pictura poesis*, to be complemented by a written or literary portrait. The ideal form for this was evolved in the course of the seventeenth and eighteenth centuries, an age of great portraiture in the art of painting, of moralists writing literary portraits, and novelists turning out entire galleries of portraits. But in both the painted and the written portrait the presentation is static, the original endowed with a fixed character so that in both instances, in the outward appearance as well as in the presentation of the interior man, time is absent; time, that is, manifested as change affecting the character. The literary portrait was really based upon the painted portrait in this respect; it merely was its adjunct, not essentially different in intention and in result, for it too could be written *en beau* or *en vrai* and also supposed an aesthetic of art. The literary portrait completed the painted portrait, and both worked in effect to create a man, a character. In truth Clarice's suspicion of the eyes can also be applied to art — indeed, to all appearance, precisely

---

[1] *Les Caractères de Théophraste, traduits du Grec, avec les Caractères ou les Moeurs de ce Siècle,* in *Oeuvres* (Paris: Editions de la Pléiade, 1951), p. 373.

because the entire world of art of the seventeenth and eighteenth centuries created a world of appearances, that is to say, of masks. It is no wonder that the man who tore the mask off, Jean-Jacques Rousseau, associated art with civilization, rejected civilization in the name of nature, and wrote his *Confessions*, that is to say an interior portrait in time, based upon an aesthetic of nature and written to accuse art and civilization of the corruption of the original nature.

✳ ✳ ✳

See also: *Expression, Imitation, Opera, Truth and Verisimilitude; Aubignac, Du Bos, Diderot, Perrault, Rousseau.*

Bibliography: for applications of the principle of *ut pictura poesis*, Raymond Picard, "Le Brun-Corneille et Mignard-Racine," in *Revue des Sciences Humaines*, April–June 1962, 175–82; R. G. Saisselin, *Style, Truth, and the Portrait* (Cleveland, O., 1963); Jean Seznec, "Racine et Prud'hon," *Gazette des Beaux-Arts*, XXV, 1944, 349 ff.; Georges Wildenstein, "Talma et les peintres," *Gazette des Beaux-Arts*, March 1960, 169–70.

PART II

Biographical and Bibliographical Articles

ALEMBERT, JEAN LE ROND D', 1717–1783

D'ALEMBERT STUDIED, at the College des Quatre Nations founded by Mazarin, theology, philosophy, medicine, law; his personal inclination was for mathematics. At twenty-two he was *adjoint* of the Academy of Sciences, and was interested especially in mechanics. He produced several works in science and mathematics, and was a witty orator, a brilliant and original mind. He became perpetual secretary of the Académie Française in 1772. He was only an occasional writer on matters concerning aesthetics, and in this area far from original, although his essays on poetry and letters are not without interest for the understanding of those minds who approached the arts as men of science. He is thus in the line of Fontenelle and, one may say also, of La Motte. He wrote several works of criticism which bear on aesthetics, to wit the *Essai sur la société des gens de lettres et des grands, sur la réputation, sur les mécènes, et sur les récompenses littéraires*, 1753; *Réflexions sur l'usage et sur l'abus de la philosophie dans les matières de goût*, 1757; *Réflexions sur la poésie*, 1760; and, like so many others, he also wrote some *Réflexions sur l'ode*, 1762. These may be found in his *Mélanges de littérature, d'histoire, et de philosophie*, of which there were many editions in the course of the eighteenth century, two (the earliest) in 1753, four in 1759, and five or six after 1763 on to 1785.

An idea of d'Alembert's position in the development of aesthetic theory will be found in his essay on taste entitled *Réflexions sur l'usage et sur l'abus de la philosophie dans les matières de goût*. Taste he simply defines as "le talent de démêler dans les ouvrages de l'art ce qui doit plaire aux âmes sensibles, et ce qui doit les blesser." There are three things worth underlining here: the definition is restricted to man-made objects; it is applied to sensitive souls; and norms of beauty are applied which ought to be binding upon those sensitive souls. Taste is not arbitrary; its causes can be known, but must be sought within ourselves. D'Alembert's essay is reminiscent of the British empirical approach as represented by Hume, whom he knew, and Burke. His view of taste also implies the possibility of a new criticism, not founded upon the old rules but upon analysis and sensibility. He warns against two sources of error in criticism, namely lack of sensibility and of psychological analysis. For him the source of the Quarrel between the Ancients and Moderns is to be sought here. One might say, paraphrasing contemporary philosophy, that d'Alembert as well as Fontenelle saw that the Quarrel grew out of a false problem. Like Abbé Terrasson, d'Alembert believed there can be no opposition between good taste and true philosophy, for both feelings and perception belong to the realm of philosophy. Philosophy was the firm support of taste, because its task was to discern the true nature and principles of each art and the true character of each situation, to draw the proper limits between the arts, and so on. Nor would philosophy dull the sensibility or genius of those who taste or create, because the two things, feelings and creative genius on the one hand, and reason on the other, are different and separate. Cartesian dualism is thus evoked, and the distance between the effects of passion and feeling and of judgment once more stressed. D'Alembert, like Batteux, also separated the judgment of taste into two distinct moments in time: first a sensitive apprehension, then a rational, analytical discernment by the mind for a greater and conscious appreciation.

* * *

Citations are from *Oeuvres Complètes* (Paris, 1821). On d'Alembert, see, Maurice Müller, *Essai sur la philosophie de Jean D'Alembert* (Paris and Geneva, 1926); also, for his relations with Hume, R. Grimsley, "D'Alembert and Hume," in *Revue de Littérature Comparée*, October–December 1961, pp. 583–95.

AUBIGNAC, FRANÇOIS HEDELIN, ABBE D' (1604–1676)

THIS QUARRELSOME POET, occasional playwright, and author of an allegorical novel was employed by the Cardinal de Richelieu to educate his nephew the Maréchal de Brézé. It was Richelieu who gave d'Aubignac his passion for the theatre and thus induced him to write the work for which he is remembered, *La Pratique du Théâtre* (Paris, 1657).

D'Aubignac's work on the theatre is not without interest. It is indispensable, indeed, for the understanding of French Classical theatre, and an excellent summary of the rules of dramatic art as they were formulated in the first half of the seventeenth century. Its message is that the rules of the theatre are not founded upon authority, but are rational and universal. D'Aubignac attempted to formulate these rules by extracting a rationale of dramatic action from the examples of the ancients as well as of the moderns. His work is filled with allusions to contemporary practice; the rules are not only deduced from first principles as, for example, in Aristotle, but are also based upon experience. He was interested in perfecting the dramatic art, but also in making it worthy of state support. The two interests were indeed complementary, for the Abbé d'Aubignac, much like the *philosophes* of the later eighteenth century, believed in the utility of the stage: it was to be a means not only of pleasing the public, but also of instruction. He conceived of the stage in terms of what we would call propaganda value directed to the idle, to keep these from mischief, while the lower orders of the population were to be educated by visual means, since these classes were generally incapable of understanding general principles or maxims. Thus the principal end of dramatic action was moral: "La principale règle du poème dramatique, est que les vertus y soient toujours récompensées, ou pour le moins toujours louées, malgré les outrages de la fortune, et que les vices y soient toujours punis, ou pour le moins toujours en horreur, quand même ils triomphent." Thus, like his contemporary Pascal, d'Aubignac thinks of art in terms of a theory of *divertissement*; only, in his case, the citizens are to be diverted from themselves and their potential of mischief and disorder for the greater profit of the state. He went as far as to write a *Project pour le rétablissement du théâtre français*, in which he recommended state control of the stage, supervision of the lives of the actors, of decor and theatres, and the creation of an intendant to take charge of this policing.

His *Pratique du Théâtre* is divided into four books. The first treats of the author's intentions, the rules of the ancients, the practise of the theatre, the public. This is a book of general considerations. The second book is concerned especially with the rules of the dramatic poem, verisimilitude, and the unities. The third book is a detailed analysis of the parts of tragedy. The final book deals with characters, discourses, deliberations, narrations, and also the spectacle, the machinery and decor, of the stage.

The term "rules," in the view of d'Aubignac, takes on the meaning we are familiar with from the literary manuals and histories of aesthetics: the rules are normative and Abbé d'Aubignac proceeds on

228 BIOGRAPHICAL AND BIBLIOGRAPHICAL ARTICLES

the assumption that rules extracted from the practise of the ancients and verified from the moderns can be successfully used and applied to produce correct, regular, perfect plays. Thus he advises that the poet study Aristotle and Horace, and their later commentators Castelvetro, Vida, Heinsius, Vossius, La Ménardière, and the greatest of them all, Scaliger. After this he ought to read all the plays of the ancients. In short, d'Aubignac poses the ideal of the learned playwright, just as others posed the notion of the learned painter. In point of fact, however, it must not be supposed that the rules, while normative, were regarded by him as prescriptive and always constraining. They reflected current practice and were as much the work of the poets themselves as of the learned critics. That these rules were not inimical to genius or to great drama, and certainly not to art, may be gleaned from the example of Racine, whose plays represent the perfection of the type of drama the rules supposed on the technical level. D'Aubignac insisted on *vraisemblance* (see article "Truth and Verisimilitude") and on the unities. He presented his argument well, basing it on the analogy of the stage to painting. He stressed continuity of action and thought that the ideal, as far as unity of time was concerned, might be in the rapprochement of the duration of the action and that of its representation. The playwright ought to start the action as close to the catastrophe as possible. This was argued on the basis of the need for illusion.

* * *

On d'Aubignac, see Charles Arnaud, *Les Théories dramatiques au XVIIe Siècle. Etude sur la Vie et l'Oeuvre de l'abbé D'Aubignac* (Paris, 1888).

CARTAUD DE LA VILATTE, FRANÇOIS (1700–1737)

LITTLE IS KNOWN of him; he was a canon and a philosopher who published two works, the *Pensées sur les mathematiques* of 1737 and the *Essai historique et philosophique sur le goût* of 1736 and 1751. It is only the latter that concerns us here.

This essay on taste is a curious and confused book which deals more with general culture, the *esprit des nations*, than it does with taste considered as the exercise of critical judgment in the arts. There are certain parallels to Rousseau's later *Premier Discours*, for Cartaud also considers the relation of the arts to the development of society from the earliest times, through the Egyptians, Greeks, Romans, to the Europeans of his own era. Taste is associated with history and climate, and if any theme is to be gleaned, painfully, in the first rambling part of this essay, it is that taste is relative and that in the course of time it refines itself. What we thus have is, in effect, a very thin *essai sur les moeurs* and a variant of Du Bos' discussion of the *grands siècles*. The *essai* is not only narrative and descriptive, it is also critical: Cartaud is no unquestioning admirer of the Greeks; he does not accept the habitual praise given Greek painting, no example of which had survived, but thought the Greeks never really mastered that art. He concedes their strength in sculpture. He discusses the Spartans, Athenians, and Sybarites, and then passes over to Carthage, which he dismisses as a mere commercial power of no interest to persons of taste, then comes to Rome, which is examined in some detail. At this point in his narrative one begins to discern what his book is about: it is a history of taste, regarded as an aspect of *perfectionnement* relative to the mores and climates of peoples. The achievement of the Romans is judged in terms of the point of perfection attained in the seventeenth and eighteenth centuries, and they do not emerge in a favorable light: we may conclude that Cartaud was a partisan of the moderns. We are left in no doubt as to this upon reading his amusing and satirical portrait of Madame Dacier, the champion of Homer, and his praise of Fontenelle, whom he likens to an eagle.

In the second part of his essay he discusses various types of beauty and the relation of temperament and passions to works of art and literature. This section is not clear, and he does not always distinguish between the beauties of nature and those of art. He touches briefly on the sublime in art and in life, and both beauty and the sublime are discussed in terms of morality. Another section of the second part deals with taste, not as a social and historical phenomenon, as in the first part, but rather in terms of preferences: Cartaud is a materialist, and we are reminded of his contemporary La Mettrie and of Diderot. There are also sections on harmony in language, poetry, and sound, sections in which he once more touches upon the relation of the passions to the arts. He uses mechanistic metaphors to make his points: man is compared to a *clavecin*, reacting to certain sounds, or to a *petite machine* which can be made to play by way of a secret spring that sets the passions in motion. His materialism is at times ludicrously simple: if the French do not like Italian music it is because their physiological organs are less flexible than those of Italians. He ends his essay with an apology for luxury along the lines of Mandeville's *Fable of the Bees*, and a final section is used to argue that learning is better for the state than ignorance.

When the second edition of Cartaud's *Essai* came out in 1751, Grimm reviewed it in the *Correspondance littéraire* and opined that the author was in a continuous delirium, that he had a great deal of imagination and little judgment, that the most sublime matters were often mixed with the most burlesque.

* * *

Cartaud de la Vilatte has recently been reedited in Berlin by Werner Krauss; *Cartaud de la Vilatte. Ein Beitrag zur Entstehung des geschichtlichen Weltbildes in der französichen Aufklärung* (Berlin, 1960).

CHABANON, MICHEL-PAUL GUY DE (1730–1792)

CHABANON'S TREATISE *Observations sur la musique et principalement sur la métaphysique de l'art* (Paris, 1779), is important in that it shifted a great deal of emphasis away from the notion of imitation to that of genius and interior sentiment. In this sense he followed and carried further the notions of Du Bos concerning genius and sentiment; he echoed certain aspects of Diderot's thought, and generally speaking is representative of an aesthetic of nature rather than of art, emphasizing genius rather than the rules of art. Chabanon, in short, drew certain lessons from reading philosophers such as Du Bos and Batteux, among others, stressing that "l'esprit philosophique, appliqué aux beaux arts, ne peut jouer qu'un rôle secondaire: le premier rôle appartient à cet instinct créateur, dont l'esprit n'est qu'un faible disciple, condamné à ne savoir que ce qu'il apprend de son maître" (p. 3). He clearly belongs to another generation from that of Fontenelle and the Abbé Terrasson. He separates poetry from poetics to stress the difference between the rules of art and the sentiment for it. He shows a great deal of sympathy for the practising artist, musician, or painter, and antipathy for theorization about the rules of art. The philosopher, when judging of the arts, must be sceptical of his reason and follow his instinct. On the other hand, it is possible for the philosopher to create an aesthetic, that is a higher criticism or theory of the arts, founded upon the knowledge of our sensations; he can instruct men of taste as to the causes of their pleasures: "La théorie des arts, considerée sous ce point de vue, devient la théorie de nos sensations les plus délicates, et de nos goûts les plus exquis" (p. 12).

Chabanon questioned the near-sacrosanct doctrine that art was an imitation of nature. This he thought but a specious truth, built upon a verbal foundation. It made for a simple axiom: "Mais cette simplicité même qui le fait admettre indistinctement pour tous les arts, afin de les soumettre à un principe commun, forme peut-être le défaut de cet axiome trop généralement appliqué" (pp. 13–14). The axiom, in short, meant little because it embraced and explained too much.

What Chabanon did was to break down the supposed unity of the arts. He implies an aesthetic for each of the arts rather than the universal aesthetic of all the arts summed up in the dictum, "Art is an imitation of nature." His critique is really more thorough than that which Diderot levelled against Batteux in his article "Beau" in the *Encyclopédie*. However, even Chabanon, like so many of his contemporaries, could not free himself completely from the doctrine of imitation. He thought that music could imitate nature, if only imperfectly through certain effects, such as by evoking the sound of the waves or the wind. This was not, however, he insisted, imitation for the ear, but merely musical depiction for the mind; the musician's first task was song. Music really pleased without imitation through the sensations it gave the listener. In short, his book was a critique directed against those who would use music imitatively, as one might use painting, and as was sometimes done in opera to create atmosphere. He thus was led to make a distinction between imitation and expression: "La peinture des effets soumis à nos sens, s'appelle *imitation*; la peinture de nos sentiments s'appelle expression" (p. 53). Song is not an imitation of the spoken word, or of inarticulated passions; it has its proper conventions: "il a des procédés à part, et qui ne dépendent pas de la prononciation des mots" (p. 80). Even dance was but one aspect of the one art of music founded upon song: "La musique et la danse, si j'ose dire, s'entendent à merveille; elles disent la même chose, l'une à l'oreille, et l'autre aux yeux; mais toutes deux ne disent à l'esprit rien de positif" (p. 97). Their effect is merely a sensation, and consequently something rather vague. If one wished to attach meaning to these sensations one should need the intervention of mind, and it is only such intervention which can turn music and dance into arts of imitation.

One is tempted to say that Chabanon unwittingly arrived at the notion of the autonomy of art by arguing against the theory of imitation as applied to one art, music. Not so. He merely expounded the naturalistic fallacy. Music ceased being an art of imitation only to become a universal and natural language whose principles and effects are not conventional, but derive directly from the organizations of human beings and certain animals. Musical proportions, for example, are the same everywhere and are innate to music itself and to man. Melody has everywhere the same base and foundation, as indeed does rhythm, and it is this existence of a universal base, natural rather than conventional, which makes of music a universal language whereas the other arts are conventional and therefore less universal. However, Chabanon did stress something his contemporaries did not underline, namely that this universal language is nondiscursive and nonutilitarian. It merely produces pleasure, and its sole utility is the expression of joy. But it is part of universal beauty, and thereby we see that Chabanon also restated for music the neoclassic creed of his time whereby the universality of beauty is joined to the fundamental goodness of nature.

CHAPELAIN, JEAN (1595-1674)

CHAPELAIN, NOT BOILEAU, was the true legislator of Parnassus, especially in the period between 1630 and 1660, and the term "legislator," in his case, is the proper one to use, for his prose has a scholastic and legalistic style which makes it practically unreadable for us. He is an excellent example of dogmatic criticism. His turn of mind was closer in spirit and manner of procedure to the scholars and humanists of the sixteenth century than to the thinkers of the seventeenth, and in reading him one comes to understand why Molière and Perrault both opposed and disliked savants and erudition. He was a savant, an erudite and a voracious reader who gained great authority among men of letters and women of fashion, and also with Richelieu and Colbert. He was an expert who believed and argued that experts were the proper judges of the value of a poem, and he also believed that the value (or lack of value) of a poem was an object of rational demonstration. A case in point is his preface to Marini's epic poem *Adonis*. Chapelain was asked to write a preface, and after protesting, in the manner of the day, that he was unworthy of this honor, that he was merely a humble man, without name, authority, or consideration in the world, he proceeded to prove that the *Adonis* was a good poem. This he did by first stating the premise that it was indeed a good poem, and then demonstrating the premise in a scholastic manner:

Je dis donc . . . que je tiens l'*Adonis*, en la forme que nous l'avons vu, bon poème, conduit et tissu dans sa nouveauté selon les règles générales de l'épopée, et le meilleur en son genre qui puisse jamais sortir en public.

Or pour procéder avec quelque lumière à la preuve de cette mienne opinion, il serait ici comme besoin de dire ce que c'est que poésie, de combien d'espèces il y en a, et quelle est la nature que les Grecs appellent *épopée* et à laquelle nous n'avons point encore trouvé de nom, afin de voir, demeurant dans ces principes, – accordé que ce poéme ne soit de l'espèce reçue d'icelle, – de quelle façon il a pu être loisible au poète d'en introduire une nouvelle différente de la reçue, laquelle fut néanmoins embrassée par l'épopée comme par genre, qui est ce qu'il nous faut montrer pour établir sa bonté.

And so on, point by point, tedious definition by tedious definition, for some thirty-five closely printed pages, only to come back to the premise, which now becomes the conclusion. It is a good poem because it is according to the rules of the epic as set forth by Aristotle, and generally to the examples given by the ancients and by some of the more modern poets and critics, such as Scaliger, who, were he still alive, would no doubt approve of the *Adonis*. The more a poem conforms to the rules or to the nature of poems, the more it approaches perfection. You decide this by analyzing the poem into its constituent parts, testing each part in terms of its rules, and judging the whole by its parts.

Chapelain's reputation in the world of letters and erudition was such that he was called to settle the quarrel of the *Cid* which had arisen between Corneille and Scudéry. He was asked to write the official view of the Academy and produced another forty pages of small print, the gist of which was that the *Cid* was a good play, but that it was not perfect, and that both the opponents of the *Cid* as well as its partisans were right and wrong, and, in conclusion, according to the doctrine of Aristotle the subject is defective, the denouement not worthy of praise, the play weighed down with useless episodes, decorum not fully observed, the disposition not faultless, and some passages stylistically impure; but that, on the other hand, the naiveté and vehemence of the passions, the elevation and delicacy of several of its ideas, and an inexplicable *agrément* which is mixed with its faults give it a notable advantage over most of the works which have appeared upon the French stage.

The advantages of dogmatic criticisms may be readily gleaned from the writings of Chapelain: a work may be judged in terms of rules spelled out by noted philosophers, pronouncements may be made, opinions proved to be right or wrong, and works of the imagination discussed without personal involvement, that is without any need for taste. Criticisms may thus be impersonal, impartial, and legalistic; the critic, as the judge of the poet, is his superior. The supposition here is that poets really write for critics. But there is a further assumption involved which proved Chapelain's undoing, namely that the rules, being prescriptive, need only be applied to produce a poem. Thus Chapelain also wrote an epic poem, *La Pucelle*, which at the insistence of friends he consented to make public in 1656. The poem proved unreadable, and dogmatic criticism never recovered from the *Pucelle*.

* * *

Chapelain's critical works are published in a volume entitled *Opuscules critiques*, published by the Société des Textes Français Modernes (Paris, 1936); this volume also includes some of his correspondence bearing on criticism. His criticism has also been treated by René Bray in his book on French Classical doctrine. See also Auguste Bourgoin, *Les Maîtres de la critique au XVIIe Siècle* (Paris, 1889).

CONDILLAC, ETIENNE BONNOT, ABBE DE (1715-1780)

LIKE FONTENELLE, Condillac has not fared well in histories of aesthetics. He is given one page in Gilbert and Kuhn, Professor Beardsley mentions him only in connection with Diderot, and Raymond Bayer mentions him only once as precursor of the Idéologues. Yet, if one wished to find a systematic, lucid, well-written and elegant French aesthetic from the eighteenth century one should turn to Condillac. Du Bos, to be sure, wrote more than Condillac, who relied on Du Bos a great deal, but where Du Bos was an *érudit*, critic, and historian, Condillac, as a philosopher who reflected upon Du Bos' writings upon the arts, was an aesthetician in the sense in which we have come to understand the term, in the sense that Hume was one. (Hume also used Du Bos and, like Condillac, went beyond erudition and the knowledge of facts and history to probe the assumptions of critics and artists and the mechanism of taste and art.) Condillac possessed a quality which Du Bos lacked, namely clarity of definition and also, one might add, method. He was, of the French *philosophes*, perhaps the least literary and most systematically philosophical or, as might have been said at the time, the most metaphysical.

A reading of Condillac will also readily show that it is not possible to maintain the nearly sacrosanct distinction between aesthetics from below as specifically British and aesthetics from above as specifically German, unless one is to regard Condillac as an Englishman. To be sure, he is sometimes discussed as a disciple of Locke, and the assumption that he merely systematized Locke in French undoubtedly hurt his reputation. But Condillac, in fact, did more than to frenchify Locke, and his contribution to aesthetic theory is as important as Hume's.

Hume, indeed, usually accepts only one standard, that of taste, while Condillac has a great deal to say, not only about imagination, genius, and taste, but also, and more importantly, about language and style, nature and art. His aesthetic theories will be found in two of his major works, the *Essai sur l'Origine des Connaissances humaines* of 1746, and the "Traité de l'Art d'écrire" of his *Cours d'études* of 1775, a work he had devised for the Prince of Parma whose preceptor he had been for several years.

Condillac not only owed something to Locke; he also owed something to Fontenelle and other French thinkers. One may say that he fused certain aspects of British empiricism with French criticism. He went beyond the erudite and historical attitude of Du Bos to delineate the development of the arts, in terms of sensationist psychology, within the historical framework of civilization. His psychology of art is inseparable from social and historical perspectives, just as knowledge is inseparable from language. There is no transcendentalism in Condillac: he deals with a wholly human world, made by man wholly on the basis of what a man, or men, can know and have known. This is especially well brought out in the second part of his *Essai sur l'Origine des Connaissances humaines*, which deals with the origins and nature of language and the implications of these for the arts and sciences. Condillac founds knowledge on the senses, but regards it as important also to stress that with what the senses give man is able to construct the world he lives in and the knowledge he possesses. One may put it this way: in the beginning there was perception, and on the basis of this man constructed a world of which the fine arts are but one aspect, for Condillac considers art in wider terms, namely also as a species of methodology: "L'art n'est que la collection des règles dont nous avons besoin pour apprendre à faire une chose" ("Traité de l'Art d'écrire," in *Oeuvres*, V, 470). Knowledge, art, civilization derive from a common source and are inseparable though they may be distinct, while the transmission in historical time of knowledge in the form of language may vary in type from lyrical poetry to philosophical analysis.

Condillac takes aesthetic speculation beyond problems of beauty, the sublime, taste, imitation, rules, or even *le Vrai*, because he says, in effect, that the entire world of man, including even our concept of nature, is the result of art, that is to say of thought and imagination, of conventions created by men. Like Fontenelle, he was one of the freest minds of the eighteenth century, one who was not afraid to be modern because he was not afraid to think. He was, it goes without saying, wholly free of the superstition of antiquity. He thus made possible what can only be described as an open theory of art and thereby prepared the way, as Lanson pointed out, for early nineteenth-century French critics who exhorted the Germans, Italians, and Russians to develop their own literature rather than imitate foreign models. Consequently Condillac was a relativist on one level and an absolutist on another. As we saw in connection with beauty, taste, and nature, the eighteenth-century thinkers ever sought to reconcile the opposite claims of the particular and the universal, just as they sought to reconcile the heart and mind. Condillac devised an elegant solution to this problem, and was able to do so because he abandoned the imitative theory of art for what we might well term a language theory. It was because the arts could be considered as aspects of language, according to this theory, that they could take various forms ranging from lyrical poetry to philosophical analysis, a differentiation based upon the degree of freedom allowed the imagination. Thus beauty became a function of language. It became universal only insofar as it became more and more philosophical, analytical, and mathematical; beauty remained conventional, tied to sentiment and national languages insofar as it remained close to the imagination and to lyricism. Philosophy was a universal language, supposing an analytical style, describing true rapports between objects and showing true beauty, while poetry was the particular language of peoples, supposing a style of images, of expressions determined by conventions, variable taste, and relative beauty. This dualism of beauty is obviously nothing new. We have had occasion to find similar distinctions in the work of Crouzas and Father André. But Condillac avoided the old opposition between universal and particular beauty by accounting for the variations of beauty in terms of different languages. Dualism was replaced by structure. Knowledge, art, civilization were seen as structures built up in the course of historical time, and the old opposition between a concept of beauty derived from intuition and one derived from sense impressions was replaced by something different, namely a conflict between imagination and reason and, as a result of such conflict, such tension, the possibility of various languages or styles.

The victor of the conflict between reason and imagination, given Condillac and the time in which he wrote, ought, one might suppose, to be reason. Yet this does not mean that Condillac was a "cold man," without sensibility, an anti-poet or geometric mind like La Motte, Terrasson, or Fontenelle, assuming for the sake of argument that these were indeed cold rationalists, insensitive to the beauties of poetry (they were not, they could not be, because in truth poetry at the time was not supposed to be warm or lyrically romantic). Not so. Condillac strictly separated the prerogatives of philosophical analysis and taste: "Il faut le dire, rien n'est plus contraire au goût que l'esprit philosophique: c'est une vérité qui m'échappe" (Ibid., 476). Condillac's reasoning led him to a pluralist world of art no longer dominated by a universal concept of beauty, but rather a world of diverse genres, diverse conventions, each possessing its own beauty. One might say, borrowing from the language of the Existentialists, that it was the end of an essentialist view of beauty:

Le style poétique est donc, plus que tout autre, un style de convention; il est tel dans chaque espèce de poème. Nous le distinguons de la prose au plaisir qu'il nous fait, lorsque l'art, se conciliant avec le naturel, lui donne le ton convenable au genre dans lequel un poète a écrit; et nous jugeons de ce ton d'après les habitudes que la lecture des grands modèles nous a fait contracter. C'est tout ce qu'on peut dire à ce sujet. En vain tenterait-on de découvrir l'essence du style poétique; il n'en a point. Trop arbitraire pour en avoir une, il dépend des associations d'idées, qui varient comme l'esprit des grands poètes; et il y en a autant d'espèces qu'il y a d'hommes de génie capables de donner leur caractère à la langue qu'ils parlent [Ibid., 478].

The arts were conventions invented by men; the rules governing them were themselves inventions which varied from language to language, nation to nation, genre to genre, and the long-established and venerated doctrine of the imitation of the ancients turned out to be mere prejudice, founded on the erroneous assumption of a universal beauty and leading to such nonsense as supposing that in order to write French poetry one first had to know Greek and Latin. One attempted in vain to recreate antique genres while despising those proper to the national character, such, for example, as the operas of Quinault and Lulli. In fact, in spite of the efforts of the French writers of the *Grand Siècle* to be Greeks or Romans, they remained French and produced French works. For only the names of the genres had remained the same over the years, while the genres themselves had changed. The taste of a nation was nontransferable; philosophy was universal, but poetry was national and nontranslatable. Every nation had its own language and the taste proper to it. (All of which did not mean that within a national taste and literature there were no standards; it did mean that French criticism had finally gone beyond the prejudice of thinking itself to be in possession of the historically most recent emanation of true and universal taste.) As Lanson summed up Condillac's lesson: "Tous les goûts ne sont pas égaux, mais tous les goûts nationaux sont légitimes, parce qu'ils sont naturels. Il y a un bon goût, mais tout ce qui n'est pas le bon goût n'est pas nécessairement le mauvais goût, ni méprisable."[1]

Condillac's aesthetics were those of a civilized Frenchman of the mid-eighteenth century. He was devoid of dogmatism; his mind was modern, rigorous, and remarkably free of various forms of cant. "Un seul homme," writes Lanson,

fit un effort vigoureux pour construire une théorie qui répondît à l'état réel de l'intelligence et du goût en France, et qui, sans demander aux lettrés français le sacrifice de la tradition classique, lui donnât le moyen de ne pas mépriser les oeuvres étrangères auxquelles il était arrivé à prendre plaisir: ce fut Condillac [Ibid., 212].

He managed to do this in part because he did not allow himself to be bewitched by the still established language of the old criticism. He questioned terms such as imitation, nature, beauty, rules, and came to the conclusion that sensationist psychology, artistic convention, language, and society offered better explanations of the arts than concepts derived from metaphysics, supposing essences. Classical French criticism thus reached the point where it recognized the freedom of the arts from metaphysical tutelage. Poetry knew itself to be decor; beauty gave up its pretensions to universality; nature was recognized to be a convention; imagination was bound to language, time, and place, and all human activity; and thought and knowledge were recognized to be the work of man's power of invention.

* * *

Oeuvres complètes (Paris, 1821). On Condillac's literary theories see: Gustave Lanson, "Les Idées littéraires de Condillac" in *Etudes d'Histoire Littéraire* (Paris, 1929), pp. 210–23. See also, for more general studies: Raymond Lenoir, *Condillac* (Paris, 1924). Georges Le Roy, *La Psychologie de Condillac* (Paris, 1937). The most recent work on Condillac is Isabel F. Knight's excellent study: *The Geometric Spirit: The Abbé de Condillac and the French Enlightenment* (New Haven, 1968).

CORNEILLE, PIERRE (1606–1684)

THIS FAMOUS French dramatic poet was occasionally his own critic, if only in order to justify his practise and explain his modification of the rules. His place in the history of aesthetic theory is important above

[1] *Etudes d' Histoire Littéraire*, p. 272.

all in connection with the discussion of the rules of the dramatic genres, especially tragedy. His critical writings will be found in the various *examens* he wrote for his plays as well as in three discourses which appeared in the first three volumes of his collected works in the 1660 edition. These are first the *Discours de l'utilité et des parties du poème dramatique*; secondly, the *Discours de la tragédie et des moyens de la traiter selon le vraisemblable ou le nécessaire*; and finally, the *Discours des trois unités d'action, de jour, et de lieu*. These three discourses are, with the work of d'Aubignac and Chapelain, an excellent summary of the entire problem of rules as these were thought of in the first half of the seventeenth century in France. Corneille knew his rules very well, but he also knew they were one thing and that practise was another. While he accepted the principle that rules existed, that they ought to be observed, he also questioned their meaning, and in practise he modified the letter of the rules wherever he saw fit to do so without too radical a departure from the general precepts of Aristotle and Horace. What he did in his three *Discours* was in effect to examine and criticize the rules in the light of his own knowledge and experience of the theatre. He put his attitude rather well at the beginning of his first discourse on dramatic poetry:

Il est constant qu'il y a des préceptes, puisqu'il y a un art; mais il n'est pas constant quels ils sont. On convient du nom sans convenir de la chose, et on s'accorde sur les paroles pour contester sur leur signification. Il faut observer l'unité d'action, de lieu, et de jour, personne n'en doute, mais ce n'est pas une petite difficulté de savoir ce que c'est que cette unité d'action, et jusques où peut s'étendre cette unité de jour et de lieu. Il faut que le poète traite son sujet selon le vraisemblable et le nécessaire, Aristote le dit, et tous ses interprètes répètent les mêmes mots, qui leur semblent si clairs et si intelligibles, qu'aucun d'eux n'a daigné nous dire, non plus que lui, ce que c'est que ce vraisemblable et ce nécessaire.[1]

His three discourses deal precisely with the ambiguities of the rules such as those prescribing unity of time, place, and action, as well as verisimilitude and necessity. Corneille defines them in terms of his interpretation of Aristotle as well as of his own practise and knowledge of the theatre. His approach is directed to widen the meaning of the rules as these were set forth by Aristotle. He also justifies changes in the rules, new interpretations, on the basis of historical change, arguing

---

[1] *Discours de l'utilité et des parties du poème dramatique*, in *Théâtre Français Classique* (Paris: Club Français du Livre, 1958), I, 5–6.

that what held true for the times of Aristotle did not for his own. Regarding the rules, those who modified and questioned them were moderns, and Corneille was a modern in this sense. What differentiates his attitude from that of the later moderns of the early eighteenth century is that he did not justify his modernity in terms of perfection and rationality; his attitude is based upon practise and the notion of historical change. At the same time his treatment of the question shows that one could find a modus vivendi with the rules without completely rejecting them. His position is halfway between complete acceptance and complete rejection. In contrast with Molière's attitude, Corneille argues the matter within the rules set by the scholars: he writes treatises, he examines, reasons, comments on texts, interprets, and draws distinctions. Molière attacks the rules by making fun of the pedants and critics and by demonstrating that a play may be successful irrespective of the rules. Corneille's *Discours* may be regarded as a species of counter-criticism, and one may consider them as works of aesthetics, in that they are second-order discourse: he examines the assumptions of the philosopher and the critics. The result is, given the times, a rather undogmatic approach to the rules. Authority is still respected, but freedom of action is derived from freedom of interpretation:

Je tâche de suivre toujours le sentiment d'Aristote dans les matières qu'il a traitées, et comme peut-être je l'entends à ma mode, je ne suis point jaloux qu'un autre l'entende à la sienne. Le commentaire dont je m'y sers le plus est l'expérience du théâtre et les réflexions sur ce que j'ai vu y plaire ou déplaire [Ibid., 34].

The impression one gets is that Corneille managed to defend and justify the French theatre of his times rather well. His *Discours* are not repetitions of Aristotle, but rather the theory of his own theatre, even though written in language and with concepts inherited from Aristotle and the ancients, made over to fit the designs of the public of his own day. The result neither resembles Aristotle nor for that matter another philosopher, Descartes: it is Corneille, appearing as a theoretician or aesthetician in his own right. The whole distance between Greek antiquity and seventeenth-century France comes out well in the matter of mores, purgation, and verisimilitude.

Commenting upon Aristotle's precept to the effect that mores must be *bonnes, convenables, semblables et égales,* Corneille argued that the term *bonnes,* did not imply, as some thought, that they must be virtuous. This seems to be an answer to d'Aubignac's attitude concerning the theatre as a means of teaching virtue. Corneille argued that if evil, vice, or weakness were removed from the stage there would be little left of ancient as well as modern theatre. He thus interpreted "good" in terms of elevation of character, as that of Cleopatra in his play *Rodogune*, or of the liar in *Le Menteur*. Neither of these is good or virtuous, but they do have greatness, even in crime. One thinks of Sganarelle's characterization of Don Juan as a "grand seigneur méchant homme"; he is more than merely a *méchant homme*, because he is such with style. Corneille here points to a problem which later beset Diderot in connection with moral monsters; though Corneille thought of it in terms of dramatic action, while Diderot considered it in terms of a moralist of the Enlightenment. What Corneille put on the stage were not Greek victims of fate at all, or for that matter moral monsters in a world posited as fundamentally good, but proud feudal nobles or historical characters driven to commit crimes because of ambition, and it is probably Corneille's own situation in history and his own knowledge of men and also of the theatre which made him interpret the difficult term "purgation of the passions" as he did.

Regarding purgation, a link with Descartes' *Treatise of the Passions* may certainly be drawn, though we do not suggest that one influenced the other. What we do mean is that Corneille and others thought of purgation as a warning concerning the passions by presenting to sight, upon the stage, their possible effect. But Corneille admitted it was a difficult question and that the opinion he had to offer as to the meaning of the term was only *une opinion probable*:

La pitié d'un malheur où nous voyons tomber nos semblables nous porte à craindre d'un pareil pour nous; cette crainte, au désir de l'éviter; et ce désir, à purger, modérer, rectifier, et même déraciner en nous la passion qui plonge à nos yeux dans ce malheur les personnes que nous plaignons, par cette raison commune, mais naturelle et indubitable, que pour éviter l'effet il faut retrancher la cause.[2]

There follows an interesting and revealing critique of *Oedipus*. Corneille could not understand why Aristotle should have picked this piece to demonstrate the notion of the tragic flaw, or for that matter the notion of purgation. For Oedipus really does not make any mistake that plunges him into misfortune; he could not possibly know that he

[2] *Discours de la tragédie et les moyens de la traiter selon le vraisemblable ou le nécessaire*, in *Théâtre Français Classique*, I, 36.

242 BIOGRAPHICAL AND BIBLIOGRAPHICAL ARTICLES

killed his father when he killed that stranger on the road. Also, no one can really purge his passions on the basis of this tragedy because it is so unusual. What Corneille really seems to mean is that not only *Oedipus*, but the whole question of purgation, does not make sense. In fact, he doubts there is such a thing at all: "Si la purgation des passions se fait dans la tragédie, je tiens qu'elle se fait de la manière que je l'explique; mais je doute si elle s'y fait jamais, et dans celles-là même qui ont les conditions que demande Aristote" (Ibid., 39–40). He then goes on to argue that no one is ever really cured, for example, of the passion of love. In truth, the implication of all this is that the aim of the theatre is perhaps less purgation than it is the pleasure of the spectator. Thus Corneille's position points to the later question posed by Du Bos: why do we feel pleasure in witnessing the misfortunes of others on the stage?

Turning next to the question of what Aristotle meant by *le vraisem-blable et le nécessaire* in connection with dramatic action, Corneille was led to an interesting digression on the novel. Since the novelist was not restricted by the rule of the three unities, he was always bound to follow that of verisimilitude. Not so the dramatic poet: in his work, verisimilitude may be modified by necessity, that is by continuity of action, but is also by the convention of the stage. Also, since theatre is obviously not reality, Corneille makes various distinctions within the rule of *vraisemblance*, so that the poet might be free to modify history for presentation on the stage. And since the stage could also be thought of in terms of a picture, and the dramatic poem be considered as a portrait of the actions of men in time, he also modifies the supposed rule of unity of time so as to give it more flexibility. Here he also espoused the notion already set forth by d'Aubignac, namely that the closer the duration of the representation is to the original action, the closer the imitation is to the original, the more perfect the representation. Thus Corneille, while saying that he would not opt either for the twelve or the twenty-four hour day, and writing that the best idea would be to shorten duration as much as possible, also opined that the wisest course was to leave the question of time to the imagination of the spectators.

Corneille's approach to the rules may be described as that of a casuist: distinctions may be drawn wherever the rules are considered too strict, and ways may always be found to bend the letter of the rule. In essence his ideas may be reduced to three arguments: one can say that Aristotle's terminology is not clear; one can say that one must rely on experience as well, and that, times having changed, the rules no longer apply in all instances; and finally, you can always argue that the playwright works for a public who must be pleased.

* * *

See also: *Dramatic Poetry, Rules, Truth and Verisimilitude; Aubignac, Chapelain.*

DESCARTES, RENE (1596–1650)

DESCARTES CONTINUES TO BE considered an aesthetician. Ever since the appearance of Emile Krantz's work of 1882, *Essai sur l'esthétique de Descartes*, he has been given space in histories of aesthetics. He is discussed by Gilbert and Kuhn in their monumental history of aesthetics, by Cassirer in his work on the Enlightenment, and most recently by Monroe C. Beardsley in his short history of aesthetics. The latter's treatment is by far the most judicious, for the author points out that Descartes himself did not produce any aesthetics and that he touched but slightly on the subject. However, Professor Beardsley persists in the error of considering Boileau a Cartesian, an error which may be attributed to Krantz and which then passed to Cassirer and others. It may thus be useful to treat of this Cartesian aesthetic riddle once more in the hope of bringing some light and clarity to bear upon it. Fortunately for us, this was done some sixty years ago by Lanson in an article reprinted in a collection of his essays, *Etudes d'Histoire littéraire*, in 1929, and more recently in 1965. The article in question is a judicious examination of Krantz's thesis, entitled "L'Influence de la philosophie cartésienne sur la littérature française."

Lanson alluded to Krantz's thesis only to refute its premises and method:

M. Krantz . . . n'a pas résisté à la tentation de rapporter tout à Descartes dans la littérature du XVIIe siècle et d'en rattacher tous les caractères comme des effets immédiats et nécessaires aux principaux articles de la méthode et de la doctrine cartésiennes. Descartes devenait ainsi comme la cause unique et universelle du génie classique. La thèse ainsi présentée n'était guère soutenable.[1]

It was nevertheless published, and was influential upon histories of aesthetics written by philosophers. Lanson analyzed the relations be-

[1] Pp. 58–59 in the 1929 edition.

tween Cartesian thought and literature in a manner still enviable today, which resulted in findings still generally acceptable and certainly illuminating. He warned that identity of vocabulary does not imply identical conceptions; that certain general characteristics discernible in the literature of the time could be attributed to causes other than the Cartesian method and the insistence on clear and distinct ideas, and finally that the psychological orientation of literature in the seventeenth century was not due only to the Cartesian preoccupation with mind, but could be explained as well in terms of social, historical, and artistic factors. The rule of the three unities, for example, forced the author to concentrate on mental events quite independently of philosophy.

Lanson's conclusions were detailed and well thought out. Poetry and art were seen as escaping Cartesian influence, for both really depended on the doctrine of the imitation of the ancients. Boileau's *Art poétique* was not described as being Cartesian, and the poet's thought was assimilated to the values and tradition of classical antiquity rather than of modernity:

Son idéal n'est pas "l'idée" cartésienne, distincte, claire, un pur intelligible. S'il réduit le beau au vrai, il entend par le vrai le naturel, et par la nature, la forme réelle des choses. Il veut que le poète s'attache au vrai universel: mais les vérités universelles de la poésie, ce sont pour lui les types constants des espèces, non pas l'essence abstraite, mais la forme normale. Si bien que ce qu'il appelle raison en poésie, c'est en définitive, non point l'exactitude de la notion, mais la ressemblance de l'image. Et le sublime n'est précisément que l'expression qui peint le plus sensiblement la chose ou l'action [Ibid., 78].

Aestheticians would thus do well to associate Boileau with Plato or Aristotle rather than Descartes. Lanson did not think that the clarity and general characteristics ascribed to French Classicism could be associated with Descartes and argued that, on the contrary, Cartesianism eventually destroyed the very foundations of French Classicism. He considered the Quarrel of the Ancients and Moderns in this light and saw in the triumph of the moderns the triumph and revenge of Cartesians over partisans of the ancients and of the doctrine of imitation. Fontenelle and Perrault were both Cartesians, and they were surely the most thorough of the moderns. Consequently, Lanson thought that the triumph and characteristics of Cartesianism in literature could be discerned in the eighteenth century rather than in the *Grand Siècle*. This Cartesianism may be characterized as follows: defiance of authority; the introduction of the idea of progress into literature; the positing of a constant nature making for equality of genius among ancients and moderns; the posing of the criterion of evidence and clarity in both letters and criticism, so that what is not clear may be accounted false; the creation of a literature of ideas, intellectual rapports, and method; and finally, an ideal suited to prose rather than poetry: "Ainsi c'est le cartésianisme qui, à la fin du XVIIe siècle, porte le coup mortel à la littérature classique, en ruinant le respect de l'antiquité dans les esprits, en leur faisant perdre le sens de la poésie et le sens de l'art" (Ibid., 81). The Cartesian writers said to represent the new trend in letters were Fontenelle, Montesquieu, Voltaire, Duclos, d'Alembert, and Madame Du Deffand. The eighteenth century, from about 1700 through 1760, was seen as dominated by Cartesianism, even though Descartes's doctrines had largely been abandoned for those of Newton. It is curious and amusing to note that this very period and some of the writers cited would today be called "Rococo" by certain critics, while their procedures of thought would by still other critics be associated with empiricism rather than Cartesianism. Note, too, that Lanson's explanation of the decline of French Classicism had its forerunners in the eighteenth century, just as did Krantz's view of the blessings of philosophy for literature. Lanson's article can, however, still serve as a corrective to those who write histories of aesthetics. It must, however, be supplemented by other considerations for, as Professor Beardsley points out, however ironical it may have been that Descartes himself did not produce any treatise of aesthetics, he must nevertheless be considered in a history of aesthetics because his thought and influence were pervasive. Indeed, one can construct a Cartesian aesthetics. Lanson, in a sense, accepted it and found its influence in the eighteenth century. His essay was an attempt to untangle what was and what was not to be attributed to Descartes's influence. But there is one passage in this essay which is worth pondering because it throws light upon the presuppositions of Lanson himself:

En effet, je n'aperçois dans la doctrine de Descartes aucune possibilité d'esthétique. Le beau se confond dans le vrai. Le système cartésien est une expression mathématique de l'univers. Et une littérature procédant du cartésianisme ne peut être qu'une littérature d'idées pures, où les mots ne seront que les signes aptes à représenter les objets intelligibles, où la phrase ne sera que des combinaisons de signes exprimant les rapports intelligibles: une idéologie en substance, et dans la forme une algèbre, voilà ce que peut être une littérature cartésienne [Ibid., 77].

Lanson was writing in the 1890s, and seems to have associated aesthetics with a concept of beauty which he took to be the norm of artistic production; and such production he took to be its own end. It is as if he unconsciously supposed French literature of the *Grand Siècle* to have been a protoform of art for art's sake so that *le Beau*, in his mind, was separated from *le Vrai* and by extension also from *l'utile*. Despite the positivism and scientism he is often associated with, Lanson seems rather to have espoused post-Kantian idealism in the above passage. Yet, his description of the Cartesian aesthetic, in which he himself refused to believe, is an excellent description of an aesthetic ideal possible for others.

In truth, the situation of letters and philosophical speculation about art, history, and letters during the time of the Quarrel of the Ancients and Moderns, in which Lanson perceived the triumph of Cartenianism, was actually the triumph of Platonism over Aristotelianism. Perrault can be made into a Platonist *malgré lui* as well as into a Cartesian, and the victory of the moderns *qua* Cartesians can be questioned if only we look beyond 1760. The idea of progress in the arts can be argued on grounds which have nothing to do with Descartes and be explained as an effect of an official policy in the arts, as an establishment doctrine which allowed Louis XIV to be elevated to the level of an Augustus and his reign to that of a *Grand Siècle*, comparable to those of Alexander, Augustus, and Leo X. Lanson failed to see that Descartes's influence was not to be sought for in the artistic and literary production of this period so much as in certain critical opinions and in the elaboration of metaphysical aesthetics. Descartes, it seems to us, made possible, perhaps in spite of himself, aesthetics from above in the modern manner rather than in the ancient manner of Plato — though this does not mean that the ancient heritage of antiquity did not linger on, even in the new aesthetics.

Consider, for example, the first part of the *Discours de la Méthode* in which Descartes writes of his intellectual formation and his love of eloquence and poetry:

J'estimais fort l'éloquence, et j'étais amoureux de la poésie: mais je pense que l'une et l'autre étaient des dons de l'esprit, plutôt que des fruits de l'étude. Ceux qui ont le raisonnement le plus fort, et qui digèrent le mieux leurs pensées afin de les rendre claires et intelligibles, peuvent toujours le mieux persuader de ce qu'ils proposent, encore qu'ils ne parlassent que bas-breton, et qu'ils n'eussent jamais appris de rhétorique: et ceux qui ont les inventions les plus agréables et qui les savent exprimer avec le plus d'ornement et de douceur ne laisseraient pas d'être les meilleurs poètes, encore que l'art poétique leur fut inconnu.[2]

In short, eloquence and poetry are gifts or natural dispositions or genius, whereas philosophy is the result of method. Descartes separates one type of thought from another: poetry is separated from philosophy. Poetic creation is not of the same order as the solid, disciplined, methodical reasoning of the philosopher; the object of the orator is persuasion; the object of the poet is beauty; the object of the philosopher is truth and certainty. There is as yet no question of ranking these activities in terms of their relative merit or superiority vis-à-vis each other. Descartes became a philosopher because he did not find himself gifted for poetry or eloquence. It would almost seem that, in those far-off days, those who could not make good in poetry and *belles lettres* slipped into philosophy. Hume too, we recall, had always wanted to be a writer first. And today we know how much Wittgenstein admired Tolstoy. The *philosophes* of the eighteenth century changed the relation of letters to philosophy somewhat, and poetry hardly ever recovered fully from the change.

Lanson was right to see that Descartes implicitly separated beauty from truth; he did not see that men like Bouhours, Perrault, and Fénelon, would reunite the two in one or another manner, just as he did not see that the Cartesian disinterest in matters of poetry and eloquence implied a certain liberty in the arts indispensable to poetic creation and which would eventually be turned against certain Cartesian suppositions concerning letters. Fontenelle may have been a Cartesian, but he was careful to distinguish between progress in the sciences and perfection in the arts. La Motte, a truly Cartesian poet, did not make the same distinction; but Du Bos and his followers certainly did, and this allowed the development of the doctrine that taste, rather than rules and reason, were to be the judges of the arts. The distinction, implicit in Descartes, survived and showed up even in the work of Batteux in his formulation of the respective provinces of taste and intelligence:

Le goût est dans les arts ce que l'intelligence est dans les sciences. Leurs objets sont différents à la vérité; mais leurs fonctions ont entre elles une si grande analogie, que l'une peut servir à expliquer l'autre.

Le vraie est l'objet des sciences. Celui des arts est le bon et le beau [*Les Beaux-Arts*, 56].

[2] In Descartes, *Oeuvres et lettres* (Paris: Editions de la Pléiade, 1953), p. 129.

Thus Cartesianism did not so much destroy Classical French literature and the doctrine of imitation, in reality, as it made possible the future autonomy of art through the distinctions drawn between the faculties of the soul. The philosophers, in other words, by assuming that philosophy was applicable to all the objects of mind and reason, including therefore poetry and eloquence, which Descartes did not even bother discussing because he considered them gifts, created metaphysical or empirical aesthetics from above or from below and thereby changed the nature, not so much of literature, as of criticism.

What this means, regarding the supposed Cartesianism of Boileau and the supposed victory of the moderns over the ancients, is that one must carefully distinguish between an aesthetic built on a concept of art which might also be termed a poetics, and an aesthetic built on such terms as truth, beauty, and nature. As for the reuniting of the True and the Beautiful, whether by philosophers termed Cartesians or by Platonists, this may be considered as an aspect of Cartesianism used in defense of religion and directed against various types of freethinkers more likely to be associated with Epicureanism than with either Plato or Descartes. Lanson himself pointed out that the first result of Cartesian influence was a revival of religious thought, and that what can be termed a Cartesian critique of Christian assumptions came later. At the time of the battle between the ancients and moderns it is certainly possible to see a Cartesian manifestation in aesthetics, but this can hardly be thought of as inimical to the doctrine of imitation, for it was associated with churchmen and with the refutation of what was called Pyrrhonism, or libertinism, in matters of taste, rather than with the triumph of the moderns. We are alluding to the work, first of Crousaz, and later of Formey in Berlin and Father André in Rouen; André was a Cartesian, but his aesthetics can hardly be considered modern and anti-Classical. He is, indeed, a fine example of how one can be a Cartesian and an Augustinian at the same time, and yet be a Jesuit. What all these aesthticians from above have in common is a distrust of relativism in taste and beauty. They draw distinctions between true and false taste, intellectual and sensual beauty, in order to stress the truth and universality of intellectual beauty, an ideal surely not inimical to the suppositions of French Classicism.

But another inference may be drawn from the passage relative to poetry and eloquence taken from the *Discours*. Descartes implies that if you possess the gift of eloquence and poetry, success in those arts is assured irrespective of rhetoric or poetics. One may say that these two forms of criticism, rhetoric and poetics, stand in relation to the potential Cartesian aesthetics much as the old scholasticism stood in relation to his method. Paraphrasing Batteux, we may say that genius is to the arts what method was to Descartes and philosophy. Lanson thought that Cartesianism undermined the bases of French Classicism. It did undermine something, to be sure, but it may well have been the rules rather than literature itself, the authority of the ancients, and also of the pedants who interpreted them, rather than poetry itself. Fontenelle is pertinent in this matter, for he opined that one wrote first and elaborated rules later, and that the existence of rules did not oblige one to follow them. If this is so, then Cartesianism was a boon. One thing may be admitted with certainty, irrespective of whether it may be attributed to Cartesianism: the rules, by the early eighteenth century, were a dead issue. Indeed, the rules of Chapelain, d'Aubignac, Le Bossu, and others hardly derived from Descartes to begin with, and French Classicism was not the work of pedants who elaborated rules. It was accepted that rules existed but, as Montesquieu put it later on, art gave the rules but taste gave the exceptions to the rules. Condillac, a Cartesian, saw that they were mere conventions, a view which makes less for the undermining of literature than its autonomy and liberty.

The problem of the relation of Descartes to letters and aesthetics is thus not without paradoxes and nuances. The Cartesian method is first used to buttress and expound a doctrine of beauty more likely to be associated with Plato than Descartes, e.g., in the work of Crousaz, Formey, and Father André; it is used by Batteux to reduce all the arts to one fundamental principle which restates the assumptions of French Classicism; it is also used by some, such as Fontenelle, to liberate criticism, and therefore judgment, therefore taste, from the authority of the ancients, tradition, and rules. And on the whole, as regards the eighteenth century, we may say that the method was used to reconcile the rational requirements of the mind for an intelligible beauty with the evidence, provided by taste and history, of the diversity and variability of beauty in art and nature. Cartesianism in literature was thus reduced, in the end, to perhaps only one aspect of letters, namely method or clarity as an aesthetic ideal — one which can hardly be thought inimical to literary values. It did not make for Romantic poetry to be sure, but then the poverty of poetry in the eighteenth century can be explained without blaming Descartes.

But the questions raised by Krantz and Lanson cannot be ended here, for in addition to these general relations between Cartesianism and French Classicism, there is one aspect which has been generally neglected by aestheticians in their accounts of Cartesian aesthetics. It concerns the passions of the soul and their relation to objects of art and nature. Indeed, one might do well to look for a much more substantial Cartesian influence on aesthetic speculations here than in his views of music or in the general influence of rationalism, mechanism, or the mind-body problem.

Descartes, among others, supplied through his treatise on *The Passions of the Soul* a vocabulary and a psychology which influenced the discussion of aesthetic problems in the seventeenth and eighteenth centuries. This psychology supposed certain moral values which were inseparable from aesthetic values. The passions of the soul have to do with aesthetics insofar as they are caused by the perception of exterior objects; what ensues upon such a perception is a reciprocal action between the passions set in motion, the will, and the judgment. This implies a psychology of consciousness and also an aesthetics independent of mere pleasure: for in the view of Descartes a pleasing and beautiful object may not necessarily be a good one, precisely because the moral and the aesthetic are inseparable. The merely pleasing belongs to sentiment and to the passions. The moral is associated with the mind: the treatise on the passions was conceived as a method whereby to master the passions. The Cartesian psychology, based upon free will, thus makes possible aesthetic judgment, that is to say judgment free from the effects of the passions, sensual titillation, and the prejudices of sentiment. It supposes the judgment to be, so to speak, an impartial and lucid aesthetic observer within the soul itself, ever watching the passions and able to guide the will. Thus, in the affective scale of values will and judgment stand higher than the pleasures of the passions of the soul. Man may be presented with objects capable of pleasing or displeasing him, of setting his passions in motion in varying degrees, but he retains his free will to judge of these passions and perhaps to master them. The mind is the critic of the heart, and the Cartesian concept of the soul makes, in fact, for a suspicious aesthetic observer.

Cartesianism makes possible criticism in the various arts, because it supposes a detached, impartial, though affected, observer or spectator, capable of being moved by the perception of beautiful, terrible, or merely pleasing objects in art or nature, yet at the same time free to judge and analyze the worth of the passions set in motion by the objects seen. We may readily see why moral and aesthetic considerations were inseparable in criticism. Suspicion of the novel in the eighteenth century, for example, need not be explained in purely Christian terms as a concern for its sinful nature; there was also the fear that the images presented in the novel might arouse strong passions which would prove irresistible to those who had not yet exercised their will. We may also see how the aesthetics of Du Bos, based on the notion of art as a therapeutic of the passions, can be associated with the same psychology of the passions. The emotions caused by the perception of objects of art are effectively reduced because the judgment knows them to be artificial passions, caused by art, caused by illusions of reality rather than by the True itself. Where Descartes set up a rather stoic morality to combat the passions, Du Bos with the same psychology set up their therapy by way of art. He and Pascal were obviously less optimistic about what men could do with themselves, about their self-mastery, than was Descartes.

But there are other aspects of this psychology and the structure of the soul it supposes which have a bearing on the aesthetics of the time. For example, if the seventeenth century paid less heed to a universal standard of beauty it was in part because beauty was closely linked to the seat of the passions, the body which, Descartes thought, was not exactly the same in all men. Thus beauty as the object of the passions was relative, and universal beauty could thus only be based upon judgment and reason.

But the Cartesian soul may also be taken as the model of the very structure of artistic thought in the *ancien régime*. Consider the relation between an object, the maker of the object, and the observer of that object — or, if you will, between a work of art, its maker, and the judge, the "public" of that work. This relation is easily explained in terms of the mechanistic psychology of the passions: the work of art is the object perceived; it arouses in the soul certain passions which are judged and classified, and accepted or rejected, by the "public" within the soul itself, namely the will in cooperation with the judgment. Because such objects, in the Cartesian psychology, could be either natural or man-made, the artist or maker of an object played little role in this scheme. However, the same scheme applied to the world of art is also illuminating, for then the artist might be considered in terms of his will and judgment, mastering his passions in order to perceive clearly and distinctly and in order to produce only acceptable passions as far as the public was concerned. Obviously, this implied a doctrine of imitation rather than of expression. With the emphasis put on sensation and sentiment rather than will and judgment in the later eighteenth century, the role of the artist would change, and genius would be associated more with expression than with mastery.

Finally, one may say that among the six primary passions of the soul, as outlined by Descartes — admiration, love, hatred, desire, joy, and sorrow — the first is of especial interest to aesthetics; it may indeed be called an aesthetic passion par excellence, because it is the only one which is disinterested. Descartes defined it as follows: "L'admiration est une subite surprise de l'âme, qui fait qu'elle se porte à considérer avec attention les objets qui lui semblent rares et extraordinaires" (*Traité des Passions*, Article 70). Now, a singular property or characteristic of this passion is that it does not produce changes in the blood or the heart because it is not connected with good or evil, and therefore with danger or security to the body; it is a passion connected with mind:

N'ayant pas le bien ni le mal pour objet, mais seulement la connaissance de la chose qu'on admire, elle n'a point de rapport avec le coeur et le sang, desquels dépend tout le bien du corps, mais seulement avec le cerveau, où sont les organes des sens qui servent à cette connaissance [Ibid., Article 71].

Admiration thus corresponds to values associated with reason, judgment, the soul, rather than with sensation. We may suppose that if Descartes had elaborated on aesthetic he might have done it on the basis of this passion of admiration, one which indeed might well serve to characterize a great part of the artistic psychology of the seventeenth century. For admiration alone produces a disinterested pleasure connected with knowledge. The link with religion and the admiration for the work of God as supreme architect is obvious, but admiration may also be linked with lesser objects of beauty that are rare and striking, and that have the power to surprise the soul. We may therefore understand why emphasis was put on the striking qualities of certain objects of beauty, why artistic quality and value were often associated with the *effet de prime regard*, and why the duration of admiration, that is lasting interest in a work, was considered an aesthetic standard and the criterion par excellence of artistic worth. Works which stood the test of time were works forever admired.

Admiration also acted as a limit: it stopped at astonishment. Astonishment was an excess of admiration. Whereas admiration merely fixed the attention upon an object, astonishment went further; it was considered vicious because it implied uncritical, unreflective admiration, and a passion, however unharmful basically, must ever be known lucidly and assessed by the mind. Admiration was not to be confused with mere curiosity for the new, the rare, and the extraordinary: it had to lead to knowledge of the object admired, and was perhaps in this sense weaker than the passion aroused by the sublime, which might astonish. The distinctions made between a *connoisseur* and a *curieux*, established by 1720 and discussed by Caylus and others, thus also find psychological justification and make admirable sense within the Cartesian aesthetic. Note that the *curieux* were held in little esteem. Descartes indeed speaks of those who are *aveuglément curieux* in terms of a malady which pushes men to seek objects of admiration without an understanding or knowledge of such objects. These men are insatiable collectors, whereas the *connoisseur* is a man who knows his objects and collects for other reasons than mere curiosity and unsatisfied passions.

A passion, then, must be mastered by the will and known by the mind, and we see that the Cartesian aesthetic comprises two major elements: passion and judgment — in short, that constant duality of heart and mind, ever represented in the language and art of the time, which makes of the seventeenth and eighteenth centuries something more than an Age of Reason or Enlightenment, namely an age of tension between heart and mind.

* * *

The Lanson article is reproduced in *Etudes d'Histoire littéraire* (Paris, 1929); on the Platonism of French Classicism, see Jules Brody, "Platonisme et classicisme," in *Saggi e ricerche di letteratura francese* (Milan, 1961); also Jean Ehrard, *L'Idée de Nature en France dans la première moitié du XVIIIe Siècle* (Paris, 1963), especially Vol. I, 260 ff.; on Boileau and links to Descartes, viewed in a new light, see Nathan Edelman, "L'Art poétique: Longtemps plaire, et jamais ne lasser," in *Studies in Seventeenth Century French Literature*, edited by J. J. Demorest (Ithaca, N.Y., 1962). For a still different view of the question of Cartesianism in the Quarrel of the Ancients and Moderns, see my essay "Critical Reflections on the Origins of Modern Aesthetics" in *British Journal of Aesthetics*, IV, I, 7–21. For a wholly different view of aesthetics in seventeenth-century France as posed by Lanson, see Arsène Soreil, *Introduction à l'histoire de l'esthétique française: Contribution à l'étude des théories littéraires et plastiques en France de la Pléiade au XVIIIe Siècle* (Brussels, 1955).

DIDEROT, DENIS (1713–1784)

IT HAS BEEN WRITTEN that Diderot stood at the very heart of eighteenth-century aesthetics. This suggests the difficulty of trying to find a coherent view of his thought concerning aesthetic and artistic problems, for it is doubtful that eighteenth-century aesthetics was a thoroughly coherent structure. Diderot has also been characterized as a paradoxical writer, though it has also been argued that his aesthetics is not para-doxical at all, while others have pointed to the contradictions between his ethics and his aesthetics. Need we stress that it is highly difficult to write about Diderot in general as well as about his aesthetics in par-ticular? For he was not primarily an aesthetician, nor was he an art critic; but he was both, occasionally, and ever a man of letters, an editor, an aesthete sometimes, quite often a sentimental bourgeois, and on top of all that, a *philosophe*.

It may be, however, that viewing Diderot's thought on matters aes-thetic and artistic within the context of Classical aesthetics may bring some clarity into what may be described as the muddle of his own aesthetics. We may say that when he thought about art in general he still tended to think in terms of the Classical doctrine of imitation; that when he thought about painting he tended to be antiacademic and pronaturalistic, with an implied penchant for a strict imitation; that when he wrote and thought about beauty he often blurred the lines of demarcation between the beauties of metaphysics, art, nature, and mo-rality, so that he sometimes confused *le beau* with *les belles choses* (or even *les bonnes choses*); that, regarding genius, he emphasized na-ture rather than art, and sensibility, emotion, expression, and inspiration rather than rules, thus upsetting the balance between genius and taste, and between genius and society, in favor of genius; that when he thought of nature in relation to art he no longer had in mind *la belle nature*, but more likely nature as a fund of motifs, moral as well as physical, or else nature as a creative force manifesting itself through genius; and finally, that when he thought of the relation of art to mo-rality, he insisted upon utility, morality, and grandeur, but when he thought of the relation of morality to nature he saw very well that the two had little relation to each other. In Diderot, indeed, one perceives the opposition of an aesthetic constructed on the notion of art and one which would build upon the concept of nature. One may go further and say that the moral and the aesthetic realms came into conflict, although this conflict was not the result of an opposition of art and nature, as with Rousseau, but rather of a view of morality as inseparable from art and a view of nature as inseparable from aesthetic pleasure. The at-tempt to reconcile the truth, beauty, and the power of nature with the morality of art explains Diderot's own rather poor, or even kitschy, taste in painting, his putting of Richardson on a level with Shakespeare, his attempt to create a new dramatic genre. The above-delineated out-line of Diderot's aesthetic muddle may be confirmed by various of his works, many of which, read singly, are fascinating, and not internally contradictory, but which in the end seem to cancel each other out on a theoretical level, so that Diderot hardly serves as a good introduction to eighteenth-century aesthetics.

Diderot's writings dealing with problems of aesthetics may be divided into three parts: literary criticism, art criticism, and aesthetics proper. Under the first heading we may put the eulogy of Terence and Richardson, writings on the drama such as *De la poésie dramatique*, the *Paradoxe sur le comédien*, the *Entretiens sur le Fils Naturel*, and various passages from the *Neveu de Rameau* and other fiction; under art criticism we may place the *Salons*, the *Essais sur la peinture*, and the *Pensées détachées sur la peinture*; while the article "Beau," two pieces on genius, and the correspondence with Falconet (published as *Le Pour et le Contre*) can be considered under the heading of aesthetics, for the first concerns a metaphysics of beauty, the second the psychology of creation, and the third the destiny of art. There are remarks pertinent to aesthetics also in various passages of the *Neveu*, the *Lettre sur les aveugles*, and the *Rêve de d'Alembert*, just as there are passages on painting and imitation in the novel *Jacques le Fataliste* and passages on various aspects of literature in the *Bijoux indiscrets*. It is obvious that no reader of Diderot can escape aesthetic problems, and these are evident even in the style of the writer, in his use of metaphors, his images, and his very lively dialogues which present different views of nature, drama, creation, and morality.

Diderot was not one of the most lucid expositors of aesthetic doctrine, but he was surely one of the most stimulating writers in the area. It may also be said to his credit that part of the difficulty of dealing with his aesthetics comes from a virtue: that of attempting to go beyond formulas. He perceived that the writings of Father André and Batteux, indeed much of Classical thinking on the arts, were only superficially clear and coherent only verbally. He said, with reference to Batteux, that he never tells us what *la belle nature* really is. And when Diderot pondered the word "nature" and looked at nature and then at works of art, or imitations of nature, he also perceived that the word "imitation" was not very clear either. He was equally acute when he turned his attention to the supposed link between art and morality and saw the potential power for evil in art. Art was one thing, nature another, and ethics something else still. Still, he did not draw the lines of demarcation with philosophical rigor and precision, as did Kant. We may surmise he did not wish to draw such distinctions at all, and it is perhaps this very unwillingness which makes for some of the difficulties of his aesthetics. The old distinctions which aestheticians had been careful to make, between pure and ideal nature, mind and sensibility, intellectual and sensuous beauty, truth and fiction, and so on, tend to be blurred in the writings of Diderot. In other words, the dualism of mind and heart upon which the old aesthetics had been elaborated no longer obtains — as is evident in his concept of nature. It is in part because of this that Diderot does not distinguish between stylization and artificiality, just as it is because of this rejection of dualism that he creates a rapprochement between art and nature and yet shrinks from the separation which ought to follow, namely that between art and morality. For the result of this end of dualism was not a world of multiplicity, a coexistence of cultures such as exists today, nor even the relative freedom of taste which had obtained in the seventeenth century and which manifested itself in a hierarchy of beauties, various schools of painting, and diverse styles; on the contrary, the age of Diderot was avid for unity, and for Diderot this meant an aesthetic built on a monistic view of nature, in which the artistic norm was not given by an objective view of nature at all, but rather by social utility and moral considerations that were justified in the name of nature. Thus it is that Diderot's aesthetic of art conflicted with his fascination for nature, and the moralist was doubled up with the aesthete, making possible that delightful dialogue between the *philosophe* and Rameau's nephew, a product of nature, part genius, part failure, a connoisseur of men and of music, amoral yet delightful, to the confusion of the bourgeois *philosophe*, who would like to see morality, talent, genius, and beauty harmoniously united and naturally one for the greater benefit of mankind.

Diderot tried to surmount this contradiction between morality and nature but only succeeded in creating Dorval, that genius of sensibility far less credible than the nephew. The contradiction between an aesthetic built on the concept of art and an aestheticism of nature remained, though we may suppose that Diderot thought that he had surmounted the difficulty by betting on the ancients. Indeed, if we consider his writings on painting and take these as indicative of his aesthetic assumptions, but keeping these distinct from the article on beauty, which is a metaphysical problem, we see that Diderot did not escape his times and that, in spite of his much-praised understanding of Chardin and the allusions to Diderot as a forerunner of Baudelaire in criticism, he was in fact a product of that second reform of the Academy in Rome carried through by Hallé under the direction of d'Angiviller. Diderot was among those who preached the *retour à l'Antique*, which ironically makes of him a man not so much of the future as of the past, merely a more dedicated academician than Boucher, who had quite rightly warned the young Fragonard on his way to Rome to watch out for the Italians lest he become as mannered as they — meaning thereby that an artist must first of all be himself rather than an example of some doctrine or school. Regarding art then, one can make a case for Diderot as a partisan of the ancients; at the same time, though, one can make another case for him as a man who confused imitation with the accurate copying of nature. This is possible because it was then often believed that the ancients had copied nature best, having been closest to it in its uncorrupted state. By the imitation of the antique, in short, one could have one's cake while eating it: nature and grandeur all in one. The allusions are to be found in various of his writings that leave no doubt as to his meaning: "La beauté n'a qu'une forme," he writes in his *Pensées détachées sur la peinture*,[1] but he had already voiced a similar thought in connection with dramatic poetry: "Mais où prendre la mesure invariable que je cherche et qui me manque? . . . Dans un homme idéal. . . . Oui. Prenons cette statue, et animons-la."[2]

He accepted not only the standard of beauty of the antique, but also the hierarchy of painting subjects of his day, with history the highest genre: for Diderot, as for the *philosophes* in general, this genre was the most susceptible of use for the instruction of mankind. We have noted that Diderot associated art with morality: he felt that one could misuse art, to be sure, but thought that the highest art was truly moral, just as he thought that taste also was related to morality. Consider this remark on Nero: "Néron fit dorer et gâter la statue d'Alexandre. Cela ne me déplaît pas; j'aime qu'un monstre soit sans goût. La richesse est toujours gothique" (*Pensées détachées*, 812). This type of approach to art explains his esteem for the paintings of Greuze, his ambivalence towards Boucher, and a remark such as this from the *Pensées détachées sur la peinture*: "Je voudrais que le remords eût son symbole, et qu'il fût placé dans tous les ateliers" (Ibid., 769). Why? because licentious pictures and statues were more dangerous than licentious books, being closer to the model in nature. For this theory, unlike that of Du Bos, the artificial signs of language proved an advantage, and it is obvious that Diderot was more aware of the possible dangers of art than was Du Bos, who was concerned mainly with banishing ennui. For Du Bos the question of the relation of morality to art is hardly touched upon except with reference to Plato and the relative desirability of avoiding ennui; but in the mind of Diderot and his con-

[1] In *Oeuvres esthétiques*, p. 830.
[2] *De la poésie dramatique*, in *Oeuvres esthétiques*, p. 284.

temporaries the moral content was inseparable from beauty and from the uses of art. Thus Diderot's concept of the artist, for example, was in accord with that of the reforms of the Academy in the 1770s, and here again he was in line with the *retour à l'Antique*, insisting that the artist must work for posterity, mankind, and honor. He was not to think of personal ambition, or merely to please the present: "L'éloge de nos contemporains n'est jamais pur. Il n'y a que celui de la postérité, qui me parle à présent, et que j'entends aussi distinctement que vous, qui le soit," wrote Diderot to Falconet.[3] As for riches in the present, let the artist beware: "Au moment où l'artiste pense à l'argent, il perd le sentiment du beau" (*Pensées détachées*, p. 824). One trembles for innumerable successful artists who turned out highly respectable works and were wealthy: but Diderot did not always think about what he was writing, for he was not always immune to enthusiasm. In any case, he thought of the artist, not as a craftsman or an artisan, but as a man with a vocation and a misson, just as he did not think of beauty as a mere product of art for the delight and pleasure of the leisured of society: as the artist was a man with a vocation, so beauty was inseparable from morality. He said much the same about the man of letters and the *philosophe*: "La vérité et la vertu sont les amis des beaux-arts. Voulez-vous être auteur? Voulez-vous être critique? commencez par être homme de bien" (*De la poésie dramatique*, 281). So much, we might think, for Diderot's theory of art as constructed upon the *beau idéal*. In this realm, far from being the precursor of Baudelaire, he was but a reader of Winckelmann and a precursor of Quatremère de Quincy and Victor Cousin. Indeed, had Diderot rewritten his essay on beauty in the 1770s he might well have retitled it *Du Vrai, du Beau, et du Bien*. This is what the *philosophes* aspired to in the aesthetic realm. Diderot not only read Winckelmann, he also admired Plato, who had in the 1760s and 1770s recovered from Perrault, Fontenelle, and Du Bos. This trinitarian aesthetic of art, however, is but one aspect of Diderot's aesthetics.

If we turn elsewhere, to the *Neveu de Rameau, Jacques le Fataliste*, and his numerous speculations on genius and nature we shall see that this trinity is reduced to a monism founded on an ambiguous concept of nature. We thus find a different attitude towards art and painting: a critique of academic art as he knew it in the name of nature, and a

[3] Diderot and Falconet, *Le Pour et le Contre, Correspondance polémique sur le Respect de la Postérité, Pline et les Anciens*, Introduction and notes by Yves Benot (Paris: Editeurs Français Réunis, 1958), p. 53.

suspicion that art and morality really have nothing to do with each other. The first leads not only to a criticism of academicism and the rules but also to a reevaluation of genius and its function in the arts and society; the second leads to an aesthete's fascination with beauties outside the realm of art and morality.

Because nature did nothing incorrect, as Diderot wrote in his *Essai sur la peinture*, it stood to reason that the idea of correct poses, attitudes, and gestures was merely conventional. Thus his critique of art, which may be gleaned in the *Salons* and in the various writings on painting, amounts to a questioning of the conventions of art as then understood in the name of the natural. This was far from new, for people had always criticized mannerisms of one type or another in the name of nature. What is new is that Diderot does not tell us which nature to copy or imitate. Sometimes it is ideal nature, but sometimes it seems to be the nature to be seen outside the window or in the street. He takes nature seriously; it is the norm of artistic value, and one suspects that at times imitation comes close to meaning copying: "Il n'y aurait point de manière, ni dans le dessin, ni dans la couleur, si l'on imitait scrupuleuse-ment la nature. La manière vient du maître, de l'académie, de l'école, et même de l'antique." [4] Nature is obviously the norm; but which nature is it? "Toute composition digne d'éloge est en tout et partout d'accord avec la nature; il faut que je puisse dire: 'Je n'ai pas vu ce phénomène, mais il est.'" (*Pensées détachées*, 773). An academician could hardly have disagreed with either of these statements, though he might have wondered about the "scrupulous imitation of nature," for that is pre-cisely what the Dutch and Flemish painters had supposedly been doing, and they were usually placed on the lowest rung of the artistic scale of values. But Diderot had, in a moment of enthusiasm, exclaimed that he would give ten Watteaus for one Teniers, so that one could interpret his views on the scrupulous imitation of nature as meaning that the painter ought to paint in the manner of the Dutch painters and restrict himself to the imitation of *le vrai simple*, to use the vocabulary of de Piles. (De Piles did not mean by this mere copying, however.) On the other hand, if copying is what Diderot meant, then this hardly squares with his exaltation of the *beau idéal*. The only thing which re-mains certain is that nature becomes an artistic norm: "Nous disons d'un homme qui passe dans la rue, qu'il est mal fait. Oui, selon nos pauvres règles; mais selon la nature, c'est autre chose. Nous disons

[4] In *Oeuvres esthétiques*, p. 673.

d'une statue, qu'elle est dans les proportions les plus belles. Oui, d'après nos pauvres règles; mais selon la nature?" (*Essais sur la peinture*, 666–67.) Diderot's naturalism led him to criticize the conventions of art and to place nature above art as a standard of beauty. This was hardly an improvement over what he found in the world of art theory; all it meant was that one academicism was to be replaced by another. Indeed, this is precisely what happened in the development of eighteenth-century painting: the feminine nudities of Boucher, Natoire, Detroy, and Pierre were replaced by the manly nudities of the antique; gracious and coquettish gestures were turned into declamatory expressions, while the happy hazards of the swing were balanced by demure Athenian ladies dipping their feet in marble baths. Opera was turned into historic melodrama. There are times when Diderot's words seems to imply views of poetry akin to those of Hugo and visions of painting reminiscent of Delacroix, but look at the pictures he admired and you know he really meant something else. It is tempting to see in him a man waiting for David, Géricault, and Delacroix. Are there not in his work passages which announce these painters' works, call for them, just as in poetry he seems to call for Victor Hugo? "La poésie veut quelque chose d'énorme, de barbare et de sauvage" (*De la poésie dramatique*, 261). And did he not appreciate Doyen's canvas at St. Roch in which "one can already discern," as professor Seznec writes, "the scattered elements of those great melodramas, the *Massacre at Chios*, the *Plague-Stricken of Jaffa*, and *The Raft of the Medusa*?"[5] But Diderot was not the sole critic to call for grandeur in the arts. One wonders, besides, whether it is justifiable to infer from his writings on Doyen's *Miracle des ardents* his possible reactions to the Romantic works named. To do so is to assume that the works of Delacroix, Gros, and Géricault have a common element with the work of Doyen which answered to one aspect of Diderot's sensibility, in this case his delight in violence and tumult, in the savage, the enormous, and the barbaric. He could have found these qualities in various Baroque painters, and it is hardly necessary to make of Diderot a man whose aesthetic announces on the one hand David and on the other Delacroix and whose criticism evokes Baudelaire. He was not that original, and the only thing that such reasoning proves is that there are affinities between what he wrote and what others painted — which proves very little, at most a similarity of imagination. He was not the only man to have such thoughts in the eighteenth century, just

[5] "Diderot and Historical Painting," in Wasserman, *Aspects of the Eighteenth Century*, p. 140.

as he was not the only man to realize that poetry needed conditions other than those which obtained in his time in order to flourish.

Consider, too, his interesting remark about Polyphemus: "Qui pourrait supporter sur la toile la vue de Polyphème faisant craquer entre ses dents les os d'un des compagnons d'Ulysse. . . ? Ce tableau ne récréera que des cannibales; cette nature sera admirable pour des anthropophages, mais détestables pour nous."[6] Obviously this nature is no longer the one which the painter ought to copy scrupulously and which never makes a mistake. And one wonders what Diderot, who supposedly would have taken delight in the *Raft of the Medusa* and other such melodramas, would have said to Goya's "black" paintings and his frightening *Saturn*? Diderot seems to forget that art is art and that nature is nature, and that a motif from nature does not have the same effect on a spectator within the convention of art as it does in nature:

> Il n'est point de serpent ni de monstre odieux,
> Qui, par l'art imité, ne puisse plaire aux yeux.

But then, the blurring of the lines between art and nature was a product of his monistic view of nature. It also led him, as we said, to revise the concept of genius and upset the balance between genius and rules. Rules are still associated with art, but they now become the fetters of genius: "Les règles ont fait de l'art une routine; et je ne sais si elles n'ont pas été plus nuisibles qu'utiles. Entendons-nous: elles ont servi à l'homme ordinaire; elles ont nui à l'homme de génie" (*Pensées détachées*, 753–54). Diderot ends up with an expression theory of genius which is hardly in accord with his view of the *beau idéal* or his moral view of art. These discords show up in his *Neveu de Rameau*, where his aestheticism and moralism contribute to the vitality of the work because they are evidently irreconcilable.

Diderot's aestheticism may be described as a fascination with characters that possess a unity of character and action and yet are morally evil; such are the Père Hudson, Madame de la Pommeraye, the renegade of Avignon, and the Neveu de Rameau himself, though he is less evil than amoral. Diderot looked at certain characters in terms of art, judged them on artistic criteria, and doing this separated their moral value from their aesthetic value. He has done this by creating these types, yet he cannot quite accept this possibility in reality, for the narrator asks the Neveu: "Comment se fait-il qu'avec un tact aussi fin, une si

---

[6] Quoted in Jean Ehrard, *L'Idée de nature en France dans la première moitié du XVIIIe Siècle* (Paris, 1965), I, 325.

grande sensibilité, vous soyez aussi aveugle sur les belles choses en morale, aussi insensibles aux charmes de la vertu?"[7] The man who poses the unity of beauty, truth, and goodness in the arts cannot help but perceive that you can have one without the other two, that you can have beauty without goodness. He also perceives the possibility of a perverse use of art: since art is an amiable lie and illusion, could it not be used for selfish, dishonest, and evil purposes? Abbé Du Bos and his generation had thought of the danger of art in terms of its capacity to arouse passions which were of themselves dangerous to society. Diderot and his generation think of the dangers of art in terms of deceit: art might be used as a form of immoral education. Thus the Neveu explains that if he had had instruction he would have been a much more successful man, for he might have modeled himself upon fictional characters to become a success in the world: "Ainsi, quand je lis l'*Avare*, je me dis: Sois avare si tu veux, mais garde-toi de parler comme l'avare. Quand je lis *Tartuffe*, je me dis: Sois hypocrite si tu veux, mais ne parle pas comme l'hypocrite" (Ibid., 467). Since art could be used for such purposes it became extremely important to reinforce the moral element of a work of art, be it a painting or a drama, a novel or a short story: the moral had to be underlined, stressed, so as to leave nothing in doubt. Precisely because morality could be separated from art, art had to become more and more moral, and the element of pleasure countered by the greater and stronger insistence upon instruction. The aestheticism of Diderot was thus complemented by moralism in the arts: he perceived beauties in nature which had a certain artistic quality about them, and part of the beauty of characters such as Father Hudson comes from their behaving in real life as one might on the stage: but precisely because of this, for the salvation of mankind and society, the stage had to become a school of moral and civic virtue. The difference between Du Bos and Diderot thus turns upon a concept of man. For the first, man is still close to the Christian conception; in a sense, man is corrupt, he cannot be changed, and therefore must be diverted from himself. For Diderot and the *philosophes*, however, man is malleable; therefore he must be educated, perfected, taught to function as a useful citizen of the state. Du Bos' salon, where men may be diverted, has given way to the forum, where they may be exhorted to virtue.

✳ ✳ ✳

Oeuvres esthétiques, ed. Paul Vernierès (Paris: Classiques Garnier, 1959).

[7] *Le Neveu de Rameau* (Paris: Editions de la Pléiade, 1951), p. 489.

There is a huge Diderot bibliography, and we shall mention here only the more important works concerning Diderot and his aesthetics and criticism: Yvon Belavel, *L'Esthétique sans paradoxe de Diderot* (Paris, 1950): well argued, well constructed, but in the end somehow not convincing; Mario Busnelli, *Diderot et l'Italie* (Paris, 1925); Lester G. Crocker, *Two Diderot Studies: Ethics and Esthetics* (Baltimore, 1952): indispensable; Herbert Dieckmann, *Cinq Leçons sur Diderot* (Paris and Geneva, 1959): a major work on Diderot; Hubert Gillot, *Denis Diderot. L'Homme: Ses Idées philosophiques, esthétiques et littéraires* (Paris, 1937): very useful; Georges May, *Quatre Visages de Diderot* (Paris, 1951): good; Jean Seznec, *Essais sur Diderot et l'Antiquité* (Oxford, 1957): an excellent work on this theme, and by extension on the *retour à l'Antique*; see also, by the same author, "Diderot and Historical Painting" in Wasserman (ed.), *Aspects of the Eighteenth Century* (Baltimore, 1965).

His work as an art critic has been treated in various works, one book, and several articles, namely: Gita May, *Diderot et Baudelaire critique d'art* (Geneva, 1957); Jean Seznec, "Falconet, Voltaire, Diderot," in *Studies on Voltaire and the Eighteenth Century*, II, 43–59; also, "Le Musée de Diderot," in *Gazette des Beaux Arts*, Mai–Juin 1960, pp. 341–56; Jacques Proust, "L'Initiation artistique de Diderot," in *Gazette des Beaux Arts*, Avril 1960, pp. 224–32. See also, in connection with this, Virgil C. Topazio, "Art Criticism in the Enlightenment," in *Studies on Voltaire and the Eighteenth Century*, in Transactions of the First International Congress on the Enlightenment, XXVII, 1934–56.

DU BOS, JEAN-BAPTISTE, ABBE, (1670–1742)

DIPLOMAT, HISTORIAN, CRITIC, member of the Académie Française, the Abbé Du Bos is chiefly known for his *Réflexions critiques sur la Poésie et sur la Peinture* (Paris, 1719), and for his *Histoire critique de l'établissement de la Monarchie française dans les Gaules* of 1734. Historians know him for the latter, aestheticians for the former work. Since we have used his work liberally in this dictionary we shall not summarize his work in aesthetics here, but merely indicate his importance and role in the history of aesthetics, and especially in the eighteenth century. His *Réflexions critiques* are indispensable reading for those who would understand eighteenth-century French and other European aesthetics, even the British, for he was translated into English as well as being read in Germany, Italy, and Switzerland. He was used by everyone, although not always cited, footnoted, or acknowledged. He is well known to scholars of French literature and art, but has been unduly neglected by aestheticians, who often tend to write the history of aesthetics "from above." Happily, this trend seems to be less prevalent today, as witness the recently published short history of aesthetics by Professor Beardsley (New York, 1965).

Du Bos did not compose any formal, rationally constructed, metaphysical system of aesthetics. His approach was empirical and historical. There are no essays on beauty in his *Réflexions critiques,* and he is not too concerned with what is called aesthetics from below, that is with the sensationalism of the British school, even though his aesthetics is founded on the notion of pleasure. He does not go deeply into the mechanism of this pleasure, but rather uses pleasure as a starting point for considerations of the various arts and their relation to society, history, genius, taste, and to each other. Judging his approach from the viewpoint of later French aesthetic theories it is possible to think of Du Bos as the founder of the French tradition — though this is not to say that the occasional aesthetics of the seventeenth century should be forgotten. His *Réflexions critiques* draw together various aspects of aesthetic speculation, namely poetics, the discussion of rules, and the newly developed discussion of painting; he elaborates on genius, taste, and artistic pleasure, and draws conclusions from the Quarrel of the Ancients and the Moderns. His work in this respect may be seen as the summa of aesthetic discussions up to his time, but he also sets up or reveals certain personal constants, such as a historical and critical approach to the arts and taste. His discussion of the *Grands Siècles* anticipates all of French aesthetic speculation in the eighteenth century, and if we read Taine we soon perceive that his *Philosophie de l'Art* owes a great deal to Du Bos, though the vocabulary is different, the method more thorough, and the results perhaps more off the point. In Du Bos' discussion of genius and art, we are reminded of the definition of aesthetics by Véron: "L'esthétique est la science qui a pour objet l'étude des manifestations du génie artistique." Du Bos could hardly have disagreed, though it is significant that his discussion of genius went beyond merely artistic manifestations.

While it is quite true that Du Bos posits a hedonist concept of art, it must not be thought that he was merely the spokesman of the Régence; he was that but he was also more, for like his contemporaries Montesquieu and Fénelon he viewed antiquity and its achievement with great respect and generally thought the Greeks and Romans worthy of emulation, in the practise of the arts as well as in their artistic policy. He learned the proper lessons from the Quarrel of the Ancients and Moderns, too, but did not dismiss the past or the ancients, or assume the attitude of a Perrault. He sided rather with Fontenelle, using the separation of art and science to save the ancients from the geometric spirit. His work is filled with allusions to various aspects of the Quarrel, as well as to that between the Poussinists and the Rubensists in the Academy of Painting and Sculpture. Thus, while he insisted upon the effect of a work of art on the spectator or reader as being all-important in the determination of its artistic value, there is also another side to Du Bos which points to the later *retour à l'Antique*, the call to greatness in art. He was not only a worldly abbé, but also a scholar and historian. If he sided with the aristocracy against the opinions of the pedants, if he opposed the judgment of taste to the authority of the critics, he also posed connoisseurship and genius as prerequisites to artistic judgment and production. He also thought that the state ought to support the arts seriously, even though he had doubts that this would do much good if genius were lacking. While he thought that the merit of a poem lies in its capacity to please and touch, he did not mean that it should amuse or titillate. With Du Bos, as with so many others, one must take care not to confuse his personal inclinations and taste with the seemingly revolutionary implications of his words. His taste was that of his own times, probably more on the lines of the *grand goût* than of the *goût moderne*. His ideas and words, when read from the perspective of today, often seem to bring to mind such terms as relativism, sensualism, even historicism, but their meaning was bounded by the society he lived in. Teubner referred to Du Bos as the aesthetician of the Baroque. This seems not unfounded when one considers his insistence upon moving the spectator, upon touching him; it also recalls his interest in opera, declamation, and mime. But Du Bos was an admirer of Quintilian, which would also align him with the partisans of the ancients. In his case, as in that of Fontenelle, we see the example of personal attitudes towards art which may be termed hedonistic accompanied by a capacity for critical and historical detachment. This trait was quite important, for it was something lacking in the Cartesians of the day, and it was this historical sense which allowed Du Bos to save the ancients from geometrical reasoning. As Caramaschi ably put in his excellent essay "Du Bos et Voltaire," "Il sent en honnête homme et formule en savant."

* * *

Réflexions critiques sur la Poésie et sur la Peinture (Paris, 1755) is used throughout this book. There are several studies of Du Bos: Marcel Braunschvig, *L'Abbé Du Bos, rénovateur de la critique au*

XVIIIe Siécle (Toulouse, 1904); Enzo Caramaschi, "Du Bos et Voltaire," in *Studies on Voltaire and the Eighteenth Century*, X, 113–236; N. Jonard, "L'Abbé Du Bos et l'Italie," in *Revue de Littérature comparée*, XXXVII, No. 2, 177–201; Armin H. Koller, *The Abbé Du Bos: His Advocacy of the Theory of Climate* (Champaign, Ill., 1937); Alfred Lombard, *L'Abbé Du Bos, un initiateur de la pensée moderne* (Paris, 1913); B. Muntenao, "L'Abbé Du Bos ou le Quintilien de la France," in *Mélanges d'histoire littéraire et de bibliographie* offerts à Jean Bonnerot (Paris, 1954); Eugen Teubner, "Die Kunstphilosophie des Abbé Du Bos, in *Zeitschrift fur Ästhetik und Allgemeine Kunstwissenschaft*, XVII, 361–410. The latest study of Du Bos is that of Enrico Fubini, *Empiricismo e Classicismo: Saggio sul Du Bos* (Turin, 1965), a work which renders justice to the greatest of the French aestheticians of the *ancien régime*.

FENELON, FRANÇOIS DE SALIGNAC DE LA MOTHE (1651–1715)

CHURCHMAN, MYSTIC, TUTOR of the Duke of Burgundy, and author of *Télémaque*, Fénelon held a view of art and beauty that is much more important and revealing for eighteenth-century aesthetics than might at first be supposed from the place accorded him in histories of literature. His views on matters concerning aesthetic theory were set forth in his *Dialogues sur l'Eloquence en général et sur celle de la chaire en particulier*, his *Lettre écrite à l'Académie Française*, and in various letters written to La Motte on the occasion of the quarrel over the translation of Homer. There are also pertinent passages in his treatise on the education of girls, the *Traité de l'éducation des filles*, while an aesthetic is implied in the *Télémaque*. His point of departure is the art of eloquence and his admiration for the ancients and the Bible. In the Quarrel of the Ancients and Moderns, Fénelon sided with neither party; his ideals were fixed above these contentions upon nature and beauty, which transcend such purely literary and rhetorical disputes. This attitude to the Quarrel differs from that of a Du Bos, in that it is not founded purely on taste, but also on the unity of truth and beauty as well as on a moral concept of art derived from Plato and the ancients. Fénelon, it must be recalled, was a churchman, not a man of letters: the relative merits of ancients and moderns were of lesser importance to him than the possibilities of the uses of art and beauty in the dissemination of the word of God and of virtue. It is this use of art which determined his aesthetics, which rests on two fundamental points: beauty is associated with simplicity and truth; eloquence is the key to a theory of art whereby men may be persuaded of the truth by touching their souls. Beauty is truth made visible, touching, moving to man. The only true art is that which leads man to truth and goodness. It is obvious that Fénelon owes a great deal to Plato, and it is not for nothing that he admired Raphael and Poussin. But beauty here on earth is but an imperfect shadow of the greater beauty of God and the life beyond. Art must serve religion, and Fénelon's *Dialogues on Eloquence* set forth how this may be done; these dialogues are far from being a technical treatise on the rules of rhetoric. He is concerned with touching the passions in order to make a durable impression on the minds of men. The way to truth is not through abstract reasoning, but through persuasion by eloquence, an art close to poetry which appeals not only to the mind but to the heart as well, and which is much more than an art of pleasing or of gaining glory for oneself, for it must also improve men. The orator, consequently, must unite the subtlety of the dialectician and the knowledge of the philosopher, be endowed with a diction nearly equal to that of the poet, and possess the voice and gestures of the great actor. It is obvious that Fénelon's view of eloquence is little different from that of Pascal, and its importance for aesthetics may be readily understood once we consider it as but a sacred version of the profane theory of art of the *philosophes*, who also wished to move men, persuade them of the truth, though less by the eloquence proper to the church than by that closely connected with the stage. The philosopher's view of the uses of theatre owes much to a theory of the function of art based upon the power of eloquence. As for the relation of Fénelon to *divertissement*, it is obvious that for him art is not to be used to divert men from their own *néant*, but rather to persuade them to have faith. Yet inasmuch as he insists upon touching men, and as the beauty and simplicity of the antique is accounted the most capable of appealing to men and stirring their imagination, *divertissement* is also implied. But it is not an end in itself, nor is it useful only insofar as it keeps men from thinking about themselves. Quite the contrary; it is used to move them to the truth. Pleasure is an integral part of beauty, produced through art by touching the passions, but since it is associated with truth, the pleasure produced, whether through painting, poetry, or eloquence, must lead to truth. The disinterested love of God, with which Fénelon's name is associated, together with the aesthetic experience, may be considered as the profane parallel of the mystical experience. In a sense art is but a poor substitute, though a useful one, for such a pure experience; it may be used as an intimation of the pure love of God and the contemplation of truth and beauty. From the perspective of our own times it is obvious that Fénelon's view of art and beauty corresponds to what is sometimes referred to as the Baroque aesthetic. The image conjured up by his views of art and beauty is not only that of Poussin, or Raphael, which corresponds to but one aspect of his aesthetics, namely the association of beauty with the nobility, simplicity, and naturalness of antiquity. But as concerns his insistence upon touching one thinks of Bernini's *St. Theresa in Ecstasy*.

* * *

Les Aventures de Télémaque, fils d'Ulysse. Nouvelle edition (Paris, n.d.); *Dialogues sur l'Eloquence en général et sur celle de la chaire en particulier* (Paris, 1753). On Fénelon see: Jeanne-Lydie Goré, *L'Itinéraire spirituel de Fénelon: Humanisme et Spiritualité* (Paris, 1957), especially the chapters dealing with the *Dialogues sur l'Eloquence* and the *Lettre à l'Academie* — both are excellent summaries of his aesthetic views; Alfred Lombard, *Fénelon et le Retour à l'Antique au XVIIIe Siècle* (Neuchâtel, 1957); Arnaldo Pizzorusso, *La Poetica di Fénelon* (Milan, 1959).

FONTENELLE, BERNARD LE BOUVIER DE (1657–1757)

FONTENELLE WAS SO WISE that he lived to be a hundred years old. He was the nephew of the great Corneille, and was destined to law, but instead became a philosopher, man of the world, man of letters, amateur of the sciences, and poet and playwright. A member of the Académie Française and the Académie des Sciences, he was appointed perpetual secretary of the latter in 1699. His role in the history of thought, literature, society, and by extension, of aesthetics, ought not to be underestimated.

In aesthetics he played an important role in the disputes of the ancients and moderns. His views on poetry and the new cosmos are indicative of the problems of the time, as are his attitudes towards rules and enthusiasm. Fontenelle is in fact an excellent introduction to the beginnings of modern aesthetics. His position derives from Descartes, and it may be said that what Descartes did not do in the area of aesthetics Fontenelle did. Needless to say, he was a partisan of the moderns, but a reasoned and reasonable one. He refused to accept the superiority of the ancients on faith; he analyzed the assumptions of the partisans of antiquity and demonstrated their absurdity, sought for the causes or reasons which might explain differences between the works of the ancients and those of the moderns, not among the authorities but from empirical sources, and distinguished carefully between genres that were susceptible of perfection according to fixed standards and those that were not. In short, he clarified confused issues and showed that the essential problem had been badly posed. His refusal to accept on authority the superiority of the ancients is akin to the methodical doubt of Descartes. The result was not a complete rejection of the past and its works, but a more discerning and critical approach to the works of the ancients and a greater liberty of examination. We may say that Fontenelle made possible liberty of critical judgment. It became possible to assert seriously that certain passages of Homer were not beyond criticism. Taste came to be seen as more than a function of the pleasure taken in works of art, the position that had been defended, for example, by Molière, expounded by Boileau, and developed by Du Bos; it was also something reasoned, arising from the examination of works of imagination. Fontenelle also carefully distinguished between those works of the ancients which had been perfected and which might not be surpassed by the moderns, and those that were still susceptible of perfection. He did not, like Perrault, pose a simple doctrine of progress; he was much more *nuancé*. In this, too, he suggests Descartes, who in his *Discours de la Méthode* implied different bases for the sciences on the one hand and for works of eloquence and poetry on the other: the former are associated with method, the latter with talent. Fontenelle was careful to distinguish between progress in the sciences and the attainment of knowledge, and progress or *perfectionnement* in the works of the imagination. Where he posed the possibility of indefinite progress in the sciences, he supposed, on the contrary, only limited possibilities in the realm of imagination. There is no end to the search for truth and knowledge, but the arts, being directed to the imagination of man and his pleasure and depending upon his powers of imagination, are limited to and by his nature. Fontenelle thus was instrumental in defining the concept of the fine arts, and in separating science from the fine arts.

His attitude to the rules and enthusiasm is also based upon Cartesian distinctions and attitudes. He did not care for enthusiasm. He associated it with the instinct of animals. Man's nobility lay in his reason. It follows that his poetry was rather weak, to say the least, from our point of view. And one senses that while he would have liked to believe in rules, he could not; he said that one usually wrote first, then made up the rules, and that even if the rules did exist, this did not mean one was obliged to follow them. His scepticism went further, for he doubted even the utility of speculations upon beauty, which he saw as a pleasant game. Reason might be extended to cover all the arts, but in the end these depended upon the genius of the artist. However, Fontenelle was of his time and therefore prized clarity, organization, and lucidity of exposition, virtues in letters which he attributed to the spread of philosophy and which, he thought, should also be applied in poetry. The result of these aesthetic assumptions may be seen in his literary works: they are examples of the Cartesian insistence on clarity, the demands of worldly taste, and may be thought of as *haute vulgarisation*. An example is his celebrated *Entretiens sur la pluralité des mondes* of 1686. Fontenelle was thus instrumental in creating the style of the eighteenth century, lucid, easy, sometimes facile, sometimes even precious for, Cartesian influences aside, there was also a new public to be reached and pleased, the women. The dualism between philosophy and rigor, and *mondanité* and pleasure, reflects that Cartesian dualism of method and talent, science and eloquence, and Fontenelle devised a prose to bridge the gap. What this implies is a certain distance, a perspective, embracing both savants and poets, philosophy and the arts. He had resolved the Quarrel of the Ancients and the Moderns precisely by assuming a certain distance. Unlike the partisans of the battle on both sides, he remains detached, as the reader of his *Digression sur les Anciens et sur les Modernes* will see, and it is this which makes his criticism possible. Fontenelle may be regarded as an example of what contemporary aestheticians often write about, namely an ideal aesthetic observer: but one, let us stress, who not only observed the fine arts detachedly, but also science, men, manners, and opinions. He is somewhat like Montesquieu's Persians, and we may also think of him in connection with an aesthetic attitude going much beyond the arts and even the concept of beauty. The only thing which saves him from being an aesthete is the fact that he goes beyond the concept of and desire for beauty; he is totally lacking in the religious attitude which was inseparable from the love of beauty in the later eighteenth century. There is no fervor in Fontenelle, no warmth at all perhaps, and certainly there is no hint of the sublime or of enthusiasm. One might say, viewing the fate of aesthetic theory after him, that eighteenth-century aesthetics are in part to be explained as a reaction against the type of detachment he represented. Thus history, enthusiasm, the insistence on the grandeur of antiquity, the new concept of genius, the new fervor for beauty and art may be regarded as attempts to go beyond Fontenelle, to save the heart from the lucidity of reason. As Madame de Tencin used to say, tapping the spot where Fontenelle's heart beat, *c'est encore du cerveau que vous avez là*. One may think of Fontenelle as an eighteenth-century Monsieur Teste, though, significantly enough, unmarried. Eighteenth-century French letters and aesthetic theories are what they are because of men like him and because others could not live in the rarefied atmosphere he breathed.

It is significant that he wrote no aesthetic treatises, no articles on beauty and taste, nothing on the sublime, merely passages on rules, enthusiasm, poetry, the ancients and moderns. His mind was essentially that of a critic, his philosophical stance that of an analyst.

* * *

Oeuvres (Paris, 1754). Fontenelle has been neglected lately by students of literature as well as by aestheticians. Yet he deserves a monograph in this area. His work in the history of science has been appreciated, however, as well as his significance for the history of ideas and the eighteenth century. See Herbert Butterfield, *The Origins of Modern Science* (London, 1960); J-R. Carré, *La Philosophie de Fontenelle, ou le sourire de la raison* (Paris, 1932), the best general introduction to his work and philosophy.

LA MOTTE, ANTOINE HOUDAR DE (1672–1731)

LACOMBE, IN HIS POCKET DICTIONARY of the arts, calls La Motte one of the most brilliant and fecund geniuses of his day. We would hardly concur in this opinion. We might say he was perhaps too rational to be truly poetic, but he was a poet, playwright, critic, worked for the theatre as well as the opera, and was involved in the famous quarrel about Homer which marks an important phase of the Quarrel of the Ancients and the Moderns. It is here and in his views of poetry that his importance for aesthetic theory and criticism lies. La Motte was more Cartesian than Descartes, and while a contemporary of Du Bos and a participant in the Quarrel of the Ancients and the Moderns, he had little sense of history. Thus he must be placed on the side of the moderns along with Fontenelle, who was much more discerning and fine-minded than La Motte, and with Perrault, who has much in common with La Motte. The Cartesianism of La Motte shows up in his views of poetry, which he associates with technique, *difficulté vaincue*, and method. His non-historical approach to Homer, his correcting of Homer to suit the public of his day, is partly Cartesian and partly a product of the social milieu; it is the former insofar as La Motte believed, like Perrault, in the superiority of the present over the age of Homer, not only in the sciences, but in the arts. It is in this respect, however, that he goes beyond anything Descartes ever said. La Motte, in short, is an example of the geometric spirit in the realm of letters. Needless to say he rejected enthusiasm, associated the sublime with *le vrai et le nouveau,* and saw no reason why Racine's tragedies might not be equally effective in prose as in verse. His insistence on method, clarity of purpose, and organization led him to defend the French epics of the seventeenth century (poems even the partisans of the moderns were doubtful of) on these grounds, but he had to admit that they were boring and made tedious reading. He also argued, however, that if the *Iliad* were really read it would suffer the same fate as the French epics of the seventeenth century: it would be found boring, and the book would fall from the reader's hands. "Personne presque n'a le courage de la lire. . . . Il n'y a que quelques savants qui se plaisent à l'admirer dans le Grec, parce qu'ils prennent le plaisir historique et celui d'entendre une langue savante, pour un plaisir purement poétique." This point had been made by Perrault in different terms, and it seems obvious that where Descartes and Fontenelle, for example, had strictly separated the imagination from science, La Motte strictly separates poetic pleasure from historical interest. His entire poetic theory rested on the concept of *la belle nature.* The poet must imitate objects which make an agreeable impression, though La Motte insists that the term *agréable* be not restricted merely to something to bring on smiles: "Il y a des agréments de toute espèce, il y en a de curiosité, de tristesse, d'horreur même." Nevertheless the *agréments,* to judge from his treatment of Homer, were bounded by the requirements of decorum. Even horror was to be refined. In sum, we may say that La Motte rationalized and refined poetry almost out of existence, and certainly out of his verses. He is an excellent source for those who would understand the dilemma of poetry in an age given to the spirit of geometry.

* * *

For his poetics see, in his *Oeuvres* (Paris, 1754), the following essays: Vol. I: "Discours sur la poésie en général et sur l'ode en particulier"; Vol. II: "Discours sur Homère"; Vol. III: "Réflexions sur la critique" and "Discours sur l'Eglogue"; Vol. IV: "Discours préliminaire-suivis de quatre Discours sur la tragédie et Suite de Réflexions sur la tragédie"; Vol. VIII: "Discours sur le différent mérite des ouvrages de l'esprit."

LE BOSSU, RENE (1631–1680)

LE BOSSU WAS A CANON of the Church of Sainte Geneviève in Paris and a professor of the humanities; he is known chiefly for two works, his *Parallèle des principes de la physique d'Aristote et de celle René Descartes*, 1674, and the one which interests us directly, namely his *Traité du poème épique* (Paris, 1675), republished in 1695 and 1708, and also at The Hague in 1714, which was probably used as the point of departure for most discussions of the epic in the eighteenth century, even though one might have modernized the epic as did Voltaire in the *Henriade* (see article "Epic Poetry").

Much as d'Aubignac does, Le Bossu begins by asserting that the arts are founded upon reason: "Les arts ont cela de commun avec les sciences, qu'ils sont comme elles fondés sur la raison, et que l'on doit s'y laisser conduire par les lumières que la nature nous a données" (*Traité du poème épique*, 3). There are, nevertheless, certain notable differences between the arts and the sciences, namely that the former do not rest upon reason and natural perceptions alone, but also upon other factors, such as the genius and choices of those who invented them (i.e. the ancients) and the general approbation of mankind. Le Bossu thus attempts to extract rational rules from the work of the ancients, to conciliate reason and the authority of the ancients. His position is one which precedes the Quarrel of the Ancients and the Moderns. Reason is being used, not to deny the authority of the ancients, but rather to buttress it. This does not mean he is a Cartesian; rather, he is a partisan of a modified or modernized Aristotelianism, as may be readily gleaned from his third chapter in which he gives us a definition of the epic:

L'EPOPEE est un discours inventé avec art, pour former les moeurs par des instructions déguisées sous les allégories d'une action importante, qui est racontée en vers d'une manière vraisemblable, divertissante et merveilleuse.

C'est ici la définition de l'épopée, et non de la poésie, qui est l'art de faire toutes sortes de poèmes, au nombre desquels est l'épique. L'Epopée n'est donc pas un art, mais une chose artificielle, comme on le voit exprimé dans la définition, qui dit que c'est un discours *inventé avec art*.

Elle est une espèce de poème, c'est aussi ce que la définition marque en ces mots, *un discours en vers*; le reste la distingue d'avec les autres espèces de poèmes [pp. 14–15].

Le Bossu is obviously much indebted to Aristotle. He may seek to arrive at clear and distinct ideas of what an epic poem is and thereby seem to be Cartesian, but he continues to use scholastic terminology and to rely upon Aristotelian concepts. His work, like that of d'Aubignac or de Piles, is an excellent example of one type of philosophy applied to the discussion of poetic forms. He begins by a general definition and then goes on from there to the various parts of the epic as implied in the definition. Thus the epic is distinguished from other genres of poetry, such as comedy and tragedy, but also from other didactic poetry such as that of Lucretius or the *Georgics* of Virgil, as it is from histories in verse such as the *Pharsalia* of Lucan or the *Punic War* of Silius Italicus. The elements of the epic are then discussed, namely, its nature, matter, form, and manner. The nature of the epic is double: it is fable and poem; that is to say, fable constitutes the nature of the epic, while the poem as such is the specific treatment of the fable, comprised in its turn of three elements, namely thought, expression, and verse. The matter of the epic is an action reproduced with verisimilitude and imitated from the actions of kings, princes, and divinities; this, in turn, implies two sub-elements, those of action and characters. Form, in turn, requires that the characters be not introduced to the public as acting by themselves, without the poet in evidence as in tragedy, but that the action be narrated by the poet. The purpose of the epic was to give moral instruction to mankind.

Obviously, each of these elements was susceptible of lengthy treatment, but Le Bossu decided to concentrate on six subjects which correspond to the six books of his *Traité*: the nature of the epic, in which he treated of fable; the matter or action of the epic; form or narration; mores and character; machines, or the presence and action of divinities; and finally, thoughts and expression. Each book, of course, is itself subdivided into many chapters, for each part of the epic is susceptible of further analysis. The entire work thus takes on the aspect of a rather complex scholastic treatise, which is precisely what it is. One feels that Le Bossu has exhausted the possibilities of analysis, that he has described everything and treated all aspects of the epic susceptible of rational treatment. It is a completely rational approach; there is no question of taste or sentiment, or of touching the reader, and the final impression is that the epic is itself some sort of machine which can be readily taken apart into its constituent parts and put together again. It is a completely objective work, in the sense that there is no question of a personal reaction on the part of Le Bossu to his reading of Homer and Virgil, for his examples are taken from these two authors and their more famous poems, the *Illiad*, the *Odyssey*, and the *Aeneid*, while the theoretical buttresses of Le Bossu's ideas are Aristotle and Horace. As far as general aesthetic theory in the seventeenth century is concerned, Le Bossu must be put among those who were closer to poetics than aesthetics. He might be described as one of those who elaborated an aesthetic of art based upon the notion of rules derived from the examination of established works which were either Cartesian or Aristotelian in orientation.

MONTESQUIEU, CHARLES LOUIS DE SECONDAT, BARON DE LA BREDE ET DE (1689–1755)

LIKE MANY OTHER writers of the eighteenth as well as of the seventeenth century, Montesquieu was above all an occasional aesthetician. His main interest and work had to do with history and social institutions. He did, however, write one treatise on aesthetics, the *Essai sur le goût dans les choses de la nature et de l'art*, and his essay *De la Manière gothique* may also be subsumed under the heading of aesthetics or art history. There are a great many notes as well which have a bearing on matters pertaining to aesthetic theory, taste, art history, and literary criticism, both theoretical and personal in nature. Montesquieu travelled widely in Europe and took notes of what he saw, felt, thought, and read, so that it is possible to construct a more or less unified view of his taste on the basis of the theoretical as well as the more personal works. He did not really think very systematically about the arts in general, as did Batteux, nor did he attempt to range over the whole subject of the arts, taste, genius, society, as did Abbé Du Bos, his contemporary, but he touched on the same matters. The materials for a possible *Goût de Montesquieu* will be found in his notebooks, the *Spicilège, Mes Pensées*, and his travel journals, as well as in various chapters of the *Esprit des lois*, while examples of his literary taste are evidenced by such works as the *Lettres persanes* (which is also a source for his views of poets, writers, writing, and so on) and *Le Temple de Gnide, Histoire véritable*, and *Arsace et Isménie*. The result of such gleanings is an impressive picture of a scholar, man of taste, keen observer of the arts, and critic, but also of a man with a poetic turn of mind, interested in the past and sometimes able to find a striking metaphor to make a point concerning some poet or aspect of art. His writings on matters related to art, aesthetic theory, and taste reflect an analytical and empirical as well as a historical turn of mind. He belongs to the generation of the Régence, that of Du Bos and Fénelon, sharing certain views with Fontenelle and perhaps even with La Motte, especially his rather cool approach to the arts and his suspicion of enthusiasm. But on the whole he is, by inclination and by poetic feeling and sentiment, more of a partisan of the ancients than of the moderns, though he took no part in the dispute concerning precedence and was not himself a firm believer in rules. Politics and religious questions aside, Montesquieu has certain affinities of mind and spirit with the British Augustans, with Swift and Addison. His views of art are not as hedonistic as those of Du Bos; there is always an air of nobility and grandeur about him. The *Lettres persanes* were often thought of as lacking in respect for religion and established social values, but as Montesquieu moved on in years an increasing gravity and nobility of mind and soul became evident.

His aesthetic preferences may be summarized by saying that he did not like Versailles. His taste and his politics were similar; he was a conservative in the best and perhaps truest sense of the term. What this means, in matters of taste, is shown in his manner of going beyond the disputes of the ancients and the moderns to adopt the good in both, while rejecting the pretensions of the moderns such as Perrault. As far as Versailles was concerned, he favored, rather, keeping to modesty and noble simplicity and avoiding a search for effects:

Ce qui me déplaît dans Versailles, c'est une envie impuissante qu'on voit partout de faire de grandes choses. Je me ressouviens toujours de dona Olympia, qui disait à Maldachini, qui faisait ce qu'il pouvait: "Animo! Maldachini. Io ti faro cardinale." Il me semble que le feu Roi disait à Mansard: "Courage! Mansard: Je te donnerai cent mille livres de rente." Lui, faisait ses efforts: mettait une aile; puis, une aile; puis, une autre. Mais, quand il en aurait mis jusques à Paris, il aurait toujours fait une petite chose [*Oeuvres complètes*, I, 1264].

This opinion is not purely aesthetic, to be sure, for Montesquieu was also conservative in matters of expense. Versailles had too much magnificence, was too expensive and too much a monument of and to Louis XIV and absolute monarchy. Montesquieu was not a partisan of the *grand goût*, and we may suppose that he must have rather liked the *goût moderne* in the decorative arts and in architecture, however opposed to his love of antiquity this may seem. Consider, for example, this entry in his book of notes, *Mes Pensées*:

La trop grande régularité, quelquefois et même souvent désagréable. Il n'y rien de si beau que le ciel; mais il est semé d'étoiles sans ordre. Les maisons et jardins d'autour de Paris n'ont que les défauts de se ressembler trop: ce sont des copies continuelles de Le Nôtre. Vous voyez toujours le même air, *qualem decet esse sororum*. Si on a eu un terrain bizarre, au lieu de l'employer tel qu'il est, on l'a rendu régulier, pour faire une maison qui fût comme les autres. Nos maisons sont comme nos caractères [Ibid., 1265].

This feeling about regularity was not peculiar to Montesquieu. He shared it with his generation, and a similar view is presented by Marivaux on the *je ne sais quoi* (see article, "*Je ne sais quoi*"). Yet for all this criticism of the grand manner and of regularity, Montesquieu did not espouse the *goût moderne* without reservations: "La Place des Victoires est le monument de la vanité frivole. Il faut que ces sortes de monuments aient un objet: le Pont de Trajan, la voie Appienne, le Théâtre de Marcellus" (Ibid.). It was not for nothing that he was called *le petit Romain* by Madame de Tencin, for Montesquieu's taste for grandeur, like his poetic inclinations, was centered upon the ancients. He thus stands partway between the rejection of the *grand goût* and the later *retour à l'Antique*, which he probably helped, quite unwittingly, to bring about. He finds a certain charm and *je ne sais quoi* lacking in the *grand goût* as represented by the art of Versailles, but he finds greatness of soul in the memory of the antique. Yet this did not mean he was a partisan of the ancients in quite the same way that one was before the Quarrel for, as his essay on the Gothic manner implies, he also believed in the perfectibility of art and of genres. His views of their development are similar to those of Du Bos on the *Grands Siècles* and are essentially cyclical: the arts were intimately tied to social and historical changes; once an art was perfected decline was inevitable; and the moderns of today will someday be the ancients of still other moderns. Like La Bruyère he thought that most subjects had been exhausted and that new subjects and forms would only come with a new society. He was suspicious of the influence of women on the arts, for they were too fond of ornamentation, whereas he sought above all the *grand simple*. He admired Michelangelo, the only sculptor who could be compared to the ancients, an artist who did not work within the rules but who nevertheless succeeded: "C'est qu'il avait le goût excellent et faisait toujours, en chaque lieu et chaque occasion, ce qui devait se faire pour plaire" (Ibid., 954). Genius, in short, always knew when not to follow rules, just as genius usually managed to do something beyond the common or average production of a century. As he said of Shakespeare: "Quand vous voyez un tel homme s'élever comme un aigle, c'est lui. Quand vous le voyez ramper, c'est son siècle" (Ibid., 1244). Art was bound to history, but genius sometimes broke the bonds. This implicit dualism between genius and rules, the *je ne sais quoi* and regularity, may be thought of as a balance between nature and art, avoiding too much of either. Montesquieu's essay on taste treats of the objects of taste in both nature and art, but he did not confuse beauty in art with beauty in nature. They were different, and art, for Montesquieu as for most of his contemporaries, was *la belle nature*:

Je suis plus touché quand je vois une belle peinture de Raphaël qui me re-présente une femme nue dans le bain, que si je voyais Vénus sortir de l'onde. C'est que la peinture ne nous représente que les beautés des femmes, et rien de ce qui peut en faire voir les défauts. On y voit tout ce qui plaît, et rien de ce qui peut dégoûter. D'ailleurs, dans la peinture, l'imagination a tou-jours quelque chose à faire, et c'est un peintre qui représente toujours en beau [Ibid., 1257].

This marks the difference between art and nature: "Ce qui fait la beauté, c'est la régularité des traits; ce qui fait une femme jolie, c'est l'expression du visage" (Ibid). It is obvious that Montesquieu was *nuancé* and often quite poetic in the application of aesthetic theories. His *Pensées* and his various observations are characterized by the ap-plication of general aesthetic theories and assumptions to particular cases in art and nature but, as in the case of Diderot's many writings pertaining to art and aesthetics, it is difficult to extract a coherent system or aesthetic from his remarks. It is possible, however, to arrive at some conclusions concerning his attitudes towards art, history, the ancients, rules, and taste, though it does not follow that these attitudes will always be consistent. Montesquieu's nostalgia for the ancients, for instance, is hardly consistent with his attitude towards perfectibility and all that this implies in the arts. Nor is his attitude to art and his marked preference for noble subjects, for grandeur and simplicity, quite in accord with his rather relativistic view of taste, a phenomenon which under his pen becomes quite complex, abstract, and often seemingly unrelated to his judgments on works of art or literature. Yet in spite of these superficial conflicts, or perhaps because of them, one gains the impression that more insight into the artistic and aesthetic mentality of the age is to be gained here, as in Diderot, than in the more formal treatises of a Batteux or a Père André. One sees in these remarks the exceptions to the general principles of aesthetics and rules of art. How much more readable and lively are Montesquieu's personal remarks on the art of writing than the usual dictionary articles on eloquence, rheto-ric, and style.

In his considerations of the art of writing and on literature in general, Montesquieu shows the same preference for what we would today call indeterminacy, which was then called the *je ne sais quoi*. What is involved is a sense of play between the rules and one's own choice, between what is required of reason and what the heart also seeks. Thus, to be a writer, for example, implies a reciprocity between society and private meditation: "On gagne beaucoup dans le monde; on gagne beaucoup dans son cabinet" (Ibid., 1218). In the privacy of one's study one learns to write with order, to reason well and truly, and to order one's thoughts; but in the world one learns to use one's imagination: "On y est pensant par la raison qu'on ne pense pas, c'est-à-dire que l'on a les idées du hasard, qui sont souvent les bonnes" (Ibid.). The result might be described as a happy mixture of the *esprit de géometrie* and that of *finesse*. It is a prose which may be read in a salon; the ennui of too much regularity is avoided by the proper degree of surprise, variety, and wit. One might consider such prose a written version of what Montesquieu defined admirably as the wit of conversation, namely "un esprit particulier qui consiste dans des raisonnements et des déraisonnements courts" (Ibid.). If prose would not allow the *déraisonnements* because it is subject to scrutiny and analysis, whereas conversation is an art of thought in motion, prose would nevertheless need some equivalent of the delight given by *déraisonnement*, and it too would have to be brief: "Pour bien écrire, il faut sauter les idées intermédiaires, assez pour n'être pas ennuyeux; pas trop, de peur de n'être pas entendu" (Ibid., 1220). As in painting, this type of brevity leaves something to the imagination of the reader, and just as what to present in painting is determined by taste, so is what to say in writing.

Montesquieu's taste, like his position in historical time, stands between the *grand goût* of the age of Louis XIV and the *goût de l'antique* of the closing decades of the eighteenth century. While he helped prepare the cult of the antique, it is doubtful that he would have appreciated the use made of the ancients by the *philosophes*. For Montesquieu was too discreet to preach, and the virtuous tone of the *philosophes* might have shocked him as being too blatant. He did not like Voltaire, because he considered him always to be writing for his own party: "Il est comme les moines, qui n'écrivent pas pour le sujet qu'ils traitent, mais pour la gloire de leur ordre; Voltaire écrit pour son couvent" (Ibid., 1252). His taste was for happy, attenuated fictions, discreet moral lessons, a touching style, a poetic vision of the past, perhaps such as that expressed in the *Télémaque* of Fénelon and in his own *Temple de Gnide*. And yet, this is not all of Montesquieu. One finds in his mind and work the same dualism which is observable in the work of the greater of the eighteenth-century French writers: a modern, strong mind, coupled with a taste for past and established artistic forms and genres. The writer of the *Temple de Gnide* is also the very analytical and "modern" writer of the *Esprit des Lois*; the poet who loves the ancients is also the historian who analyzed the process of the growth and decadence of Rome irrespective of his feelings for antiquity.

$$* \quad * \quad *$$

Oeuvres complètes (Paris: Editions de la Pléiade, 1949). Little has been done on Montesquieu's aesthetic theories, implicit or explicit. There are pertinent passages in Robert Shackleton, *Montesquieu, A Critical Biography* (Oxford, 1962) and in Paul Barrière, *Un Grand Provincial: Charles de Secondat, Baron de la Brède et de Montesquieu* (Bordeaux and Paris, 1946); the last chapter of this work is devoted to aesthetic questions and material. There are two works directly concerned with aesthetics: the first is dated — Edwin Preston Dargan, *The Aesthetic Doctrine of Montesquieu: Its application in his writings* (Baltimore, 1907); the second is an article especially on his concept of taste — Jean Charles Beyer, "Montesquieu et le relativisme esthétique," in *Studies on Voltaire and the Eighteenth Century*, XXIV, 171–82. The latest work touching on Montesquieu's aesthetic theories considers his art criticism: Jean Ehrard, *Montesquieu critique d'art* (Paris, 1965).

PASCAL, BLAISE (1623–1662)

PASCAL DISMISSED DESCARTES in one brief note: "Descartes inutile et incertain" (*Pensée* 78). The words might serve to characterize his views on aesthetics, not merely the Cartesian, but all aesthetics: "useless and uncertain." Indeed, one might put it even more strongly: impossible. And yet Pascal really wrote more on matters pertaining to aesthetics than did Descartes. If the latter mentioned eloquence and poetry, it was merely to be able to write about his method: poetry and eloquence were the result less of rules than of natural gifts; therefore they were not worth discussing. They did not belong to reason and certainty; they belonged to the realm of ornament. Pascal's attitude was different, but the result was much the same. Eloquence, to Pascal, could be a useful tool, as it was to churchmen who had to preach; it was necessary for the service of truth. For him, the ideal eloquence was colorless; it was simplicity itself; it was persuasion of the truth with the least possible deviation from the message. What was important to Pascal was truth, not beauty, and it is this which explains his impossible aesthetics. He speaks of beauty only to make clear that it belongs to the realm of the imagination, and therefore to that of uncertainty, deception, fashion, fiction.

Pascal's aesthetics is based upon his concept of the imagination: "L'imagination dispose de tout; elle fait la beauté, la justice, et le bonheur, qui est le tout du monde" (*Pensée* 82). Imagination created the world of *divertissement*. But this, for Pascal, was not praise, for the truth was elsewhere, not in the sinful nature of man, his uncertainty, his weakness, his incapacity to be at rest with himself. Reason was of little help against the creative power of the imagination, which was a source of errors, follies, misfortunes, foibles, and false values: a source, indeed, of the entire world of man, a creator of a veritable second nature within man. Men go to war, to sea, to spectacles and games only because man cannot remain at rest alone in a room. He must find diversion, and the entire realm of art belongs to the realm of diversion, of deception, of the false comforts created by sinful man.

To be sure, this world of *divertissment*, or more narrowly, of beauty, is not without a certain rationality in its relationships. It is arguable that an aesthetic is possible if one fixes one's attention on the relation of beauty to human nature:

Il y a un certain modèle d'agrément et de beauté qui consiste en un certain rapport entre notre nature, faible ou forte, telle qu'elle est, et la chose qui nous plaît.
Tout ce qui est formé sur ce modèle nous agrée: soit maison, chanson, discours, vers, prose, femme, oiseaux, rivières, arbres, chambres, habits, etc. Tout ce qui n'est point fait sur ce modèle déplaît à ceux qui ont le goût bon [*Pensée* 32].

It might be possible to construct an aesthetic built on the concept of beauty, given such an outlook. It would involve a treatise on beauty in art and beauty in nature, and it would also require an investigation of taste. But read on in Pascal and you begin to have doubts, for no one really knows what this model is:

Comme on dit beauté poétique, on devrait aussi dire beauté géométrique, et beauté médicinale; mais on ne le dit pas: et la raison en est qu'on sait bien quel est l'objet de la géométrie, et qu'il consiste en preuves, et quel est l'objet de la médecine, et qu'il consiste en la guérison; mais on ne sait pas en quoi consiste l'agrément, qui est l'objet de la poésie. On ne sait ce que c'est que ce modèle naturel qu'il faut imiter; et, à faute de cette connaissance, on a inventé de certains termes bizarres: "siècle d'or, merveille de nos jours, fatal," etc.; et on appelle ce jargon beauté poétique [*Pensée* 33].

Thus an aesthetics built upon the rapports between human nature and what men call beauty, upon taste and *agrément*, would be a purely verbal construction, as uncertain and useless as its foundation, the human imagination. If Pascal was at all interested in eloquence it was for the same reason that Descartes was interested in his method: both were ways, passages, tools: in the case of Pascal, a way to persuade others of the truth of faith; in the case of Descartes, a way to find certainty.

Yet we may say of Pascal what we said of Descartes, that he makes a certain aesthetic possible. If Descartes makes an aesthetic from above possible because he strictly separates the mental from the physical realm, Pascal makes possible an aesthetic built on the concept of art. But it becomes possible only if the Christian attitude to art and *agrément* is abandoned. Thus, if Father André is the Cartesian as an aesthetician, one may say that Abbé Du Bos is the Pascalian turned aesthetician. Where one used the Cartesian insistence on clear and distinct ideas in order to draw distinctions between various types of beauty, the other used the Pascalian notion of *divertissement* to construct a theory of art.

* * *

Pensées. Texte de l'edition Braunschvicg. Introduction and notes by Ch-Marc Des Granges (Paris: Classiques Garnier, 1952).

PERRAULT, CHARLES (1627–1703)

FAMOUS FOR HIS TALES of Mother Goose, Charles Perrault also deserves to be remembered for one of the most important works produced by the Quarrel of the Ancients and the Moderns, namely his *Parallèle des Anciens et des Modernes*, which he published in four volumes over a period of nine years, from 1688 through 1697. He was the brother of Claude Perrault, the famous and justly celebrated architect of the colonnade of the Louvre, and was a member of the Académie Française and also of the Academy of Inscriptions. He showed a lively interest in the arts throughout his life. He had, indeed, been closely associated with Colbert and was responsible for the reforms effected in the organization of the *Académie de Peinture et de Sculpture*, as well as that of architecture. He also played an important role in literary patronage. He was thus a representative and a bulwark of the state-sponsored literary and artistic establishment, and as a spokesman of the moderns defended his own accomplishments. He made many enemies through his defense of the moderns; as Voltaire wrote, in his short entry for Perrault appended to his *Siècle de Louis XIV*: "On lui a reproché d'avoir trouvé trop de défauts dans les anciens; mais sa grande faute est de les avoir critiqués maladroitement, et de s'être fait des ennemis de ceux mêmes qu'il pouvait opposer aux anciens." Among these was of course Boileau, though a reconciliation in the halls of the Academy was eventually arranged. Perrault was not only a critic, he was also a poet and a man very learned in the fine arts.

His *Parallèle* is probably the best single source for understanding the issues which divided the partisans of the famous quarrel. The work has, however, thanks to anthologies, been eclipsed by the much more succinct and manageable *Digression sur les Anciens et les Modernes* of Fontenelle. Their attitudes, positions, and arguments are much the same, though Fontenelle's short essay must be accounted much more analytical than Perrault's work in its form of reasoning. Perrault touched on all aspects of the dispute, and his *Parallèle* is not lacking in highly revealing psychological insights. He divided his work into five dialogues conducted by three protagonists. The *Président*, a gentleman from the provinces who has not been to Paris for twenty years, is a partisan of the ancients; he is learned, reads Latin, has been to Italy, but has not been in touch with the modern world for a long time. The Abbé, the mouthpiece of Perrault, is learned too, but is irreverent concerning the ancients, enthusiastic about modern developments in the arts and sciences, intelligent, sometimes ironical, and is a good dialectician and an admirer of Louis XIV's patronage of the arts. The Chevalier, a worldly gentleman of facile expression who sometimes sums up a long argument in an apt image, a metaphor, or a few *bon mots*, plays the role of mediator between the two partisans, though it is obvious that the Chevalier is inclined to the moderns by temperament. The dialogue begins on the way to Versailles, where the Abbé wishes to show the *Président* what the moderns are capable of accomplishing. The *Président* has a prejudice in favor of the ancients, a predisposition which is not rational, which must be dissipated. At Versailles he is shown evidence of the capacities and greatness of the moderns. Having seen these marvels, the *Président* is thus prepared for further arguments based on reason. The trip to Versailles is used as empirical proof in an argument touching various questions of aesthetics. This first dialogue deals with the irrational psychological grounds of the uncritical admiration of the ancients; the second dialogue deals with architecture, sculpture, and painting; the third concerns eloquence; the fourth, poetry; and the final dialogue touches on the sciences and modern philosophy. In the course of these conversations every genre, ancient and modern, is discussed and compared, and questions of aesthetics are raised. The contents of the *Parallèle* thus summarize the point of departure for much eighteenth-century aesthetic speculation, outlining, surely, the most important questions: taste, the history and progress of art, imitation, beauty, ornament, novelty, and the problem of the imitation of nature. The *Parallèle* must be counted as one of the central works in aesthetics at this time, in rank second only to the *Réflexions critiques* of Du Bos. It can also be counted as among the first writings in modern aesthetics for, unlike the *Art Poétique* of Boileau, for example, or the various treatises on rules in seventeenth century, it raises questions which belong to aesthetics more than to poetics, and is concerned with all the fine arts rather than with only one of them. It is a general reflection upon the arts and as such is an example of the *goût de comparaison*, the sign of a new spirit of critical enquiry, of true enquiry rather than dogmatic criticism. Though Perrault was obviously favorable to the moderns, the important point is that he was among those who actually dared to question the supremacy of the ancients.

$$* \quad * \quad *$$

Citations are from *Parallèle des anciens et des modernes en ce qui regarde les arts et les sciences* (Paris, 1688–97). See also facsimile edition (Eidos Verlag, Munich, 1964); the introduction is by H. R. Jauss and there are two art historical excursuses by M. Imdahl. This edition is possibly the only one available besides the first in the original. There are also pertinent passages concerning Perrault in Bernard Teyssèdre's *Roger de Piles et les débats sur le coloris au siècle de Louis XIV* (Paris, 1957).

ROUSSEAU, JEAN-JACQUES (1712–1778)

ROUSSEAU THE CITIZEN of Geneva was perhaps the only true anti-artist who ever lived. He did not produce all-black or all-white paintings; he did not write poetry made up of words picked by chance out of a hat; he did not lift common utilitarian objects out of their contexts to name them ready-mades and thereby turn them into works of arts; he did not, like his later compatriot Tinguely, fabricate self-destroying machines; he did not compose music by exploiting the effects of silence and the spacing of natural sounds or electronic noises; but on moral grounds he coherently and thoroughly opposed the entire world of art he knew, which everyone else accepted almost without question. In this he went much further than our twentieth-century anti-artists, who produce art in spite of themselves, who react against established art or arts in order to produce a truer type, and whose very existence and activities suppose the convention or institution of art to begin with. Rousseau joins the anti-artists of today only insofar as these tend to think that life as such might be more interesting than art: though here too a distinction must be made, for the life they have in mind is that of modern society, modern cities, and modern technology and science. Rousseau was more thorough, for his refusal of art also meant a refusal of civilized society. Whereas the contemporary anti-artist is a product of the modern city, the offspring of Baudelaire and Dada, Rousseau was the son of a relatively small city situated in a part of Europe which, thanks in part to him, came to be called beautiful. Rousseau's particular anti-art position is in truth the only one possible within the Classical aesthetic, which supposes art, taste, a doctrine of imitation, and a metaphysics of beauty. The alternative to art was not anti-art or no art at all, but a concept of nature incompatible with the Classical aesthetic of art, indeed one making art unnecessary because it rejects, in effect, the Classical notion of man along with the *philosophes'* supposition of the perfectibility or malleability of man. Rousseau therefore is opposed not only to Pascal and Du Bos, but also to his fellow *philosophes*.

As we may see (article "Art"), the Dubosian aesthetic was a way of meeting the challenge posed by the Christian view of man: *divertissement* is exploited to save from themselves those men and women who have not the ability to occupy their minds with study. To use an architectural metaphor, Montaigne's tower, Pascal's room, Descartes's *poêle*, are abandoned for the Régence salon of the Abbé Du Bos or the forum posed by the *philosophes*, the forum being just outside the salon. If we consider the salon and forum in connection with the aesthetic theories which may be associated with them, we conclude that these theories posit a classical space, the work of an architect, with more or less decoration, depending on the degree of Epicureanism, Stoicism, or Christian rigorism attributable to the theorist-architect. Rousseau's aesthetic supposes the abandonment of this classical space; the decorated interior of the salon is abandoned for the true, pure, and invigorating outdoors. Paneling, mirrors, overdoors, and painted ceilings are left for the wood, field, and stream, and the great sky of the Supreme Architect. True enough, Rousseau also dreamed of the forum — there is a phase of his aesthetic thought that is quite in accord with that of Diderot — but in the end he doubted the possibility of virtue in a great monarchy, and went beyond the *philosophes* and the Classical aesthetic to espouse, indeed to create, a new refuge: a nature so novel, so redefined or rethought, as to make its imitation and the product of such imitation unnecessary.

For Rousseau art is a mask, nature truth: the former corresponds to *l'homme de l'homme*, man perverted, altered by society, with powder, wig, and exquisite but false and deceitful manners; the other suggests man at peace with himself, the moral conscience, a truth still within us if we would but leave the mask imposed by society in order to find ourselves. With nature, the self is no longer *haïssable*; being with oneself is no longer frightening; solitude is no longer exile; the imagination is no longer the madwoman in the machine; one is true to one's nature once more, while to choose all the rest, all the brilliance and spectacle of art, is to become alienated from oneself. Rousseau's view of *divertissement* is akin to Pascal's, to be sure, for he also sees it as an evil, but its cause is not attributed to man fallen because of sin, but rather to man fallen through history. In the mind of Rousseau the theology of the Fall is historicized; *divertissement* is a necessary evil, not because all men have sinned and have thereby a corrupt and unstable nature, but because men unfortunately exist in society and therefore need the drugs of art, spectacle, *divertissement*. For Rousseau then, art is not a necessary second nature, it is a false nature: *la belle nature* plays no role in his aesthetic, he has gone beyond it. It is at most décor, *clinquant*, merely the gold braid, the sword, and the wig which he gave up along with that other little work of eighteenth-century art, his watch. For beauty was not in externals, it was within, and was not a sensation caused by an object of art, or for that matter by an object in nature, but by the pure sensation of being, and also, as ever, by moral beauty. "J'ai toujours cru que le bon n'était que le beau mis en action," writes St. Preux to Julie in *La Nouvelle Héloïse*,

que l'un tenait intimement à l'autre, et qu'ils avaient tous deux une source commune dans la nature bien ordonnée. Il suit de cette idée que le goût se perfectionne par les mêmes moyens que la sagesse, et qu'une âme bien touchée

ROUSSEAU 287

des charmes de la vertu doit à proportion être aussi sensible à tous les autres genres de beautés. On s'exerce à voir comme à sentir, ou plutôt une vue exquise n'est qu'un sentiment délicat et fin. C'est ainsi qu'un peintre à l'aspect d'un beau paysage ou devant un beau tableau s'extasie à des objets qui ne sont pas même remarqués d'un spectateur vulgaire. Combien de choses qu'on n'aperçoit que par sentiment et dont il est impossible de rendre raison? Combien de ces je ne sais quoi qui reviennent si fréquemment et dont le goût seul décide? Le goût est en quelque manière le microscope du jugement; c'est lui qui met les petits objets à sa portée, et ses opérations commencent où s'arrêtent celles du dernier.[1]

Beauty is moral virtue; it has little to do with the worldly values of society and its arts, and insofar as it is connected with the production of art, the subject matter becomes all-important, since the aesthetic judgment is not separated from the moral. It is therefore no accident that Rousseau's most significant work of criticism should have been directed towards the theatre, towards Molière and Racine, that he should have concentrated his attention on the supposed merits of catharsis and opposed Abbé Du Bos. He saw very clearly that art was a species of escape and that aesthetic beauty on the stage, by provoking tears among the spectators, interfered with another type of beauty, namely moral beauty, *le beau mis en action*. But then, this separation is essential to all of Rousseau's thinking. It was precisely this division within man, caused by the fall into history, by society, that the arts, being inseparable from society, reflected; they were the very manifestation of this division within the being of man. As *divertissement* was the outward sign of sin for the Christian Pascal, so the arts were the outward sign of social and historical failure for Rousseau; they merely increased the distance between the social man and the natural man, between *l'homme de l'homme* and the conscience: "Plus j'y réfléchis, et plus je trouve que tout ce qu'on met en représentation au théâtre, on ne l'approche pas de nous, on l'en éloigne."[2] It stood to reason that the claim advanced for the utility of art and the stage was false, and Rousseau was among the few who did not advance the utilitarian argument in the eighteenth century; given his premise, he could not. Besides, the corruption of man through society occurred long before the establishment of the theatre so that the theatre could hardly change anything: the arts could not instruct, or polish, or educate, or civilize men, because the arts were the products of the fall from grace; they could only hide some of the corruption,

[1] In *Oeuvres complètes*, p. 196.
[2] *Lettre à M. d'Alembert* (Paris: Classiques Garnier, 1954), p. 141.

only create a mask. Civilization itself was wrong; therefore, it was foolish to argue that the stage civilized and polished men.

It will be readily understood that the notion of perspective, of what we would call aesthetic distance, which was so important in the Classical aesthetic, was considered as a vice by Rousseau. Perspective is precisely that cleavage within the nature of man brought about by civilization and reason. Thus, "Art is an imitation of nature" changes value completely in the mind of Rousseau, and the formula might be rewritten to read: "Art is a perversion of nature." This permits us to understand the role of nature, in his aesthetic, as the device whereby the perversion might be ended, the perspective abolished, the distance between the social and the natural man bridged. Rousseau perceived the dualism on which the arts were built, but he read it quite differently from his contemporaries; he, like Diderot, is a unitarian, but a much more thorough one. Rousseau would abolish the distance between appearance and reality, between the imitation and its model, and this could only be done by dropping the former. His abandoning of wig, silk stockings, braid, watch, and sword is symbolic of this: Rousseau rids himself of ornament because nature suffices. This implies, given the attitudes of his time, a complete reevaluation of nature. For Perrault, who had participated at Versailles in the construction of the palace and the dispositions of the gardens, pure nature was chaos. For Rousseau the opposite was true: nature is truly pure, free from the interference and corrupting influence of man, and thus is no longer merely a model for imitation in art, but is opposed to art. Suddenly, the oft-repeated exhortation to painters that they follow nature came to mean something else, something associated with morality and sincerity, and a position opposed to society.

Rousseau was instrumental in the production of a new style of art and of new fashions in letters in spite of himself. Like the British writers on the sublime and the picturesque or the Swiss writers on the Alps, he helped elaborate an aesthetic sentiment for nature, thereby causing some confusion in aesthetic theory, since it was not always quite clear, in the closing decades of the eighteenth century as sometimes even today, that a taste for nature is not quite the same thing as a taste for objets d'art, and that it is one thing to enjoy a sunset by nature and quite another to enjoy a sunset by Vernet. One might put it this way: where Diderot posed a naturalistic aesthetic and all that this implied in the way of potential kitsch, Rousseau posed an aesthetic of nature with all that this implied, *malgré lui*, in the realms of Romantic interi-

ority, poetry, Biedermeier painting, and tourism. The artistic manifestations of Rousseau's aesthetic were middle-class, as in the case of Diderot's
aesthetic, but the same middle class was not involved in both: there are
so many middle classes. Rousseau's middle class loved nature, walks in
the country, Switzerland, mountains, edelweiss, children, watchmaking,
country singing and dancing, with a bit of time off for the *Turnverein*
and rifle practise on Sunday morning. Diderot's middle class, on the
other hand, also loved all the right things, Art with a capital A, Morality
with a capital M, and generally Life, Liberty and the Pursuit of Happiness, justified by Nature. One is tempted to say that the *philosophes*
transformed an aristocratic aesthetic into a bourgeois aesthetic. What
Rousseau did, wrote, and lived proved in the end more important for the
arts than his theoretical writings, though we may argue that one point
of his aesthetic theory was indeed productive of a revolution in aesthetic thought too. This is his interiority, the aesthetic of which will
be found in the *Confessions* as well as in the *Rêveries*, not theoretically
explained but artistically exemplified.

The implications of Rousseau's attitude towards nature and of his
writings may be clearer if we concentrate on his relation to the self and
to exterior nature. In the first instance we come to a new portraiture;
in the second we are led to the discussion of the aesthetic experience
of nature.

When Fontenelle, Bayle, Saint-Evremond, Montesquieu, and Voltaire
wrote about men, they had in mind men in general, and their psychology
was based upon what all men had in common and upon what might be
termed the common experience of mankind. When these men wrote they
hardly ever wrote about themselves, and if they did, as did Montaigne,
Montesquieu, or even Voltaire in his *Mémoirs*, the self-portraits they
presented were eminently social and polished by the thought that these
self-portraits would be observed or read by other men. Thus they were
hardly ever revealing about their private lives. Theirs was a psychology
of worldliness and of surface: which is not to say that it was superficial,
but merely that its parallel is to be found in the art of portraiture as
practised by the painter: as there were certain traits that could not be
shown in painting, so there were certain traits not to be revealed in
the literary portrait or autobiography. "Le moi est haïssable." The self
was not considered as interesting then as we tend to assume it to be.
What was interesting was the face you presented society, not what you
hid, because men, being sinners by definition of the theologians or fools
by definition of the sceptics, more or less hid the same things. Such

a view of man is inseparable from value put on style in being a man, and such a psychology supposes that men are to be actors and that the process of education, for example, is one of imitation. Hence the importance attributed to the stage in the formation of manners and the emphasis put on the moral lesson of literature, as well as the fear of perversion from the wrong books, especially novels. Essentially, then, we are dealing with a society in which everyone was more or less an actor, if only for the reason that everyone was supposed to have manners. Ridicule came from missing one's cue and repeating the wrong line. When a man brought up in this society sat down to write his memoirs he would not speak about his self, but rather about his social actions, and he would be careful to present a polished portrait, for he wrote with posterity in mind as well as with an idea of style. He wrote a self-portrait *en beau* or *en vrai*, to use the terminology of the painter, in either case based upon a choice, or as Rousseau said of Montaigne, a profile view with only the better half shown.

In the works of Rousseau the first person singular dominates. Voltaire, Montesquieu, Fontenelle, Saint-Evremond, Diderot even address our minds, suppose the reader to be a civilized man, with whom it is possible to have an intelligent conversation. With Rousseau, something else is involved and something different comes into literature, namely feelings, sentiments, beliefs, dreams, hopes, fears, habits, private life, childhood, adolescence, maturity, and old age, his and no one else's, his, Jean-Jacques Rousseau's. He knew very well that his *Confessions* was a novel enterprise and that he would, unlike the painter, go beneath the skin. This was a new psychology, one no longer of surface but of depth. The writer could now think of himself as interesting, and his private life, feelings, beliefs, and experience as a man and as a writer were admitted as literary motifs. This was no longer a psychology of portraiture, but one of interiorized and personal history. Time recalled came to play an important role in letters, and readers were led from the universal to the particular. The dualism between the universal and the particular, the eternal and the passing, was abolished because all men are subject to historical time. The model to be imitated was no longer outside the imitator, among the ancients, among the established masters, not even necessarily outside in the world of nature, but primarily within. This affected the Classical aesthetic of imitation radically, for it postulated an aesthetic of expression, of the sincere expression of personal truth. It went beyond the world of the imitation of *la belle nature*, beyond the whole convention of art which, given the Classical aesthetic and its accent on the universal, implied a rather impersonal, even "objective," world in which the personality of the artist and poet played a minor role. Rousseau realized that this enterprise also supposed a new language, as he put it in the first draft of his *Confessions*:

Il faudrait pour ce que j'ai à dire inventer un langage aussi nouveau que mon projet: car quel ton, quel style prendre pour débrouiller ce cahos [sic] immense de sentiments si divers, si contradictoires, souvent si vils et quelquefois si sublimes dont je fus sans cesse agité?"[3]

Rousseau did not find that tone, but it is of course precisely the same attitude, the same aesthetic which animates the search of artists and anti-artists today, for they too, like Rousseau, are interested in breaking the barriers between art and life. He did not succeed, and this fact might be a lesson for today.

Now this priority accorded the true tone of nature within is complemented by Rousseau's relation to nature without; here, what dominates is truth and what matters is, as in the former instance, the end of the dichotomy between the social and the natural self; if the *Confessions* assume an aesthetic of expression, exterior nature brings about an aesthetic of immanence. The aesthetic experience of nature may be described as a laicization of pietism. This experience is essentially interior. Nature merely prompts it; the self is the ultimate source of its resultant happiness: "La source du vrai bonheur est en nous." This true happiness is quite complex: it comes partly from the act of recalling the past, is partly an effect of imagination, of the sight of the countryside, but ultimately it comes simply from the joy of being. Examples of this type of experience are to be found in the *Rêveries d'un promeneur solitaire*, notably in the Second, Fifth, and Seventh Reveries. In such experiences the self joins with the universe, the separation effected by the fall into history is overcome, and the self no longer feels divided. Thus, when Rousseau regained consciousness after an accident just outside of Paris, he described his coming to consciousness as follows: "Je naissais dans cet instant à la vie, et il me semblait que je remplissais de ma légère existence tous les objets que j'apercevais."[4] Rousseau transformed a state of the soul usually associated with a union with God unto a union with Nature. This is totally different from the relation of taste to a work of art, and it may well be that the aesthetic experience of nature is

[3] In *Oeuvres complètes*, I, 1153.
[4] In *Oeuvres complètes*, I, 1005.

wholly different from the judgment of taste. No criticism is involved, no separation of mind and object; there is rather union of the self with nature: distance has been abolished. We may say, in other words, that Rousseau perpetrated the pathetic fallacy, a device that, Ruskin tells us, is often made use of by poets and which he defines as a "falseness in our impressions of external things." Nature could not resist Jean-Jacques Rousseau's powerful imagination and peculiar sensibility, and we might almost play with words and say that far from Rousseau being ravished by nature, it was she who was ravished by Rousseau.

Rousseau's aesthetic experience of nature may allow us better to understand the essence of taste, for it may be argued that this aesthetic experience is in fact its opposite, a conclusion which follows from Rousseau's entire attitude to art and society. It is here, indeed, that we find Rousseau the anti-artist, at a turning point in aesthetic theory. Taste supposes a certain detachment from the work of art, which is there to be judged. The aesthetic experience of nature supposes the contrary, and one may argue that people who say they are ravished by works of art are not exercising their judgment, because they have transferred a type of aesthetic experience proper to nature into the realm of art. Note too that, whereas art really separates those men who have taste from those who have not, the aesthetic experience of nature, based upon feeling, sentiment, the moral conscience, and ultimately on God and on what all men may experience, if only they will rid themselves of the constraints of society, unites all men. In terms of historical time the aesthetic experience of nature is the poor man's version of taste, and nature itself is the substitute for the works of art he cannot possess. If you can't own a Claude or a Poussin, a Vernet or a Hubert Robert, go out for a walk in the country. It is a more direct, easier, purer experience of beauty and truth than that of art, which supposes rules, connoisseurship, society, conventions, and reasoned judgment as well as an initial sensibility.

The Classical aesthetic supposed that art was a triumph over nature. Rousseau produced the reverse: nature triumphs over art.

* * *

Oeuvres complètes (Paris, Editions de la Pléiade, 1959). Rousseau's writings in which his views on art and matters concerning aesthetic theory are exposed are the following: *Discours sur cette question: Le Rétablissement des sciences et les arts a-t-il contribué à épurer les moeurs?* (Paris, 1750–51). This is often referred to simply as *Premier discours.* Essentially it may be called his anti-Renaissance view of art. Before this, however, he had written several works on music: *Projet concernant de nouveaux signes pour la musique,* 1742; *Dissertation sur la musique moderne,* 1743. Other works on music include the later *Lettre sur la musique française,* 1753, and the *Dictionnaire de musique* of 1765. He also was asked to write the articles on music for the *Encyclopédie.* Besides this theoretical work on music, Rousseau himself composed operas, namely *Les Muses galantes* and the famous *Devin du village;* he also cooperated with Rameau and Voltaire on the revision of *Les Fêtes de Ramire.* His other writing on matters pertaining to aesthetics is the *Lettre à M. d'Alembert sur les spectacles* of 1758. There are, of course, also occasional aperçus of great importance concerning beauty and taste in the *Nouvelle Héloïse,* while an aesthetic not falling within the Classical aesthetic may be gleaned in his *Confessions* and *Rêveries.*

See also the more general works on Rousseau which also have a bearing upon his aesthetic: Ernst Cassirer, *The Question of Jean Jacques Rousseau,* translated and with an introduction by Peter Gay (New York, 1954); Marc Eideldinger, *Jean-Jacques Rousseau et la réalité de l'imaginaire* (Neuchâtel, 1962); Henri Gouhier, "Nature et Histoire dans la pensée de J.J. Rousseau," in *Annales de Jean-Jacques Rousseau,* XXXIII, 7–48; Ronald Grimsley, *Jean-Jacques Rousseau — A Study in Self-Awareness* (Cardiff, Wales, 1961); François Jost, *Jean-Jacques Rousseau Suisse,* 2 vols. (Fribourg, 1961): especially valuable for the Swiss background, which considerably reduces what one might tend to think of as original to Rousseau; his views on nature and on aesthetic matters, for example, owe much to Swiss thinkers and Swiss attitudes; Jean Starobinski, *Jean-Jacques Rousseau — La Transparence et l'obstacle* (Paris, 1957): a brilliant essay stressing the problem of reality and appearance in the thought of Rousseau and his feeling of being a divided man.

On Rousseau and music see also the following: Robert Osmont, "Les Théories de Rousseau sur l'harmonie musicale et leurs relations avec son art d'écrivain," in *Jean-Jacques Rousseau et son oeuvre* (Actes et Colloques-2) (Paris, 1964); and for his role in the quarrel of the buffoons, Edward E. Lowinsky, "Taste, Style and Ideology in Eighteenth-Century Music," in E. R. Wasserman, ed., *Aspects of the Eighteenth Century* (Baltimore, 1965).

TERRASSON, ABBE (1670–1750)

THE ABBE TERRASSON belongs to the family of minds represented by such men as Fontenelle and La Motte. He was involved in the quarrel over Homer, wrote a novel called *Séthos*, published in 1731, translated Diodorus of Sicily, and was much praised by d'Alembert for being a practical philosopher and a stoic. He was a member of the Academy of Sciences. His contribution to aesthetics is indirect and will be found in his *La Philosophie applicable à tous les objets de l'esprit et de la raison* (Paris, 1754). This is written in the form of detached thoughts and short reflections, and represents on the whole an apology and praise of Cartesianism. Progress in philosophy and letters stems from Descartes, and one might define the aesthetic implied by Terrasson as one of method. Taste comes to be associated with right judgment, an idea again associated with Descartes, so that even the Academy of Sciences contributes to the perfecting of taste: "L'Académie des Sciences a perfectionné le goût, en établissant, d'après Descartes, les vrais principes du jugement; comme l'Académie Française l'a perfectionné par le choix des termes et par l'élégance du style" (p. 8). Cartesian thought and method may be applied to all areas of human endeavor, and Terrasson at times is reminiscent of Emile Krantz' thesis on the aesthetics of Descartes. He was also a thorough believer in the inevitability of progress, which he saw as the natural and necessary effect of the very makeup of the human mind.

Taste he associated with accuracy of mind, in letters due, above all, to philosophy:

C'est la justesse d'esprit qui fait trouver le vrai; et c'est le goût qui fait trouver la manière de la bien dire. La justesse d'esprit est le véritable fruit de la philosophie appliquée aux belles-lettres comme aux matières de physique. C'est faute d'avoir cet esprit que les Anciens ont dit très-élégamment des choses fausses en morale comme en physique [Ibid., 120].

This attitude is rather close to that of Fontenelle and derives from the same association of art and science, and ultimately, of judgment and imagination, truth and beauty. Terrasson associates beauty with a conformity between ourselves and some exterior object: "Le sentiment du beau ne naît en nous que de la conformité que les objets se trouvent avoir avec la conformation de nos organes. Cette définition est applicable, tant aux objets qui ne se présentent qu'à l'esprit, qu'à ceux qui frappent les sens" (Ibid). This is a definition which implies relativism and is built upon philosophical and psychological presuppositions rather than artistic canons and tradition. Beauty is, in a sense, of less importance than judgment and the discernment of truth, just as taste ultimately helps the judgment only insofar as it can give a fine turn to the expression of truth. In effect, Terrasson's aesthetic of method implies the disappearance of style and ornament, because the ultimate value and beauty is truth alone. Thus the perfect style, for example, is invisible: "Le style le plus parfait est celui qui n'attire aucune attention comme style, et qui ne laisse que l'impression de la chose qu'on a voulu dire" (Ibid., 134). Philosophy applied to the fine arts and to letters implies an art of purists and an aesthetics founded upon the notion of truth.

VOLTAIRE, FRANCOIS-MARIE AROUET DE (1694-1778)

VOLTAIRE, MAN OF LETTERS and taste, occasional aesthetician, and more than occasional critic, has disappeared behind Voltaire the *philosophe*, the liberal, the fighter of fanaticism, the sage of Ferney, the rehabilitator of Calas, and the author of *Candide*. And while his *Lettres philosophiques* are still read and commented upon as revealing England's influence on Voltaire in the realm of philosophy and social and religious thought, few pay heed to his *Temple du Goût*, the numerous prefaces to his plays, the various articles of his *Dictionnaire philosophique* which deal with subjects properly belonging to aesthetics, and other articles of criticism and countercriticism. Yet from Professor Raymond Naves' definitive study of Voltaire's aesthetics, namely *Le Goût de Voltaire*, it is clear that he was most representative of eighteenth-century aesthetic values, as was apparent to Madame du Deffand when she pleaded with him to give up writing for the philosophic party in order to restore the good and true taste of the age of Louis XIV. In his own day Voltaire was as much an arbiter of taste as a fighter for tolerance, and he probably was as much read for his style and wit as for the ideas he popularized. For us the Enlightenment is inseparable from Voltaire and from the ideas of progress and an open society. But this is to read history backwards, and it is indeed questionable to associate the light which emanated from the Enlightenment with American and French postrevolutionary views of man and society. One ought never forget that Voltaire was above all a man of taste and that taste has little to do with democracy.

Voltaire's taste owes much to the *Grand Siècle*, and his views of art owe much to Du Bos, but the expression of his views, the defense of his taste, is very much his own, and considerably more comprehensive and tolerant than were the artistic assumptions and preferences of the *Grand Siècle*: for like Montesquieu, Voltaire also surmounted the differences between the ancients and moderns. Yet his views of art and taste were not without limits; they are those of a man who has espoused, although unconsciously or without probing deeply into his assumptions, an aesthetic of art. The limits of his views are made clear by certain attitudes towards art, civilization, letters, and towards Rousseau and Shakespeare. The limits of his tolerance in matters of taste are fixed by the Temple of Taste, the concept of genius as manifest in Shakespeare, and Rousseau's view and use of nature. We might add something more; could it not be argued that the garden of Candide is the garden outside the Temple of Taste? that in a certain sense Voltaire's fight on the side of the *philosophes*, the forms used in this fight, and his involvement in the Enlightenment are directed to the purpose of maintaining the Temple of Taste? Thus a rather amusing dualism develops in the activities and mind of Voltaire: he writes novels, produces innumerable pamphlets, satirical pieces, *fusées volantes*, and what-have-you, all of which fail to fit into the forms supposed by his artistic values, in order to create a vast audience for the true artistic values and taste represented by the forms and genres inherited from the *Grand Siècle*. The garden of Candide must be cultivated, that one may have better access to the Temple of Taste. And thus Voltaire often works outside the rules, outside the great tradition of letters, in order to save what that tradition represented, a concept of civilization and life inseparable from art. Voltaire was one of the last representatives of that concept of civilization.

Voltaire rarely departed from the ideal expressed by his description of the Temple of Taste:

Il est plus aisé de dire ce que ce Temple n'est pas que de faire connaître ce qu'il est. J'ajouterai seulement, en général, pour éviter la difficulté:

> Simple en était la noble architecture;
> Chaque ornement, à sa place arrêté,
> Y semblait mis par la nécessité:
> L'art s'y cachait sous l'air de la nature;
> L'oeil satisfait embrassait sa structure,
> Jamais surpris, et toujours enchanté.

Le Temple était environné d'une foule de virtuoses, d'artistes et de juges de toute espèce, qui s'efforçaient d'entrer, mais qui n'entraient point:

Car la Critique, à l'oeil sévère et juste,
Gardant les clefs de cette porte auguste,
D'un bras d'airain fièrement repoussait
Le peuple goth qui sans cesse avançait.

This view of beauty and art is not too far from the preferences of Montesquieu and Fénelon, even of Fontenelle; it is the view of the young Voltaire, of the poet of *le Mondain* as portrayed by the painter Largillière, a worldly, handsome young man with the smile he would have throughout his life, even on Houdon's sculptured portrait that suggests a sage of antiquity. The Temple of Taste is an example of *la belle nature*: art is carefully hidden, ornamentation is discreet, the entire edifice is not too big, not too small; the eye may see it all at once. It satisfies the mind, and even though it does not hold any surprises, it enchants the soul. The same ideal of a nature inseparable from art, of a feigned naturalness which is the essence of ease, is also expressed in a letter of June 20, 1741, to Helvétius apropos of Boileau and the art of writing:

Vous ne trouvez point Boileau assez fort; il n'a rien de sublime, son imagination n'est point brillante, j'en conviens avec vous: aussi il me semble qu'il ne passe point pour un poète sublime; mais il a bien fait ce qu'il pouvait et ce qu'il voulait faire. Il a mis la raison en vers harmonieux; il est clair, conséquent, facile, heureux dans ses transitions; il ne s'élève pas, mais il ne tombe guère.

Voltaire was capable of recognizing and of being touched by the sublime, as he was touched by the greatness and also the strangeness of Shakespeare when he went to England. But on the whole, he was suspicious of enthusiasm. In his view, genius is inseparable from taste, and what he prized in Boileau was this taste, the judgment which told Boileau just what he could and could not do. Considering what the eighteenth century all too often did when it meant to be sublime, there is something to be said for Voltaire's sense of limits. But this attitude to Boileau also reveals something else. It is often said that Voltaire was not an original mind, that he had not an idea of his own, but that he borrowed and then vulgarized. The point is he did not care as much for ideas as for art:

Il ne vous coûte point de penser, mais il coûte infiniment d'écrire. Je vous prêcherai donc éternellement cet art d'écrire que Despréaux a si bien connu et si bien enseigné, ce respect pour la langue, cette liaison, cette suite d'idées, cet air aisé avec lequel il conduit son lecteur, ce naturel qui est le fruit de l'art, et cette apparence de facilité qu'on ne doit qu'au travail. Un mot mis hors sa place gâte la plus belle pensée [Ibid.].

Voltaire sometimes is close to being a purist where the language is concerned. One understands his devastating satire of Rousseau's *Nouvelle Héloïse* better when one reads letters such as the one to Helvétius. But also, his view of art, inseparable from taste, from care and the exercise of judgment, his sense of limits, also explain his attitude towards Shakespeare: he had sparks of genius, he was sublime, true, but he did lack taste, he did violate decorum, and on the whole he ought not to be imitated. But one must note that Voltaire was hardest on Shakespeare in the 1770s rather than after his first acquaintance with him during his trip to England. By the 1770s taste had changed considerably in France; Shakespeare had been translated, English novels were fashionable, even if often adapted to French tastes, nature was all the rage, and Voltaire could conclude, with some reason, that taste was lost. His attitude to Rousseau thus reveals his beliefs in matters of taste and defines his view of civilization, and perhaps also of his role in the Enlightenment.

When Rousseau sent Voltaire a copy of his *Second Discourse*, that on the *Origins of Inequality*, Voltaire chose to answer, not the arguments set forth in this discourse, but those of the *First Discourse on the Arts and Sciences*. The letter, dated August 30, 1755, is well known but it is still worth citing:

J'ai reçu, monsieur, votre nouveau livre contre le genre humain; je vous en remercie. Vous plairez aux hommes, à qui vous dites leurs vérités, mais vous ne les corrigerez pas. On ne peut peindre avec des couleurs plus fortes les horreurs de la société humaine, dont notre ignorance et notre faiblesse se promettent tant de consolations. On n'a jamais employé tant d'esprit à nous rendre bêtes; il prend envie de marcher à quatre pattes, quand on lit votre ouvrage.

And Voltaire goes on, demonstrating easily that Rousseau is all wrong because art has nothing to do with the crimes, follies, and misfortunes of mankind. The letter tells us really a great deal about Voltaire's view of art, directly and by implication. The opening remark of Voltaire's about the incorrigibility of man is revealing for a man associated with the Enlightenment. We must recall Voltaire's own thoughts on Pascal, whom he took care to refute in a chapter appended to the *Lettres philosophiques*. We must also remember the great debt he owes Du Bos.

May we not suppose that Voltaire's view of the function of art as a civilizing force is but a broadening of Du Bos' hedonism: indeed, a view going beyond hedonism, because Voltaire knew, perhaps better than Du Bos, how difficult it was to maintain the values of civilization? Voltaire represents what comes nearest to a tragic view of civilization in the eighteenth century: it is as if he perceived that civilization, and art as well, must ever be maintained by the application of will. The Goths were always trying to get into the Temple of Taste, and by the 1770s it looked as if the gates were about to be stormed, under the banners of Nature, Genius, and Enthusiasm. His view is the reverse of Rousseau's, for the loss is not that of nature, but of civilization: man does not fall from nature into civilization, but rather from civility, gained arduously, slowly, painfully, back into the original chaos of passion, prejudice, fear, and dullness, to borrow an expression from the Augustans — appropriate here, for Voltaire's view of civility, if not of optimism, is not far removed from Pope's. Voltaire ceaselessly fought what he considered the mounting bad taste of the later eighteenth century.

The sage of Ferney, Houdon's Voltaire, is thus not only a *philosophe*. When Voltaire returned to Paris, just before his death, to be crowned at the opening of his play *Irène*, was he crowned for his fight for toleration and his association with the philosophic movement, or was he crowned as a great man of letters? The patriarch of Ferney was not only the center of a campaign against the *infâme*; he also brings to mind, besides the garden of Candide, that room in which, Pascal opined, men could not bear to be alone with themselves. Voltaire's view of man is not Rousseau's; therefore his view of the function of art is not Rousseau's either, and in Ferney the personal as well as social implications of the Classical aesthetic are apparent. They probably were apparent to Rousseau too, though he came from another social class. Pascal's room, metamorphosed into Ferney, is no longer a room in which men do nothing but meditate upon or take stock of their *néant*. There is no black bile in Ferney, because there is activity, civilized and civilizing activity, inside the house and outside in the garden, for the seigneur, his friends, and for his employees. For these last there is even a church, for the Mass is really very good for the lower classes. As somebody would say later, it is their opium. Inside the house, there is no need of opium; there is study, art, leisure, play. Voltaire's conception of taste represents the surmounting of the problem posed by Pascal by assimilating the aristocratic view of art, that of a Du Bos, with the bourgeois virtue-as-necessity conception of work, this being left to the lower classes. Voltaire also recognizes the necessity of *divertissement*, for himself, for others: "L'étude a cela de bon," he wrote on February 19, 1766, to Madame du Deffand, who also needed *divertissement*, "qu'elle nous fait vivre doucement avec nous-mêmes, qu'elle nous délivre du fardeau de notre oisiveté, et qu'elle nous empêche de courir hors de chez nous pour aller dire et écouter des riens d'un bout de la ville à l'autre." And when one is tired of study, there is the theatre, or a good library.

If we turn from such general considerations of Voltaire's taste and aristic values to specific questions concerning his aesthetics, or rather his occasional sallies into the realm of aesthetics, we shall find that his views in this area are quite in accord with the premises of his taste, and a variation on his attitude towards pedantry. Here too, Voltaire is the inheritor of the *Grand Siècle* and particularly of Boileau. One may put it this way: he not only transcended the old quarrel between partisans of the ancients and the moderns, but believed that the problem of rules was a false problem, a view he shared with Du Bos. The ease and naturalness he prized so much could hardly come from following the rules of the pedants, who often did not write poetry themselves. He thought little of a metaphysical approach, of the problem of the *to kalon*, of beauty (see article "Beauty"). His article on taste in the *Dictionnaire philosophique*, or rather the renamed dictionary, the *Questions Encyclopédiques*, is very much in the historical tradition of the eighteenth century: taste is tied to history, to society; it varies in time and place, but this does not mean that anyone's opinion in matters of taste is valid; thus taste is also inseparable from connoisseurship and sensibility. There are some people who have taste and there are others who, no matter what you teach them, never will. As for rules, they are not to be used to judge or evaluate works of art. The only rules that Voltaire admitted were the precepts of craftsmanship, which were not a priori rules as to what constituted a work of art or of how to write a play, an epic, and so on. What mattered was that one execute well what one set out to do. His standards were those of excellence in art.

Madame du Deffand was right to consider Voltaire the last great representative of the age of Louis XIV. We might say that he fought its rear-guard action. It was quite hopeless, for what that age and Voltaire stood for had passed even before Voltaire himself, who perhaps overlooked only one thing, namely that even men of taste might grow bored with taste.

✳   ✳   ✳

Citations from the *Dictionnaire philosophique* are from the Classiques Garnier edition (Paris, 1959). The best single source for Voltaire's aesthetics or, more properly speaking, taste, is Raymond Naves' excellent dissertation, *Le Goût de Voltaire* (Paris, 1938). More recently another work has been published on the same subject, namely David Williams' *Voltaire: Literary Critic*, in *Studies on Voltaire and the Eighteenth Century*, Vol. XLVIII. As for Voltaire's own writings on aesthetics and criticism, they are scattered throughout his work, in prefaces, articles, letters, essays, poems, and histories. The following may be singled out: *Essai sur la poésie épique*, 1721; *Le Temple du Goût*, 1731–33, *Lettres philosophiques*, 1734, especially Letters 18, 19, and 24, on tragedy, comedy and academies; *Discours sur l'homme*, 1737, the section entitled "Sur la nature du plaisir"; *Conseils à un journaliste*, 1737; *Conseils à M. Helvétius*, 1738; *Mémoire sur la satire*, 1739; *Conseils à M. Racine*, 1742; *Connaissance des beautés et des défauts de la Poésie et de l'Eloquence dans la langue française*; several chapters on the arts in the *Essai sur les moeurs* and the *Siècle de Louis XIV*; *Parallèle d'Horace, de Boileau, et de Pope*, 1761; *Eloge de M. Crébillon*, 1762; *Commentaires sur Corneille*, 1764; *Réponse à un Académicien*, 1764; and various chapters in the *Dictionnaire philosophique*, or *Questions Encyclopédiques*, 1764–72; plus other writings too numerous to mention and for which the reader will do well to consult Naves and Williams.

Supplementary Bibliography

The bibliography which follows merely supplements those items already given in Parts I and II. A complete bibliography of writings on the criticism and aesthetics of the seventeenth and eighteenth centuries has not yet been compiled. Such a bibliography would have required a separate volume and would have been of little value unless it were a critical bibliography. Many works listed in either catalogues or partial bibliographies turned out to be very disappointing upon examination. I have consequently listed only those items which I thought of value. As for a complete bibliography of Classical aesthetics, conversations with friends in the field of electronic information machines have convinced me that compilation of such bibliographies had better be left to such machines, and that within a few years such bibliographies will be readily obtainable. I thus thought it wise not to start compiling one now.

I: PRIMARY SOURCES

André, Père Yves Marie, S.J. *Essai sur le beau*, 1741. This is a fine example of metaphysical aesthetics; well constructed, well written, it is still worth reading today as an example of such aesthetics. For my purposes I have used a 1760 Amsterdam edition of this essay.

Batteux, Abbé Charles. *Les Beaux-Arts réduits à un même principe*, 1746. Reprinted in 1747 and 1773, this little book is an excellent *abrégé* of eighteenth-century critical theory. See also his *Cours de belles lettres*, 1754, and its later version published as the *Principes abrégés de la littérature*, 1776.

Bernety, Dom Antoine-Joseph. *Dictionnaire portatif de peinture, sculpture et gravure, avec un traité pratique des différentes manières de peindre*. Paris, 1756.

Boileau Despréaux, Nicolas. *Oeuvres complètes*, Textes Français. Paris,

1960; see especially the *Art poétique, Réflexions critiques sur quelques passages du Rhéteur Longin*, as well as his Sixth Satire. On Boileau see Antoine Adam, *Histoire de la littérature française au XVIIe Siècle*, Paris, 1948–56, especially Vol. III, "L'Apogée du Siècle" and Vol. IV, "La Vieillesse de Boileau"; also René Bray, *Boileau, l'homme et l'oeuvre*, Paris, 1942; Jules Brody, *Boileau and Longinus*, Geneva, 1958.

Bossuet, J. B. "Maximes et réflexions sur la comédie" in *Oeuvres complètes*, ed. Abbé Guillaume (Paris, 1885), IX, 91–111.

Bouhours, Dominique. *Les Entretiens d'Ariste et d'Eugène*. Amsterdam, 1671. *La Manière de bien penser dans les ouvrages d'esprit*. Paris, 1687.

Bricaire de la Dixmérie, Nicolas. *Les Deux Ages du Goût et du Génie Français sous Louis XIV et sous Louis XV, ou parallèle des efforts du Génie et du Goût dans les Sciences, dans les Arts et dans les Lettres, sous les deux Règnes*. Paris and The Hague, 1769. An interesting item for cultural history and the history of criticism rather than for theoretical aesthetics. It is an evaluation of contemporary achievement in the form of a dream; at the end the poet wakes up and determines to work for glory. It is the sort of writing which was easily produced in the spirit of the Temple of Fame; see Mouhy, below.

Caylus, Comte de. *Vie d'Artistes au XVIIIe Siècle*, edited by André Fontaine. Paris, 1910. Excellent essays on several painters, but also on connoisseurship and on genius in the arts. On Caylus see Samuel Rocheblave, *Essai sur le Comte de Caylus*, Paris, 1889.

Chastellux, Jean-François, Marquis de. *Essai sur l'union de la poésie et de la musique*. Paris and The Hague, 1765.

Cochin, Charles Nicolas. *Recueil de quelques pièces concernant les arts*. Paris, 1757. Excellent satirical pieces on taste in the plastic arts and on connoisseurship.

Coypel, Charles. *Discours prononcés dans les conférences de l'Académie Royale de Peinture et de Sculpture*. Paris, 1721. Coypel was a painter; the work cited here is excellent for the artistic doctrine of that time.

Crousaz, Jean Pierre. *Traité du Beau: Où l'on montre en quoi consiste ce que l'on nomme ainsi, par des exemples tirés de la plupart des arts et des sciences*. Amsterdam, 1715. Aesthetics from above; one of the major treatises on the subject.

Dacier, Anne Lefèvre. *Des Causes de la corruption du goût*. Paris, 1714.

Taste is being corrupted because scholarship is being neglected in favor of novels and opera; if the study of the ancients is thus neglected one falls back into barbarism. Another cause of corruption is Monseiur de la Motte, who adapted Homer to the taste of the times.

de Piles, Roger. His works were numerous: *Abrégé d'Anatomie accommodé aux arts de Peinture et de Sculpture et mis dans un ordre nouveau dont la méthode est très-facile et débarassée de toutes les difficultés et choses inutiles qui ont toujours été un grand obstacle aux peintres pour arriver à la perfection de leur art. Ouvrage très-utile et nécessaire à tous ceux qui font profession du dessein, mis en lumière par François Tortebat, Peintre du Roy dans son Académie.* Paris, 1668. *L'Art de Peinture de Charles-Alphonse du Fresnoy, traduit en François, avec des remarques nécessaires et très-amples.* Paris, 1668. *Dialogue sur le Coloris.* Paris, 1673. *Conversations sur la connoissance de la peinture, et sur le jugement qu'on doit faire des Tableaux. Où par occasion il est parlé de la vie de Rubens, et de quelques-uns de ses plus beaux ouvrages.* Paris, 1677. *Abregé de la Vie des Peintres, avec des réflexions sur leurs ouvrages, Et un Traité du Peintre parfait, de la connoissance des Desseins, et de l'utilité des Estampes.* Paris, 1699. *L'Idée du peintre parfait.* Paris, 1699. *Cours de Peinture par Principes,* composé par M. de Piles, Paris, 1708. These are not all of his writings, only the more important ones, and especially those of interest for aesthetic theory. A complete bibliography will be found in Bernard Teyssèdre's *Roger de Piles et les Débats sur le Coloris au Siècle de Louis XIV*, Paris, 1957; for de Piles' relation to aesthetic theory in the eighteenth century see also my *Taste in Eighteenth Century France*, Syracuse, N.Y., 1965, especially Chapter IV.

Desfontaines, Pierre, François Guyot. *Le Nouvelliste du Parnasse ou Réflexions sur les ouvrages nouveau.* Paris, 1734. Useful for the practise of and opinions about criticism.

Du Cerceau, Jean Antoine. *Réflexions sur la Poésie Française, où l'on fait voir en quoi consiste la beauté des vers, et où l'on donne des règles sûres pour réussir à les bien faire; avec une défense de la poésie et une apologie pour les savants.* Paris, 1742. This is a clever treatise on poetry; the author attempts to define the relations between prose and poetry, one of the central problems of poetry criticism at this time. He argued it was all too easy to change prose into poetry merely through rhyme. This was probably directed at Houdar de la Motte and others experimenting with prose tragedies. Du Cerceau makes his point cleverly by turning prose passages from Bossuet's history into poetry, thus reducing the difference between eloquence and poetry and thereby demonstrating that the essence of poetry is not in verse or rhyme at all, but in what he calls the *tour de phrase*, that is transposition of certain words within the verse itself. He thereby touches on another important question of the times, namely the permissibility of the inversion of the syntax, of what was thought to be the natural order of French, subject, verb, object. "Or," he asks, "quel est ce tour de phrase qui est particulier à la poésie, et qui distingue les vers, de la prose? C'est uniquement *le tour qui met de la suspension dans la phrase, par le moyen des inversions ou transpositions reçues dans la langue et qui n'en forcent point la construction.*"

Duclos, Charles Pinot. "Essai sur le goût," in *Oeuvres*. Paris, 1821. A good essay on taste representing the views common in the second half of the eighteenth century. Duclos separates taste from the Good and the True, though both must be the foundations of beauty, which is the object of taste: "Il me semble que le goût est le sentiment du *beau*. Le beau seul est donc l'object du goût qui, dans les auteurs et les artistes, est le talent de le produire, et, dans les juges, celui de le sentir et d'être blessé du contraire; car le goût ne consiste pas moins à rejeter ce qui est désagréable, qu'à être flatté du beau." Taste is also examined in terms of historical and social development.

Estève, Pierre. *L'Esprit des beaux-arts*. Paris, 1753. Very general; see Lacombe, below.

Félibien, Jean François. *Entretiens sur les vies et sur les ouvrages des plus excellents peintres anciens et modernes*. Paris, 1666. See especially the life of Poussin.

Formey, Jean Henri Samuel. "Discours préliminaire" to the 1760 edition of Père André's *Essai sur le Beau*, which also includes his "Analyse de la notion du goût."

Gédoyn, Nicolas. "Réflexions sur le goût," in *Recueil d'opuscules littéraires*. Amsterdam, 1767. Gédoyn's little essay on taste is one of the better ones of the eighteenth century; short and clear, it summarizes the problems involved quite well. He distinguishes between natural taste and acquired taste; the former is a form of common sense and is indispensable to the latter, but will not take you very far in the world of the fine arts. There taste is a question of comparison, a *jugement de comparaison*. Taste in the fine arts is distinguished from another type of taste which obtains in the sciences and which he calls *goût de précision*, a form of taste which ought not to be used in the realm of the arts, for purely intellectual matters are not the domain of taste. Gédoyn also enquires into the nature and causes of bad taste, which is usually the fault of mental vices and ignorance, but as well of surprises caused by too much admiration; he counsels the classical *nil admirari*. Prejudice in favor of one's own nation is another cause, as is the general furor for modernity and current approval.

Helvétius, Claude. *Oeuvres complètes.* Paris, 1818. See in *De L'Esprit* (1758), Vol. I, Discours IV, Ch. xvi, "L'Influence du climat sur le génie poétique"; Vol. II, Ch. xiv, "Du Sublime"; Vol. III, *Epître sur les arts; Epître sur le plaisir.*

Lacombe. *Dictionnaire portatif des beaux-arts, ou Abrégé de ce qui concerne l'Architecture, la Sculpture, la Peinture, la Gravure, La Poésie et la Musique.* Paris, 1755. Amusing and useful. *Le Spectacle des Beaux Arts, ou Considérations touchant leur nature, leurs objets, leurs effets et leur règles principales.* Paris, 1761. Like Estève, a popularization and systematization of much of Du Bos.

Marivaux, Pierre Carlet de. *Oeuvres complètes.* Paris, 1781. See especially "Le Cabinet du philosophe" for remarks on style and the *je ne sais quoi.*

Marmontel, Jean-François. *Eléments de littérature.* Paris, 1787; *Oeuvres,* Paris, 1818–20.

Mercier, Louis Sebastien. *Le Génie, le Goût et l'Esprit.* The Hague, 1756. *Du Théâtre, ou Nouvel essai sur l'art dramatique.* Amsterdam, 1773. This is an important work on drama, indicative of changes in taste.

Moncrif, François, Augustin Paradis de. *Oeuvres* (Paris, 1791), Vol. I: "Essai sur la nécessité et sur les moyens de plaire"; "De l'esprit critique"; "Dissertations: de l'Object qu'on doit se proposer en écrivant."

Morellet, André. *Observations sur un ouvrage entitulé, "Traité du mélodrame," ou réflexions sur la musique dramatique.* Paris, 1771.

Mouhy, Chevalier de. *Apollon Mentor, ou le Télémaque moderne.* London, 1748. Another variation on the Temple of Fame theme.

Mourgues, Michel. *Traité de la poésie française.* Paris, 1754 edition.

Noverre, Jean-Georges. *Lettres sur la danse et les ballets.* Stuttgart and Lyons, 1760. This work has been translated by Cyril W. Beaumont, from an enlarged edition of 1803 published in St. Petersburg, in an edition published first in 1930, and more recently by Dance Horizons in 1966; it is this version, entitled *Letters on Dancing and Ballets*, that we have used. Indispensable for an understanding of the theory of imitation as applied to music and dancing, and generally an excellent work. Noverre reformed dancing in the name of nature and sought to raise the dance to the status of an autonomous, imitative, and expressive art.

Poinsinet de Sivry, Louis. *Traité du rire*. Amsterdam, 1768. An attempt to fix the origins of laughter and to classify its varieties.

Rapin, René. *Discours sur la comparaison de l'éloquence de Démosthène et de Cicéron*, 1670; *Réflexions sur l'usage de l'éloquence de ce temps*, 1671; *Réflexions sur la poétique d'Aristote et sur les ouvrages des poètes anciens et modernes*, 1675; *Du Grand et du Sublime dans les moeurs et dans les différentes conditions des hommes, et quelques observations sur l'éloquence des bienséances*, 1686.

Rémond de Saint-Mard. *Oeuvres mêlées*. La Haye, 1742. Various interesting essays on opera and poetry and also on the causes of the decadence of taste in opera and poetry.

Saint-Evremond, Charles de Saint Denis. *Oeuvres*, 1740. See especially the following: *De la Tragédie ancienne et moderne*, 1672, in Vol. III; *Sur les poèmes des Anciens et des Modernes*, 1685, in Vol. IV; *Sur la dispute des Anciens et des Modernes*, 1685, in Vol. V; *Sur le Merveilleux qui se trouve dans les poèmes des Anciens*, 1685, in Vol. IV; and *Quelques observations sur le goût et le discernement des Français*, published in Rotterdam in 1695 and republished in Volume V.

Saint-Pierre, Bernardin de. *Etudes de la Nature*. Paris, 1784. Fascinating; blurring of nature and art in aesthetic feeling.

Saint-Réal, Abbé de. *Oeuvres*. Paris, 1722. See Vol. V: "Sur le mauvais goût du public" and "De la Critique."

Séran de la Tour, Abbé. *L'Art de sentir et de juger en matière de goût*. Strasbourg, 1790. La Tour seems to have been influenced by Burke.

Watelet, Claude Henri. *Dictionnaire des arts de peinture, sculpture et gravure*. Paris, 1792. Very useful work.

II: SECONDARY SOURCES

Bayer, Raymond. *Histoire de l'esthétique*. Paris, 1961.

Beardsley, Monroe C. *Aesthetics from Classical Greece to the Present: A Short History*. New York, 1966.

Cassirer, Ernst. *The Philosophy of the Enlightenment*. Princeton, N.J., 1951.

Chambers, Frank P. *Perception, Understanding and Society: A Philosophical Essay on the Arts and Sciences and on the Humane Studies*. London, 1961.

Collingwood, R. G. *The Principles of Art*. Oxford, 1938.

Folkierski, Wladislaw. *Entre le Classicisme et le Romantisme, Etude sur l'esthétique et les esthéticiens du XVIIIe Siècle*. Paris, 1925.

Fontaine, André. *Les Doctrines d'art en France: Peintres, amateurs, critiques, de Poussin à Diderot*. Paris, 1909.

Foucault, Michel. *Les Mots et les Choses*. Paris, 1966.

Francastel, Pierre, ed. *Utopie et Institutions au XVIIIe Siècle: Le Pragmatisme des Lumières*. Paris and The Hague, 1963.

Minguet, Philippe. *Esthétique du Rococo*. Paris, 1966.

Mustoxidi, T. M. *Histoire de l'esthétique française, 1700–1900, suivie d'une Bibliographie générale de l'Esthétique française des origines à 1914*. Paris, 1920.

Nivelle, Armand. *Kunst-und Dichtungstheorien zwischen Aufklärung und Klassik*. Berlin, 1960.

Saisselin, R. G. *Taste in Eighteenth Century France*. Syracuse, N.Y., 1965.

Soreil, Arsène. *Introduction à l'histoire de l'esthétique française: Contribution à l'étude des théories littéraires et plastiques en France de la Pléiade au XVIIIe Siècle*. Brussels, 1955.

Sparshott, F. E. *The Structure of Aesthetics*. Toronto and London, 1963.

Wasserman, Earle, ed. *Aspects of the Eighteenth Century*. Baltimore, 1965.

Wimsatt, William K. and Brooks, Cleanth. *Literary Criticism: A Short History*. New York, 1967.